Black families in Britain as the site of struggle

MANCHESTER
1824

Manchester University Press

Black families in Britain as the site of struggle

edited by Bertha M. N. Ochieng and
Carl L. A. Hylton

Manchester University Press
Manchester and New York
distributed in the United States exclusively by Palgrave Macmillan

Published by Manchester University Press
Oxford Road, Manchester M13 9NR, UK
and Room 400, 175 Fifth Avenue, New York, NY 10010, USA
www.manchesteruniversitypress.co.uk

Distributed in the United States exclusively by
Palgrave Macmillan, 175 Fifth Avenue, New York,
NY 10010, USA

Distributed in Canada exclusively by
UBC Press, University of British Columbia, 2029 West Mall,
Vancouver, BC, Canada V6T 1Z2

British Library Cataloguing-in-Publication Data
A catalogue record for this book is available from the British Library

Library of Congress Cataloging-in-Publication Data applied for

ISBN 978 0 7190 7686 2   hardback

First published 2010

Typeset in 10.5/12.5pt Palatino
by Graphicraft Limited, Hong Kong
Printed in Great Britain
by TJ International Ltd, Padstow

To Mama and Baba

Contents

List of tables   *page* ix
List of figures   x
List of contributors   xi
Foreword – Harry Goulbourne   xv
Acknowledgements   xvi

1. **Introduction and overview of research with
   Black families**   1
   Laura Serrant-Green, Carl Hylton and Bertha Ochieng

2. **History and profile of Black families in Britain**   21
   Franklin Smith

3. **Black families and child-rearing practices**   55
   Bertha Ochieng

4. **Overcoming the 'Triple Quandary': how Black
   students navigate the obstacles of achievement**   76
   Tony Sewell

5. **Mothering and the family as sites of struggle:
   theorising 'race' and gender through the perspectives
   of Caribbean mothers in the UK**   100
   Tracey Reynolds

6. **Black UK families and the labour market: a historical
   review of the continuing difficulties of establishing
   a firm economic base**   122
   Jerome Williams

7.   Personal social services and locality: UK Black elders
     and young carers, health care and housing provision   143
     Alice Sawyerr, Carl Hylton and Valerie Moore

8.   Conceptualisation and effects of social exclusion,
     racism and discrimination and coping strategies
     of individuals and families   169
     William (Lez) Henry

9.   The cultural politics of African Caribbean and
     West African families in the UK   188
     Perry Stanislas

10. Rites of passage and family bonds   214
     Trevor Gordon

11. The Black family and sport: it's all good ... right?   234
     Kevin Hylton

12. Creating and sustaining African self-identity in
     the Western diaspora   258
     Carl Hylton

13. Black music as a key revolutionary signifier   283
     Richmond Quarshie

14. Spirituality and Black family life   305
     Garnet Parris

15. Conclusion: Can you didgeridoo?   312
     Carl Hylton and Bertha Ochieng

Index   319

Tables

2.1 Immigration to the United Kingdom from the
West Indies 1958–60   *page*   24

2.2 Regional distribution of Caribbean people in
Great Britain   28

2.3 Marital status: Caribbeans compared with Whites   31

7.1 Older people aged fifty and over in each ethnic group   149

Figures

2.1   Factors influencing migration to Britain in the
1950s and 1960s   *page*   25

2.2   Recruitment of skilled workers to the UK   27

2.3   Black migration networks in Britain and
the Caribbean   29

2.4   The transnational Black family paradigm   32

2.5   Returning residents to Jamaica between 1993 and 1997   34

2.6   Number of children per family   35

2.7   Percentages of exogamous marriage   37

2.8   UK comparison between first- and second-generation
African Caribbeans with White partners   38

2.9   Children looked after in England by ethnic origin
between 2001 and 2003   39

2.10   Percentages of young people by ethnic origin in
Tower Hamlets, London, achieving five GCSEs
grades A–C; 1994–2002   42

2.11   Young people achieving five or more GCSEs A–C
in England, 2004   43

2.12   Permanent school exclusions in England by
ethnic group, 2004–05   44

2.13   Racists incidents in the four educational divisions
in Hampshire   45

2.14   Ethnic breakdown of the socially rented sector   46

2.15   Owner-occupation by ethnic category   46

2.16   The formation of Black consciousness   47

Contributors

Trevor Gordon (MSC Sociology/Social Policy) is an education management consultant specialising in equality and diversity compliance. He is a governor in higher education and Chairperson of the Southwark Diocesan Board of Further and Higher Education, and is a former college Vice Principal. Trevor has a passion for African history and works with excluded school pupils.

Dr William (Lez) Henry was born in Lewisham, southeast London, of Jamaican parents. He is an experienced youth worker, poet, writer and one of the pioneer British reggae–dancehall DJs. Lez lectured in the Department of Sociology, Goldsmiths College for a number of years, and is a researcher, consultant and staff trainer for Nu-Beyond Ltd: Learning By Choice. He is the author of two books: *Whiteness Made Simple: Stepping into the GREY Zone* (London: Learning By Choice, 2007) and *What the Deejay Said: A Critique From The Street* (London: Learning By Choice, 2006).

Dr Carl Hylton has established an outstanding record of contributions in promoting and developing policies to enhance cultural competence care and understanding for Black families amongst health and social service providers. He is a former Lecturer in Ethnic Relations, Exclusion and Ethnicity, Leeds Metropolitan University and former Project Director of the Leeds Bi-Centenary Transformation Project (LBCTP). Carl is a freelance researcher, community activist, consultant and archivist who has recently completed editing a curriculum teaching pack (*African Achievements, Liberation and Aspirations*) addressing issues of freedom, identity, human rights, prejudice, racial discrimination and social change. Published by GBAKHANDA for LBCTP, the pack will be used in all schools in Leeds.

Dr Kevin Hylton is Course Leader for the MA in Sport, Leisure and Equity in the Carnegie Faculty of Sport and Education, Leeds

Metropolitan University. He has written and conducted research relating to diversity, equity and inclusion, and in particular critical race theory, racism and antiracism in sport and leisure, and sports development. Kevin's recent publication include *'Race' and Sport: Critical Race Theory* (London: Routledge, 2008).

Valerie Moore (formerly Valerie Blake) is an education and community activist who has contributed to research projects and publications on education, 'race' and gender. She is the former assistant director of student services at the Open University and former Senior Lecturer, Leeds Thomas Danby College. Valerie is currently involved in PhD research at Leeds Metropolitan University; she is Chair of the Afrikan Curriculum Development Association and a foster carer. Valerie is the eldest daughter of Jane and the late Wilford Cunningham, who joined the ancestors in 2008, aged 92 years. She is the proud mother of two sons, Julian and Matthew, and is married to Barry.

Dr Bertha Ochieng is Senior Lecturer, School of Health Studies, University of Bradford. Her teaching and research activities largely cover the areas of public health, families, adolescents and children, and in particular health and healthy lifestyle and the experiences of UK Black families in accessing and negotiating health and social-care services. Bertha is on the advisory board of the *International Journal of Interdisciplinary Social Sciences* and the Interdisciplinary Social Sciences Conference.

Reverend Dr Garnet Parris was born in Trinidad, and is Director of the Centre for Black/African Diaspora Theologies in the School of Philosophy, Theology and Religion, University of Birmingham. He has worked on committees across Europe on church-related activities with respect to racism, employment, and the urban and rural movement of the World Council of Churches. Garnet is currently involved (2009) in groundbreaking work with the Rastafari movement in the UK, and is coordinator of the African Diaspora in Europe. His PhD thesis was the African diaspora in Germany.

Alice Sawyerr is a Lecturer in Psychology, Mental Health and Systemic Psychotherapy in the Health and Social Care Department, Royal Holloway, University of London. Alice is also a clinician and an Honorary Consultant Systemic Psychotherapist at the Marlborough Family Services, an all-age multidisciplinary service in Central and North West London (CNWL) Mental Health NHS Trust, in St John's

Wood, London. She has a particular research interest in lifespan development psychology, development of identity, implementation of the pre-school curriculum, and ethnicity in multi-racial societies.

Dr Perry Stanislas is a Senior Lecturer at De Montfort University, Leicester and teaches policing and applied criminology. Perry's areas of research interests are international policing, policing diverse communities, and masculinity, ethnicity and crime. He has recently completed work on the perceptions and experiences of Polish and Somalian migrants of the British police, ethnicity, and masculinity and violent homophobia.

Richmond Quarshie, who holds a postgraduate qualification in management (MBA), is a business management consultant, writer, lecturer and racial and social justice activist. He was the conceiver, organiser and coordinator of the highly acclaimed Celebration Huddersfield 2000 (CK2K). Richmond served on the Joseph Rowntree Charitable Trust Racial Justice Committee for seven years. In June 2005, assisted by a group of friends, he won a landmark race discrimination case against Serco (Bradford LEA).

Dr Tracey Reynolds is Senior Research Fellow with the Families and Social Capital Research Group at London South Bank University. Her research interests are in the areas of 'race' and gender identities, motherhood and family, employment, education and qualitative research methods.

Professor Laura Serrant-Green is Professor of Community and Public Health Nursing, University of Lincoln, and Visiting Professor, University of the West Indies. She is editor of the journal *Nurse Researcher* and a member of INVOLVE, which ensures effective user involvement in research. Laura has received various national research awards and has been the UK government national advisor on Black and minority-ethnic issues relating to sexual health and HIV. She has worked closely with several health, education and social-care organisations around the needs of BME communities, and continues to work as a community mentor.

Dr Tony Sewell is the Manager of the charity Generating Genius. The programme seeks to support the needs of Black boys in the UK and Jamaica by using science and technology. Tony is a former high school teacher and lectured at the University of Leeds in Education.

He has written extensively on 'race', education and social anthropology. Tony is also columnist for the *Voice* newspaper; his best-known
book is *Black Masculinities and Schooling: How Black Boys Survive Modern
Schooling* (Stoke-on-Trent: Trentham, 1977). His new book, *Generating
Genius*, will be published in 2009. Tony, who was born in London, lives
happily between Croydon, London and Kingston, Jamaica.

Dr Franklin Smith is an Irish national and a graduate of Oxbridge and
other universities, with qualifications in education, archaeology and
theology. He was formerly a practising archaeologist in the Caribbean
before moving into education and race relations in the United Kingdom.
Franklin's main academic interests are archaeology and African
Caribbean history.

Jerome Williams is a double graduate in accounting, business development, project and programme management and public policy. Since
the 1980s he has successfully worked with Black businesses in the
creation of new 'start-ups', organisational development, producing
development plans to help existing businesses to survive, and developing action plans and management skills training initiatives to assist
business growth and generate sustainable employment and wealth.

Foreword

Increasingly, and rather interestingly, in the post-imperial world of North America and Europe, the concepts of 'family' and 'Blackness' are becoming subjects of debate, covering a wide range of issues – parenthood, childhood, education, caring, identity, and so forth. While, however, in US and Caribbean scholarships the combination of these concepts (the Black family) is readily understood and has historical contexts, the concept of the 'black family' in Britain is highly problematic and therefore raises intriguing questions. For example, what does this construct represent? Where does blackness begin and end along a wide spectrum of peoples from the Caribbean, various parts of Africa, Asia, Latin America, and beyond? Blackness, like Whiteness, denotes social consciousness, and in general Black consciousness has come to represent opposition to Whiteness. As this volume shows, the juxtaposition of 'racial' or colour consciousness and identity is being carried over into British popular and academic discourses.

But the book represents more than this particular problematic. Bertha Ochieng and Carl Hylton bring together here an impressive collection of individuals engaged in public and academic debates and concerned about the conditions of families who describe themselves as Black or are so depicted by the wider communities in our changing nation. This collection, therefore, raises a number of theoretical issues that many will want to question and discuss, and thereby stimulate a significant contribution to the growing literature on the diversity of family or living arrangements springing up in Britain with their attending problems and opportunities.

Harry Goulbourne
Professor of Sociology
London South Bank University
September 2008

Acknowledgements

We people of African descent have travelled a long way in space and time to arrive at our present physical destination in the United Kingdom. For this we are thankful to our ancestors and the creator who imbued us with spirit, fortitude and endurance. We give thanks and praise that we are able to complete this important book project, which could not have been achieved without the support and collaboration of all the brilliant and spiritual chapter authors, Professor Harry Goulbourne (foreword), Oluseyi Ogunjobi (front cover image), and everyone at Manchester University Press who sustained their faith in the project during a three-year period. We have arrived at our appointed destination but the journey continues.

Dr Bertha Ochieng and Dr Carl Hylton
February 2009

1

Introduction and overview of research with Black families

Laura Serrant-Green, Carl Hylton and Bertha Ochieng

Introduction

Although many family practitioners and academics in the United Kingdom (UK) now recognise and concede the value and need for an understanding and appreciation of Black family life, there still exists a significant challenge to produce a comprehensive book about Black families that goes beyond the negative stereotypical views that have been held on the position of Black families in the UK. This edited work progresses the debate on a number of significant issues experienced by Black families. It relies on the contribution of fifteen African-descent authors who do not hesitate to speak against the negative images that are held against Black families. Various synopses of the key issues identified by chapter authors are provided at the end of this introductory chapter.

This introduction provides an overview and introduction to the context of research with Black families of African descent where, historically, Black families are always seen in the light of other minority ethnic groups or the dominant 'race'. The authors discuss how Black families have been the targets of a deficit-oriented research model that measures them and their performance against an idealised standard of the behaviour of White families living in adequate economic and educational environments. They will argue that it is against the background of such work that Black families have been judged dysfunctional and pathological, despite the fact that little empirical evidence supports this assumption. The chapter demonstrates how earlier research conducted 'on' Black families was at first descriptive and that this was later replaced by comparative deficit-oriented research. In addition, the issues raised in this chapter will provide detail to argue that the volumes of research on 'race' in Britain have not produced dividends either in explaining differences in experiences or in improving provision to Black families. Unfortunately, when researchers started to incorporate ethnicity and 'race' in their studies, they tended to view minority ethnic families as monolithic, with many studies not specifying the 'ethnicity' of the participants. Few studies considered socioeconomic differences in their investigation of Black families, and to date there is evidence to suggest that issues of institutional and individual racism as determinants of Black people's lifestyles are still ignored. The authors will demonstrate how, currently, the literature is often still heavily skewed, reflecting the interests of professionals across a range of disciplines that remains at odds with the 'true' priorities of Black communities. The chapter concludes by suggesting future research strategies that may be used with Black families, and areas for further reading.

Black family identity

One of the purposes of research is to provide a reliable evidence base to inform and influence policy, practice and decision-making that affects the lives of individuals and communities. It is through research that we begin to understand and make sense of how people live in various societies by assessing their hopes and expectations to measure the impact that social, economic or political changes have on their communities. Nonetheless, families vary in size, ethnic identity, number of parents, gender mix and many other factors. They thus contain a rich source of potential information that may be useful to research studies due to the wide variation of experiences, viewpoints and values housed within them.

In the multi-ethnic context of the UK many forms of family unit exist. Examples of families encompassing the wide range of formats identified above can be found in all ethnic groups in the twenty-first century. A history of migration to the UK from across the globe means that minority ethnic families are a well-established component of British society. Statistical research studies focussing on family structure and functioning in the UK, such as the national survey of minority ethnic communities, are a key source for identifying the diverse family structures currently resident in the UK (Smith and Prior, 1996). These surveys and other research projects often report statistical differences and variations among minority ethnic groups in relation to family norms and attitudes to family life; they demonstrate the many ways in which minority ethnic families represent diverse family identities that differ from the majority UK population and each other. The issue of homogeneity in representations of Black families in research sits as one example of how Black identity has been marginalised around debates on 'race' and ethnicity.

The negativity associated with Black families through research studies in the past has not remained confined to the annals of history or discussions about the structures and functions of families in the UK. Over time these negative 'differences' have acted as blueprints to inform a range of sociological debates resulting in economic and health-care policies based on consideration of the 'problems' arising out of the ways in which specific Black communities differ from the White UK majority population (Richeson and Pollydore, 2002; Santelli *et al.*, 2000).

Homogeneity and the invisibility of racism

'Race' and 'ethnicity' are complex terms that have been and continue to be used to denote characteristics of people in society (Bhopal, 1997). Their complexity lies in the lack of consensus as to their definitions and in the often confused or contradictory ways in which they have been used to include some and exclude others from society. Writing and speaking about 'ethnicity' and 'race' is preceded by a long history of concentrating on specific aspects of an individual's culture or ancestral origins, and using this as a basis to constrain the identity of minority communities and the individuals who comprise them within three to five bounded categories (Ahmad, 1993). Historically, much of this categorisation has been imposed by people belonging to majority ethnic groups who themselves have not been constrained by such categories. These categories have then been used to establish grounds for inequality and maintain the status quo in a range of areas including health, social care, education policies and law.

The outcome of this approach in relation to research is that minority ethnic populations have been routinely homogenised within racial stereotypes. This homogenisation has been criticised for taking little or no account of the effects of other socially determined factors such as gender, occupation or socioeconomic group in their lives (Balsa and McGuire, 2002). Researchers in the twenty-first century are thankfully encouraged to employ a much more critical and reflexive approach to research centred on ethnicity and 'race' research in order to more effectively appraise the purposes and outcomes of their work in relation to minority ethnic groups (Nazroo, 2001).

The labelling of minority ethnic people within categories that differentiate them from majority populations but not from each other is not exclusive to issues of academic research, but is within the lived experiences of many people who are members of minority ethnic groups. For example, in the experience of one of the authors (Serrant-Green) this meant that, from an early age, being of Caribbean origin and living in the Midlands area of Britain meant being taken to be

Jamaican. Dominica, the island of her ancestors, differs from Jamaica and many of the other Caribbean islands in relation to language, dominant religions, climate and economics. Thus, while sharing with other Caribbeans the common experiences of being Black in Britain, she is in many ways culturally and ethnically dissimilar to Jamaicans who comprise the largest group of Caribbeans in the Midlands. Many of the authors in this book can claim similar experiences. As Black researchers they have found themselves in situations where their approach to research is conceptually, experientially and overtly conducted from the perspective of a Black person of African descent living through and with this history. The same can be said for the individuals and communities that comprise the 'families' noted in research on Black families. Problems of 'assigned ethnic identity' permeate their experiences of research itself and the policies and practices that arise from it. The complex situation in which 'race', ethnicity and family norms are experienced is acknowledged as a continuous and influencing factor underpinning the writing of this chapter and the book as a whole.

Identifying 'race' and ethnicity in social research

The origins of 'race' as a term are disputed, but it is believed to be a much older term than 'ethnicity' (Sollars, 1996). In the UK, understanding of 'race' was based on definitions from the United States of America (USA), where 'race' identity was initially associated with phenotypical characteristics and 'races' were deemed to be distinguishable on physical grounds (Woodward, 1999). Thus, from the outset 'race' was presented as an objective term associated with physical and fixed characteristics. The linking of the term 'race' to notions of fixed, differentiated and identifiable traits underlines the traditional ways in which 'race' is understood and was used from very early on to justify the difference and superiority of one 'race' of people from another (Estes, 2000; hooks, 1992). The value of using this essentialist or fixed notion of 'race' to identify specific groups in society has been discredited for a long time, particularly in the sociological literature on many fronts (Barot, 1996; Rose *et al.*, 1984; Whitehead, 2000).

Many of the criticisms directed at this traditional approach to 'race' focus on the fact that many of the categories used to determine racial identity were less self-evident and objective than was claimed. While appearing to be based on fixed and objective measures, the characteristics such as skin colour or country of origin depend on both internal and external definitions, which in turn are not fixed or self-evident but determined by degrees of interpretation that vary between people, different societies and over time (Pratto and Espinoza, 2001). 'Race' as a descriptive term has been further discredited due to its association with racism and the persecution and victimisation of people that occurred (and continues to do so) in Britain and elsewhere on the grounds of racial identity or categorisation. This culminated in the coupling of the term 'race' with degrees of negativity that has been difficult to overcome, and to some extent the exploration of 'race' as a concept still remains shackled to and substituted for racism and oppression in the minds of the general public (Afshar and Maynard, 2000).

The negative connotations and inadequacies associated with the use of the term 'race' as an effective way of identifying groups in society resulted in people in both academic and social spheres avoiding the use of the word and seeking out other ways of locating individuals. During this period of time 'ethnicity' emerged as a less rigid way of describing social groups. The term ethnicity is closely linked to the Greek noun *ethnos* from which it is derived. This word was used to refer to people in general but also to 'others' who were different from the self (Sollars, 1996). The literary origins of the term ethnicity are non-specific about the nature of 'others' and give no indication as to the traits associated with particular groups or the identity. This would seem to invite the development of concepts of ethnicity that exclude no one and make no attempt to determine absolutely who or what is included in the term.

However, in practice there have been various attempts to define ethnicity by setting boundaries to contain it that have then been applied to limit its association to specific groups (Pickering, 2001). In relation to research on families in the UK the term ethnicity has regularly been used with these connotations resulting in the selective application of the term 'black and minority ethnic' populations, to the exclusion of people from White communities. Definitions of ethnicity used in researching families and society in the UK have attempted over the years to incorporate the value of cultural difference and diversity missing from approaches based on 'race'. However, this was often carried out uncritically with little reference to the political and social constraints that affected people's experiences (Ahmad and Atkin, 1997). This approach to ethnicity has been criticised as denying a full exploration of the positive and challenging aspects of ethnic identity and family life in the UK that are equally part of Black people's experiences (Afshar and Maynard, 2000; Balsa and McGuire, 2002; Karlsen and Nazroo, 2002a, 2002b).

Early research on Black families and communities therefore attempted to define 'race' and ethnicity based on a particular physical trait, belonging to a defined social group or other pre-defined characteristics. This has resulted in research that extols a view of the existence of a stereotypical Black family experience that has been inconsistent over time, between and within social groups. This suggests that 'race', ethnicity and identity are more closely determined on the basis of culturally, historically and politically derived perceptions of a society rather than on 'objective' facts. If this is the case, then there is a need to know much more than 'who' is denoted by racial or ethnic categories and to move towards activities that focus on how, why and what effects this has on the families involved and the research in which this categorisation takes place.

Over the years educational and social-science research on families and Black experiences has widened the discussion of 'race' and ethnicity beyond the boundaries of categorisation. Ethnicity, in particular, has been explored much less as an issue in itself but increasingly and extensively reviewed and explored in relation to other concepts such as class, identity and life experiences. Research is evident that has investigated, debated and explored the impact of 'race' and ethnicity on a range of issues including feminist thought (Bryant *et al.*, 1985; Carby, 1997), educational achievement (Sewell, 1995) and youth culture (Richeson and Pollydore, 2002). This broader revised focus has moved debates, particularly in the social sciences, beyond the question of terminology or difficulties associated with definition into contemplation of the theoretical and experiential nature of these concepts and their effects. The long history in these disciplines of engaging in debates that recognise and appreciate the differences in experiences brought about by the effects of society on individuals and groups underpins the fluidity inherent in an anti-essentialist view of 'race' and ethnicity. An anti-essentialist approach allows an understanding of 'race' and ethnicity to emerge where their 'definitions' are identified as being contextual and forever changing (Nazroo, 2001).

This has enabled the discussion in the social sciences to move beyond exploration of 'race' and ethnicity as concepts in themselves or attempts to define them absolutely. Instead, current thinking accepts that there are not one, but many 'races' and ethnicities existing at an individual, group and societal level (Mac an Ghaill, 1999). The acceptance of multiple 'races' and ethnicities has been identified with post-structuralist approaches which accept that there are many different experiences and viewpoints in understanding the world (May and Williams, 1998; Mulholland and Dyson, 2001). This is the approach to researching ethnicity and the experiences of Black families in particular that will be taken in this chapter.

Incorporating multiple views of the world allows for alternative or even simultaneous aspects of ethnicity to emerge in a society, or be located in individual experience and identity. As part of this fluid and changeable view of ethnicities and racisms different aspects of these experiences relating to an individual's identity may become more prominent or pertinent depending on the context. The experience of Black families and the communities that comprise them can be appraised therefore in the light of their differing phenotypical characteristics, and cultural, racial and social situations. Research should encompass these aspects and not view them as contradictory but accept them as components of the unified whole that is the experience of Black individuals and families.

Researching Black families

Many of the currently available reports and surveys about minority ethnic communities focus on a broader range of minority ethnic families than those of Caribbean or African decent who are the subject of this publication. These descriptive reports attempt to plot or record the 'nature' of a range of Black communities and families in Britain. In doing so they highlight some generally held beliefs about minority ethnic families that are also commonly reported in the findings of studies focussing on Black Caribbean experiences alone. These findings include:

- minority ethnic families are 'Black'; and classified as African, Asian, Caribbean or Dual Heritage Parentage
- minority ethnic families differ from White families, who are the majority population families in the UK
- the 'difference' between Black families and White families is implicitly or explicitly problematic
- Black family structures are static and strongly related to past 'homeland' living styles.

On the surface it may appear that there is a great deal of consensus concerning the make-up of Black families and the commonalities that exist between minority ethnic groups. However, closer examination of some past research studies reveal that within the 'sanitised' reporting of statistics, there are several issues related to researching Black families that require further consideration.

One of the key issues particularly visible in historical research of Black families is the positioning of White families from the majority population as the standardised norm against which Black family experiences are measured (Beishon *et al.*, 1998). This is a common approach taken in many research projects in the past, both qualitative and quantitative. White (majority) families, particularly in the UK and other 'western' nations, were used as an ever-present reference point against which the activities, beliefs and choices of Black families were held up for scrutiny (McAdoo, 1997). Even in studies where the purpose was declared to be geared towards determining the needs of Black families, this was translated in practice to judging how closely their requirements 'fitted' with the existing and established White family norms (Song and Edwards, 1997). The underlying message generated by this practice in research was that for Black families to approximate to White families was morally worthy and a sign of their progress towards assimilation into (White) British society. Conversely, the greater the distance or deviation of their lifestyles and needs from the White majority, the more 'deviant' the families and, by association, the communities to which they belonged. The continuous comparison of Black families with the 'White' norm contributed to the development on a broader scale of a close association, made implicitly or explicitly, of Black family identity as negative.

Research in which the complexities of Black family experiences and the impact of political or social change are explored from the perspective of both the family members and the communities to which they belong have received comparatively less attention than the broad surveys of whole communities. Unlike other social groupings, for example, in relation to class and gender, centralised studies conducted to provide an insight into the Black and other minority ethnic family perspective experiences in the UK still remain relatively unexplored outside epidemiology. Some of the reasons for this in a range of situations will form the subject of discussions in later chapters. Failure to establish a range of other types of studies focussing on Black families and communities alongside the epidemiological approaches available has resulted in the predominance of deficiency in models of Black family research. The lack of research into the experiences impacting on the life chances of Black populations occurs within a wider sphere where, in terms of studying families and communities, exploration of Black families against the yardstick of 'White' experiences is the norm. From a starting point where Black families are the 'negative' to the White 'positive', much of the information available to underpin social service policies and developments in the UK relies almost exclusively on incidence and prevalence data across ethnic groups, with minimal exploration as to the causes and effects of these on life experiences. As a result, the wider health, welfare and political implications for Black families resulting from the interplay of ethnicity, class or gender on different aspects of community life in the UK have received little attention.

Epidemiological studies alone are inadequate in providing an indication of why family health, welfare and life experiences vary between social groups or how the socialisation process affects our beliefs and behaviour (Pitts, 1996). Researchers in the twenty-first century need to look beyond the statistics and explore the mechanisms and symbols that influence them; in this way we can gain a better understanding of the values, needs and experiences of Black families. Sociocultural studies of Black family experiences in Britain need to be politicised (in similar ways to how those addressing the broader issues concerning gender, class and ethnicity have been) in order that they may be better able to illustrate how social inequality affects the nature and scope of life chances of individuals from different social groups. This need offers an ideal invitation for researchers to explore the interplay between social groupings, ascribed or acquired identities and Black families. It follows then that in order to fully understand the issues associated with Black families in the UK, research studies need to explore the social dimensions under which they are constructed and how they relate to the specific subjects at the centre of the research. The possible variations in experiences arising out of the interplay between gender, ethnicities and family identities in society makes it important that any research set within these contexts makes explicit the ways in which researchers identify their research in relation to these concepts. To this end, at the very least it is essential that, early on in the research, the research team begins by identifying how the terms 'black' and 'minority ethnic' are used throughout the study.

The need for participatory and ethnicities-based approaches

The use of quantitative methods of enquiry has become part of the established mode of research into ethnicity in the UK, particularly within education, law and public health. Epidemiological research on Black families, while not answering many of the pertinent issues about Black experiences, has been invaluable in bringing to the attention of health service providers, politicians and the general public the very real need to address a variety of issues pertaining to the lived experiences of Black communities in Britain. Many of the studies included in this book and the wider debates about Black family experiences take place at a time when social research and explorations of family life in the UK are still inextricably linked with morality and social expectations concerning what is appropriate and acceptable behaviour in society. The use of surveys as a key form of enquiry in Black community experiences in general has become established for a variety of political and social reasons relating to the sensitive nature of many of the social inquiry subjects such as sexual health, delinquency, low educational achievement and domestic violence. This has resulted in reluctance on the part of governments to take political risks on this platform. The use of epidemiological approaches in studying Black families may be seen as a way of facilitating the study of a sensitive subject by removing the need to ask probing or personal questions about the experiences of an individual or specific ethnic group, thereby reducing the threatening aspects of studying what are still deemed to be potentially contentious issues. By confining research about Black families or Black communities in general to the more 'objective' scientific paradigm, it may be possible to avoid public discussion or exposure of embarrassing and politically sensitive issues.

The exposure of variations in health, education and welfare across ethnic groups brings with it a challenge to understand why rates differ so significantly in particular groups. Policy-makers, educationalists and service providers need to understand why these differences exist and the impact on the lives of Black families in order to devise appropriate changes in statute or provide care and advice to Black clients. One of the issues that impact on the effectiveness of this process is the tension between the factual risk data provided by epidemiological studies and the way people make sense of their life experiences. At a personal or group level, 'perceived risk' arising from individual or shared feelings, expectations and beliefs about an issue is as important as 'actual risk' based on scientific calculations in determining actions. These aspects of decision-making are neither quantifiable nor measurable in any absolute sense. This means that the questions required to be answered by policy-makers, educationalists or service providers in relation to the needs and experiences of Black families cannot be addressed by quantitative data alone. What is required is that other methods of enquiry which ensure that the individual, social or political aspects of family life for particular ethnic groups are introduced into the discussion. In order to do this a variety of perspectives are required, including, most importantly, those of the Black families themselves.

User involvement in research is a key change in research governance and good practice through which the voices of users are encouraged as an essential aspect of each stage in the research process. User involvement is particularly championed in health and public service research, where involvement is taken to mean that people who use services are active partners rather than just the 'subjects' in the research (Steel, 2004). In user-focussed research, the emphasis is on conducting studies 'with' or 'by' the public rather than 'to', 'about' or 'for' them. This exists in sharp contrast to the historical models or approaches described earlier where definitions, actions and conclusions of research were conducted often without any reference to the Black families who were the subjects of the studies. Combined with recommendations in research ethics procedures where convenors of research studies are advised to ensure their research ethics committees not only engage user involvement processes, but reflect the ethnic profile of the subjects of research (Economic and Social Research Council, 2005: 11), there is ample scope for those conducting studies involving Black families to incorporate 'internal' perspectives in their research designs.

Therefore, this book does not claim or even seek to present or resolve all issues of Black family life in the UK, but to assert that the experiences of Black families in the UK are dynamic, sparkling, fluctuating and volatile. With a continued Black population in the UK signified by the arrival of new migrants of Black families from Africa and other countries, arguments in this edited work ensure the continuation of theoretical and practical debates of Black family life in the UK. It takes into account the many important historical developments that have taken place across the centuries, from trans-Atlantic African enslavement, to the publication of the McPherson Report and beyond, including examples of good practices that are beginning to meet at least some of the needs of Black families. The organisation and structure of the chapters attempt to cover topics of national and international interest in historical and theoretical conceptualisation, economic and educational aspects, socialisation within families, social policies and its effect on families, music, sports, racism, religion and much more. Most significantly it is a departure from work that stigmatises Black families, and argues from various viewpoints that the strength and resilience of Black families are responsible for some of their successes in the UK. However, it also points to some important problematic areas for families that are pertinent not only to students but to family practitioners, professionals and researchers interested in understanding the lives of Black families.

Guide to chapters

The book commences with Franklin Smith's (Chapter 2) examinations of the nature and forms of Black family structures as well as some of the problems families confront and how they attempt to resolve them. Smith argues that, until quite latterly, African and African Caribbean family forms and their 'transmogrifications' have received, and continue to receive, scant attention. Much of the literature is preoccupied with the lone-parent nature of African Caribbean households and the absenteeism of Black fathers. This is indeed surprising given the inestimable proportion of Black people in the UK and their relationship to the British Empire. The chapter argues that many Black family forms are being replicated in Britain. It also attempts to provide a discussion on how Black family forms at a point of cultural traction show signs of changes in order to adapt, simultaneously retaining the strength of the consanguineous networks endowed by history and culture. This chapter also asseverates that, whatever impact locality may confer, there are some cherished ideologies and beliefs that form a web of support to both the individual and group members who, because of racism and racial discrimination, feel themselves outside the ambit of what is described and defined as British culture.

Bertha Ochieng's research with Black families (Chapter 3) revealed that on a daily basis children are socialised to negotiate discontinuities in their role demands at home, neighbourhood and school, as they are expected to learn and navigate courses of actions acceptable to Black and White cultures. In essence, this entails a socialisation that encompasses a dual existence of multiple normal cultures. Ochieng's findings suggest that Black families have mutual and relatively communal believes about child-rearing. For instance, families' child-rearing styles were rooted and reflected their own life experiences, values and beliefs. An understanding of the nature of Black children's socialisation processes for both parents and children is discussed.

Whereas Tony Sewell (Chapter 4), in analysing the education of Black children in the UK, asserts that one of the key factors for success in the British education system is the degree of family support. It is noted that recent research on African Caribbean underachievement has been dominated by research that has focussed on in-school factors. However, a new discourse is emerging that has taken on the complexity of these students and their contexts. By examining the 'Triple Quandary' of dominant mainstream peer group pressure and low aspiration comfort zone, educational researchers, including Sewell, are able to produce a framework of success. The chapter ends with a social navigational guide based on the experiences of Black students who have succeeded in spite of the risk factors they face. It also poses the question of whether we are exacting too high a price for Black success in schools.

The work of Tracey Reynolds (Chapter 5) argues that for African Caribbean mothers, similar to other mothers belonging to minority ethnic groups in the UK, the family and their mothering experiences represent a key site in which they continue to struggle against social constructions of mothering and the experiences of racial discrimination in their everyday lives. Caribbean mothers are the central focus of debate in the study, which reveals that mothering is equally racialised as it is gendered. Yet contemporary mothering discourses generally overlook this factor, and universalistic claims of mothering are based on White, middle-class and heterosexual practices. The specific focus of the study on Caribbean mothers also demonstrates that White, middle-class mothering issues have only recently encompassed themes such as balancing and negotiating work and family roles, lone mothering, and kinship and community networks and extended family relationships. These themes are intrinsic to Caribbean mothers who have longstanding traditions in these areas. This chapter documents the experiences of a cross-section of first-, second- and third-generation Caribbean mothers in the UK, to illustrate that the practices performed by these mothers represent their attempts to maintain established cultural, social and kinship links to their cultural and ethnic origins, whilst at the same time adapting to the social circumstances of being part of a Black minority ethnic community in the UK. The analysis begins by highlighting and examining the cultural, historical and social contexts of Caribbean mothering, where 'race', ethnicity and gender are integral to understanding Caribbean household patterns and family relationships. The second part of the discussion examines how Caribbean mothers experience and respond to issues of racism and racial discrimination in their everyday lives. An important aspect of these women's mothering is concerned with socialising, and transmitting their Caribbean cultural values. Examples of this aspect of Caribbean mothering are provided in the final part of the analysis.

Jerome Williams (Chapter 6), in exploring Black families' experiences of the labour market, identifies that the levels of unemployment and deprivation experienced by African Caribbean migrants and their families are of paramount importance primarily to that community, but also to the wider UK society. The lack of material success, especially financial, among the UK African Caribbean community has been noticeable since the early 1980s. As a group their socioeconomic positions in society are virtually unchanged. Other migrant groups living in western societies have sought to develop themselves as a group, employing hard-work ethics and cultural awareness as the vehicles to achieve employment and wealth to overcome social disadvantages. They key question asked in this chapter is: why are UK African Caribbean residents entrenched at the foot of the socioeconomic ladder? The main evidence supporting this claim mainly derives from a range of publications and case studies that focus on the views and shared experiences of members of the African Caribbean business community. Arguments are also advanced from a sample of the experiences of present and former business entrepreneurs, and other African Caribbean community members, and the observations of the writer, who is a business management professional. Jerome's key results and conclusion indicate that much work is left to be done amongst the African Caribbean community, including the UK Government and social policy institutions that should provide key support required to enhance future development.

Alice Sawyerr, Carl Hylton and Valerie Moore (Chapter 7) examine the history and patterns of changes in the culture of care provision for Black families of African descent in the UK. They focus on two generations: Black young people and the elderly, with the elderly being the primary focus. The chapter explores the extent to which the needs of Black elderly people of African descent are being met by Black families, Black organisations as providers, and the personal public social services. The extent to which the younger generation will be able to continue with the tradition of providing familial support for an ageing Black population is in question. The implications for policymakers in terms of meeting the housing, health care and welfare needs of Black families, particularly the elderly, are examined. The chapter also offers recommendations for meeting the specific needs of Black families of African descent in a multi-ethnic society.

It is impossible to provide analyses of the life experiences of any Black and other minority ethnic families in the UK without making reference to social exclusion, racism and discrimination. William 'Lez' Henry (Chapter 8) analyses the conceptualisation and effects of social exclusion, racism and discrimination, and coping strategies of individuals and families, by providing a thorough examination of 'race', race-relation issues and how they have shaped Black family life. While social exclusion, racism and discrimination reverberate across the different chapters, the analysis in Henry's work becomes the central and key issue to illustrate how racism and discrimination have been embedded in UK society. Henry provides special understanding of the problems experienced by Black families due to racism and examines and articulates the impact and influence of racism on different aspects of Black family life across generations.

Perry Stanislas (Chapter 9) explores the problems experienced by African Caribbean and West African families in the UK since the migration following the Second World War, specifically the impact of socioeconomic and cultural issues and their implications for bringing these communities in contact with the legal justice system. He examines the direct impact of government policies on family patterns and social behaviour, both in terms of their adverse consequences and the successes of these minority ethnic communities and their families. Stanislas highlights many of the obstacles that people of African Caribbean and West African origins face in their efforts to influence the social policy decision-making agenda. In terms of a conclusion, the author calls for matters related to the Black family and how it is adversely affected by policy and cultural changes to be given higher priority both from within the communities themselves, but also in the context of research and official decision-making. In the case of West Africans, Stanislas calls for greater acknowledgement of their presence, which should be reflected in closer attention to their specific experiences and problems in the areas of their family lives and interconnections with UK society.

Trevor Gordon (Chapter 10) explores the historical development of the Black family from trans-Atlantic enslavement and colonialism to the recent arrival in the 'mother country' and subsequent treatment and assimilation into the 'host' or 'mother culture'. The chapter examines the denial of fair, just and equitable structures that have deliberately prevented equal 'rites of progress' or 'rites of passage' in the host culture. Gordon argues that historically the notion of a Black family never really existed in the psyche of the British until late into the twentieth century due to the dehumanisation and demonisation of enslaved Africans that lasted more than 400 years. This process of trans-Atlantic African enslavement commenced with the separation of African families, followed by a period of forced transition from a matriarchal to patriarchal family structure, and again this was followed by the forced assimilation and incorporation of British cultural values and norms. The rights to housing, education and employment are examined, as these are the three main areas of the host society that Black families have to successfully navigate if they are to survive successfully, develop and make a meaningful contribution while in the host society. The chapter concludes by arguing for more scientific rigour and African-centred or Black academic methodologies and approaches to be used, including an understanding of the importance of positive 'rites of passage' programmes for Black families' survival. Gordon's work makes an important contribution to this area of study, sets out the historical and contemporary mind-set of the 'host subject' towards these new arrivals and begins to give a sense of the many physical and psychological barriers that Black families have had to face in seeking fair and equitable treatment on arrival in the UK.

Kevin Hylton (Chapter 11) considers a number of issues that present sport as a double-edged sword that concerns the African Caribbean family in its widest sense. This critical reading of sport and the Black family outlines sport's function in our collective consciousness as it explores how sport contributes to our sense of 'Self' and 'Other' identities. Hylton finds that sport, unlike other key arenas in society, has been viewed as a vehicle for Black people in the UK to become integrated or even assimilated into 'British culture'. Hylton's arguments draw upon an emerging body of work in the sociology of 'race', sport sociology, critical 'Whiteness' studies and cultural studies to examine the phenomenon of 'race' and sport in relation to the Black family. He reflects key debates in relation to racism, Whiteness, the media and public policy development in relation to sport and its impact upon individual and collective identities. It is demonstrated that 'race' logic pervades sport and its major related institutions such as governmental bodies, the media and education. The impact of this racism includes the administration and spectatorship of mainstream sport. The duality of sport is further played out here as we consider how it is used as a tool of resistance, control and community cohesion. This chapter concludes that sport can be used as a tool to subjugate by creating an arena for oppressive social relations, and likewise it can empower as a force for social transformation. A sense of contrariness and ambivalence towards Blackness and Black Britishness is played out in sport in multifarious ways. It is concluded that where an uncritical acceptance of sport's purported social contribution is left unexamined it can become a cloak to hide dysfunctional racialised social attitudes.

Carl Hylton's chapter (Chapter 12), on the other hand, posits that in creating self-identity, it has become widely accepted that ethnic identity is a multi-faceted concept, with cultural, structural, symbolic, psychological and functionally instrumental dimensions. This chapter focuses on the influences that ethnic identity has on Black people in the UK. It demonstrates how, for Black families just as for any other group of people, their identity is of crucial importance; however, to be of value identity needs to be recognised as a context, itself flexible, interacting with, shaping and being shaped by other social and structural contexts. The chapter analyses ways in which Black identity is portrayed in public and its effect on individuals and families. It demonstrates how families are preparing their children's identities. It argues for the recognition of the strength of ethnic identity, by stating that social identities and participation have the potential to serve as important mechanisms for social change. It demonstrates the need for a positive identity and acceptance and recognition of Black identity at the intersection of social services targeted for Black families.

Richmond Quarshie (Chapter 13) constructs a view of music above all things as being a powerful indicator and documentary of the Black experience. Quarshie's arguments come from an artistic perspective whilst drawing on the beliefs, traditions and practices that underpin 'African spirituality'. A number of themes are developed in presenting the thrust of these arguments, the most fundamental being that music is a potent force and spiritual medium that should be revered. This chapter also maintains that music and Black freedom struggles are intricately linked, hence giving rise to the notion of revolutionary artistes of music. Entering into the realms of spirituality, Quarshie contends that music is a conduit allowing for connection to higher forces, elevating the status of some of those gifted in the craft as having a divine mission, with 'serious consequences' when this is compromised. There is also a focus on the oratory skills that makes Black music unique as a voice of struggle. Examination of reggae's lyrical content indicates the complexities and implications for the struggle of African spirituality, and cultural and practical liberation, whilst acknowledging the dynamism pushing in several directions. Certain developments are presented as beneficial in terms of 'the struggle' whist others raise serious questions. The music industry is a major factor in any such discussion, notwithstanding the racism and hints of a conspiracy to undermine 'the struggle' for African liberation with the negativity that is around today. Whilst acknowledging the contribution across all genres, the chapter concludes on a note that moves for music to be more in tune with its true essence, including the aspirations of 'the struggle'. With a culture enriched with traditions dating back to creation itself, it is easy for certain themes to be taken as a given. However, looking at 'the struggle' in detail, there are those who believe that the Black community is undergoing something of a cultural crisis, in particular when looking at the music scene. Perhaps what this chapter does best is to create a context for discourse on that proposition, ensuring that this process does not take place in an abstract vacuum. Moreover, it opens an interesting debate by examining the multitude of genres that make up Black music as a point of struggle. Essentially, this chapter seeks to spark off some form of a literary revolution for the documentary of where things stand as of today and for the future.

Garnet Parris (Chapter 14) seeks to alert the reader to the presence of African Indigenous Churches and their Caribbean counterparts. Additionally, Parris explores the significant presence of the Nation of Islam as well as mainline Islamic influences in the African Caribbean population. Black churches provide people of African descent with a home and a safe space in which to be engaged culturally and spiritually, as well as affirmation; although now they are moving into an area of engagement with those in power, as representatives of a people who should benefit positively from changes in society. In terms of relating to multidisciplinary approaches by Black religious community leaders, Parris notes the direct role played by Islamic organisations and the specific role that the African/African Caribbean faith communities have carved out for a national para-church organisation; methodologically he uses both desk research and informal discussions with faith and community leaders to fashion this chapter.

Carl Hylton and Bertha Ochieng (Chapter 15), use the final chapter, *Conclusion: can you didgeridoo?*, to draw together the main tenets of the diverse arguments of the previous chapters. This concluding chapter relies on linking, acknowledging and exploring the overlap between authors' individual activist experiences and academic arguments from research data. The key theme that emerges is the need to ensure that policies and strategies aimed at Black families should be planned and delivered with the use of a much clearer understanding of their 'everyday' experiences while respecting their individuality and encouraging their participation.

Conclusion

Finally, in relation to this publication and the focus on research involving Black families, we resist attempts to define or determine the nature of the relationship between ethnicity and Black family experiences absolutely. Instead the variety of projects and perspectives explored in the following chapters reflects the pragmatic views adopted by the various authors. These incorporate an acceptance of variety and diversity in the ways ethnicity and family life interplay and are experienced in the UK. Exploring the realities, experiences, viewpoints and personal decisions of Black families from this standpoint enables the contributors and encourages future researchers to conduct studies incorporating Black families' perspectives as well as their own situated positions. In doing so, researchers will add to a growing evidence base of divergent studies of Black family life in the UK, which are recognised as being neither objective nor unique but which provide one of many possible interpretations from which social policies and practice may be developed to benefit Black families and ultimately the wider multi-ethnic society of twenty-first-century UK.

References

Afshar, H. and Maynard, M. (2000), 'Gender and ethnicity at the millennium: from margin to centre', *Ethnic and Racial Studies*, 23:5, 805–19

Ahmad, W. I. U. (ed.) (1993), *'Race' and Health in Contemporary Britain* (London: Open University Press)

Ahmad, W. I. U. and Atkin, K. (eds) (1997), *'Race' and Community Care: 'Race', Health and Social Care* (Buckingham: Open University Press)

Balsa, A. and McGuire, T. (2002), 'Prejudice, clinical uncertainty and stereotyping as sources of health disparities', *Journal of Health Economics*, 22, 89–116

Barot, R. (ed.) (1996), *The Racism Problematic: Contemporary Sociological Debates on Race and Ethnicity* (Lewiston: Edwin Mellen Press)

Beishon, S., Modood, T. and Virdee, S. (1998), *Ethnic Minority Families* (Westminster: University of Westminster, Policy Studies Institute)

Bhopal, R. (1997), 'Is research into ethnicity and health racist, unsound, or important science'? *British Medical Journal*, 314, 1751

Bryant, B., Dadzie, S. and Scafe, S. (1985), *Heart of the Race: Black Women's Lives in Britain* (London: Women's Press)

Carby, H. V. (1997), 'White women listen! Black feminism and the boundaries of sisterhood', in Mirza, H. S. (ed.), *Black British Feminism: A Reader* (London: Routledge)

Economic Social Research Council (ESRC) (2005), *Research Ethics Framework* (Swindon: Economic and Social Research Council)

Estes, S. (2000), ' "I AM A MAN!"'! Race, masculinity, and the 1968 Memphis sanitation strike', *Labor History*, 4:2, 154–70

hooks, b. (1992), *Black Looks, Race and Representations* (London: Turnaround)

Karlsen, S. and Nazroo, J. Y. (2002a), 'Agency and structure: the impact of ethnic identity and racism on the health of ethnic minority people', *Sociology of Health and Illness*, 24:1, 1–20

Karlsen, S. and Nazroo, J. Y. (2002b), 'The relationship between racial discrimination, social class and health among ethnic minority groups', *American Journal of Public Health*, 92:4, 624–31

Mac an Ghaill, M. (1999), *Contemporary Racisms and Ethnicities, Social and Cultural Transformations* (Buckingham: Open University Press)

May, T. and Williams, M. (1998), *Knowing the Social World* (Buckingham: Open University Press)

McAdoo, H. (1997), *Black Families* (California: Sage Publications)

Mulholland, J. and Dyson, S. (2001), 'Sociological theories of "race" and ethnicity', in. Culley, L. and Dyson, S. (eds), *Ethnicity and Nursing Practice* (Basingstoke: Palgrave Macmillan)

Nazroo, J. Y. (2001), *Ethnicity, Class and Health* (London: Policy Studies Institute)

Pickering, M. (2001), *Stereotyping: The Politics of Representation.* (Basingstoke: Palgrave Macmillan)

Pitts, M. (1996), *Sexual Health – The Psychology of Preventive Health* (London: Routledge)

Pratto, F. and Espinoza, P. (2001), 'Gender, ethnicity and power', *Journal of Social Issues*, 57:4, 763–80

Richeson, J. A. and Pollydore, C. A. (2002), 'Affective reactions of African American students to stereotypical and counterstereotypical images of Blacks in the media', *Journal of Black Psychology*, 28:3, 261–75

Rose, S., Lewontin, R. and Kamin, L. (1984), *Not in our Genes: Biology, Ideology and Human Nature* (Harmondsworth: Penguin)

Santelli, J., Lowry, R., Brener, N. and Robin, L. (2000), 'The association of sexual behaviors with socioeconomic status, family structure and race/ethnicity among US adolescents', *American Journal of Public Health*, 90:10, 1582–8.

Sewell, T. (1995), 'A phallic response to schooling – Black masculinity and race in an inner city comprehensive', in Griffiths, M. and Troyna, B. (eds), *Antiracism, Culture and Social Justice in Education* (Stoke-on-Trent: Trentham Books)

Smith, P. and Prior, G. (1996), *The Fourth National Survey of Ethnic Minorities: Technical Report* (London: National Centre for Social Research)

Sollars, W. (ed.) (1996), *Theories of Ethnicity: A Classical Reader* (London: Palgrave Macmillan), 425–59

Song, M. and Edwards, R. (1997), 'Comment: raising questions about perspectives on black lone motherhood', *British Journal of Social Policy*, 26, 233–44

Steel, R. (ed.) (2004), *INVOLVE: Involving the Public in NHS, Public Health and Social Care Research* (Eastleigh, Hampshire: INVOLVE)

Whitehead, S. (2000), 'Masculinities, race and nationhood – critical connections', *Gender and History*, 12:2, 472–6

Woodward, K. (ed.) (1999), *Identity and Difference: Culture, Media and Identities* (Milton Keynes: The Open University)

2

Historical profile of Black families in Britain

Franklin Smith

Introduction

The aim of this chapter is to investigate and describe Black families and the extent to which family patterns are being replicated or changed, as well as their disamenities compared with other families in the United Kingdom (UK). Indeed, it is true to say that racism still narrows and complicates the sociological integration pattern of Black families.

This investigation is an amalgam of qualitative and quantitative data, constructing a picture of the social milieu. The data consist of information on various aspects of Black families such as education, migration, demographic distribution, employment, and patterns of childbirth and housing. The research can also be described as descriptive, simply because it relies overwhelmingly on library sources coupled with quotations from relevant primary-source materials and comparative tables. The findings illustrate that African and Caribbean cultural norms and values are echoed in Britain. The sense of feeling excluded and being on the periphery of society means that, often, behaviour-oriented ideas are brought into play, thus reinforcing kinship bonds and tabus. Emanating from this research is the finding that cultural proximity has resulted in more exogamous marriages than occurs in other ethnic groups as well as in changing patterns akin to the establishment of multi-generational households owing to shifting family and cultural patterns. For example, whereas in Africa, married partners may choose to establish matri- or patri-local residence, according to culture, in Britain this has taken the form of neo-local residency. Thus it is indeed right to question whether long residency in Britain is transforming the structure of the Black extended family (Ochieng, 2005: 34–6).

This chapter deviates from the weaknesses with which major studies in the past are preoccupied. Preoccupation with pathology as seen in M. G. Smith's *West Indian Family Structure* (1962) misses and obfuscates some excellent areas for research. Instead this present work focuses on their resourcefulness by addressing topics such as factors influencing migration networks in Britain, kinship networks, Black family transformations, endogamy, exogamy, discrimination and politicised folk traditions. Only an infinitesimal amount of research has been done in these areas. Most concentrate on Caribbeans while excluding continental Africans. Equally, there is no reliable up-to-date source of information concerning education, schooling, housing and employment that focuses on Black families. What sources do exist suffer from serious limitations. For example, the 2001 Census and the data on school exclusions have been criticised for being out-of-date as well as failing to take account of the reasons for exclusions (OREC, 2005). The fact that these data are controversial could have implications for policy and resources. Inevitably, it may provide the background for reduced grant funding to one ethnic group and an increase to another, resulting in inequity (Smith, 1996: 15).

The rationale for this review stems from a few salient factors. To begin with, the problems of racism have their provenance in historical relationships. Equally, the writer desires to respond to why Black families migrated to Britain in the post-war period, coupled with a desire to discuss and record issues around the Black family and discrimination. For example, to what degree do social exclusion and racial prejudice pervade educational, employment and housing provisions? Latterly, such questions have assumed a central position in general discourses.

This chapter maps out the debate on issues pertaining to Black family transformations and racial discrimination. Since the late 1990s there has been a burgeoning of the literature on Black families in Britain, most notably Goulbourne's *Caribbean Transnational Experience* (2002) and Chamberlain's *Narratives of Exile and Return* (1997). Nevertheless, few books on this salient area describe linked frameworks for comprehending the nature and structure of Black families as well as their transmutations. For example, I have attempted to discuss the search for consciousness, racial discrimination and early Black migration to Britain, beginning in the Romano-Celtic period and not from the 1940s as many texts surmise.

Sociologists and sociology students who choose this field cannot abstain from posing the basic question: are Black families treated inequitably, despite anti-discriminatory legislations such as the Race Relations Amendment Act 2000? Racism is indeed rife, and simply introducing and amending legislations should not be construed as an adequate response. Furthermore, policies designed to assist tend to have an adverse effect on Black families whose social and cultural structures differ in configuration. Certainly, in Occidental quasi-scientific terms, kinship is construed as a people belonging to the same household.

Until latterly the varying nature of African and African Caribbean family forms received minor attention. Much of the literature is preoccupied with the lone-parent nature of Caribbean households and the supposed absenteeism of Black fathers.

This chapter contends that some aspects of Black family forms are being replicated in Britain, simultaneously providing a discussion on how Black family forms at points of cultural contact change in order to adapt; retaining the strength of the consanguineous networks endowed by history and culture. Moreover, whatever impact locality may confer, there are cherished ideologies that support group members who feel excluded from British culture.

Black migration to Britain

Black migration to Britain is not new. Archaeological and historical evidence substantiate the presence of Black people during the Romano-Celtic period. For example, Smith (1993) opined that African and Asian presence can be attested by archaeological remains discovered in cities such as York, London, Woodeaton (Oxford) and Wall (*Lecocetum*). Some important officials during Roman governance were Black (Allason-Jones, 1989: 52). Vibia Pacata, who followed an African cult of the Punic Tanit, was of African origin. She was married to Flavius Verecundus, a Hungarian of the Sixth Legion Victrix. It is possible that during centuries of Roman occupation inter-racial marriages between Africans and indigenous Britons might have occurred (Allason-Jones, 1989: 15). Thousands of Black people also lived in Elizabethan England, residing in major towns and cities such as Barnstaple, London and Plymouth. Their numbers augmented to the point that the Queen (Elizabeth 1st) ordered their deportation from England in 1596 (Adi, 1995: 6–7; Fryer, 1984: 1; Saunders, 1984: 16). Britain's involvement in trans-Atlantic African enslavement equally resulted in Africans being transported to the UK from approximately 1550 (Fyson, 1984: 3). In 1555 the merchant John Lock returned to England with a number of enslaved Africans. More Black people came to Britain during the First World War to assist with the war effort. After its culmination many remained, forming small communities in Cardiff, London and Liverpool, but found themselves in competition for jobs with White men who resented their presence. Tensions between the two resulted in 'race' riots in Cardiff and Liverpool in 1919. Small-scale

Table 2.1 Immigration to the United Kingdom from
the West Indies 1958–60

Territory	1958	1959	1960	Total for 3 years	%	1960 as % of 1958
Antigua	422	353	741	1,516	2	176
Barbados	1,147	1,514	4,340	7,001	8	378
Dominica	577	1,116	1,946	3,639	4	337
Grenada	680	594	1,809	3,083	4	266
Jamaica	10,137	12,573	31,447	54,157	66	310
Montserrat	323	455	620	1,398	2	192
St Kitts, Nevis, Anguilla	928	779	1,508	3,215	4	163
St Lucia	541	970	1,308	2,819	3	242
St Vincent	304	310	838	1,452	2	276
Trinidad & Tobago	939	973	1,892	3,804	5	202
Total West Indies Federation	15,998	19,637	46,449	82,084	100	290

Source: Davidson, 1962: 7

disturbances were also reported in Glasgow, London and Tyneside. Black men found it difficult to obtain work during the inter-war years and their numbers did not increase until the Second World War (Fletcher, 1930: 14–35; Senior and Manley, 1956: 6; University of Liverpool, 1940: 10). However, the biggest movement of Black people to Britain occurred during the 1950s and the 1960s. For Davidson (1962: 6), 'the net inward movement of West Indians into the United Kingdom was estimated to be about 16,000 in 1951, 1,000 in 1952, 2,000 in 1953 and 10,000 in 1954' (See Table 2.1).

Exodus from the Commonwealth was precipitated primarily by the demand for labour during and after the Second World War (Davidson, 1962: 2; Sewell, 1998: 7). In order to salve wartime shortages, the then Ministry of Labour recruited Black people to work in munitions factories. Arnold R. Watson (1942) states that 188 West Indians were brought to Britain mainly from Jamaica to be employed in the technical industries. This leads me neatly to the hypotheses concerning Black migration to the UK in large numbers during the 1950s and the 1960s.

For Hooper (1965: 10–13), economics was the singular reason prompting migration to the UK following the Second World War. Hooper believes that large-scale migration was possible because rudimentary socioeconomic conditions in the colonies constricted opportunities for advancement. Similar reasons have been cited by Anwar (1986: 13) and Halstead (1988: 8–9).

Recent scholarships have discountenanced this facile, almost racist exposition. Revisionists have eloquently argued that the metamorphosing of cultures rather than economics impelled migration. Migration was psycho-cultural, premised on a yearning to visit the 'mother country', as people in the Caribbean were indeed British subjects (Smith, 1996: 12–15). This entitlement was restricted in 1962 when the first in a series of Immigration Acts were promulgated to curtail 'New Commonwealth' transients (Adi, 1995: 43). Visualising migrants in purely economic terms means eschewing important variables such as overlapping territories and intertwined histories (Said, 1993: 1–72) (Figure 2.1).

We cannot ignore the historical symbiotic relationship that existed and which still exists well after 1945 especially in countries considered to be part of the British territory or living space. Centuries of African enslavement inculcated the notion that the 'Other' had to be experienced within an established phenomenological space. The 'mother country' became a geographically detached but poignant variable that had to be embraced as well as demythologised. Black people, existing in

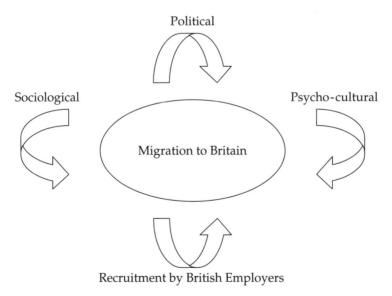

Figure 2.1 Factors influencing migration to Britain in the 1950s and 1960s

a state of depersonalisation, had been nurtured to regard Britain as a society constructed on tolerance and benevolence towards strangers (Haynes, 1987: 2). According to Hill:

> What is more natural than that he should turn in his distress to his mother country, for the West Indian is enormously proud of being British. He reveres our Royal Family and is proud of the Union Jack. The vast majority also respect the Englishman and look to him for example in ordinary matters of conduct, as well as in the academic field. A nurse who has done her training in England is held in much higher esteem in the West Indies than one in America or any other country. This is not merely because the Jamaican believes that our academic standards are higher, but because he esteems England and looks upon her as being his mother country. (Hill, 1958: 17)

Thus migration for the colonised was also socio-diagnostic. It meant social status and acquiring the *savoir faire* of the British (Fanon, 1967: 147; Glass, 1960: 96). Examples of this are seen in the education systems of Commonwealth countries, towering monuments to colonialism (Figueroa, 1991: 7). However, Khan (1982: 202–9) expounds how psycho-cultural forces influenced migration, asserting that colonialism warped self-conceptualisation which in turn precipitated the evolution and crystallisation of an attitude that is intrinsically White. Migration must therefore be comprehended within the context of a colonial relationship (Rex, 1970: 76–80).

Black people were invited to come to work in the UK as post-war reconstruction required a large workforce that the internal labour market could not provide (Field and Haikin, 1971: 6–13). To fill the gap, both state and private industries such as British Rail, London Transport, the British Hotels and Restaurant Association and the National Health Service began formal recruitment programmes abroad (Byron, 1994: 1; Dodgson, 1984: 3–8; Saunders, 1984: 20). Many recruited were doctors, nurses, teachers, dentists, technicians and engineers (Hill, 1969: 31–61) (see Figure 2.2).

According to Watson (1942: 6–7) those recruited to work in Britain during and after World War Two were highly trained technicians. In fact, 65 per cent of those recruited to the UK from Jamaica in 1953 were classified as skilled workers (Peach, 1968: 49; Rose, 1969: 51).

Nevertheless, migrants set in motion sociological forces that would affect and redefine family patterns and kinship relationships both in Britain and abroad. Additionally, many transients were confronted with the harsh realities of racism but the government did not respond to the problems they encountered. The assumption was that newcomers over time would become indigenised. In other words, familiarity

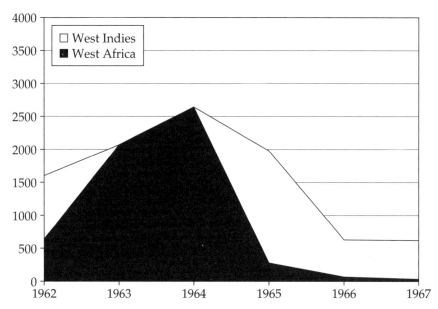

Figure 2.2 Recruitment of skilled workers to the UK
Source: Rose, 1969: 86

would ameliorate their situation. This did not materialise and by the 1950s and the 1960s Britain began experiencing 'race' riots. Black people became disquieted about what they saw as a racist police force, a racist education system and, more than all, institutional racism. This is well attested by publications such as *Nigger Hunting in England* by J. Hunte (1966) and *How the West Indian Child is Made Educationally Subnormal by the British School System* by Bernard Coard (1971).

Newcomers settled in major conurbations such as London, Birmingham, Liverpool, Leeds, Sheffield and Manchester. Indeed, there was a notable urban bias in their location. For example, currently, more than half of the population of African Caribbean descent reside in Greater London and the West Midlands (Owen, 2001: 71). In fact those arriving between 1961 and 1966 settled in areas with an established migrant population (see Table 2.2).

Those areas still predominantly retain descendants of the earlier migrant population. For Rex and Moore (1967), kinship and cognate reticulations were salutary in the determination of settlement. Sheila Patterson's *Dark Strangers: A Study of West Indians in London* (1963) reveals that many Black migrants settled in Brixton because they already had family members residing there. Likewise, Senior and Manley (1956: 5) claimed that approximately 60 per cent of new

Table 2.2 Regional distribution of Caribbean people in Great Britain

Region, county and metropolitan county	Total population	Minority ethnic groups (000s)	Percent regional population	Share of GB total (%)	Caribbean population (000s)	Percent of regional population	Share of GB total (%)
South East	17,208.3	1,695.4	9.9	56.2	432.4	2.5	63.7
Greater London	6,679.7	1,346.1	20.2	44.6	371.6	5.6	54.8
East Anglia	2,027.0	43.4	2.1	1.4	12.1	0.6	1.8
South West	4,609.4	62.6	1.4	2.1	19.0	0.4	2.8
West Midlands	5,150.2	424.4	8.2	14.1	96.9	1.9	14.3
West Midlands MC	2,551.7	373.5	14.6	12.4	87.9	3.4	13.0
East Midlands	3,953.4	188.0	4.8	6.2	35.1	0.9	5.2
Yorkshire & Humberside	4,836.5	214.0	4.4	7.1	31.7	0.7	4.7
South Yorkshire	1,262.6	36.2	2.9	1.2	8.6	0.7	1.3
West Yorkshire	2,013.7	164.1	8.2	5.4	21.3	1.1	3.1
North West	6,243.7	244.6	3.9	8.1	37.7	0.6	5.6
Greater Manchester	2,499.4	148.2	5.9	4.9	26.3	1.1	3.9
Merseyside	1,403.6	25.9	1.8	0.9	6.4	0.5	0.9
North	3,026.7	38.5	1.3	1.3	3.0	0.1	0.4
Tyne & Wear	1,095.2	19.9	1.8	0.7	1.3	0.1	0.2
Wales	2,835.1	41.6	1.5	1.4	6.8	0.2	1.0
Scotland	4,998.6	62.6	1.3	2.1	3.6	0.1	0.5
Great Britain	54,888.5	3,015.1	5.5	100.0	678.4	1.2	100.0

Source: 1991 Census of Population (quoted in Owen, 2001: 72)

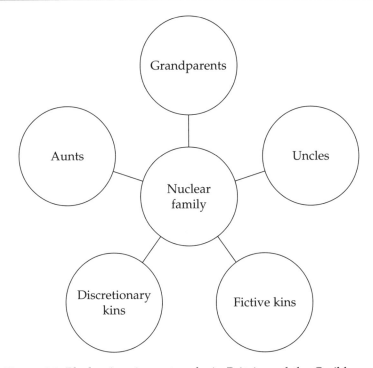

Figure 2.3 Black migration networks in Britain and the Caribbean

arrivals from the Caribbean arriving between 1953 and 1954 had addresses of friends and relations in London. In *Newcomers: West Indians In London* (1960: 44–5), Glass maintained that 'When newly-arrived West Indians are asked on the boat-train to London if they have an address to go to, they usually produce an air-mail letter from a relative or friend' (Figure 2.3).

These affined or kindred bonds were and still are intrinsic to the existentialist traditions as well as ensuring fealty. As illustrated in Figure 2.3, aunts, uncles, grandparents, fictive and discretionary kins all played their part in the migration chain and, as we shall see later, the links between Black families in Britain and families in Africa and the Caribbean are still being maintained.

Black families and kinship networks

The family is regarded as one of the most important primary groups in society. According to Gelles (1995: 10), the family can be defined as a social group and a social institution that possesses an identifiable structure composed of positions such as breadwinner, child-rearer, decision-maker and nurturer between whom there are constant inter-actions. However, Gelles' depiction is Eurocentric, as it does not encompass the family forms exhibited for Africans and African Caribbeans. In both ethnic groups, the socialisation of children extends beyond the consanguinean structure (Commonwealth Student's Children Society, 1995: 9). An example of this is evident in scaffolding behaviour, where children are sent from the Caribbean and Africa to be raised by family members in Britain as a type of inter-state adoption bypassing all the State's formalities.

The Black family structure in Britain whose roots are in both Africa and the Caribbean is matriarchal and extended. The extended family is premised on a collaboration of shared social allegiances and values that are transmitted from birth. Reciprocal and bi-directional socialisation is fundamental to the functional importance of the group, providing a psychological and sociological provenance, advantageous in determining life-goals (Weisner *et al.*, 1997: 21–2). Allied to this is respect for older people, especially among Africans, and for the highly valued prudence of the elderly. The educated person who genuflects before an elder does so not as a matter of subservience but as a sign of respect. Another indicator of reverence is the lowering of the eyes when addressing an elder. To Europeans, this is misconstrued as insincerity, but raising one's eyes to an elder is regarded as insolence (Stapleton *et al.*, 1978: 17–18).

Matrifocality arose as a result of historical and socioeconomic conditions. For example, plantation slavery undermined the role of Black males and transformed African family organisation, resulting in women becoming the omphalos of the family structure; during slavery in South Africa women reproduced on the understanding that maternity is primary but paternity is secondary and unimportant. Legislations in Africa and the Caribbean did not recognise enslaved African marriages, and it was customary for slaveholders to sell enslaved Africans away from their kin. The Black male's role was perfunctory. Any cementing of the union between two enslaved Africans would indubitably upset the social and political construction of plantation polity (Scully, 1997: 19–30). Family patterns therefore had to be responsive by adapting to the assigned roles for an enslaved person in an imperialist dominated society. Thus it may be said that trans-Atlantic enslavement and imperialism expunged the authority of African males, since the shape, composition and nature of the family form was governed and dictated by the volition of the slave master (Smith, 1962: 12). The result has been that gender roles have evolved and are defined somewhat differently from those that occur in British or European family forms. To the outsider, fathers (a point which I shall discuss later) are not visualised as fulfilling their roles and are sometimes described as marginal (Barrow, 1996: 2–3). Accumulative evidence suggests that some Black living arrangements are similar to those that exist in both Africa and the Caribbean (Goulbourne, 2002: 234). It also appears that some Black family cultural values from the Caribbean are being replicated (Berthoud, 2006: 9). For example, in Britain as in the Caribbean there are high rates of lone parenthood and low rates of marriage. Pauw drew attention to the fact that a number of the households researched in the UK were ones that were in the main matrifocal (Pauw, 1975: 146). Notwithstanding, even if households are in the main matrifocal, mothers still do retain the love, affection and assistance of the extended family. A survey of kinship revealed that 72 per cent of those interviewed were residing only an hour from their mothers. Approximately just over a half spent time with their mothers several times per week or at least once a week, and 58 per cent said they telephoned or corresponded weekly (Family Policy Studies Centre, 2006: 1).

Richard Berthoud's research (2006) indicated that African Caribbean families compared with White families have very low rates of marriage; he concluded that: 'Two thirds of White men and women in that age group [their late twenties] had lived with a partner; little more than one third of Caribbeans had done so'. Only half the African Caribbeans he surveyed were in a formal marriage. The numbered separated or divorced was greater for Caribbeans than it was for Whites (Table 2.3).

Be that as it may, Black families, as a unit of collateral relations, retain close links with those abroad, either through frequent visits to what

Table 2.3 Marital status: Caribbeans compared with Whites

	Percentages	
	Caribbeans	Whites
Ever had a partner (age 25–29)	38	68
Is or was married to their partner (age 25–29)	51	73
Separated or divorced from their spouse (16–59)	18	9

Source: Fourth National Survey of Ethnic Minorities (quoted in Berthoud, 2006: 6)

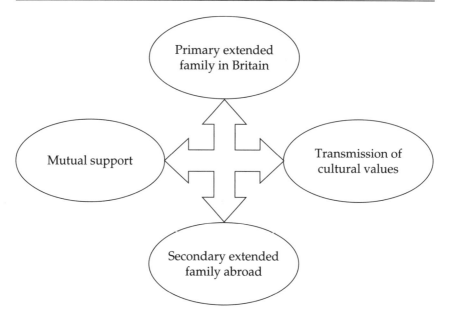

Figure 2.4 The transnational Black family paradigm

is often referred to as 'home', or by regular exchange of missives
and presents (Patterson, 1963: 298–9). In the years since the major
migrations from Africa and the Caribbean, Black British families continue to augment their kinship networks in two basic ways. Firstly,
although the empirical data may indicate that Black African Caribbeans
are over-represented as lone parents, there is indeed evidence to suggest that family members continue to reside in geographical proximity and this may assist in reinforcing the support of the extended family
being a unit of self-reliance (Chamberlain 2001: 131). Secondly, Black
people have evolved into transnationals, illustrating that political
boundaries cannot harness traditions (Figure 2.4).

There are indeed a plethora of reasons why Black families in Britain
desire to remain in close contacts with relatives outside Britain. These
links are relevant to the transmission of cultural values as well as providing an arena and paradigm for psychological, economic development and emotional aid in times of need (Goulbourne, 2002: 161–72).
For example, among Ghanaians, family life is arranged within a
synallagmatic structure, salutary in a milieu that eschews African
traditional values. Where citizenship does not translate into rights
and entitlements then consanguinity becomes more cogent. Layton-
Henry's research (2003) in Birmingham revealed that many African

Caribbeans believe it is important to maintain links with family members in the Caribbean because it assists in the maintenance of their patrimony and identity. Such networks are important in initiating strategies and multi-dimensional problem-solving. Support is translated into assistance such as foreign exchange remittances to family members abroad. Occasionally, the duties performed are tantamount to a political act. For example, Black families in Britain are constantly blighted by the problems of racism and underachievement in the education system. Many Black parents disappointed with the education system in Britain have begun to send their children 'home' to be educated. One headline in the Telegraph (19 March 2006) reads: 'British children sent to the West Indies for a better education'. The report intimated that children sent to the West Indies reside with families who provided them with opportunities to be in receipt of a more disciplined and traditional form of existence. Here is certainly evidence for what is sociologically termed 'child-shifting'. 'Child-shifting' is another form of fosterage, which involves the re-allocation of dependants to a household that does not include a natural parent (Gordon, 1987: 422–7). 'Child-shifting' in this sense is certainly not new. Early migrants from the Caribbean and Africa relied on 'child-shifting' arrangements to ease the burden of travel to the UK. Children in both Africa and the Caribbean remained in the care of family members until their parents arranged for them to settle in Britain. Another classic example of the importance of consanguineous or kinship links is the desire of some Black people to return to their primary societies in Africa and the Caribbean. The empirical evidence appears to suggest that hundreds are returning each year to what are considered their primary societies. Figure 2.5 gives us some indication of the numbers returning to Jamaica between 1993 and 1997 from the UK and the United States of America (USA) to settle permanently. Resettlement in Africa or the Caribbean should be conceptualised as a kind of spiritual contract between the primary and secondary units of the extended family.

The extended family in Africa and the Caribbean is not only a sociological unit; it is equally a complex spiritual outfit with opportunities and economic connections. Land is a key aspect of the extended family's collective social memory. It concretises their sense of incorporeal identity, which in turn inspirits consciousness, rejuvenates connections and reaffirms solidarity. Those returning are restoring cultural harmony, imperative to their spiritual, social and emotional memories. To be interred after death in the same spiritual space as your ancestors is to further strengthen the ancestral bond as well as to repair the link fractured by incongruous circumstances. As these specific events

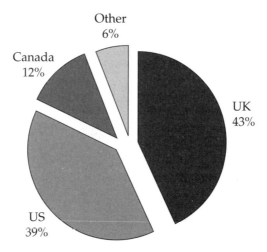

Figure 2.5 Returning residents to Jamaica between 1993 and 1997
Source: Ministry of Foreign Affairs, Jamaica (quoted in Goulbourne, 2002: 185)

such as birth and death rituals, paramount to the existence and function of the family, occur outside Europe, then the need to be more fully involved as some Black people get older becomes ever more alluring. This in my opinion indicates the cogency of extended family structures but it also provides us with some evidence to show that the Black family in Britain is itself witnessing some degree of transformation as western social and cultural spaces circumscribe some of its norms and values; and it is this point I shall now attempt to address.

Black family transformations

Family size changes
Analogous to other primary groups, Black families are undergoing changes some of which are useful in meeting and dealing with new challenges. The Black family structure is not static. Its metastable configuration has led many writers on the subject (among them Berthoud, 2006) to conclude that Caribbean cultural values are abating. Generational changes alloyed with increased length of settlement and acculturations have combined to effect these changes. Some of the transformations I wish to moot here are palpable while others are not as conspicuous. For example, unlike the first generation of Africans and Caribbeans who came to the UK, Blacks are now having fewer children. The notion of male virility and female fertility salient in traditional societies as symbols of divine blessings is beginning to

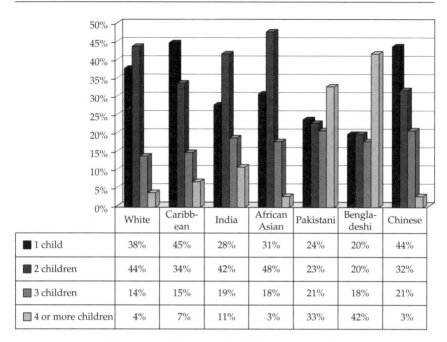

	White	Caribb-ean	India	African Asian	Pakistani	Bengla-deshi	Chinese
■ 1 child	38%	45%	28%	31%	24%	20%	44%
■ 2 children	44%	34%	42%	48%	23%	20%	32%
▨ 3 children	14%	15%	19%	18%	21%	18%	21%
▨ 4 or more children	4%	7%	11%	3%	33%	42%	3%

Figure 2.6 Number of children per family
Source: Madood *et al.*, 1997: 4

wane in Britain. Figure 2.6 indicates that Black Caribbean reproduction patterns are analogous to White reproduction patterns. Whereas 4 per cent of Whites have four or more children, the figure for African Caribbeans is 7 per cent; 11 per cent for Indians, 42 per cent for Bangladeshis and 33 per cent for Pakistanis. According to the Family Policy Studies Centre (2006: 9) fertility rates for African Caribbean and African women have been plummeting since the 1970s.

Additionally, Black household sizes compared with, say, South Asians are much smaller. A 2001 survey revealed that Bangladeshi households were the largest of all, with an average size of 4.5 people. For Pakistanis the figure was 4.1, while for Indians it was 3.3. The study of 2001 highlighted that the smallest households were African Caribbeans and White British, both with an average size of 2.3 individuals (Office for National Statistics, 2007: 5).

Exogamous partnerships
Another major transformation is the numbers of exogamous relationships. Inter-ethnic partnerships have been occurring for centuries but they were comparatively few and were discouraged by those whose pejorative

ratiocinations about Africans were premised on pseudo-scientific arguments. For example, Edward Long, the planter–historian, remarking about Dual Heritage said:

> Let any man turn his eyes to the Spanish America dominions, and behold what vicious brutal and degenerate breed of mongrels has been there produced, between the Spaniards, Blacks, Indians and their mixed progeny; and he must be of opinion, that it might be much better for Britain, and Jamaica too, if the White men in the colony would abate of their infatuate attachment to the black women, and instead of being graced with a yellow offspring of their own, perform the duty incumbent on every good citizen, by raising in honourable wedlock a 'race' of unadulterated beings. (Long, 1774: 327)

Research in 1940 by the University of Liverpool showed that inter-ethnic marriages were occurring in that city on a large scale, between West African men and English women. The children of these unions were stigmatised as semi-savages with inferior mental abilities. Fletcher's study (1930) noted that the thinking at the time was that Dual Heritage children should be trained for specific ignominious tasks. Inter-ethnic marriages are more common now and contend with far less prejudice than they did during the twentieth century. Data from the Office for National Statistics (2005: 2) attest to the fact that Black men are much more likely to engage in exogamous relationships compared with other ethnic groups (Figure 2.7).

Figure 2.7 illustrates that, compared with other ethnic groups, Dual Heritage men and Black men demonstrate a greater propensity for exogamous relationships. The question is, why are Blacks marrying outside their ethnic group? The reasons, facile as they may appear, are to do with sociocultural assimilation (Muttarak, 2003: 4–13). White culture is definitely the Black man's solatium in the sense that Black culture is not without its echoes of imperialism. This markedly illustrates the magnitude and anfractuosities of the colonial and neo-colonial relationship. Certainly, colonialism repositioned Black people's frame of reference, composing a new dialectical situation that produced stereotypes and narratives of civilisation. Examples of this are the religion and system of nomenclature that have been adopted by Black people. This resulted in the birth of 'Black British people', a term first coined by William Knibb, a radical English Baptist missionary who served in Jamaica and vehemently opposed African enslavement (Hinton, 1847). Thus acculturation assisted in shaping homomorphic mores to those of the coloniser. This cultural conscription makes it less difficult for Blacks compared with other

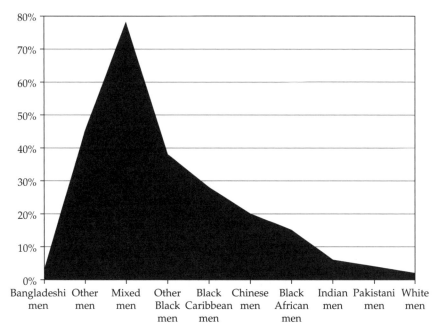

Figure 2.7 Percentages of exogamous marriages
Source: *Guardian*, 2006

ethnic groups to bridge the sociological hiatus. More assimilation will indubitably augment exogamous marriages. Figure 2.8 highlights that those born in Britain, compared with the first generation of immigrants, have a higher propensity to marry or cohabit with a White partner.

Elderly: changed relationships

Another aspect of change is the role and function of the elderly. In Africa and the Caribbean the elderly are revered, keeping alive conventions and tabus. In Britain there is some evidence to suggest that the influence and position of the elderly has declined. In some families, grandparents contributed to the household economy. However, migration alloyed with acculturation to norms and values in British society have modulated the role of the elderly and disrupted the current of continuity (Plaza, 2001: 219–31). In Britain the State plays a more dominant role in family arrangements; it could be argued that the State has taken over the power the elderly once held. Unlike Africa and the Caribbean, grandparents do not have the power to determine social outcomes in major disputes. Furthermore, grandparents cannot, given current regulations, structure child-shifting arrangements; such arrangements must be conducted via the State. The State is a cogent

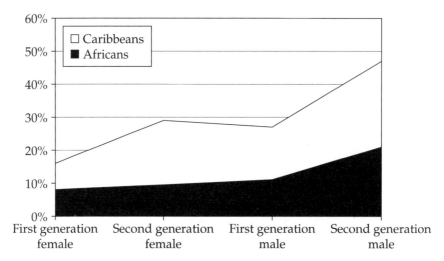

Figure 2.8 UK Comparison between first- and second-generation
African Caribbeans with White partners

Source: *The Fourth National Survey of Ethnic Minorities*, 1994
(quoted in Muttarak, 2003: 13)

partner whose indomitable influences cannot be eschewed. State intervention and bureaucracy unwittingly have the effect of constraining
the ambit of influence the elderly once possessed in child-rearing
decisions. Legislation in Britain has assisted in marginalising the
roles of the elderly and grandparents. Increasingly, owing to shifting
family and cultural patterns such as an inestimable reduction in
multi-generational households, the more elderly African and African
Caribbeans are being placed in care homes (Department of Health,
2006: 7). Traditionally, ethnic minorities prefer to care for the elderly
in their own homes and most share the belief that it is disgraceful to
place the elderly in residential care (Fyson, 1984: 24). Indeed, the Black
elderly have a number of special needs and problems beyond the general issues confronting elders (Fyson, 1984: 21). For example, many find
it difficult to participate in mainstream activities given the inimical recep-
tion they often receive. This can sometimes mean that older Black
people feel unwelcome and isolated.

Growing old in Britain is certainly difficult for Black people. Many
who came here regarded themselves as transients. As Plaza (2001: 231)
opined, elderly Black people laboured under the belief that 'they
would accumulate sufficient savings to return to the Caribbean'.
However, for the vast majority this has not materialised and many are
trapped in Britain and often made to feel as if they do not belong.

Children in residential social care

Another issue that I wish to discuss here is the increasing number of Black children currently ending up in the social care system, including secure children's and foster homes, many with disastrous consequences (Barn *et al.*, 1997; Barn, 2001). Fyson (1984: 21) notes that by the mid-1970s almost half the children in care in Wandsworth were of Caribbean origins, while in Wolverhampton a third of the children in care were classified as Black. Stapleton *et al.* (1978: 119–31) have documented extensively the difficulties experienced by many West Africans, notably Nigerians and Ghanaians who leave their children in foster care to pursue their studies. This indicates that the Black family's authority over the socio-political environment is diminishing. These arrangements are becoming more common: according to *Black Britain* in its discourse about London (2006: 1), in the social care system there are approximately 4,500 Dual Heritage children and 3,900 children of Black Heritage (Figure 2.9).

What this indicates in my opinion is that government policy continues to disempower Black families (Morgan, 1995). It may also suggest

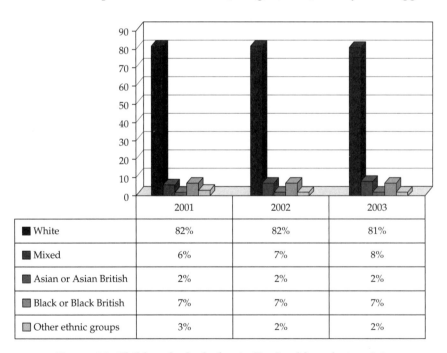

	2001	2002	2003
■ White	82%	82%	81%
■ Mixed	6%	7%	8%
■ Asian or Asian British	2%	2%	2%
■ Black or Black British	7%	7%	7%
☐ Other ethnic groups	3%	2%	2%

Figure 2.9 Children looked after in England by ethnic origin
between 2001 and 2003

Source: Department of Health, 2007: 10

that growing economic and social pressures are forcing many Black families to conform to norms and values irrelevant to them. Most certainly in Africa and the Caribbean with a less anfractuous and powerful social care system the breath of family support is considerable via the conduits of 'rites of passage' such as naming ceremonies and the interment of the navel cord (known as the 'navel string' in Jamaica). Burial of the navel cord or string consolidates the family's socio-spiritual networks.

It is believed that racial stereotyping and poverty may be responsible for the growing numbers of Black children in the UK social care system. For example, Barn (2001: 207–17) notes that statutory agencies utilise a more rigid assessment framework in the referral of Black families. Based on an analysis of admissions patterns, Barn (2001: 206–9) maintains that Black young people not only entered the social care system more rapidly compared with other ethnic groups, they also spent longer periods and were less likely to be returned to their families.

Racial stereotyping – in terms of viewing African and or African Caribbean males as aggressive, especially where child abuse is mentioned – often mean that assessment frameworks employed by UK social workers are specious. For example, Black males will often employ hyperbolical statements, which are not meant to be taken seriously or literally. As Arnold (1982: 109) intimates:

> The West Indian parent who threatens to beat the living daylight out of a disobedient child, or asks to leave 'if he thinks himself a man' seldom means to be taken literally. These are his or her attempts at imposing discipline in the hope that the threats will serve as a deterrent for the delinquent behaviour.

It has also been suggested that the high numbers of African Caribbean children in the social care system may be due to Black people's misconception about its operation. Certainly, Fitzherbert (1967: 69–72) intimates that Black parents in the early period, displaying the attachment complex of colonised people, were placing their children in the State's social care system as they believed the children would acquire habits and skills that would equip them for a better life in the UK. Yet even if this was not the case as Barn (2001) appears to believe, the fact that large numbers of Black children are entering residential care does seem to indicate that the theory and scope of the Social Service's culture excludes Black families from the channels of a participatory working partnership. Transformation must not, however, be visualised in a negative light as all social institutions are confronted by new challenges. Black families have certainly had to cope with racial harassment, poverty and discrimination and it is to these I shall now turn.

Discrimination and the Black family

Black people have been facing racial discrimination in Britain since their arrival on British shores in large numbers between and after the two World Wars. In the 1950s and 1960s advertisements for rented accommodation stated that 'coloureds' would not be welcomed (Smith 1977: 287). The activities of right-wing political parties and their views on Black and other ethnic minorities in Britain are well documented (*British Patriot* 1978: 11; Jones, 1977: 23–44; Maher, 1996: 13–45; Smith, 1996: 13). Signs such as 'Niggers go home' and 'Pakis out', were routine in the 1960s. Many anti-Black groups such as the *White Defence League*, via its publication *Black and White News*, increased the pressure on government by printing headlines such as '*BLACKS MILK THE ASSISTANCE BOARD*'. One right-wing publication known as *Action* printed in 1959 a number of hostile headlines against Blacks. These included; '*MORE SPENT ON BLACKS THAN ON BRITISH HOMES*' and '*IS BRITAIN TO BE A BLACK CESSPOOL*'? These emotive headlines may have played their part in the racist murder of Kelso Cochrane, a young Caribbean carpenter murdered in London on the night of 17 May 1959 (Glass, 1960: 158–71). As late as 1978 the *British Patriot* published the following racist poem:

> The Lord God Almighty
> gave him Africa
> The treacherous British
> governments gave him
> Britain and said that
> he was British
> By opposing the coloured
> invasion and
> by instituting a policy
> of repatriation, the
> British Movement
> is defending the Lord's work.
> Whose side are you on?
> (*British Patriot*, 1978: 11)

In the 1950s, Black children were regarded as educationally subnormal and treated less fairly compared with their White counterparts. In the 1970s, 34 per cent of the 'educationally sub-normal' school population in the Inner London Education Authority area were children of migrants, despite the fact that they only composed 17 per cent of the total school population (Littlewood and Lipsedge, 1997: 152). Today there is much discourse about Black educational underachievement and their disproportionately high rates of exclusion from mainstream schools (Mamon, 2004: 78–9). Soon after the publication of the Macpherson Report, the Office for Standards in Education (Ofsted), documented that less than a quarter of the twenty-five Local Educational Authorities visited had a lucid strategy for raising the academic attainment of ethnic minorities (Mamon, 2004: 80).

Accumulated evidence suggests racism is responsible for the relatively low rates of Black academic attainment. For example, only 25 per cent of African Caribbean boys obtain five good General Certificates of Secondary Education (GCSEs) compared with 51 per cent of the population as a whole (BBC, 2006: 1). Figure 2.10 illustrates the low level of attainment by Black Caribbean pupils in Tower Hamlets, East London, between 1994 and 2002. Whereas the figures improved for Bangladeshi and White children in Tower Hamlets, for Black Caribbean pupils improvement was only marginal. For example, in 1994 16 per cent of White pupils gained five GCSEs grades A

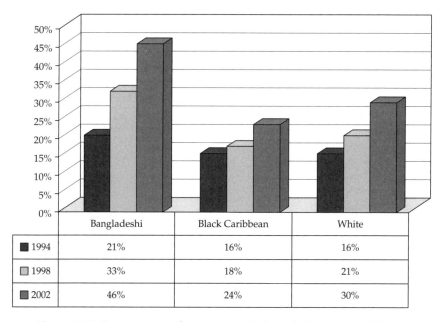

	Bangladeshi	Black Caribbean	White
■ 1994	21%	16%	16%
□ 1998	33%	18%	21%
■ 2002	46%	24%	30%

Figure 2.10 Percentages of young people by ethnic origin in Tower Hamlets, London, achieving five GCSEs grades A–C; 1994–2002

Source: Dench, 2006: 142

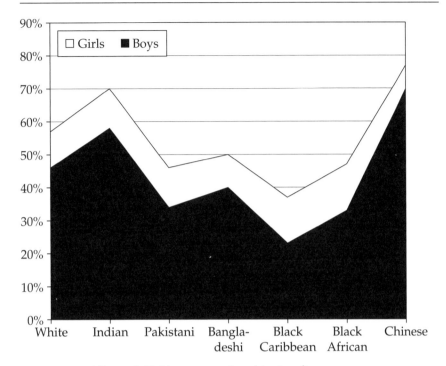

Figure 2.11 Young people achieving five or more
GCSEs A–C in England 2004
Source: Dobbs *et al.*, 2006

to C. In 1998 this increased to 21 per cent and, in 2002, to 30 per cent. For Black Caribbean pupils 16 per cent gained five GCSEs grades A to C in 1994, 18 per cent reached the same level in 1998 and only 24 per cent achieved the same results in 2002. In contrast, in 2002 the percentage of Bangladeshi pupils who gained five GCSEs grades A to C was 46 per cent.

The statistics in Figure 2.11 for 2004 covering England as a whole show that, analogous to the situation in Tower Hamlets, children of Caribbean heritage are under-performing. For example, only 40 per cent of girls and 25 per cent boys obtained five or more GCSEs at grades A to C, compared with 70 per cent for girls and 60 per cent for boys from the Indian community.

Concerning school exclusions, Black children are over-represented in the exclusion statistics and are four times more likely to be excluded compared with their White counterparts (Brown and Sessions, 1997). Figure 2.12 corroborates the fact that school exclusions are indeed higher for Black and Dual Heritage children (notably White and Black Caribbean). Underachievement and exclusion comes at a cost. It

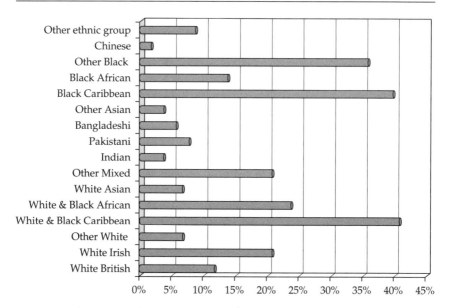

Figure 2.12 Permanent school exclusions in England by
ethnic group, 2004–05

Source: Office for National Statistics, 2007: 29

exacerbates the tensions between Black families and the State by creating an army of unskilled young people who will face exclusion in their adult life.

Aside from exclusion, Black children are confronted daily by racial harassment and racial discrimination from their peers. Research in Hampshire between 1993 and 1996 by Smith (1996) emphasised the fact that children even within the so-called safe confines of the State's education system are not free from racial abuse (Figure 2.13). The incidents ranged from name-calling to physical abuse and incitement to racial hatred.

Black families are also lower down the economic scale. A study in Leicestershire evidenced that the economic position of African Caribbean men is considerably worse compared with their White counterparts. For example, whereas only 8 per cent of White men were unemployed, for Black men it was 22 per cent. The study also showed that a greater proportion of Black people occupy manual and lower manual positions compared with White people. For example, whereas 11.7 per cent of employed Black people are categorised as employers or managers, the figure for Whites is 15.5 per cent. In manual occupations the figures were Blacks, 53.2 per cent and Whites, 45.5 per cent (Benyon, 1996). Ethnic minorities are confronted with major difficulties

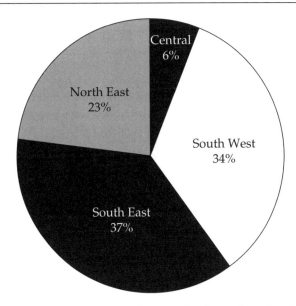

Figure 2.13 Racist incidents in the four educational
divisions in Hampshire

Source: Hampshire County Education Department, 1993: 4

when they apply for jobs. One *Guardian* article with a headline that
read 'Racist firms keep Black unemployment high' went on to state,
based on government figures, that Black men are five times more likely
to be unemployed compared with White men (*Guardian*, 2001). On the
whole, UK minority groups are more vulnerable to unemployment compared with Whites. All these findings appear to suggest that racism
is an impediment to Black families (Smith, 1977: 104).

Discrimination is replicated in other areas such as housing. Black
families are over-represented in the rented housing sector compared
with Whites and most other minority ethnic UK groups, and under-
represented in the home ownership sectors (see Figures 2.14 and 2.15).

Although the data are based on research carried out in London they
nonetheless highlight what is regarded as a basic problem and convey the fact that people of African descent fare far worse compared
with most other ethnic groups (Owen, 2001: 75). What is interesting
here is that discrimination in housing against Black families is not new.
In the 1960s and 1970s Black families waited much longer than White
families to be housed and were frequently allocated accommodation
in the more squalid areas (Ali, 1979: 23). These disadvantages have
facilitated social vehicles to propagate identity consciousness and it
is these that I will now discuss.

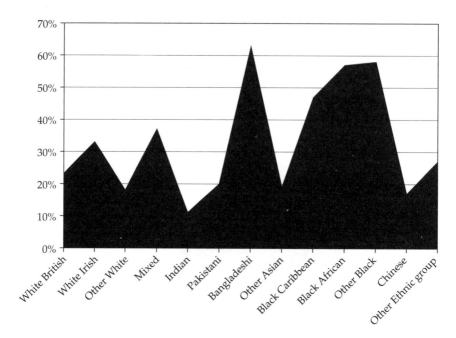

Figure 2.14 Ethnic breakdown of the socially rented sector
Source: Dobbs *et al.*, 2006

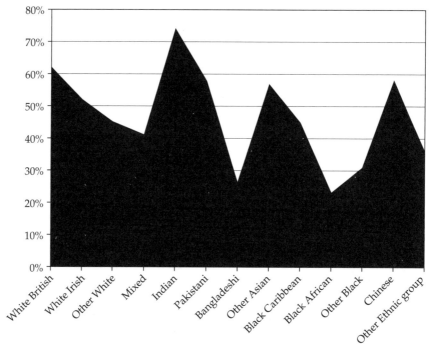

Figure 2.15 Owner-occupation by ethnic category
Source: Dobbs *et al.*, 2006

Black families and the search for national consciousness

Supplementary schools

Given the levels of socioeconomic exclusion to which they have been subject, Black families are now beginning to undergo a process of conscientisation. The emergence of racial consciousness is due to the antidialogic nature of society and institutional racism (Figure 2.16).

The reasons for counter-hegemonic structures are to counteract inter-group conflict and maximise commonalities to challenge oppression. Evidence of this is seen in the burgeoning numbers of supplementary schools across the UK providing academic support for Black children. They also indicate the gravity of political activity given that the current educational climate hardly augurs well for Black children. Supplementary schools provide what is now commonly known as Black History. The belief is that equipping Black children with their history and culture will give them self-confidence to cope within a European-centric education system. There are calls from sections of the Black community for the State education sector to make Black History available at General Certificate of Education (GCSE) level (Minutes of the Oxfordshire Black History Group Meeting, 2006). More importantly, supplementary schools make a fundamental contribution to children's learning. Schools such as the Marcus Garvey Supplementary School in Birmingham, the Chapeltown Independent After School (CIAS) in Leeds and the Motherland Project in London have for many years been operating Saturday classes and after-school and remedial classes in mathematics, English and science, long before the State sector even started on the idea. Supplementary schools demonstrate shared sociological imperatives for Black families in order that social communication should become possible about matters such as school exclusions and racism (Black Information Link, 2006: 2; Dodgson, 1984: 57–8).

Connected to supplementary schools are the numerous parents' support groups around the UK. The aim is to promote group loyalty and solidarity to confront the generalised 'other', as well as to provide assistance for parents and young people.

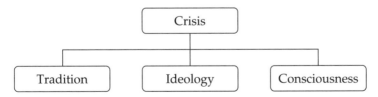

Figure 2.16 The formation of Black consciousness

Black fathers

Among the many important changes and challenges are the roles of Black fathers. Once regarded as feckless and irresponsible, fathers of African descent are now engaged in a self-righting drive for dependability and this can only be helpful in correcting some of the deficits. The literature in the past failed to link the fact that Black fathers' absenteeism was connected to their exclusion from the labour market that resulted in their emasculation and displacement (Reynolds, 2001: 134).

While it is indeed wholly specious to treat Black men as a homogenous group, it is fair to say that on the whole Black men are beginning to take seriously their role as fathers. Organisations such as the Leeds Black Men's Forum have for a long time been disseminating information about the importance of fathers as positive role models. According to Trevor Gordon, keynote speaker at the 1998 Black Men's Forum National Conference held in Leeds, not only must Black men begin to respect women, they must also assist in rejuvenating the extended family and take their responsibilities seriously (Hylton, 1999: 24–39).

Reynolds' research (2001: 133–53) illustrates that Black fathers' roles in the family is on the increase. Reynolds advances the view that 'despite the existence of a significant gender difference between men and women involving childcare provision, there appears to be no significant ethnic difference between Black and White fathers concerning the amount of childcare they provide' (Reynolds, 2001: 138). The amount of time spent caring for children has increased since the late 1990s for both Black and White fathers. This growing consciousness is linked to an awareness and realisation among Black men of how racism and racial discrimination play their part in both trivialising and subverting their roles and functions (Hylton, 1997: 2–24).

Housing

Another point I wish to mention here is about Black Housing Associations. Their main remit is to provide accommodation for Black families. Black Housing Associations such as Karibu in Southampton were born out of political processes, recognising that Black families had to wait longer to be housed or re-housed. Black Housing Associations are a political statement; an ontological act to gain mastery over events and restore an acceptable level of social independence.

Spirituality

There is some evidence to indicate that Black families are using religion as a vehicle to mould cultural identity and politicise activities. Caribbean families are now turning to Kwanza, a festival rooted in an East African tradition (ESRC, 2006: 1). Many will attend church on Christmas Day as part of what they visualise as British tradition but later participate in Kwanza celebrations to counter what they see as rabid materialism of the festive period. Those who identified Kwanza as a time for family festivities voiced cynicism about Christmas because it is imbued with European values and embroidered with materialism. Kwanza celebrants intimated there are strategic benefits to this ceremony as it facilitates more poignantly their reaffirmation of Black unity and culture. In particular, young Black people are beginning to employ their families as cultural provenance points from which to reaffirm their continuous relationship with the Caribbean and Africa.

The growth of the Rastafarian movement in Britain among young Black people is a synthesis of ideology and tradition. Rastafarians believe social ills can be tackled by a rejuvenation of cultural identity, and the movement provides a cultural space for sacralisation, comradeship energies and self-identity. The Bible becomes a cultural register to valorise Black people in a manner conducive to their racial identity and consciousness.

Of equal importance is the proliferation of Black Majority Churches (BBC News, 2006). Black people are also turning to the religious and spiritual tenets of their progenitors such as 'Obeah'. Indeed, Pauw (1975: 54) asserts that belief in sortilege did not dissipate even with high academic attainment. Pauw found that a substantial proportion of the mothers interviewed believe that certain ailments lay outside the scope of medical doctors and hence they frequently resorted 'to traditional Bantu doctors, particularly when sorcery is suspected' (Pauw, 1975: 87).

The questions here are: why are some Black families turning to Obeah? Is this a sign of cultural retrogression? In my opinion it is simply because they reside in an intractable environment that devalues their identity; cosmological reality has to be reconstructed to give meaning and purpose to their social life. Allied to this is the psychological assurance that alleviates suffering. Thus the Obeah practitioner becomes the thaumaturge, whose spirit and eudemonic mediation between the social and the spiritual formulates a comprehensive identity infrastructure for racial and cultural consciousness and self-determination.

Conclusion

In this chapter, I have examined the Black family by examining migration. I have also, with the use of empirical data, highlighted some of the structural changes and challenges confronting families of

African descent in Britain. What certainly clearly holds true is that the Black family, similar to many primary groups, is 'facing-up' to challenges. Equally important in this discourse is the fact that the Black family is confronted with racial discrimination and racism, and these carry with them severe repercussions. The poor employment figures for Black men and the underachievement of Black boys in particular are of particular concern. Yet what is most certainly true here is that Black families are not resigned to their fate. Despite the fact that the empirical data may indicate that large numbers of African Caribbean and Dual Heritage children are entering the social care system, there is yet no evidence to prove that a process of forisfamiliation is occurring, or that Black family structures are beginning to break down. What it does show is that some of the formalisms are being re-created and adapted to fit into Western structures. They too show notions of resilience and psychological resolve. Black people are, in the words of that famous Black Jamaican poet Claude McKay (1959), 'pressed to the wall, dying but fighting back'.

References

Adi, H. (1995), *The History of the African and Caribbean Communities in Britain* (London: Hodder Wayland)

Ali, A. (1979), *West Indians in Britain* (London: Hansib Publications)

Allason-Jones, J. (1989), *Women in Roman Britain* (London: British Museum Publications)

Anwar, M. (1986), *Race and Politics* (London: Tavistock)

Arnold, E. (1982), 'The use of corporal punishment in child rearing in the West Indies', *Child Abuse and Neglect*, 6: 141–5

Barn, R. (2001), 'The Caribbean family and the child welfare system in Britain', in Goulbourne, H. and Chamberlain, M. (eds), *Caribbean Families in Britain and the Trans-Atlantic World* (London: Macmillan)

Barn, R., Sinclair, R. and Ferdinand, D. (1997), *Acting on Principle: An Examination of Race and Ethnicity in Social Services Provision for Children* (London: BAAF/CRE)

Barrow, C. (1996), *Family in the Caribbean* (Oxford: James Curry Publishers)

BBC News (2006), *Minorities Prop Up Church Going* (18 September) (London: BBC)

Benyon, J. (1996), *African-Caribbean People in Leicestershire: Summary of the Final Report* (Leicester: University of Leicester)

Berthoud, R. (2006), *Family Formation in Multi-Cultural Britain* (Essex: Institute for Social and Economic Research, University of Essex)

Black Britain (2006), *Unemployment and Ethnicity* (17 October) (London)

Black Information Link (2006), *Supporting Black Parents* (London: 1990 Trust)

British Patriot (1978) newspaper of The British Movement, No. 65

Brown, S. and Sessions, J. (1997), 'A profile of British unemployment: regional versus demographic influences', *Regional Studies: The Journal of the Regional Studies Association*, 31:4, 351–66

Byron, M. (1994), *Post War Caribbean Migration to Britain – The Unfinished Cycle* (Aldershot: Avebury)

Chamberlain, M. (2001), 'Narratives of Caribbean families in Britain and the Caribbean', in Goulbourne H. and Chamberlain M. (eds), Caribbean families in Britain and the Trans-Atlantic World (London and Oxford: Macmillan Education Ltd)

Chamberlain, M. (1997), *Narratives of Exile and Return* (London: Macmillan)

Coard, B. (1971), *How the West Indian Child is Made Educationally Subnormal in the British School System* (London: New Beacon Books)

Commonwealth Students' Children Society (1995), *Report of a Seminar on the African Child in Great Britain* (London: Commonwealth Students' Children Society)

Davidson, R. B. (1962), *West Indian Migrants: Social and Economic Facts of Migration from the West Indies* (Oxford: Oxford University Press)

Dench, G., Gavron, K. and Young, M. (2006), *The New East End: Kinship, Race and Conflict* (London: Profile Books)

Department of Health (2006), *A Sure Start to Later Life: Ending Inequalities for Older People; A Social Exclusion Unit Final Report* (London: Office of the Deputy Prime Minister)

Department of Health (2007), *Social Care Statistics: Children Looked After in England* (London: TSO Publications)

Dobbs, J., Green, H. and Zealy, L. (2006) *National Statistics: Focus on Ethnicity and Religion* (London: Palgrave Macmillan)

Dodgson, E. (1984), *Motherland: West Indian Woman to Britain* (London: Heinemann)

ESRC (Economic and Social Research Council) (2006), *Caribbean Families Embrace Kwanza as Christmas Becomes Materialistic* (Swindon: ESRC)

Family Policies Studies Centre (2006) *Family Poverty and Social Exclusion*, Briefing Paper No. 15 (London: Family Policy Studies Centre)

Fanon, F. (1967), *The Wretched of the Earth*, trans. C. Farringdon (Harmondsworth: Penguin)

Field, F. and Haikin, P. (1971), *Black Britons* (Oxford: Oxford University Press)

Figueroa, P. (1991), *Education and the Social Construction of Race* (London: Routledge)

Fitzherbert, K. (1967), *West Indian Children in London* (London: Bell Publications)

Fletcher, M. (1930), *Report on an Investigation into the Colour Problem in Liverpool and Other Ports* (Liverpool)

Fryer, P. (1984), *Staying Power: The History of Black People in Britain* (London: Pluto Press)

Fyson, N. (1984), *Multi-Ethnic Britain* (London: Batsford Academic Books)

Gelles, R. (1995), *Contemporary Families* (London: Sage Publications)

Glass, R. (1960), *Newcomers: The West Indian in London* (London: George Allen and Unwin Ltd)

Gordon, S. (1987), 'I Go To "Tanties": The economic significance of child-shifting in Antigua, West Indies', *Journal of Comparative Family Studies*, 18:3, 427–43

Goulbourne, H. (2002), *Caribbean Transnational Experience* (London: Pluto Press)

Guardian (2006), 'First Figures for Inter-Ethnic Marriages' (22 March)

Guardian (2001), 'Racist Firms Keep Black Unemployment High' (11 January)

Halstead, M. (1988), *Education, Justice and Cultural Diversity: An Examination of the Honeyford Affair* (London: Falmer Press)

Hampshire County Education (1993), *A Hampshire Approach to National Curriculum History at Key Stage 3: Materials on Black peoples of the Americas* (Winchester: Hampshire County Education)

Haynes, A. (1987), *The State of Black Britain* (Antigua: Hansib)

Hill, C. (1969), *Immigration and Integration: A Study of the Settlement of Coloured Minorities in Britain* (Oxford: Pergamon Press)

Hill, C. S. (1958), *Black and White in Harmony: The Drama of West Indians in the Big City from a London Minister's Notebook* (London: Hodder and Stoughton)

Hinton, J. (1847), *Memoir of William Knibb* (London: Houlston and Stoneman)

Hooper, R. (1965), *Colour in Britain* (London: British Broadcasting Corporation)

Hunte, J. A. (1966), *Nigger Hunting in England?* (London: West Indian Standing Conference)

Hylton, C. (1999), *Black Men's Forum 1998 National Conference Report: Men of African Descent Overcoming Social Exclusion* (Leeds: Gbakhanda Publishing)

Hylton, C. (1997), *Black Men in Britain: Marching into the Millennium* (London: Bogle L'Ouverture Press)

Jones, C. (1977), *Immigration and Social Policy in Britain* (London: Tavistock Publications)

Khan, S. (1982), 'The role of culture dominance in structuring the experience of ethnic minorities', in Husband, C. (ed.), *Race in Britain: Continuity and Change* (London: Hutchison and Co. Ltd)

Layton-Henry, Z. (2003), 'Transnational communities, citizenship and African Caribbeans in Birmingham', in Doomernick, J. and Knippenberg, H. (eds), *Migration and Immigrants: Between Policy and Reality* (Amsterdam: Aksant)

Littlewood, R. and Lipsedge, M. (1997), *Aliens and Alienists: Ethnic Minorities and Psychiatry* (London: Routledge)

Long, E. (1774), *The History of Jamaica or the General Survey of the Ancient State of that Island* (London: T. Lowndes)

Madood, T., Berthoud, R., Lackey, J., Nazroo, J., Smith, P., Virdee, S. and Beishon, S. (1997) *Ethnic Minorities in Britain: Diversity and Disadvantage* (London: Policy Studies Institute)

Maher, V. (1996), *Immigration and Social Identities* (London: Oxford University Press)

Mamon, S. (2004), 'Mapping the attainment of Black children in Britain', in Sivanandan, A. and Waters, H. (eds), *Race and Class* (London: Sage)

McKay, C. (1959), 'If we must die', in Johnson J. (ed.), *The Book of American Negro Poetry* (New York: Harcourt, Brace & World, Inc.)

Minutes of the Black History Group Meeting (2006), *Black History* (29 June) (Oxford: EMAS)

Morgan, P. (1995), *Farewell to the Family? Public Policy and Family Breakdown in Britain and the USA* (London: IEA Health and Welfare Unit)

Muttarak, R. (2003), 'Who intermarries in Britain? Ethnic intermarriage' (MSc dissertation, University of Oxford)

Ochieng, B. (2005), 'The Strength of the Black Extended Family and Its Influence on Well-Being', *The Northern Journal* (Spring): 34–46

Office for National Statistics (2007), *Social Trends* (London, Palgrave Macmillan)

Office for National Statistics (2005), *Ethnicity and Identity* (London: OfNS)

OREC (Oxfordshire Racial Equality Council) (2005), *Three Years of Business Planning* (Oxford: OREC)

Owen, D. (2001), 'A profile of Caribbean households and families in Great Britain', in Goulbourne, H. and Chamberlain, M. (eds), *Caribbean Families in Britain and the Trans-Atlantic World* (London: Macmillan)

Patterson, S. (1963), *Dark Strangers: A Study of West Indians in London* (London: Harmondsworth)

Pauw, B. (1975), *The Second Generation: A Study of the Family Among Urbanized Bantu in East London* (Oxford: Oxford University Press)

Peach, C. (1968), *West Indian Migration to Britain: A Social Geography* (London: Oxford University Press).

Plaza, D. (2001), 'Ageing in Babylon: Elderly Caribbeans in Britain', in Goulbourne, H. and Chamberlain, M. (eds), *Caribbean Families in Britain and the Trans-Atlantic World* (London: Macmillan)

Rex, J. (1970), *Race Relations in Sociological Theory* (London: Weidenfeld and Nicolson)

Rex, J. and Moore, R. (1967), *Race, Community and Conflict: A Study of Sparkbrook* (Oxford: Oxford University Press)

Reynolds, T. (2001), 'Caribbean Fathers in Family Lives in Britain', in Goulbourne, H. and Chamberlain, M. (eds), *Caribbean Families in Britain and the Trans-Atlantic World* (London: Macmillan)

Rose, E. (1969), *Colour and Citizenship: A Report on British Race Relations* (Oxford: Oxford University Press)

Said, E. (1993), *Culture and Imperialism* (London: Chatto & Windus)

Saunders, K. (1984), *Indentured Labour in the British Empire, 1834–1920* (London: Croom Helm)

Scully, P. (1997), *Liberating the Family? Gender and British Slave Emancipation in the Rural Cape, South Africa* (Oxford: James Curry)

Senior, C. and Manley, D. (1956), *The West Indian in Britain* (London: Fabian Colonial Bureau)

Sewell, T. (1998), *Keep on Moving: The Windrush Legacy* (London: The Voice Enterprises Ltd)

Smith, F. (1996), 'Racial Harassment and Racial Discrimination in Education in Hampshire' (MSc thesis, University of Oxford)

Smith, F. (1993), 'Has Britain Always Been a Multi-Faith Society?', in Klein, G. (ed.), *Multicultural Teaching* (London: Trentham Books)

Smith, D. (1977), *Racial Disadvantage in Britain* (London: Penguin)

Smith, M. (1962), *West Indian Family Structure* (Seattle: University of Washington Press)

Stapleton, P., Ellis, J. and Biggs V. (1978), *West African Families in Britain: A Meeting of Two Cultures* (London: Routledge and Kegan Paul)

Telegraph (2006), British Children sent to the West Indies for a Better Education' (19 March)

University of Liverpool (1940), *The Economic Status of Coloured Families in the Port of Liverpool* (Liverpool: Liverpool University Press)

Watson, A. R. (1942), *West Indian Workers in Britain* (London: Hodder and Stoughton)

Weisner, T., Bradley, C. and Kilbride, P. (1997), *Families and the Crisis of Social Change* (London: Bergin and Garvey)

3

Black families and child-rearing practices

Bertha Ochieng

Introduction

For Black families (Africans and African Caribbeans) in the United Kingdom (UK), child-rearing occurs within the ambiguities of a cultural heritage that is formed both from their own cultural background and British heritage, a social system that espouses democratic equality for all citizens and institutional racism for its minority citizens (McPherson, 1999). The environment of most Black children includes not only the special stress of poverty and discrimination (Beishoon *et al.*, 1998; Haskey, 2002), but also the ambiguity and marginality of living simultaneously in two worlds – the world of their Black community and the world of the mainstream White population. Consequently, for most Black parents, child-rearing involves mediating between two contradictory cultures. Using findings from a larger study conducted by the author (Ochieng, 2005) and drawing on other published work, the chapter will present a critical analysis of African Caribbean families' child-rearing practices. By means of an in-depth ethnographic interviewing process, ten African Caribbean families, comprising eighteen adults (eight men and ten women) with age range thirty-nine to sixty years and twenty-three adolescents (twelve to seventeen years of age), from West Yorkshire participated in the study with interviews conducted in their homes. The participants were not randomly selected and cannot therefore be regarded as 'typical' or representative in the statistical sense. However, they are typical in that their lives reflect the history and experiences of the social and the economic life of working-class African Caribbean families within West Yorkshire.

The concept of family has changed historically across cultures and classes, and family representation also alters with the life stages of its members. The consequence of this was that, before exploring African Caribbean families' child-rearing practices, it was essential to examine their family networks. Equally, in order to place Black children as central players within research and gain an insight into Black families' influences on their child socialisation process, the study commenced by inviting thirty Black adolescents, not associated with the ten families who participated in the study, to describe their families. The gender split was equally distributed between female and male; however, ten were classified as African and the remainder as African Caribbean. Questions that were posed related to the adolescents' gender, age and ethnicity, the ethnicity of their mother and father, the country of origin of both mother and father, and their household and family structures. Each interview lasted approximately forty-five minutes and was conducted by the author. The method used for data analysis was a comparative analysis; this involved constantly comparing the themes that emerged from the findings, thus allowing for diverse aspects of both household and family formations. Findings from adolescents in relation to their family dynamics were in line with Goulbourne and Chamberlain (1999) and Hylton's (1997) work, which both found that Black families comprise different households and have multiple parenting and interfamilial consensual adoptions.

In relation to child-rearing, the findings highlighted a number of contrasting multidimensional factors that acted as key determinants for African Caribbean families' child-rearing decisions. This was particularly significant since UK research with Black families has generally failed to take into account the central aspects of their life experiences. Similar to other ethnic groups, the mother was noted to have the most prominent role in child care and socialisation. The African Caribbean mothers appeared to value the role of a mother, viewing it as an important part of their sex-role identity. A number of other studies have also confirmed that Black mothers frequently prioritised the mother role over the wife and worker roles. In instances of inter-role conflicts, mothers would attempt to resolve the conflict by putting their children's needs before those of their husbands or employers (Dosanji, 1996; Harrison, 1981; Reynolds, 2001a). However, since there is a dearth of information on the role of Black fathers in child socialisation and the role of the extended family in childrearing, this is here a specific focus. Other key areas that emerged and are discussed include family–child interaction, racism, discipline, spirituality and identity. Education was also another key area; however, this has been considered by Tony Sewell in chapter four. This chapter concludes by stressing the need for a greater awareness and understanding of the nature of the socialisatin process for Black children.

Black adolescents' family dynamics

In describing their family structures, the thirty Black adolescents went beyond their household structures and mentioned their step-dad/ mum, grandparents, uncles, aunts, in-laws and step-families. In lone-parent households, the adolescents would include the non-resident parent and described the nature of contact with the non-resident parent and the role the non-resident parent family played in their welfare. This at times was even without the desire or support of the resident parent. One child, whose non-resident father had died three to four years previously, described how he continued to maintain contact with his paternal grandparents and (step-) sisters and brothers from the father's side of the family. Further confirmation of this process of socialisation was indicated by the continued involvement of fathers with children whether or not they were married to their children's mother. Fathers' relatives also had a role in their lives even after marriages and relationships had been dissolved and in some cases where they were never formalised. Nearly 90 per cent of adolescents also included their parent's friends, friends' children, and elders within the community where they lived as part of their family. Other notable family members were identified as friends of the adolescents and friends of the wider family. When prompted why they had included certain individuals as members of their families, the adolescents' narratives demonstrated that a family unit was in part not only a strategy for meeting physical, emotional and economic needs of families, but also seemed to commit family resources to crisis situations and played a key role in child-rearing.

Traditions such as maintaining the extended family were clearly very strong amongst these particular Black adolescents, which is perhaps an indication of the Black community ethos as a whole. These practices appear to have survived the process of westernisation into what is now for some adolescents the third or fourth generation of Black families living in Britain. Family structures and systems, which at first glance may seem antiquated, appear to exist for a purpose. It is argued that issues such as socioeconomic status and persistent discrimination have encouraged the survival of these structures. Thus, in the absence of an adequate welfare state, families continue to depend upon the integrity and collective responsibilities of their own people. This creates a strong sense of belonging and, possibly unlike many western families, members may not discuss problems or communicate personal hopes or fears to outsiders.

The adolescents were able to articulate a family system that seemed to mirror the traditional African extended family system. Authors such as Dodson (1981), Harrison *et al.* (1990) and Hylton (2000) have also documented this phenomenon. Hylton's (2000) study, which involved discussions with sixty women and men of African descent, also acknowledged the presence of extended families; however, participants in Hylton's study also stated that the traditional extended family systems are difficult to reproduce in an individualist environment. Similarly, Barn *et al.* (2006), whose study involved 446 minority ethnic parents (Asian, African, African Caribbean and White), found that for some families the process of migration from their countries of birth to Britain had resulted in the fragmentation of the wider family networks. However, the strong presence of extended networks different from the studies by Hylton and Barn *et al.* can be explained by the differences in age of participants, in that, in this present study, it was the adolescents and not the parents or adults who articulated the description of their family systems. The adolescents, who were either second- or third-generation migrants, confirmed that, for Black families in the UK, the support of children was an issue that kin, in spite of past experiences, can rally around. Within this extended network, the adolescents were able to describe the nature of the ties that existed and give reasons why these individuals were seen as legitimate members of their family. This circle of family was seen as relevant and involved a reciprocal network of sharing and contributing tangible help, such as material support, household maintenance assistance and most significantly childcare. Child-rearing included non-tangible help such as interaction, emotional support, shelter, companionship, counselling, instruction and social regulation, while at the same time providing the adolescents with a sense of personal identity, behavioural rules, roles, responsibilities, emotional affiliation and attachment. Though it may appear complex, this kind of set-up was functional, highly valued and with strong ties beneficial to the socialisation process of the adolescent.

It is not uncommon for Black children to describe people who are not blood relatives as mother, auntie, uncle, sister or brother (Freeman, 1990; Ochieng, 2004; Othieno, 1998). Othieno (1998) states that, in the absence of the extended family, most Black families in the UK have complex family relationships with people of the same ethnic group, discovering common ties or alliances. Such networks provide mutual support and an extended family system within this country, offering the individual a sense of belonging. This unique feature of Black families also described by the thirty adolescents regarded non-blood social ties as family. Other complex family relations including friends, friends of the family, and 'sisters and brothers' from church were also significant in providing emotional and spiritual support. Friends who were willing to be obligated as family appear to have achieved social recognition as family members and were referred to by the adolescents as grandmother, grandfather, uncle, aunt, sister or brother. Such arrangements appeared to enhance the family system and the adolescents' socialisation processes.

Families are never static (Chamberlain, 2001), but are reconfigured from generation to generation, in response to need, circumstance and convenience. Notwithstanding the most recent findings of Hylton (1997), Chamberlain (2001) and Barn *et al.* (2006), the adolescents who participated in this study indicated that the traditional Black extended family appears to have been replicated in Britain. In their descriptions, Black family households and family ties were not only a systematic and logical response to the experiences of people of African descent in the UK, but it is within the family that their values and priorities are learnt and handed down, and through which they learn most of their deeply felt ideas about their roles and duties in life.

African Caribbean extended families and child-rearing

The extended family system described by the thirty adolescents was again confirmed by the twenty-three adolescents who participated in the larger study. Findings from both sets of adolescents indicated that the extended family mandated family members to be involved in the care of children. It was not uncommon, in the narratives of both groups of adolescents, for them to describe how in instances where their parents were not on speaking terms they still remained central and would be welcomed in the different households; this strong attachment to children in Black families has also been recorded in other studies (Beishoon *et al.*, 1998; Fernando, 2000; Grace, 1983). On the other hand, because half of the households that participated in this study were headed by lone parents, they appeared to rely on the extended networks for childcare support and this may have created much more interaction with extended families.

From the adolescents' point of view, extended family networks are child-centred and have flexible interchangeable role definitions and performance aimed at the care of children. The adolescents narrated how the extended networks were also central in promoting good behaviour, stating that parents, grandparents, family friends, aunts and uncles expected the children, for instance, not to smoke, take drugs or use alcohol excessively. Conversely, all adolescents cited their parents and other family members as a source of knowledge and a reason for not engaging in certain behavioural patterns. However, it was apparent that the family and its extended networks, in socialisation, actually reflected the families' values and beliefs. Childcare within extended families included non-tangible help such as interactions, emotional support, counselling, instruction and social regulation, at the same time providing the children and other members of the family with a sense of group and personal identities, behavioural rules, roles, responsibilities, emotional affiliation and attachment. This finding has also been demonstrated by Atkin and Ahmad (2000), who highlighted that many parents (African Caribbeans and South Asians) in their study mentioned the importance of support from other family members when their child was ill. In the studies by Allen (1994) and Hylton (1997) on Black families' views on parenting, it emerged that – from a choice of categories including Black professionals, friends, family and self-help sources such as books – the majority of respondents stated that the family would be best suited to providing childcare. This support was practical, emotional and financial and usually helped the parents cope with caring for their child.

Though there is a paucity of studies analysing the influence of the African Caribbean extended family on child-rearing styles, Wilson (1986) examined the direct and indirect effects of the Black extended family on children and child development. The findings suggested that the effects on children are more indirect than direct. That is, single mothers who are active participants in an extended-family system have a greater opportunity for self-improvement, work and peer contact than the other single mothers. While Plaza (2000) found that, though African Caribbean grandmothers may no longer be relied upon to take over the long-term responsibilities of childcare for their grandchildren, many still provide short-term care when needed. Whilst this area of Black children's socialisation still requires further exploration, the presence of the extended family in childcare cannot be ignored by practitioners working with Black children.

Child-rearing and Black fathers

Similar to other studies (Grace, 1983; James-Fergus, 1997; Reynolds, 2001a; Wilson *et al.*, 1990), it emerged that the African Caribbean fathers took an equal part in the child-rearing decisions of their family, and whenever the fathers were present as members of the household they were equally involved in making child-rearing decisions. Though most of the African Caribbean men involved in the study appeared to be disenchanted in their role as economic provider, this did not appear to preclude failure in all aspects of their father role. Findings from the adolescents suggest that their fathers were taking an equal part in decisions about their care and in all instances they cited actions he had taken and so forth. In essence, African Caribbean fathers, whether present in or absent from the household, were described as active participants in their children's lives; their representation as marginal or absent was not evident. The adolescents relied on them for supervision, advice and security. The fathers who were not residing in the same household were still able to contribute to their families and undertake a significant role in adolescents' lives. In this study, the conventional constructions of Black fathers by media and policy-makers positing them as absent or marginal from the family home (Reynolds, 2001b) were not evident. The adolescents' perceptions of their fathers, uncles and grandfathers appeared to challenge this media representation. Evidence from the adolescents suggests that their fathers were fundamentally family men, that child-rearing was important to them and in some instances that they might work many hours in two or three low-paid jobs in order to support their families. In the early 1980s, Grace (1983) analysed the role of Jamaican fathers in the socialisation of their children. Grace's (1983) findings, which were later collaborated by Wilson *et al.* (1990) and Reynolds' (2001b) work, demonstrated that whenever the fathers were present, they were found to be equally involved in making child-rearing decisions. However, according to James-Fergus (1997) and McAdoo (1981), there is a significant variation based on socioeconomic status, with a higher involvement by middle-income families compared to lower-income families.

Nonetheless, the support provided by Black men as husbands, fathers, brothers or uncles has received little attention. The exploration of the Black fathers' role in the socialisation of his children is almost non-existent in social science literature and there still remains a dearth of information relating to African Caribbean fathers' expectations and parenting styles. According to Reynolds (2001b), it is almost as if Black men have been written out of discourses and debates on Black family life, and instead discourses on Black men tend to restrict them to the specific realms of urban youth culture, sport, music and entertainment. The research work by Goulbourne and Chamberlain (1999) and Reynolds (2001b) represents some of the few attempts to reassert Black fathers into construction of the Black family. In addition, consistent with the customs of their culture, most Black men have assumed the paternal role in the status of 'boyfriend' and as members of a kinship network system. However, a number of factors including the socioeconomic issues in Britain appear to affect the role of Black men in child-rearing. These factors have resulted in the documented variation of the numbers of Black men giving practical help and emotional support to their partners as opposed to White men.

Black families' child-rearing approaches

Black families' child-rearing practices rest on a range of social, political and economic factors and life experiences, including their values and beliefs. Although the cultural and historical heritage helps to explain the child-rearing practices of Black families the mistaken comparison of Black families against White standards has distracted attention from the influences of economic deprivation and racism and has ignored Black families' adaptive strengths. In analysing child-rearing styles the author's research study highlighted a number of key themes. This chapter will focus on five main areas: family–child interaction, racism and child-rearing, discipline approaches, spirituality and child-rearing approaches, and identity and child-rearing.

Family–child interaction

The adolescents involved in this study described close social ties and interaction patterns with their parent(s) and wider family members, as well as other social ties. Other evidence in relation to close family and child interaction was the presence of other family members and friends living within the neighbourhood. All adolescents and their parent(s) identified relatives such as grandparents, aunts, uncles and close friends who lived within the neighbourhood and contributed to an active family–child socialisation process. During the author's visits to conduct interviews, family members would point out, from their living rooms, where other relatives and close social friends lived. Living in close proximity was noticeable and this facilitated opportunities for social exchanges. This socialisation with family and social networks indirectly enhanced the adolescents' mental well-being and was evidenced by sharing in childcare, psychological support and expressions of love. Family and social network members provided aid not only in times of crisis but also in an ongoing fashion, easing stressful situations and directly promoting a positive child-rearing process.

The ability for family and other social networks to interact and respond to children was seen as an essential feature of development for the child and a buffer against discrimination from the wider society. Frequent interaction between family members was noted in this study and is perhaps an indication of a more meaningful feature for Black families, in general, than White families in Britain. Earlier on Grace (1983) found that Jamaican parent–child interactions were characterised by an attitude that emphasised strong family-ties, unconditional love, respect for self and others and the assumed natural goodness of the child. Stinnett *et al.* (1973), in analysing the parent–child relationships of Black and White high school students in the United States of America (USA), found that the African-descent students experienced closer parent–child relationships than did the other students. In this study there was some evidence of willingness to provide friendship and care for children. In instances where grandparents or other relatives lived very close by, regular short care occurred when adolescents visited on a regular basis; for example:

> I go to my nana, I see them a lot, well I see all my grandparents, aunts, uncles, friends, cousins, mum and dad's good friends. (Trevor, age 12)

> I don't mind either, I am happy here and I like it, my family and nana and friends live around also and I like the place. (Jamal, age 14)

In most instances the interactions were perceived as functional; however, as expected within this particular age group, there was a lot of disagreement between parents and adolescents about the adolescents' friendship networks, school work and general behavioural traits. Nonetheless, within the household and wider family network of most families, the adolescents played a role in mundane decision-making, such as diet. For instance, some parents stated that in making decisions of food choice; they took likes and dislikes into consideration, with the result that the adolescents saw themselves as having more decision-making power about matters within the household. It was found that achieving or sustaining a harmonious relationship was often a priority and influenced the wider family decisions. However, in all households, parents still set certain rules for their adolescents and would expect certain obligations even if the adolescents did not like them. Yet most parents, while acknowledging their children's views, also encouraged their children to adopt African Caribbean values and beliefs, believing this is an important part of their heritage. On sensitive issues such as sexual behaviour, most parents, to an extent, discussed these subjects with their children, despite all claiming that they were not provided with sex education either from their own parents or at school. This shift in culture may have been contributed by their experiences whereby most expressed how they were ill-equipped to deal with issues of sexual behaviour as their parents did not discuss the subject with them. A number of parents confirmed that they did not want to make the same mistakes their parents did and were therefore *open* with their children:

> Well, I am open to my children I talk to them about all sorts, including sex education, boyfriends, sexual behaviour in a wider sense and I hope if they have any questions, I will be able to answer. If I can I will. If I can't then I can't, but I will try to find some solution for them, I do that anyway. So I treat sex as I treat anything else, I feel it should be the parents who should tell their children what they need to know, they should not leave it to somebody else, what they need to know the parents need to tell them. My parents did not tell me and because of that I decided to do it with my children. (Diane, age 39)

Interestingly, it was the mothers who were more likely to communicate messages about sexual behaviour to their children than the fathers. Perhaps this is not surprising, because numerous studies across cultures point to the mother as the key player in closeness and communication with their children, and monitoring the process of their sexual socialisation, especially their daughters (Dittus and Jacard, 2000; Resnick *et al.*, 1997; Whitaker and Miller, 2000). The focus of discussion between parents and children was on expectations, family values and the negative implications of engaging in early sexual activity. All parents promoted abstinence during adolescence as a delay to sexual activity and it was seen as a positive and desirable outcome, since the likelihood of responsible sexual behaviour increases with age (Howard and Mitchell, 1993; Silva, 2002). Some parents in this study, while encouraging abstinence, were still aware of the societal pressures present during adolescence and discussed with their children strategies for healthy sexual behaviour:

> I am not naive to think that they may not want to try it but as Christians, we do not encourage sex before marriage, but it may not be easy and if for some reasons they have to have sex before marriage, then they have to be aware of the preventative factors. But it is also about being ambitious so that one enjoys a healthy life and they are in control of things like that; I don't think we are naive in thinking that they won't want to try it. (CiCi, age 43)

This finding suggests a degree of acculturation in particular amongst Black parents, who view their role as communicating the dire consequences of sexual activity to balance the glamorisation of such activity in the media.

Racism and child-rearing

The findings suggested that African Caribbean families teach their children to be aware of and at times imitate the White majority culture whether they accept its value or not. This involved parents finding methods of warning children about racial dangers and disappointments without overwhelming them or being overtly protective. All parents reported that being Black made a difference in the way they raised their children. They reported that special facilities were required to prepare their children and that this placed additional stresses on their lives as well as their children. Parents further argued that the supportive child-rearing strategies of families buffer some of the cruel and demeaning messages received by their children. However, they also argued that it is particularly difficult in contemporary environments where the signposts of racism are less visible and more subtle than in previous generations. Racial socialisation was further complicated by great differences between the parents' racial experiences and those of their children. While it is questionable if any amount of preparation can sufficiently dull the pain of racism, families felt that it was important to prepare and teach their children to recognise the existence of racism and its sequel and to understand how it continues to survive.

It can be argued that the burden of racism, discrimination and marginalisation appeared to have influenced African Caribbean childrearing practices: issues such as culture that have traditionally been overemphasised as causative factors were established as ignoring the main issues of inequality, racism, disadvantage and power differences between African Caribbeans and the White majority. Findings from studies such as Grace (1983) and Reynolds (2001a) suggest that the tendency to concentrate upon weaknesses and disorganisation of some Black families, by almost exclusively using demographic characteristics as the index of family strength, is questionable. As Grace (1983) clearly stated in her study, if Jamaican child-rearing practices are viewed within the total context of families' socioeconomic conditions (as they must be), it can be seen that the parents' efforts alone will not enable their children to escape from the cycles of socioeconomic and cultural deprivation in which so many minority ethnic people find themselves. Unfortunately, there is still a dearth of information and lack of interest or recognition among social scientists on the validity and functionality of Black families (Barn *et al.*, 2006). This suggests that child-rearing policies are likely to affect them differently in comparison with White families. According to Ahmad (1996), the adaptations of Black and other minority ethnic families to the circumstances of poverty, racism and the subtle behavioural patterns that reflect their heritage, which differ from behaviours and living patterns of the majority population, have been viewed by social scientists as the source of 'their problem'. Research priorities, therefore, have often emphasised educating Black and other minority ethnic families to conform to the values and behaviours of the indigenous population. Nonetheless, the mistaken comparison of Black families against White standards continues to give little attention to the existence and influence of racism and economic deprivation in the child-rearing practices of Black families.

Discipline approaches

In child-rearing, discipline emerged as a primary factor; all parents believed that appropriate discipline was a necessary child-rearing socialisation process:

> The other thing is our attitude towards training children and the attitude of the English towards training children are too different, we sort of have control of the children so we instruct them what's right from what's wrong and they tend to grow up in that atmosphere compared to most children in this society. Training a child is very important to the child's health. You see in this country, the parents do not have control of their children as such because looking at the attitude and their behaviour, it shows and the children grow-up very unhealthy, the process of bringing up a child is very important. We discipline our children by sometimes whipping them, which here in England they will call an abuse, but I tend to disagree; training children and abusing children are two different things, now that is what I wanted to say so you know where we are, our religion is very important towards our health and also disciplining the child. (Carlton, age 60)

> Of course it does help, if children start smoking when they are young and you punish them by hitting them, you think they will never pick up that cigarette again; of course not, they are not daft. They may do it when they are older, but by then they will have learnt what is right or wrong, same with going out with the opposite sex or drinking alcohol at a young age. The thing is they tell us not to hit the children, but if they are caught with marijuana, they go to prison, why not prevent it, proper disciplining of a child can help to straighten them and that will enable them to have a better future and increase chances for a healthy lifestyle. (Joshua, age 52)

> We do not abuse our children; most of us discipline our children so that they can have a better life, a better healthy life. (Seth, age 59)

> I mean you discipline a child to make them better and by making them better, you will make them have a better life a better healthy lifestyle;

the Bible also tells us, we should not shy away from disciplining our children. (Khandi, age 43)

For most parents, discipline was seen as an element of an effective socialisation process and parents felt that the establishment of regular and routine habits and patterns was viewed to be largely the role of the parents with the use of appropriate discipline mechanisms. Child discipline was therefore fundamental to all families. Parents felt that it was within the house that reward, punishment and direction of a specific lifestyle was reinforced or discouraged. This finding was in keeping with other studies, which confirmed that most Black parents believe that strict discipline is necessary in child-rearing, simply because of the severe consequences that their children face in the wider society if they misbehave (Yoos *et al.*, 1995). Spencer *et al.* (1990) argue that a discipline style that fosters children's obedience in a hostile inner-city context may serve as a protective mechanism in such situations. They further state that Black families tend to adopt a discipline style that they believe will benefit and adequately prepare their children for future roles in society. This is mostly characterised by more emphasis on obedience and parent-defined rules, namely greater orientation towards interdependence, reciprocity, obligation and sharing, which are the essential elements of social interactions; this also includes a more inclusive perception of assimilation to family, household and community.

Physical punishment was mainly used as a last resort and the discipline styles adopted by most families who participated in the study varied according to the child's age. This may be viewed as harsh and old fashioned; however, families stated that their experiences suggested that any bad behaviour by their children would normally be dealt with much more severely than that of White children by members of the social and public authorities. Therefore, addressing bad behaviour by a discipline style that appears harsh may ensure future good behaviour and less likelihood of confrontation with authority figures such as school teachers and police officers:

> White children might spit on the face of somebody and the parent will say, you can't do that Johnny, but for a Black child you know that you do not put your hand on your parent, you know you'll be a dead person and if you do it outside, the police will be on you as if you have stolen the crown jewels, so we have to be tough with the children, we cannot pretend, man. (Claudette, age 40)

> The police in this country will not hesitate to jail a Black child if they feel that the child has committed a crime, do they? No, . . . As I said before,

you are better off to correct the actions now rather than pay later, just
as in racism, the Black child will be punished more, the punishment is
more severe! (Isaiah, age 42)

On the issue of physical punishment, the African Caribbean parents
appeared to adopt some clear guidelines, such as age of the child and
personality, with parental control and demonstration of love as key,
and in addition making references to their spiritual beliefs. One
mother stated; 'you do not abuse them or use an iron rod, you know
what I mean, you discipline them without abusing them. Taking
things from them, sending them to their room or denying them food
and shouting all the time is not good, that will not help, it can mash
their brain'.

Parents felt that the accepted other forms of discipline, though appropriate, at times were limited and did not allow a safe environment
for correcting bad behaviour. They argued that though the system pro-
hibits them from physical punishment, they must later watch when
their children are punished severely by members of social and civic
authority. In general, parents believed that the State has interfered with
child-rearing and their role as parents is constantly being challenged,
while their personal circumstances and struggles to bring up their
children are ignored. There was a strong feeling that their styles of
child-rearing were not recognised or welcomed as a valid useful
resource, especially their methods of discipline. Parents felt that
the UK law has undermined their rights and that if they disciplined
their children (physically) they could be reported and arrested and
their children taken into 'care'. Fernando (2000) suggests that when
African Caribbean methods of parenting are not recognised or welcomed
as a valid resource, parents may become reluctant to seek help because
of the fear of attracting criticism about their parenting methods. This
creates extra pressures to the struggles they have to overcome as a
normal part of parenting, because their cultural values are undermined.
Hylton (1997) found that parents believe that, after destroying parental
authority, the State has been unable to successfully replicate it and
has therefore left a vacuum, resulting in some children being out of
control. Interestingly the study by Barn *et al.* (2006) did not document
any real differences between ethnic groups with regard to physical
punishment of children. Less than two-fifths of parents in that study
reported that they used physical punishment as a last resort.

Nonetheless, there appeared to be a continuing generational
change in child discipline strategies amongst African Caribbean families who participated in the author's study. The present generation

of parents with young children appeared to emphasise cooperation rather than physical control. According to Hylton (1997), part of this change can be attributed to a changed 'moral' consensus, which some Black parents view as being very child-centred and also as double-edged as a consequence. In the author's study, families felt that this change has undermined their parental authority and loosened the control they once had over their children. Within this new climate, physical discipline or the threat of such discipline from parents to their children was viewed as being liable to result in children being removed from their parents. This perceived loss of parental control can to an extent explain the identified need for appropriate role models among the adolescents and their parents. However, while the adolescents in the study recognised discipline, seeing it as an integral part of their socialisation process, none of them agreed to physical punishment as a form of discipline and they were observed to openly and very strongly disagree with their parents. There were very strong feelings from the adolescents and they advocated for the more conventional forms of discipline that included banning from certain treats and/or being grounded. Discipline remains an important element of Black families' child-rearing and all informants regarded the discipline experienced in childhood as vital to ensuring certain important values. Most significantly, strategies for discipline were always in flux throughout the child-rearing process.

Spirituality and child-rearing approaches

Spirituality was found to play an important part in the life of this group of African Caribbean families and in particular appears to heavily inform their child-rearing practices. Families who described themselves as Christians cited the similarities between the teachings of the Bible and their child-rearing styles; these included their attitudes towards consumption of alcohol, cigarette smoking, illicit drugs and sexual health. They advocated the need to promote an environment for better mental health for their children and love and security. The influence of spirituality as a social order prerequisite was described as important and it was the basis for child-rearing practices. Indeed, religious beliefs and practices seemed to be interwoven into the family's way of life, and such beliefs united them and gave them a purpose for life. They view their faith as a source of strength and as a rationale for indirectly engaging in certain aspects of child-rearing practices. In general, spirituality and the church were important elements; spirituality reinforced their child-rearing values of sharing, caring, obedience and hard work. This was often described by the respondents:

... the correct way of correcting a child is to give them a proper punishment, the Bible teaches that spare the rod and spoil a child, if you
need to whip a child then you should but only when the child is
younger, the age of the child matters; and it is not a Black form of punishment, it comes from the Bible and Christianity is not just for Black
people is it? (Hosea, age 47)

Our religion remains important to us and we more or less rely on it to
give us direction on how to bring up the children, but we also recognise that we live in a real world, we know the children will be tempted,
that is why I feel that we need to talk to them about these things, especially when they ask questions. (Esther, age 42)

A number of studies suggest that spirituality is primarily the
means by which Black and minority ethnic communities are able to
adapt and respond to marginalisation and widespread social discrimination. In Hylton's (1997) study of African Caribbean families,
spirituality was used to refer to wider feelings that included religious
adherence and a way of life that may assist the families to survive
life within a context of discrimination and marginalisation. Because
of discrimination even within the UK majority churches, African
Caribbeans have tended to set up their own congregations, which offer
another lifestyle (Stebbins, 1997; Weinbender and Rossignol, 1996). This
distinctive form of Christianity appeared attractive to members of
the community since there is evidence that the early migrants were
treated less warmly by the native congregation (Gerloff, 1992). This
led to a greater identity of the community with churches that were
more likely to express their interests and sentiments (Hunt and
Lightly, 2001). Struve (2001) demonstrated that social support, psychological functioning and religious involvement directly influenced
the individual's quality of life. Since Christianity and spirituality in
general play a large part in the Black community and are important
in beliefs and practices as well as an important social focal point,
there is a need for a greater understanding of how they influence Black
families' child-rearing practices.

Identity and child-rearing

Parents felt that in order to counteract a strong British identity, it was
their duty to promote an African Caribbean identity. They recognised
that their children were integrated with their White counterparts at
the level of friendship, leisure and culture; indeed, their children's
culture and identity were much more mainstream. This seemed to contribute to strong feelings towards ensuring the survival and recognition of African Caribbean identity by the parents and wider family

network. Most argued that adopting and acknowledging a different identity would not protect them or their children against discrimination and racism; however, it would result in conflict, pressure and low self-esteem. While the parental role in identity construction was acceptable to the adolescents the author observed how in most instances they would interject and reassert their identities as both British and African Caribbean. The adolescents felt that they were more 'bi-cultural'. It appeared that, on a daily basis, children experienced discontinuities in their roles demanded at home and in the wider community.

In general a strong and positive African Caribbean identity existed amongst all family members, including the adolescents who described themselves as having Caribbean and British identity. In a way, it could be argued that some of the negative experiences in the UK may have actually provoked strong feelings of the need to assert this identity. For most, this was an important point of defiance and resistance that was shaped by the external forces they experienced on a daily basis. Therefore, not only was their identity based on country of origin, or traditions, but it was also an important element of the need to assert their rights in this climate of equality for all. Similarly, in Hylton's (1997) study, the Somali young men who came to this country as refugees indicated that their parents have become more rigid in some aspects of their Islamic beliefs and culture in Britain than they were when they lived in Somalia. A part of the explanation of such behaviour was that in Britain the Somali parents were surrounded by British liberal values and racism, so it required greater effort and was of more importance to retain their own cultural heritage.

Male and female adolescents shared mutual and partial rather than absolute identification with their parents. They did not identify in an all-or-nothing fashion with the values and beliefs of their parents. Instead, they identified with some values and way of life and dissociated with others. This was an indication that their socialisation experiences have involved two cultures, their parents' and that of the indigenous population. In Weinreich's (1979) study on ethnicity and adolescent identity conflicts, it emerged that West Indian girls in Bristol differed from the boys, in that the girls were more likely to have conflicted identifications with their parents as well as with general representation of their own identity. In this study, such gender difference was not observed. This may suggest that though the girls, in general, claimed to experience less discrimination than the boys or men, their awareness of the level of discrimination and racism experienced by members of the opposite sex in their family appears to have invoked a stronger identification with their parents. Nonetheless, both the girls and boys appeared to be converging in their experiences in Britain, and 'race' consciousness appeared to have been awakened in these particular African Caribbean adolescents.

Conclusion

Though Black and other visible minority ethnic children constitute the largest group of children in the UK affected by social and welfare policies, their family networks remain relatively obscure. It is critical that practitioners working with Black children and families appreciate the structure of Black families and their existing strengths. As a starting point, practitioners need to understand and assess appropriately the diversity and functions of the Black extended family in child socialisation and, whenever appropriate, work with the family to ensure that this is sustained. This should subsequently help minimise threats to this structure during the care of children. However, if this is difficult to achieve then perhaps attempts are being made to apply conventional family policies in situations where they will not work because they are inappropriate, with a resultant effect of unnecessary stress for Black children, their parents, the wider family network and professionals who work with them.

In various studies on the child-rearing practices of Black families, behavioural factors have been implicated while other social determinants such as social class, poverty or racial discrimination have been inadequately controlled for, with the result that the way of life or 'culture' of the group has been prematurely identified as the basis for their child-rearing practices. Similar to most Black families in the UK, the African Caribbean families who participated in this study had fewer options in their working, domestic and social lives than many White people. The families are in general struggling under conditions of economic inequality where economic and social stratification constitute a permanent feature of the economy, and if there is a trend for the new century and beyond it is clearly towards further inequality. Issues such as 'culture' have traditionally been over-emphasised – as contributing to 'bad parenting', for example, resulting in some Black children being taken in care – while in most instances the main issues of socioeconomic status, inequality, racism, disadvantage, and power differences between the Black minority and the White majority and their role in structuring their life experiences have been ignored.

It must be emphasised that Black families are beginning to modify their traditional child-rearing practices, partly in response to the diminished role of the extended family and their present socioeconomic status and experiences of racial discrimination. However, given the critical importance of child-rearing practices and orientation in shaping the personalities, behaviours and values of future Black children there is a need for a greater understanding of the influences of child-rearing practices. Currently there is a dearth of research focusing on Black families' adaptive strategies and their influence on child-rearing styles. In this chapter it was found that African Caribbean families' child-rearing styles have normally developed out of the exigencies of the community's unique economic, cultural and racial circumstances, demonstrating a multiplicity of inter-linked factors, which include socioeconomic status, along with historical, political, religious and cultural factors, experiences of racism and so forth.

Black families are heterogeneous, the result of their unique cultures and histories, yet relatively few researchers have undertaken any systematic, empirical research on the families' styles of child socialisation. Though most researchers emphasise that family structures do not uniformly predict family functioning or socialisation of children, more work is needed to explore the influences of Black family-networks, structures and functions on child-rearing.

References

Ahmad, W. I. U. (1996), 'Family obligations and social change among Asian communities', in Ahmad W. I. U. and Atkin K. (eds), *Race and Community Health* (London: Open University Press)

Allen, E. (1994), *A Summary of the Research Relating to the School Experiences of Young African-Caribbean Males* (London: Positive Image Education Project Youth Aid)

Atkin, K. and Ahmad, W. I. U. (2000), 'Family care-giving and chronic illness: how parents cope with a child with sickle cell disorder or thalassaemia', *Health and Social Care in the Community*, 8:1, 57–69

Barn, R., Ladino, C. and Rogers, B. (2006), *Parenting in Multi-Racial Britain* (London: National Children's Bureau)

Beishoon, S., Modood, T. and Virdee, S. (1998), *Ethnic Minority Families* (London: Policy Studies Institute)

Chamberlain, M. (2001), 'Narratives of Caribbean families in Britain and the Caribbean', in Goulbourne H. and Chamberlain M. (eds), *Caribbean Families in Britain and the Trans-Atlantic World* (London and Oxford: Palgrave Macmillan)

Dittus, P. and Jaccard, J. (2000), 'Adolescents' perceptions of maternal disapproval of sex: Relationship to sexual outcomes', *Journal of Adolescent Health*, 26, 268–78

Dodson, J. (1981), 'Conceptualisation of Black families', in McAdoo, P. H. (ed.), *Black Families* (California: Sage)

Dosanji, J. S. (1996), *Child Rearing in Ethnic Minorities* (London: Multilingual Matters Limited)

Fernando, C. (2000), *Racism and its Effect on Parenting* (London: Coram Family-Moyenda Project)

Freeman, E. M. (1990), 'The Black family's life cycle: operationalizing a strengths perspectives', in Logan, M. L. S., Freeman, M. E. and McRoy G. R. (eds), *Social Work Practice with Black Families – A Culturally Specific Perspective* (London: Longman)

Gerloff, R. (1992), *A Plea for British Black Theologies* (Frankfurt: Peter Lang)

Goulbourne, H. and Chamberlain, M. (1999), *Living Arrangements, Family Structure and Social Change of Caribbeans in Britain* (Swindon: Economic Social Research Council)

Grace, M. A. (1983), 'Jamaican Immigrant Child Rearing Practices: A Study of Two Hundred Seven Year Olds in Relation to their Daily Lives at Home and at School' (PhD dissertation, University of Nottingham)

Harrison, A. (1981), 'Attitudes toward procreation among Black families', in McAdoo, P. H. (ed.), *Black Families* (California: Sage)

Harrison, A. O., Wilson, M. N., Pine, C. J., Chan S. Q. and Buriel, R. (1990), 'Family ecologies of minority children', *Child Development*, 61:2, 347–62

Haskey, J. (2002), *Population Projections by Ethnic Group: A Feasibility Study* (London: Stationery Office)

Howard, M. and Mitchell, M. (1993), 'Preventing teenage pregnancy: some questions to be answered and some answers to be questioned', *Pediatric Annals*, 22, 109–18

Hunt, S. and Lightly, N. (2001), 'The British Black pentecostal "revival": identity and belief in the "new" Nigerian churches', *Ethnic and Racial Studies*, 24:1, 104–24

Hylton, C. (2000), *Black Men's Forum, Black Family Debate and Roles of Mothers and Fathers* (Leeds: Gbakhanda)

Hylton, C. (1997), *Family Survival Strategies: A Moyenda Black Families Talking Project Exploring Parenthood* (London: Coram Family Moyenda Project)

James-Fergus, S. (1997), 'Rebuilding the African-Caribbean family in Britain', in Dench G. (ed.), *Rewriting the Sexual Contract* (London: Institute of Community Studies)

McAdoo, L. J. (1981), 'The roles of Black fathers in the socialization of Black children', in McAdoo L. J. (ed.), *Black Families* (California: Sage)

McPherson, W. (1999), *The Stephen Lawrence Inquiry Report: An Inquiry* (London: Home Office)

Ochieng, B. (2005), 'A Healthy Lifestyle: the Attitudes and Experiences of African Caribbean Adolescents and their Families in West Yorkshire' (PhD dissertation, University of Leeds)

Ochieng, B. (2004), 'Making healthy lifestyle the easier option for the Black community', *The Northern Journal*, Winter, 6–9

Othieno, G. K. (1998), *African Social and Cultural Structures* (London: African Culture Promotions)

Plaza, D. (2000), 'Transnational grannies: the changing family responsibilities of elderly African Caribbean born women resident in Britain', *Social Indicators Research*, 51:1, 75–105

Resnick, M. D., Bearman, P., Blum, R. W., Bauman, K. E., Harris, K. M. and Jones, J. (1997), 'Protecting adolescents from harm: findings from the national longitudinal study of adolescent health', *Journal of the American Medical Association*, 278:10, 823–32

Reynolds, T. (2001a), 'Black mothering, paid work and identity', *Ethnic and Racial Studies*, 24:6, 1046–64

Reynolds, T. (2001b) 'Caribbean fathers in family lives in Britain', in Goulbourne, H. and Chamberlain, M. (eds), *Caribbean Families in Britain and the Trans Atlantic World* (London and Oxford: Palgrave Macmillan)

Silva, M. (2002), 'The effectiveness of school-based education programs in the promotion of abstinent behaviour: a meta-analysis', *Health Education Research*, 17:4, 471–81

Spencer, M. B., Dornbush, S. M. and Mont-Reynauld, R. (1990), 'Challenges in studying minority youth', in Feldman, S. S. and Elliot, G. R. (eds), *At the Threshold: The Developing Adolescent* (Cambridge, MA and London: Harvard University Press)

Stebbins, R. A. (1997), 'Lifestyle as a generic concept in ethnographic research', *Quality and Quantity*, 31:4, 347–60

Stinnett, N., Talley, S. and Walter, S. (1973), 'Parent-child relationship of black and white high school students: a comparison', *Journal of Social Psychology*, 91:2, 349–50

Struve, J. K. (2001), 'The future of the church as a primary health place', *Journal of Religious Gerontology*, 13:2, 17–24

Weinbender, M. L. M. and Rossignol, A. M. (1996), 'Lifestyle and risk of premature sexual activity in a high school population of Seventh-day Adventist: Value genesis', *Adolescence*, 31:122, 265–81

Weinreich, P. (1979), 'Ethnicity and adolescent identity conflicts: a comparative study', in Khan, V. S. (ed.), *Studies in Ethnicity* (London and Basingstoke: Palgrave Macmillan)

Whitaker, D. and Miller, K. (2000), 'Parent-adolescent discussions about sex and condoms: impact on peer influences of sexual risk behaviour', *Journal of Adolescent Research*, 15:2, 251–73

Wilson, M. N. (1986) 'The Black extended family: an analytical consideration', *Development Psychology*, 22:2, 246–58

Wilson, M. N., Tolson, T. F., Hinton, I. D. and Kiernan, M. (1990), 'Flexibility and sharing of childcare duties in Black families' special issue, gender and ethnicity, perspectives on dual status', *Sex Roles*, 22:7–8, 409–25

Yoos, H. L., Kitzman, H., Olds, D. L. and Overacker, I. (1995), 'Child rearing beliefs in the African-American community: implications for culturally component paediatric care', *Journal of Pediatric Nursing*, 10:6, 343–53

4

Overcoming the 'Triple Quandary': how Black students navigate the obstacles of achievement

Tony Sewell

Introduction

One of the key factors for success in the British education system is the amount and quality of family support. Recent research on African Caribbean underachievement has been dominated by research that has focused on in-school factors. However, a new discourse is emerging that takes on the complexity of the students and their personal contexts. By examining the Triple Quandary – of dominant mainstream, peer-group pressure and low-aspiration comfort zone – we can construct a framework of success. The chapter ends with a social navigational guide based on the experiences of Black students who have succeeded in spite of the risk factors around them – and it asks whether we are exacting too high a price for Black success in schools.

The complexity of African Caribbean underachievement continues to perplex policy-makers and teachers. This chapter challenges the notion that teacher racism or institutional racism alone can explain the achievement gap of African Caribbean students, especially boys. According to the theory of the Triple Quandary, underachievement is located as a cultural-ecological notion of school performance. Racism or systematic explanations are not dismissed, but I suggest that Black children are open to a number of risk factors that are far wider than the school environment. In order to get a deeper understanding of why Black boys in the United Kingdom (UK), United States of America (USA) and Jamaica have an academic performance gap with their peers, we need to look to a more complex set of hypotheses.

The work of Ogbu (1995) and Boykin (1986) in the USA are key to developing a cultural-ecology approach to Black achievement. Ogbu's anthropological work into minority groups and education spans three decades. He began by looking at differences between the school performances of minority and dominant-group students before refocussing on attempting to explain differences in school success between and among minority groups. His research has looked at many different minority groups in several countries.

The cultural-ecological theory sets out to understand the differential school performances of minority groups in the light of two intersecting factors. The first is 'the system': the broad societal and school factors such as policies, pedagogy and educational outcomes. The second is community dynamics as played out in perceptions and responses to schooling in the light of the conditions under which certain groups became a minority and remain a minority.

Ogbu observes that collective problems faced by minority groups are differentiated according to their histories. These histories are influenced by the way they became a minority group and are often closely connected with their subsequent treatment by dominant groups. Relationships with education are then affected by how different minority groups work on collective solutions to their collective problems. Within his framework Ogbu classifies minority groups as either 'voluntary' or 'involuntary' minorities, as determined by their histories and power status in society.

This line of thought is developed by Wade Boykin's work *The Triple Quandary and the Schooling of African American Children* (1986). Based on research, he developed six hypotheses that told us why and how African Caribbean children succeed in the system. He believes that the academic achievements of Black students are enhanced for those Black students who:

1. are in safe and reinforcing environments;
2. in their homes experience high academic achievement as a greatly valued standard of performance by their parents or parent surrogates, and as a very high priority for investment of family resources;
3. associate with and can identify with peers who value and invest in such achievement;
4. can identify and utilise academic support services at their school and in the school community;
5. experience strongly supportive interactions with key classroom teachers and heads of year; and
6. successfully negotiate the Triple Quandary, which consists of the following theoretical constructs: mainstream (White) culture, minority experience and Black cultural experience.

African American students who successfully negotiate the Triple Quandary are more likely to:

- develop peer relationships across racial, ethnic, class and gender boundaries;
- participate in homogeneous and heterogeneous extracurricular activities;
- develop coping strategies to overcome inconsistencies between mainstream (White) values and their home and community values; and
- internalise only those mainstream (White) values that they define as necessary for their academic achievement.

Testing Boykin's theory, I conducted a short survey of African Caribbean students in the UK at Township High School and found that the successful students matched his hypotheses and the unsuccessful ones could not navigate the choppy waters.

Black boys in the UK

It could be argued that the Triple Quandary has just as much resonance amongst Black students in the UK as it has in the USA.

What the African American students said provided the research team with a deep understanding of the multiple ways in which African Caribbean students perceived and experienced the school. For some students, the complexity of climate and safety issues was difficult to navigate. Others who found navigation less difficult were the students who were involved in extracurricular activities.

There is evidence that African Caribbean students benefit from parental support in terms of providing resources in the home and of being engaged with the school in significant ways. The students in our sample underscored the importance of parental investment in academic achievement. Another important aspect of the lives of students in the sample involved their keen awareness of the roles their peers play in their academic experiences.

During their interviews, African American students repeatedly showed that they were sensitive to and savvy about peers with whom they should either associate or disassociate, as well as about the need to keep peer activities aligned with academic activities and expectations. This is also true in the UK. British television Multicultural Commissioning Editor Farrukh Dhondy wrote in the *Times Educational Supplement* in 1999 about the need to look wider than institutionalised racism in schools to find the cause of Black underachievement. He maintained that:

> The other possibilities need a hard and scientifically passionate examination. It has never been done. Instead we have notions about 'culture', 'role models', 'stereotyping', 'positive images', 'low expectations' and 'unwitting racism' floating about which are grasped from the fashionable ethos and put into play in every circular discussion of the wretched subject.

He goes on:

> Doesn't any institution want to draw up some correlative tables about class conditions, family conditions, details of parenting, cultural pursuits at home, amount of homework done, behaviour in class, voluntary attention spans, respectful and polite behaviour, however animated or lively, and the great goal of achievement?

What emerged from the research in the USA and confirmed my own work in the UK (Sewell 1996) was that there existed a set of multiple skills that students had to have at their disposal. It was essential that they:

- developed peer relationships across racial, ethnic, class and gender boundaries;
- participated in homogeneous and heterogeneous extracurricular activities;
- developed coping strategies to overcome inconsistencies with mainstream (White) values and their home and community values; and
- internalised only those mainstream values that they defined as necessary for their academic achievement.

It was clear that even if these skills were applied, they were not an absolute guarantee of success. Succeeding often meant valorising one identity, that of the mainstream (White), over all others. The lessons for schools are clear both for the USA and the UK. The characteristics and skills necessary to navigate the Triple Quandary are easier for White middle-class students and certain ethnic minorities.

Ogbu (1995) still gives the best reasons for this difference by his distinguishing between voluntary and non-voluntary minorities. This explains the position or case of African Caribbeans, who are non-voluntary minorities unable to feel part of the mainstream but connected to little else that is outside of it. Put simply, Black academic success will be more likely if Black children have significant and positive adults who are able to guide them. The rest seems to be a lottery and Black children too often have the losing ticket.

The literature on Black achievement does seem to have been dominated by a simple race agenda that fails to account for Black children with all their complexities. It does not take us far from the rather dry liberal perspectives according to which the Black child is a kind of educational theoretical victim, unable to do wrong and unmoved by family, peers and human instinct. This approach has spawned a raft of masters and higher research that – problematically – seeks to uncover racism as the cause for Black underachievement. I've read little in the literature that has had the courage to break from this cycle. The best to date is on the internet in blogs. A fine example is www.tomisswithlove.blogspot.com, who describes herself thus:

> I'm a black teacher in inner-city London and here are some of my stories . . . I love my job and I love these kids. But boy, do I sometimes wonder why.

This kind of work should be encouraged because it comes from the chalk face and resonates with the critical honesty that has been missing in the literature for many years. This is how 'tomisswithlove' deals with this issue of competition in education:

> I will never understand why in schools across the world, from China to Africa, from the Caribbean to our private sector, children are ranked. Everyone knows who is at the top, and who is at the bottom. Consequently, children compete to raise their scores. In the state sector, and particularly in the inner city, we are encouraged to praise everyone. Everyone gets a certificate. Everyone gets a prize. So everyone feels good about themselves. And they keep on feeling good about themselves until they fail their GCSEs. Suddenly, they feel pretty damn bad.

Results from videotaped interviews show that African Caribbean students in the Township High School sample who could manage and negotiate the Triple Quandary are academically successful. They are conscious of the images and the subtle messages of their group and they develop strategies from their family and community to successfully negotiate both a mainstream (White) and a minority experience in the learning community at the school. When not successfully negotiated, these two experiences can threaten the academic achievements of the school's African Caribbean students. Results of this short survey confirm the perception that African Caribbean and White students experience different levels of safety in the school climate and that African Caribbean students are less likely to feel happy about their teachers.

There was a systemic performance gap at Township High School. This performance gap in the learning community suggests that there are in reality two separate learning communities at the school – one for White students that places them 'at academic promise' and one for African Caribbean students that places them 'at academic risk'. The learning community performance gap is further exacerbated by differential outcomes in the success rates for African Caribbean and White students in accelerated courses and the gifted and talented registers.

The Triple Quandary

The Triple Quandary is an ecological-cultural theory used to understand African Caribbean student achievement and the learning community performance gap. This approach recognizes a set of distinct orders, patterns and meanings ascribed to a complexity of behaviours that underpin the bi-cultural status of African Caribbean and African American students in most school settings. Because of their unique social position in Britain and the USA, theses students are bi-cultural:

> One ever feels his two-ness – an American, a Negro; two souls, two thoughts, two un-reconciled strivings; two warring ideals in one dark body, whose dogged strength alone keeps it from being torn asunder. (DuBois, 1903: 17)

In order to be successful within and outside their own culture and social climate, African Caribbean students at Township High are hypothesised to confront a Triple Quandary within which they must negotiate three experiences:

- **Mainstream (White) experience** entails the conventional assumption of assimilation into the dominant culture. The end result is a melting pot in which cultural difference and diversity are integrated into a homogeneous environment with shared rules, goals and values. Black students and members of other groups of colour may perceive the melting pot as a forced conformity to a set of rules applied unevenly and typically to keep them behind.
- **Minority experience** consists of being exposed to a set of culturally, politically, socially and economically oppressive conditions that have reduced Black people's life chances. These conditions – such as African enslavement, anti-miscegenation laws, segregation, restrictive covenants, redlining, lynching, political disenfranchisement, racial profiling and racial balancing – place Black groups in an out-group position in the wider community, society and

schools. This situation becomes a vicious cycle. African Caribbeans are labelled inferior and are victimised by discrimination. The label of inferiority and the discriminatory treatment are subsequently used to blame them for not trying hard enough. Failure is then attributed to their inferiority.

- **Black cultural experience** relates to the complex ways in which African Americans develop certain coping strategies to negotiate the multiple contexts and demands by a perceived White middle-class mainstream. The reliance on groups or gangs as an alternative family is the next logical step.

Some of these coping and negotiation strategies resemble efforts to 'cross over' and negotiate mainstream (White) experiences by inter-nalising only those rules and cultural values that lead to success. As Boykin (1986: 34) states, 'some passive strategies that derive from mental colonization are connected to the mainstream (for example, "a piece of the action"), and some active strategies are related to Black culture (for example, identification with Black Nationalist movements)'.

Some coping strategies used by African American students may appear to be conforming or 'passive'; these are usually perceived and understood as acceptable by mainstream (White) society. Other strategies, such as identification with Black cultural experience, are usually labelled radical or militant in the context of the mainstream experience because on appearance they are defined as abrasive; these are too often interpreted harshly and result in disciplinary action or expulsion. If African American students come from a bi-cultural experience within which they are hypothesised to negotiate a Triple Quandary, their academic achievement must be investigated from this broader social context.

The Triple Quandary for me has close parallels with the way Foucault (1980) explained the workings of disciplinary power. He says:

> In thinking of mechanisms of power, I am thinking rather of its capil-lary form of existence, the point where power reaches into the very grain of individuals, touches their bodies and inserts itself into their action and attitudes, their discourses, learning processes and everyday lives. (Foucault, 1980: 39)

Foucault described disciplinary power as not just an abstract concept but one that functions in all actions, particularly at the level of the body. He argued that this disciplinary power emerged with the advent of modern institutions and extended throughout society, such that we can see a continuity of power relations in schools, hospitals, prisons, factories and other institutions. He observes that:

A certain significant generality moved between the least irregularity and the greatest crime: it was no longer the offence, the attack on the common interest, it was the departure from the norm, the anomaly; it was this that haunted the school, the court, the asylum or the prison. (Foucault, 1977: 299)

Foucault talks about eight major techniques of power, namely: surveillance, normalization, exclusion, classification, distribution, individualization, tantalization and regulation. It is my contention that Black boys in the UK, the USA and the Caribbean found their masculinities defined by these techniques of power. What is more interesting is to understand this in nautical terms. These power-plays tested African Caribbean boys as they sailed into the Triple Quandary. The task of sailing through the all-White mainstream tides can be hazardous; its currents are so strong that it can suck away all elements of your Black identity. The minority experience is one of feeling isolation or invisibility. It is summed up in the words of DuBois:

The history of the American Negro is the history of strife. . . . The Negro is a sort of seventh son, born with a veil, and gifted with second sight in this American world. It is a peculiar sensation, this double-consciousness, this sense of always looking at one's self through the eyes of others, of measuring one's soul by the tape of a world that looks on in amused contempt and pity. One ever feels his twoness – an American, a negro, two souls, two thoughts, two unreconciled strivings, two ideals in one dark body, whose dogged strength alone keeps it from being torn asunder. (DuBois, 1903: 21)

DuBois wrote this passage more than a century ago. It is best understood by those of us from a Caribbean background that saw identity as the eventual birth of an assimilated European and African marriage. For Black boys in the USA and Britain this would be made even harder when it came to nationality. Not only do you know that you are a distinct evolution of the British project but you know that you are constantly challenged about your legitimacy as a Black Briton.

To return to things sea-worthy – Black boys in the USA and Britain have clung to the lifeboat of community identity. This has been a source of strength and encouragement for some; for others it has been a source of confinement. I am reminded of the words of James Joyce in *A Portrait of the Artist as a Young Man*. He says of Irish nationalism: 'When the soul of a man is born in this country there are nets flung at it to hold it back from flight. You talk to me of nationality, language, religion. I shall fly by these nets' (Joyce, 1916: 19). In contrast, Black identity and Black communities have been the source of tremendous creativity and comfort to Black people in a hostile world.

The Triple Quandary theory can literally be sexed up if we use it to unravel the deeper issues around masculinity. First, the notion of the mainstream could be redefined as civil society (not necessarily 'white' but any civil society). Second, the idea of a discriminated or marginalised minority is certainly a reality for working-class boys, both Black and White, in Britain and the USA, while, among the Black majority of Jamaica, working-class Black males face mainstream institutions from university to middle management that are female populated and run. Third, the notion of a Black comfort zone based around tight norms within communities is still characteristic of many Black communities in the USA, for example in Baltimore and parts of Chicago.

In the UK, however, Blackness is not necessarily the cultural comfort zone it used to be. Second- and third-generation Caribbean immigrants have become more embedded in a Britishness which no longer questions their waving the Union Jack with pride. The downside is that it may well have attached itself to a White working-class low aspiration around education and work. In Jamaica, class, education and 'skin tone' still define a Black male underclass that is locked into certain ghetto areas. It has helped to develop a popular culture of resistance, which is both liberating and in some instances a source of self-confinement.

Uprace High School and TrueBrit College – student voices

To understand the Triple Quandary as a lived experience we undertook some qualitative research at Uprace High School. The school is a superbly resourced high school in a middle-class suburb in the USA. Yet African descent students with all these advantages still perform below the White average in their test scores, with one in three boys unable to gain the equivalent of five GCSEs in the UK.

I also looked at data taken from interviews of 16-year-old African and African Caribbean boys who attended TrueBrit College. Unlike Uprace this is a predominantly Black college, with most of the students from economically poor backgrounds.

During the interviews, students were challenged to speak candidly about their exam scores. Most of them blamed themselves for what they perceived as failing to work up to their academic potential. However, when probed for details, they spoke more about the nuances of their practices and their everyday lived experiences that were important explanations for poor performance. The following discussion of the six hypotheses formulated by the research team includes supporting quotations drawn from students' videotaped interviews. These selected quotations represent the responses offered and the sentiments expressed by students in the entire sample. Clearly, the following quotes are just a sample of those accumulated during the interview process.

In Uprace School, Black students are struggling with what seems to be an alien ethos of the school and the comfort zone culture of their peers and home. Ethos is related to how students feel and how they express their feelings in situations in and outside the classroom. Students who believe that they can share their feelings and intellect openly and honestly with faculty and staff are more likely to experience the school as a safe and reinforcing environment. Students who feel that they are not able to express openly and to share candidly their feelings and intellect are more likely to perceive and experience the school as uncomfortable.

First hypothesis

Consequently, the research team's first hypothesis seeks to ascertain the degree to which school ethos is perceived and experienced by students as a safe and reinforcing environment in sharing both one's feelings and intellect:

> **The academic achievement of Black students is enhanced for those who find school (peers, teachers, staff, administration) to be both a safe and a reinforcing environment in sharing and expressing feelings and intellect.**

The quotations below from students at Uprace High School and TrueBrit college reflect the alienation and separation from the school's ethos that many students in the sample expressed in their interviews. One student feels completely helpless and powerless while another feels that involvement in extracurricular activities that 'cross over' challenges his social identity and group boundaries. Clearly, students who enter the school with a need to get involved often articulate the consequences of their involvement as impacting on their identity.

> And then when I get here, it's like just a wall and I ain't got no arms to climb it. I ain't trying to disappoint my family. I want to be able to achieve in school and get good grades and stuff, but there is a part of me that is saying the hell with it, if I have to do all this work and still get nowhere. It's like having a dead end job, not going anywhere, and having to do so much and getting nothing out of it.

> I think a lot of it is, like you said, they need to say, 'we want you involved'. A lot of people feel reproach and they don't want to follow other students because they don't think they'll be accepted and that's a big thing – especially being a teenager and being in the environment. You want to be accepted and wherever you fit in is where you're comfortable. And

because a lot of African Caribbeans now choose not to participate, younger Black students, especially year sevens, come along and say, 'I'm Black so I'm not going to participate either because then I'm not accepted by my fellow Black people'. It's almost like they have their own colour group because it's something they identify with; it's something they're comfortable with. It's a very sad thing, but it's prevalent.

During break time at Uprace, the third-floor hallway near the gym is a common space and place for African American students to be 'down'. This area is both a contentious space and a comfort zone for Black students. Intra-group interpretations of the third-floor space and its dynamics are articulated in the following quotation. This student recognises and describes in the social ecology of the school both the positive need for the space as well as the negative external reactions that 'other races' might have because of their limited involvement with Black students. In one sense, this quotation suggests that this area is a consequence of the few spaces where African American students can openly share their feelings and intellects. Some of the actions of students when they gather in this space are likely to be perceived as disrespectful and non-intellectual, yet Black students with high grade-point averages value the space for the presence in it of a 'large amount of Black students'. In another sense, the third-floor area becomes a place where one can be absorbed into a common racial group without having to identify with the totality of the group and with what it represents to outsiders and insiders.

> The third-floor hallway – a lot of kids stand there and in my opinion, just simply act ignorant. They scream real loud, they curse, and they make themselves look bad. They make African American students as a whole look bad to other students of other races who don't know anyone Black. They see that and they think that's how we are. And maybe not completely, but those who haven't expanded their mind yet, you know, that's what they see. . . . It's tempting to get mad at those students who act wild and say, 'You know, you're making us look bad, and why are you acting like that? I know you don't usually act like that; there's no need'. But, at the same time, you have to understand that in a school that's mainly White you've got to have some where to chill.

If we contrast this with aspiring Black students from the UK, we see that TrueBrit college is not an alien space but in fact a safe haven from the madness and insecurity of the street, Black masculinity and negative aspects of youth culture.

Mario, a successful African Caribbean student, is positive about college:

> I don't feel peer pressure. I say to myself I prefer to be at the top than at the bottom. At school I used to get asked to bunk off lessons but I'd just ignore them. . . . When I said no my friends started going to lessons too. . . . No peer pressures at college . . . people are much more positive . . . most people want to go to university.

He goes on:

> Most of my friends are into education . . . I've lost contact with those who didn't stay in education . . . some of them have got into trouble which didn't surprise me . . . their attitude was very macho. . . . I'm not macho. . . . I don't focus on that, I focus on my education.

David Kofo is 16 and from a Nigerian background. There are five people in his family – Mum, Dad, brother and sister. David is the eldest child. Mum went to university after David was born. He goes to a predominantly Black college in South London:

> My Dad puts pressure on me because he believes nowadays there are more opportunities for young people than when he was young. . . . I see myself going to university to become a lawyer . . .

David's 'AS' grades were 'B' for English Language; 'C' Law; 'D' Sociology and 'U' History (which he dropped).

David feels more confident this year and wants to improve his grades. He likes college and has always enjoyed it. There are many elements of the Triple Quandary in his experience. There is a positive pressure from home to succeed:

> I worry if I'm gonna do good in my exams. . . . I worry about getting into university . . . I'm worried if I'm gonna be alive the next day? I worry something might happen, . . . I hear about the 25th teenager to die this year; I can tell Mum and Dad worry too, . . . so I say hello . . . and go straight home. In some cases keeping myself to myself is good . . . but it would help if I interacted more.

There is real tension here between the wider culture and David's own desire to succeed. He is on the tightrope, trying to meet the demands of mainstream society but also aware that a particular kind of negative street culture could literally devour him and his ambitions. No matter how academic he feels, he must be streetwise to survive. Talking about dress code he says:

> I give out the message 'leave me alone' . . . sometimes if I go out in the evening I wear dark clothes . . . some people say I look threatening. . . . I'm not angry . . . I'm just always thinking . . . dress is protection.
> If I'm in certain areas I ask a friend to come or I avoid walking there; . . . I take the bus instead . . .

> I would definitely avoid Deptford ... they just know you're not from
> the area ... they just know – I can't explain it. ... If I get asked where
> I live I would give the answer they wanted. I feel safe in Peckham because
> that's where I live.

The following student talks about the Uprace High School Code of
Conduct and discipline system. African American students are more
likely than others to be disciplined for behaviour that is described
as defiant, aggressive and disruptive. One-third of the African
American males in the school's Class of 2000–01 were involved with
the discipline system during their first year. This student's perception
of 'work harder because we is Black' suggests that the disciplinary
climate is less flexible for African American students who conclude
that they are 'outsiders' – that is, that they are restricted from participating fully in the everyday life of the school. Many who have been
heavily involved in the discipline system become estranged from the
school ethos because they feel they are bound by a behaviour contract that cuts them off from participating in school activities. An issue
that merits further investigation is whether long-term restrictions on
student involvement in extracurricular activities achieve any reduction in continued misbehaviour.

> I would say, loosen up on the code of conduct and get rid of that con-
> tract. Because the contract is basically you signing your life away ... I
> think Uprace High can do without the contract and I believe that they
> could loosen up on the code of conduct. Because the code of conduct,
> I mean, most of that is ... African American people, females and males,
> females and males do get put on contract.

Building ways to relate to students as soon as they enter the discipline system is a key intervention, as Jason from Uprace makes clear:

> Most of the time what goes on in school, the parents never find out.
> There should be more phone calls home, so the parent could know. Maybe
> if the parent would find out and know about what's going on, they may
> be able to help. But most of the time the parent knows nothing until
> the child gets in serious trouble, maybe getting expelled or suspended.
> Then the parent finds out and the parent has no idea what's going on
> and they have to explain all of the way from the beginning that may
> have started months ago.

Second hypothesis

The second hypothesis seeks to ascertain the degree to which parents and the home environment support the achievement of Black
students.

> **The academic achievement of Black students is enhanced for those who experience in the home high academic achievement as a highly valued standard of performance, and as a very high priority for investment of family resources.**

Students who consistently experience this message in their homes are more likely to experience positive academic outcomes. The following student's quotation represents the comments of others whose homes are similarly supportive environments:

> A lot of it has to do with my parents. It started long before I got here. There was always a work ethic. The rule was if my parents have to go to work, I have to go to school and so school and schoolwork was always viewed as a responsibility. My parents haven't allowed me to work during the school year because they feel my focus should be on academics. Along with that, it's a personal competitive nature that I have. I want to do well. I want to do my best and, again, that comes from my parents.

Strong parental values that encourage educational achievement in the home are often reinforced by family participation in a network of community institutions and organisations that stimulate positive student performance and behaviour. The following student's remarks echo this:

> A lot of it's from my family and my church – things like that, that built me up as a person. Because in order to go out and do extracurricular activities, you have to have a certain amount of confidence to say, you know, I can do this. So they instilled a lot of that in me. I like my voice to be heard, to be honest and I like to get involved and because I feel that my opinion is valid.

This speaker also reflects how social networks that students bring to the school are used to model student interaction and participation in school organisations that resemble parent, family and community networks. Clearly, Black students seek to find in the school a social ecology that mirrors their social interaction in family and community.

The need to experience the school as a part of their family and community network is a critical element in understanding their academic achievement, role and place in the school. Thus, social interaction in the school that 'benefits my community' is not only viewed as rewarding but can also present the student with a burden of overcoming a minority experience that challenges the value of being a full and equal member of the school. The racial identity and social networks of Black students mediate the observed practices, policies, processes and organisational structures of school. Both school and student receive messages from descriptive practices and processes about the behaviour that seems appropriate for the school. Both overt and subtle messages are communicated to students about their ability to succeed, their reliability and trustworthiness.

The following are subsets of the second hypothesis; these further explain what parents can do and what they can make available to increase their students' academic success.

Parental resources

So really it depends on the textbooks and we have like other books at home too, so I can also use those as a reference.

I distinctly remember not wanting to learn how to read. It was a real fight. Every day my mother would come home from work and she would have like a set of learning-to-read books or something like that. I didn't want to do it; I just did not want to learn to read. But she, it was a for-real battle and she won. Every day, without fail, we would read together on the couch. We would do whatever it took and because she pushed so hard, there were times that I was like, you know what; I'm not looking for my mother. I'm going to go outside. I'm going to do this. But she found me, and she made me do it and I appreciate that now. But, at the time, it was not my idea of a good time.

Yeah, sometimes when I ask, my mother will quiz me.

Positive parental experiences

Both my parents work very hard and, watching them as a young girl, I basically took it upon myself to work really hard too. I myself, I've always had an inner motivation of doing well in school and so it kind of like, it was disappointing to me if I didn't do as well as I wanted to or if I didn't live up to an 'A' on the test or, you know, a 'B'+ or something. So, it was basically both. Like my parents and it was me too.

Pretty much positive role models in my life. There is my grandfather. He is the one who doesn't try to sugar coat everything. He just gives it to me straight. Like, he explains everything to me in a way that I would want him to, to make sure I understand it. He would explain like as if one of my peers would explain it to me. My grandmother, she sort of pushes and puts so much faith in me. That's probably where I get that from. . . . My mother; I see how she works so hard because she is a single parent and she had me young, so I see how she struggles to work hard and to get the best for me.

Negative parental experiences

Well, when I first came here, I was a low grade student, like an 'F' student and a 'D' student. . . . That was because my parents were going through a divorce and I wasn't going to school or doing my work. . . .

I was getting a bunch – a lot of discipline, a lot of yelling at me during that time. It was both of my parents. They was disciplining me about my grades, . . . it was natural that they got a divorce and I should be doing my work, not to worry about them, they got a divorce. . . . I was thinking it was my fault that they got divorced and it wasn't.

Third hypothesis

The third hypothesis seeks to ascertain the degree to which peers influence a student's academic performance.

The academic achievement of Black students is enhanced for those who can identify and associate with peers who value and invest in such achievement.

The next student voice illustrates how an African Caribbean student whose peers are academically successful will likely want to emulate positive peer behaviours and choices. Conformists tended to have a mixture of friends from different ethnic backgrounds, unlike the exclusively Black peer group of the rebels. Some of these conformists tended to go to the extreme in their break from the collective, so much so that it borders on a racialised discourse. This example is taken from Britain. Kelvin, who is a Year Nine student, gives this 'individualistic' perspective as the reason why he has avoided school exclusion:

TS: Do you belong to a gang or a posse?
Kelvin: No because my Mum says I shouldn't hang around students who get into trouble. I must take my opportunity while I can.
TS: What students in this school do you avoid?
Kelvin: They are Year 10 students, you can easily spot the way they walk around in groups, they are mostly Black, with one or two Whites and in the playground they wear hoods and Bop (Black stylised walk).
TS: Don't you ever bop?
Kelvin: Sometimes for a laugh, but it's really a kind of walk for bad people. I might walk like this at the weekend with my mates but not in school in front of the teachers. It sets a bad example.

The presence of a critical mass of African American high achievers at Uprace High may enhance the potential for peer modelling. However, African American students are seriously under-represented in all the top academic activities. The same can be said of African Caribbean students in the UK, who find it difficult to get on the gifted and talented register.

That said, the successful management of peer pressure is seen as a craft. As Vance, an African Caribbean student at TrueBrit College, says:

You do tokenism to show that you are one of them but you don't get fully involved . . . say your friend is arrested, you'd help your friend . . . you'd show you are solid . . .

I deal with it by going with my instincts . . . you need to say that you are in college or that you are working so that you can pull out . . .

Until I get to university . . . if you don't move out you will never break out, . . . everyone is at risk, mostly because of where you live, . . . even those who aren't involved are at risk, . . . it's not impossible to pull out, . . . university is the way out.

You can't avoid certain people; . . . there are places I would avoid going. . . . I feel a little safe in Peckham because I went to school there (Vance lives in New Cross). Deptford is safe; . . . you are safer in Lewisham than in Catford, . . . but generally I am at risk anywhere I go.

The comments of African American students during the interviews showed that they too were keenly aware of the importance of peers and peer relationships in their lives. Students described how they tried to sustain academic progress as a priority while they remained active in their peer networks. Students valued being a good student as well as being a good friend.

Scheduling time for peers
If I want to go to this party, I have to be sure that I do have time, some time to get the work done. If I don't, then I'll try to do half and half. Like maybe I'll do some of the paper and then go to the party and then do some later or do it the next day. I try to, if something presents itself, I try to accommodate it. I have to put my work first, but usually I try to accommodate it. It's usually possible.

I don't usually go out on school nights. I try to restrict myself to not go out and do things with my friends Monday through Thursday. It's hard, but I try to restrict myself on the phone because that's really two big temptations, you know, to communicate with your friends and find out how they are and how they're doing, things that are going on. But I try to stay off the phone until I have everything done. I pick a quiet room in the house to do my homework, where there aren't too many distractions, which isn't that hard to do. Basically, just because I now know what the distractions are, I stay away from them until I have time to focus on them once I'm done with my work.

Too much socialisation. Talking to everybody. Wanting to be around girls and thinking about having money, smoking and drinking and going to parties. A lot of stuff that was distracting me. Instead of saying, OK, well I'm gonna go to this party later and I'm gonna do my work now.

The next voice indicates that the stigma of 'acting white' does not seem to influence the students' academic performance.

Acting White/racelessness

I've definitely heard it, kind of like not expected it, but kind of like expected some people to be like that. It hasn't really bothered me. I haven't had a problem with it. But some people just don't know any better, but it's sad, but I can't do anything about that. It's not my problem.

Fourth hypothesis

The fourth hypothesis seeks to ascertain the degree to which students know about and access academic support services available to them.

The academic achievement of Black students is enhanced for those who can identify and who do utilise academic support services at the school and in the school community.

The repetitive and limited commentary that students in the sample are offered on school support services is captured in this quote:

I joke about my assignment notebook being my brain. There's a lot of information that I just can't keep in my head, so I have to write it down. ... So before a week starts, I open my assignment notebook and I've already written out the long-term things – oh, I've got a paper due Wednesday, I've got a test Thursday–Friday.

Fifth hypothesis

The fifth hypothesis seeks to ascertain the degree to which students' academic achievement is enhanced by strong and supportive relationships with adults in the school.

The academic achievement of Black students is enhanced for those who experience strongly supportive interactions with key classroom teachers and counsellors.

The development of positive student and teacher relationships is often cited as a key component of student academic success and as a core component of schooling. African American students who are academically successful report positive interactions and relationships with their teachers. Those who experience strong and supportive interactions with key classroom teachers and dean counsellors note both the importance of building relationships with faculty and staff and the significance of these relationships on their academic achievement. Furthermore, African American students who do well in school often identify with and emulate teachers whom they look up to and don't want to let down. The responsibility students take in maintaining such relationships by not disappointing their teachers provides them with a set of standards to monitor their role as students continually. In this way, students receive sustained support and encouragement from their adult role models – and academic support in the school.

> I would say a lot of my relationships with my teachers are good. Most of them are positive, come from outside of the classroom. I know a lot of my teachers through extracurricular activities, other activities that I'm involved in school. So if I have occasion to actually be in their class, there's already a relationship there. With other teachers that I don't see in an extracurricular setting, a lot of times, I'm just in their room. 'You know what, Mr or Mrs So-and-So, I don't understand this'. . . . When I have questions, that's why I'm, you know, 'I don't understand number three'; 'What'd you do this weekend?' – you know – that kind of rapport. But a lot of it comes from outside of the classroom.

> Yeah, actually my [sport] coach [name] he's always been proud of anything that I do. He lives in the local area and so he reads the local papers and he sees me in them and in the hallways and congratulates me. Where other teachers notice it, but they may not mention it, but he always makes sure that I know that he's proud. That's very encouraging.

> Ms [name of teacher], she was like very quiet and gentle. She was more like a grandmother teaching you and she was just very nice in the beginning, you see . . . She was – and she told us, you have to pay attention to each and every lesson because you move on; each lesson is like a domino effect.
>
> I could really talk with her and get help with maths and she always gave me the feeling that if I really wanted to do this or if I wanted to succeed, then I can, you know, and I can do anything that I wanted to. She really helped out with that, and I just loved going to talk to her because she just always had a good word or something good to say, and actually I still keep in touch with her now, even though she's not a teacher here.

Most African American students at Uprace High care about their academic achievement. They seek out teachers and other adult role models for academic support and encouragement.

> But, for things like essays, basically I just try to get what the teacher wants from me, ask them what they want, how the test is going to be formatted, or how the essay should be completed . . . then I go from what they say.
>
> A lot of other students, like older students, my older sister, whoever I was looking at, they did that and they told me it's a good idea. Some teachers, especially the better ones, welcome students to come at certain times and they give you specific times that's more convenient for them and they encourage us to come. Just from personal experience, I

found it to be the best thing to do; . . . of course, my parents tell me I should do things like that. But a lot of it is just experience.

Students in the sample also talked frankly about their negative experiences with teachers. Their comments focused on their discomfort with such teachers and their perception of these teachers as generally uncaring about their students.

> I just didn't feel comfortable there. I didn't really talk to her. I think I tried once but, I don't know, I didn't feel that comfortable. I don't think she really has that personality that you just go up and ask her a question.
>
> You know, she was just – sometimes she would just be mad for no reason. Nobody would do anything wrong. You know, she just be snapping to be snapping.
>
> Like some teachers I know really do not care about their students. I hate to say this about teachers, but some of them, I know just really don't. Like, if they think the student is a trouble maker or bad, they'll more than likely just write the student off.

Sixth hypothesis

The sixth and final hypothesis seeks to ascertain the degree to which students that have successfully negotiated the Triple Quandary experience academic success.

The academic achievement of Black students is enhanced for those who successfully negotiate the Triple Quandary, which consists of the following theoretical constructs: mainstream (White) culture, minority experience and Black cultural experience.

Mainstream (White) culture

A measurable fraction of African American students in the sample, some of whom were in the internalised non-negotiated stream, challenged the relevance and applicability of the content of the school's curriculum to their lives and career opportunities. Voices in this fraction of the sample often cited curricular reading materials that they perceived as personally disconnected from their individual experiences and as unrelated to the experience of being Black in the USA. Both their affective and cognitive/intellectual reactions seemed to emanate from their collective need for curricular materials that were integral both to their everyday lives and to their academic experiences. While this representative group did not indicate rejection of the mainstream culture, they seemed to express the necessity for inclusion in the curriculum of lessons and examples that embraced more fully and consistently the Black experience in the learning community:

Maybe the books that the school won't let us read. There are a lot of ethnic books about Africa and what really happened between the slave trading and all that. I am really interested in that. I don't see any books on that.

I don't think that I can remember back . . . I think we were doing like the little short stories or like the plays and stuff like that we had to read, like most of Shakespeare's work. Like I can't really understand what was said and I can't really get into it . . . if I can't get into it, I can't really focus on it. So, I think that's what that was. I like to read and I like a lot of books. I like one of Shakespeare's stories, *Romeo and Juliet*, but *Julius Caesar*; I can't really catch what they are saying or what they are doing. In his sentences, he puts the verb before the noun and when we talk, we put the noun before the verb. So it's sort of backwards. So, I think that's pretty much what it was.

Minority experience

Most Black students negotiate a set of stereotypes in the learning community at Uprace High. Many see fellow African American students who perpetuate these stereotypes through actions that reinforce a group stigma. Thus, African American students perceive that they are not treated as individuals in the learning community but rather that they are viewed as a group with generalised deficits. When African American students are treated as a group, their unique and individual differences are not sought after and nurtured by all members of the learning community.

In the cases where students and adults note a particular African American student's academic qualities, values and assets on an individual basis, that student's behaviour and attitudes are often interpreted as: 'You're different from the rest', because 'You're not like one of them'. Such subtle but penetrating messages and images in the learning community at Uprace High are detrimental to the life chances of all students and in particular to African American students living in a diverse society.

Black cultural experience

Knowing and trying to understand each student's assets and accepting the whole student requires the willingness to believe that affective and cognitive processes are integrally interwoven in the fabric of every student. Recognition of the interdependency between affective and cognitive processes is at the core of a relationship model. One student's comment: 'It's not always the "academic" that make the student', is a way of saying that the learning community at the school should do much more than simply assess the academic skills of students.

Creating a caring and compassionate environment in which all human beings and their differences are embraced is central to any culture of academic achievement.

Another student's statement that 'students got to make academics to make his grades' not only connotes the affective side of the student as an individual but also highlights that one's feelings about self and others play a vital role in academic achievement. In our sample, African American students who endorse the internalised negotiated success have higher results than those who do not. This correlation suggests that these students consciously nurture their affective and cognitive development in knowledge, skills and assets to achieve academically in the learning community at Uprace High.

> As far as being good, I could say that there is some teachers in this school who care about their students more than their academics. Because some teachers would just think about, oh well, his academics are low so something is probably wrong with him. But then again, you got other teachers that are like okay, well, let me see what's wrong with the student and see why his academics are low or he's not doing good. There are some teachers here that actually want to see what's wrong with the student before the academics because it's not always the academics that make the student. The student got to make academics to make his grades and stuff.

African American students in the sample who recognise ways to manage, cope and negotiate the Triple Quandary are academically successful. They are conscious of the images and the subtle messages of their group; they develop strategies from their family and community to successfully negotiate mainstream (White) and minority experiences in the learning community at Uprace High. When unsuccessfully negotiated, these experiences can inhibit the academic achievement of African American students in the learning community. African American students who successfully negotiate the Triple Quandary are more likely to:

- develop peer relationships across racial, ethnic, 'class' and gender boundaries;

> From the time, as long as I can remember until year eight, I was the only Black student in my class. So that makes – it makes it a lot easier because a lot of the programmes are predominantly White and a lot of Black people are scared to step out of their racial boundaries and you know, explore other people, other cultures; you know things that they're afraid of or whatever. So the fact that I have been raised around different 'races' made it a lot easier.

- participate in homogeneous and heterogeneous extracurricular activities;

  > Tennis is just a passion. I always loved sports and both volleyball and basketball, but I'm very short. So since my parents had me take tennis lessons when I was younger and they enjoyed it, that was kind of a natural decision; . . . one of the things I appreciate about it is that it's a way for me to meet different people.

- develop coping strategies to overcome inconsistencies with main-stream (White) values and their home and community values;

  > It's funny, because as the acceptances started coming in, you know, I didn't tell people because, of the well, you know – if I got in and other people didn't, I don't want them to be awkward about it. I just – if it comes up, we'll talk about it, but I'm not going to bring it up. So every morning, she'd [mother] asked me, 'Did you get any college news'? And I'm like: 'Okay, well, I got into Harvard'. And she physically hit me. She'd be like, 'Are you kidding me? Why aren't you more excited'? . . . She would be ten times more excited than I was and just that kind of support really helped.

- internalise only those mainstream (White) values that they define as necessary for their academic achievement.

  > I am not saying all higher learning is all bad, I mean, some things it's like mandatory for life but it's like right now; . . . now is to be a six or seven page essay about somebody else's life. I don't have no idea what it's about. I mean I heard about Shelley, but I'm not so into his life that I just want to write about him. I mean give me something else that will help me out later on in life and not just put me in a classroom where I just sit down and listen to somebody.

Conclusion

The literature on resilience focuses on children at risk of adverse developmental outcomes and on specific factors such as children's competence as a strength. The notion of the Triple Quandary is really another way of unpacking the characteristics of resilience for Black students in the UK and the USA. Researchers have found that many young people who live in high-risk situations overcame risks. Studies of at-risk children led quickly to the recognition that certain children did not succumb in the same way as others to maladaptive behaviours. Such children seemed to be in some way protected against the negative effects of parental, social or environmental factors so that their development could proceed apparently unimpaired by difficulties. Black students face a range of pressures, mostly to do with cultural, peer and family backgrounds. There is little evidence that teachers and schools are presenting the biggest barriers to overcome. They would clearly be more effective if they provided programmes for students to navigate their way through challenges they face in and outside of school.

References

Boykin, A. (1986), 'The Triple Quandary and the schooling of African American children', in Neisser, U. (ed.), *The School Achievement of Minority Children: New Perspectives* (New Jersey: Lawrence Erlbaum Associates)

Dhondy, F. (1999), 'Institutional racism', *Times Educational Supplement* (19 February) (London)

DuBois, W. E. B. (1903), *The Souls Of the Black Folk, Three Negro Classics* (New York: Avon Books)

Foucault, M. (1977), *Discipline and Punishment* (London: Penguin)

Foucault, M. (1980) (translated by C. Gordon) *Power/Knowledge: Selected Interviews and Other Writings 1972–1977* (New York: Pantheon)

Joyce, J. (1916), *The Portrait of the Artist as a Young man* (London: Penguin)

Ogbu, J. U. (1995), 'Cultural problems in minority education – their interpretation and consequences', *The Urban Review*, 27:3, 189–205

Sewell, T. (1996), 'Mind your Language Trevor', *Voice Newspaper*, 699 (23 April) (London)

Internet sources

www.tomisswithlove.blogspot.com (accessed 12 April 2007)

5

Mothering and the family as sites of struggle: theorising 'race' and gender through the perspectives of Caribbean mothers in the UK

Tracey Reynolds

Introduction

For Caribbean mothers[1] and other mothers belonging to minority ethnic groups in the UK, the family and their mothering experiences represent a key site in which they continue to struggle against social constructions of mothering and the experiences of racial discrimination in their everyday lives. Caribbean mothers, as the central focus on debate in this study, reveal that mothering is equally racialised as it is gendered. Yet contemporary mothering discourses generally overlook this factor and universalistic claims of mothering are based on White, middle-class and heterosexual practices. The specific focus of the study on Caribbean mothers also demonstrates that White middle-class mothering issues have only recently become attentive to themes such as balancing and negotiating work and family roles, lone mothering, kinship and community networks, and extended family relationships – themes that are intrinsic to Caribbean mothers, who have longstanding traditions in these areas. The chapter documents the experiences of a cross-section of first-, second- and third-generation Caribbean mothers in the United Kingdom (UK), to illustrate that the practices performed by these mothers represent their attempts to maintain established cultural, social and kinship links to their cultural and ethnic origins, whilst at the same time adapting to the social circumstances of being part of a Black[2] and minority ethnic community in the UK.

The analysis begins by examining the cultural, historical and social contexts of Caribbean mothering. 'Race', ethnicity and gender are integral to this understanding of Caribbean household patterns and family relationships. The second part of the discussion examines how

Caribbean mothers experience and respond to issues of racism and racial discrimination in their everyday lives. An important aspect of these women's mothering is concerned with socialising and transmitting Caribbean cultural values to their children. Examples of this aspect of Caribbean mothering are provided in the final part of this analysis.

Research background

The data for this chapter form part of my doctoral thesis investigating the experiences of Caribbean mothers in the UK (see Reynolds, 1999). During 1996 to 1997 in-depth qualitative interviews were conducted with forty mothers living in four areas of London. The main advantage of a relatively small sample size of forty mothers is that it allows for an in-depth focus on the lives and experiences of these women. This is particularly important in a under-researched area of Caribbean mothering in the UK. The age group of the mothers ranged between nineteen and eighty-one years old. This wide age range facilitates the analysis of inter-generational similarities and differences:

- four mothers in the study were third-generation mothers, between the ages of nineteen and twenty-four years old;
- twenty mothers were second-generation mothers, twenty-five to forty years old;
- eleven mothers were either second- or first-generation mothers, forty-one to sixty years old; and
- five were first-generation mothers, sixty-one years old and over, and who were retired.

These retired mothers provided retrospective account of the mothering and the particular issues and concerns they faced as first-generation mothers raising Black children from the 1950s through to the 1970s. The retired mothers' retrospective accounts were also vital in highlighting the generational shifts in childcare and employment patterns that occurred for Black mothers over the years. In addition, these retired mothers were still involved in caring work with their grandchildren and great-grandchildren today, and therefore they continue to be involved in mothering work.

Caribbean mothers in context

Mothering is framed around particular social, cultural and historical contexts. There is much evidence to suggest that Caribbean mothering

in the UK represents both structural–economic and cultural phenomena: structural–economic because Caribbean mothers, as a result of their
racial and gender status, occupy a collective subordinate location
and have unequal access to resources compared to White men and
women. The collective experiences of slavery, colonialism, migration,
racism and sexism have each encouraged this unequal access to
resources. Historically, for Caribbean mothers the gendered division of
labour that traditionally separates men and women's activities according to public and private spheres is much more blurred, and the gender
roles are more interwoven (Hill-Collins, 1994; Reynolds, 2005).

Some writers have argued that this interweaving of the public and
private spheres for Black mothers is rooted in African patterns of
family organisation that have been transplanted and transformed,
and have survived the institution of African enslavement in the
Caribbean and the United States of America (USA), to continue into
the present day (Herskovits, 1941; Nnaemeka, 1997; Sudakasa, 1996),
while other writers claim that Black mothers' structural location is rooted
in and attributable to African enslavement by Europeans (Frazier, 1948;
Gutman, 1976). Those writers that support this 'Africanist' perspective refer back to studies by W. E. B. DuBois (1908), one of its earliest
advocates. DuBois stressed the importance of understanding the relevance of Western African heritage on Black family organisation in
Caribbean and USA societies. He contends that although the institution of slavery in these societies prohibited the replication of African
lineage and family life, it did not remove the core values and societal
codes underlying them. The enslaved Africans brought with them
values that highlight family membership based on consanguinity: in
other words, kinship rooted in 'blood ties'. African families were organised around consanguineal cores of adult family members that were
either patri- or matri-lineage. These blood ties have far greater importance to African family life than conjugal ties that dominated family
organisation in European societies. Under a consanguineal form of
family organisation, family members each took on different roles and
labour within and outside of the family compound that was dependent on their seniority and family status and not a gendered division
of labour. Within the family unit, both the male and female elders
wielded considerable power, authority and influence along with
mothers and adult sisters in terms of responsibility and decision-
making for the family.

Supporters of this viewpoint suggest that African patterns have
survived and continued into the present day; and they indicate
that Caribbean families have traditionally been organised around

matri-lineage structures – such as matri-focal households or family units – that comprise mother, child and extended matri-lineage kin. Smith's (1953) influential study of Caribbean family life acknowledges that within the Caribbean the concept of family primarily means relationships created by 'blood' rather than conjugal ties. Motherhood is culturally valued over and above marriage, and the organisation of family units is not necessarily dependent upon conjugal ties. Children are socialised to think in terms of obligations to mothers, siblings and other 'close kin' as more important than obligation to outsiders' such as spouses (Barrow, 1996; Clarke, 1957; Smith, 1996). These typical family structures and household arrangements mean that women's activities in public and private spaces are not so rigidly defined and their power and authority within their family are equally governed by seniority – determined by age or status, and gender (Berleant-Schiller and Maurer, 1993; Gonzalez, 1982). Of course, not all Caribbean families emphasise consanguineal relationships. Historically, factors such as class, education and social status have influenced the consanguineal or conjugal family structures. Research by Roopnarine and Brown (1997) suggests that Caribbean middle-class families are more likely to favour conjugal family units and the poor or working class are much more consanguineal-focused in their family groupings.

The relevance of Africa for understanding Black family relationships and households structures has been criticised by those writers who contend that trans-Atlantic African enslavement is the starting point of analysis of Black families. Two leading authors of this perspective, Franklin Frazier (1948) and Herbert Gutman (1976), argue that it is difficult to identify the particular ethnic groups or communities that influenced the organising principles of Black families because of the sheer diversity of cultures, language and social structural factors of the descendants of enslaved Africans. In addition, the 'Africanist' position fails to account for the socioeconomic context of slavery in which Black family structures developed and the influence of European values on family organisation. They contend that the blurring of the boundaries marking out public and private spheres that characterise Black women's relations is firmly rooted in and attributable to African enslavement by Europeans. The organisational principles of this type of enslavement created a structure whereby Black women, irrespective of their maternal status, were viewed as commodities, and alongside their menfolk they provided free labour and were positioned as 'workers' (Davis, 1981; Gutman, 1976; Shaw, 1994). The adaptation of the 'slave culture' vis-à-vis socialisation and in response to Black people's socioeconomic circumstances is responsible for women's continued worker and mother role in the public and private spheres, and female-centred households. Leading commentators of the Caribbean family return to this adaptation model to understand and explain how Caribbean mothers' long-standing status as 'workers' – whether it be free, indentured, migrant or paid labour – has continued from trans-Atlantic enslavement across successive generations and up to the present day across different societies (Berleant-Schiller and Maurer, 1993; Bryan *et al.*, 1985; Dodgson, 1984; Seguera, 1994).

Despite these contrasting perspectives concerning the origins of role relationships and family structures, both approaches suggest that Caribbean mothers and their family relationships encompass social–structural issues and cultural traditions that mark them out as 'alternative' to European or western White family models and relationships. Black feminists challenge conventional feminist claims that mothering is primarily based on sets of complex and interacting relationships between self/mother, family and child (see Ribbens, 1995). Black feminists recognise that instead, for Black mothers, mothering extends beyond this essentially private realm of the family. The care Black mothers provide for their children 'is inextricably linked to socio-cultural concerns' (Hill-Collins, 1994: 47). In this sense mothering does not merely involve the physical, mental and emotional care of the individual child but also 'strategic mothering', wherein these mothers engage in strategic child-rearing practices to encourage their children to move beyond racial stereotypes that seek to constrain them (Reynolds, 2003 and 2005).

Black feminists also argue that in contrast to White middle-class mothers, whose norms and values are mirrored and affirmed in mainstream society, Black mothers' work, irrespective of ethnic grouping, involves them actively challenging societal norms and values that identify their children and familial experiences as inferior (Hill-Collins, 1994). Consequently, these women's mothering work is not simply an individual activity, because the work these mothers undertake has important ramifications and wider implications for the Black communities at large. At a community level Black mothering represents conscious and collective modes of resistance. Hill-Collins (1994) introduces the concept 'community mothers' and Naples (1996) the term 'activist mothering' to historically map Black women's roles, across successive generations, in providing informal and voluntary care through community projects and education programmes for Black children residing in their local communities. Similarly, shared mothering has been an important mothering practice for Black mothers (Roschelle, 1997; Stack, 1974). In the Caribbean context, Lynda Pulsipher's (1993) study of multi-generational low-income 'houseyards' in the Caribbean reveals that caring for children and other kin is shared among other house-yard members. Studies by Karen Fog-Olwig (1999) and Elsie Leo-Rhynie (1997) both acknowledge that in the Caribbean a well-established feature of family life is that children regularly reside with, and are cared for by, their grandmothers or senior female relatives (such as great-aunts) on a permanent basis in order to encourage mothers to seek employment. The idea that senior female relatives should care for children so that the mother can act as economic provider for the family is regarded as a functional and pragmatic approach to child-rearing. For example, Evelyn Dodgson's (1984) analysis of Caribbean mothers who migrated to the UK in the era following World War Two high-lights that the vast majority of these women left their children behind in the Caribbean to be cared for by relatives until they could send for them to live in the UK at a later date. This practice still continues today with a new wave of Caribbean mothers who have been recently recruited to teaching and nursing posts in response to labour short-ages in these areas (Reynolds, 2005). Similarly, current research work exploring the social resources within Caribbean family relationships recognises the reciprocal nature of kinship caring.[3] Underpinning kinship relationships is the cultural expectation and obligation that care will be shared among family members (Reynolds and Zontini, 2006). Family members are 'kinscripted' (Stack and Burton, 1994), or recruited to care for family who may have previously cared for them.

Ultimately, this family and community work by Caribbean mothers represents their collective and individual resistance to societal insti-tutions, structures and processes that seek to subvert them. Unfortun-ately, in contemporary western mothering ideologies, the social and cultural significance of Black mother's practices, values and work are typically overlooked or downplayed because the mothers assume a marginal or oppositional location in the discourse. Black feminists have attempted to redress this imbalance by developing a methodological framework to study Black women's experiences and position their voices at the centre of analysis (Amos and Parmar, 1984; Griffin, 1996; Hill-Collins, 1990; Mama, 1995; Mirza, 1997; Sudbury, 1998).

Household structures and family relationships

This part of the analysis develops some of these broader issues within the context of the Caribbean household structures and family relation-ships. The discussion focuses on three household patterns: the matri-focal or female-centred family,; adaptive family forms and 'child-shifting'.

The Caribbean matri-focal family

Female-headed households are strongly embedded in Caribbean history and they exist as a longstanding and well-established cultural tradition of Caribbean families. Historically and cross-culturally, the celebratory image of the 'matriarch' who is strong, independent and the 'linchpin' of family life, continues to be the most dominant image of Caribbean mothering. In Caribbean family literature much has been written about female-centred or matri-focal families and also the child-rearing practice of 'child-shifting', but what is less explored is the diverse family models and adaptive family forms Caribbeans move through within their lifetime.

Some of the earlier studies to examine the root causes of matri-focal families emerged in the USA and focussed on family structures of enslaved Africans. Frazier (1948) and Herskovits (1941) were the first comprehensive studies of African American slaves' family structures. They identified that the mother–child unit was the primary family unit that persisted throughout the slavery period, but while Herskovits regarded this as a continuance of the domestic arrangements of African societies Frazier attributed this to men's displaced role under slavery. He draws on other historical material to suggest that, wherever possible, Black men tried to develop and maintain family structures based on strong conjugal unions and paternal headship and authority. Later work by Gutman (1976) highlights that the Black matriarch is fundamentally about the low-income families' adaptive capacities for survival. He claims that in order to survive the separation of men from their homes during trans-Atlantic enslavement, Black families culturally adapted themselves to female-headed households. This family structure continues to evolve across successive generations because of Black people's unequal access to social and material resources.

These ideas expressed by Gutman, Frazier and Hershkovits were adopted and fitted into analysis of Caribbean families from the period following World War Two onwards (Smith, 1996). Fortes (1956), for example, points to a strong cultural emphasis on blood ties such as the mother–child bond and sibling relationships, and a much lower emphasis on legally sanctioned marriage and conjugal ties to suggest that it is 'this aspect of family relations which is crucial in producing matri-focal structure across West Indian societies' (Fortes, 1956: 53). Marriage is viewed in terms of status and legal significance, but family and kinship ties have cultural significance. Gonzalez's (1982) analysis of matri-focal families in the Caribbean adopts Smith's mother-centred approach, but she also incorporates into this analysis a focus on children's expectations of female authority and dominance in households especially around household decision-making and child-rearing. Gonzalez suggests that within matri-focal households children expect that 'maternal figures would be strongest, most stable and most dominant; they would see their mothers as being not only nurturing but disciplinary figures' (Gonzalez, 1982: 233). Other writers also suggest that what characterises Caribbean matri-focal families is their longstanding tradition of maternal economic activity and financial provision to support their families (Massiah, 1986; Safa, 1986).

In the UK today, matri-focal families are one of many models of family life, family forms and household structures that Caribbean mothers move through within their lifetime. Yet the matriarch image and matri-focal families are the most pervasive image of African Caribbean mothering. On the one hand, this type of family structure could be said to represent the mothers' varied and changing understanding of families and the 'moralities and rationalities that underpin how families work' (Carling *et al.*, 2002: xiv). On the other hand, however, they also reflect a cultural and strategic response to the specific social and economic conditions Caribbean mothers face in the UK.

Adaptive family forms and household structures

Dorien Powell's (1986) analysis of Caribbean families offers a flexible and pluralistic understanding of family life by examining the dynamic and shifting nature of family and household structures. Powell develops a four-part typology of Caribbean family relations to identify that female-headed households are not static. Rather, they are one of several family forms that most Black mothers move through within their lifetime. These family forms are:

1. single (complete absence of male partner);
2. common-law (joint residence without legal sanction);
3. married (joint residence and legal sanction); and
4. 'visiting relationships'.

This last concept of visiting relationships was first introduced by R. T. Smith (1962) to represent those households where the male partner does not reside within the household on a permanent basis but is generally considered to be a part of the family by other family members and regularly visits the family household.

In the Caribbean 'visiting relationships' dominate amongst the Black poor and lower-social-class groups, and the households they produce – female headed-households – are considered as being representative of the adaptive capacities of poor, low-income Black families to survive poverty and economic disadvantage (Barrow, 1996; Waters, 1999). Writers discussing the Caribbean family in the UK and particularly the prevalence of 'visiting relationships' amongst low-income working-class Caribbean households, have applied and adopted these ideas of the correlation between the 'visiting' family patterns and poverty, and economic insecurity, to a UK context (see Dench, 1996).

The concentrated focus on female-headed households has been at the cost of ignoring the sheer multiplicity and diversity of family forms Caribbean mothers live in. For example, in this study, sixteen mothers are married and the remaining twenty-four mothers live in family structures and relationships that range from 'single' to 'visit-ing' to 'co-habiting' relationships. The dynamic and fluid nature of the mothers' relationships with their partners means that they move through different family forms during a period of time. For instance, five out of the sixteen married women in this study were in 'visiting relationships' with their partners prior to marriage. Two of these mothers commented that they primarily saw this period as a 'getting to know you' phase before moving on to a common-law relationship and finally a married relationship:

> After we had the first child, we were spending all of our time together but I was used to my independence. At that stage in our lives I don't think either of us were ready to settle down and live together like man and wife and so we sat together and decided that he would stay with us some of the time to see how things developed with us. Obviously things worked out fine for us because we got married in the end. (Anita, age forty-three, married, first generation)

> I am used to being on my own and doing my own thing and I couldn't ever imagine me being welded to a man's side. About two years with him living here part-time I thought this isn't so bad and marriage just seemed to be a natural progression. (Tina, age forty-nine, married, first generation)

The above quotations show that these mothers were not permanently fixed, in some pathological way, into a 'visiting relationship'. Instead, a 'visiting relationship' was considered as a way to adjust to a change in their relationship status. Other married and partnered Caribbean mothers interviewed moved from 'visiting' to common-law to mar-riage relationships as a consequence of external factors. For example, Georgia, a second-generation mother, also existed in a 'visiting rela-tionship' with her partner whilst he was unemployed. It was only after her partner found a relatively secure job as a car mechanic and could financially contribute towards the family income that they decided to marry. Many other unmarried mothers greatly valued their independent and autonomous status of 'visiting' and 'common-law' relationship.

'Child-shifting'

'Child-shifting' is another well-established feature of African Caribbean family life and this has been extensively documented in Caribbean family literature (Brodber, 1974; Russell-Browne *et al.*, 1997; Senior, 1991). 'Child-shifting' involves the shifting of child-rearing responsibilities from the mother to other family relatives, usually female kin, on a permanent or temporary basis. It represents an informal adoption practice that is viewed by many as a 'strategy for economic and social survival of the mother and child' (Russell-Browne *et al.*, 1997: 224). Maternal migration is an essential characteristic of Caribbean life. Mothers migrate outwards in search of employment opportunities that will provide them with financial independence and enable them to achieve better life-chances for themselves and their children (Fog-Olwig, 1999; Senior, 1991). Historically, this has involved internal migration by mothers from rural areas to urban cities and outward migration to other Caribbean territories and, principally, North America and the UK. From as early as the 1970s Caribbean mothers in the UK have also been part of a process of secondary migration to the USA and Canada, where Caribbean people who initially migrated to the UK have utilised extended family links established in these countries to seek out further social and economic opportunities (Goulbourne and Chamberlain, 2001). A large number of migrating mothers belong to low-income socioeconomic groups and they do not have the economic means or support networks readily available to take their children with them. Consequently, they consider that the child's best interest is best served by being left behind and cared for by their relatives. In the majority of 'child-shifting' cases the principal carers are the maternal grandmother or a maternal aunt (Russell-Browne *et al.*, 1997).

In my study I spoke with mothers who decided to leave their children behind in the Caribbean when they first migrated, in order to establish themselves in the UK. In each instance they saw 'child-shifting' as a temporary measure and they were in the process of sending for their children to join them here. With 'child-shifting' the mothers do not relinquish maternal responsibilities. During their time apart from their children their maternal responsibilities are framed around maintaining regular contact with their children and carers, and sending money and gifts 'back home' to them. Whilst these mothers readily acknowledge that their children's best place is with them and they highlight the emotional costs and worries of leaving their children behind, they also adopt a pragmatic approach to under-standing that benefits of improving their children's life chances far outweigh the costs of separation.

Strong reciprocal kinship relationships are an important feature of Caribbean families and 'child-shifting' practices reinforce this. For instance, it is an accepted practice for Caribbean mothers to 'give' or 'lend' their children to female relatives who are childless or require male or female children's companionship (Sanford, 1976), as the following quotation indicates:

> Aunite Vy really wanted a girl child; . . . My mum told auntie Vy that she could take me to live with her. So I really grew up around my auntie. (Enid, age sixty-nine, married, first-generation mother)

There are a number of studies that examine the negative impact of 'child-shifting'. In the Caribbean and the UK there have been documented cases of mothers who simply abandon their children to a succession of temporary carers, children who are taken into state authority care, and children who have experienced neglect and abuse (Brodber, 1974; Rhodes, 1992). Studies have also looked at the impact of 'child-shifting' on carers. Brodber's study (1986) of care-givers in Jamaican society shows that many carers are usually from low-income groups themselves and they find it difficult to make ends meet and successfully fulfil their role as carers. Potential conflicts can also arise between principal care-givers in the Caribbean and the mothers who have left their children behind (Fog-Olwig, 1993). Other studies have explored the psychological and socialisation costs of children that experience 'child-shifting' and reunification with their mothers (Arnold, 1997; Senior, 1991). On the whole, however, the Caribbean mothers welcomed 'child-shifting' as a positive solution to their social and economic circumstances.

Understanding racism as lived experiences

In my study all the mothers stated that they had encountered racism in their everyday lives, although the extent that they experienced this varied, as did the context. Social class and generation differences generally informed the mothers' experiences and their access to resources to respond to and challenge racist practices in their every-day lives. In the following quotations two mothers from different generations – first and second – reflect on this issue of racism. Doris, a first-generation mother, offers a retrospective account of racial violence and harassment she faced during the 1950s when she first migrated to the UK. Michelle, a second-generation mother, reflects on similar experiences of overt racial abuse during her childhood years growing up in East London during the 1970s.

> Things were awful in those early days because they wasn't used to Black people. We were like aliens from outer space and you could see the fear in their eyes. I was there for the 1958 [Notting Hill] riots. . . . I'm sure you heard the stories from your parents about signs landlord used to put up in their windows about 'no Blacks, no dogs and no Irish'. . . . That was how it was for Black people back then. White people were really racist because they didn't know any better. (Doris, age eighty-one, married, first generation)

> I'd be walking down the road and you have these nasty, vile people. They would have the nasty habit of spitting at you and calling you 'nigger' or 'black bitch'. East London was supposed to be a multi-cultural area but I still had to deal with that. You never knew what you was going to get when you left your house. (Michele, age twenty-eight, lone mother, second generation)

Racist encounters and practices experienced by the Caribbean mothers were not only confined to (perceived) overt or direct racial actions such as racial abuse, harassment or physical violence. Instead, the mothers recognise that racism manifests itself in more subtle 'invisible' and complex ways. Nizinga's comment is one of many viewpoints expressed by the mothers to support this claim:

> I can't really give you a clear-cut example because racism is so subtle that you can't put your finger on it and define it and say this is actually going on, but you know it's there. You just can't articulate it but it's what's going on. It's no use ranting and raving because when you're talking to those people, they want facts. Their idea of racism anyway is name-calling. I can handle that but I can't handle the subtleness, where it is coming from. It did actually make me quite paranoid for a while but I just had to learn how to deal with it. (Nizinga, age thirty-one, lone mother, second generation)

The above quotations reinforce Gilroy's (1987) view that racism is experienced as a 'changing sameness'. This reflects the fact that whilst the form and expression of racism has transformed over the years, it still continues to inform the daily lives of Black people and more specifically the lives of Caribbean mothers. The extensive literature documenting the racial inequality Black people continue to experience in British institutions such as, for example, education, social welfare services and the criminal justice system supports these claims of the 'changing sameness' of racism (Modood *et al.*, 1997).

Caribbean mothers have a longstanding tradition of responding to racial inequality by actively, and in diverse ways, challenging racist practices at personal, individual, local and collective levels. For example, during the 1970s a group of Caribbean mothers collectively organised to campaign successfully for the abolition of Educational Sub-Normal (ESN) schools where Caribbean children were greatly over-represented (Bryan *et al.*, 1985). My study throws up similar stories of Caribbean mothers collectively and individually campaigning to improve conditions for themselves. Pearl, a first-generation mother, recollected her experiences as a factory worker during the 1950s to recount how she collectively organised with the other female workers on the factory floor (many of whom were Caribbean mothers) to successfully lobby management into altering their shift working patterns so that the working day now ended at 3.00 p.m. instead of the old time of 4.00 p.m. These women's new working patterns meant that the mothers were now able to take or collect their children from school, or arrive home shortly after their children's school day had finished. Pearl's success could be viewed as a small victory. But it was a large victory in the sense that these mothers were prepared to actively take on these larger institutions and organisations to secure better rights and working conditions for themselves and confront perceived incidences of racially and sexually unjust and unfair treatment.

Similarly, Dolly, a first-generation mother, recounts how she individually and indirectly worked to challenge racist practices in her church:

> In the church I was going to, there was a lot of Black people that started to come, but there wasn't many Black people taking part, so I got myself on the PCC [parish church council] and if anything disturbed me or worried me, I got my say. . . . In a quiet way, I got changes. I did it without being too forceful. (Dolly, age seventy-six, married, first generation)

At individual and personal levels the mothers also implemented, within their child-rearing, strategies to actively respond to racism, thus subverting it and minimising the importance of it in their children's lives. This factor, the struggle against racism, unites Caribbean mothers across the differences that exist between them. Of course differences between the mothers, such as social-class and generation divisions, inform their perceptions of racism and how they respond to what they believe to be racist practices and experiences in their own and their children's lives. These divisions also have implications for the strategies the mothers devise and resources available to them in this particular aspect of their mothering work.

Mothering practices, cultural identity and belonging

The mothers consider that an important aspect of their mothering concerns involves teaching their children their historical legacies, including trans-Atlantic African enslavement and colonial migration. One way in which the mothers achieve this is by utilising cultural signifiers in their mothering so that they transmit Caribbean cultural values and identity to their children. The mothers identify respect and good manners demonstrated by their children, the use of corporal punishment to maintain the discipline of their children, food and the celebration of ethnic–racial identity as key practices they transmitted to their children.

Respect and good manners

The mothers recognise the issue of showing respect to parents, family members and community elders as a Caribbean tradition – clearly distinct from a British one, as the following quotations illustrate:

> When your parents call you and you don't say 'yeh' or 'what', you've got to say 'yes mummy' or 'yes daddy', little things like that, you had to show respect. That's the way it is in the Caribbean and my parents raised me like that, . . . little things like you make your beds in the mornings, like when you come home from school you know that you have got to take off your school clothes and you put on your house clothes. Those kind of values I want to pass onto [my daughter] because I think those kind of values carry you through life and make you a better person. (Jamilla, age twenty-five, lone mother, second generation)

It is interesting that the mothers perceive these values of good manners and respect as intrinsically Caribbean traits. However, it could be argued that Britain's colonial legacy in the Caribbean meant that Caribbean families would have incorporated British value systems into their parenting and adopted British views around family values, respect and discipline. Furthermore, critics would also suggest that many other ethnic groups uphold these values of respect for elders, good manners and discipline. Therefore, and in contrast to these mothers' views, they cannot be viewed as exclusively Caribbean values or behavioural traditions.

Corporal punishment and discipline

A historical tradition exists in the Caribbean wherein 'good parenting' relates to parents' ability to act as successful disciplinarians and produce well-disciplined children who adhere to societal norms and values (Lowenthal, 1972). The onus is on parents to show others in their community that their children are obedient and respectful (Peters-Ferguson, 1988). Physical punishment is used to ensure their children's compliance (Leo-Rhynie, 1997). Elsie Leo-Rhynie (1997) reflects: 'these beliefs are founded, for the most part, on the biblical injunction not to "spare the rod and spoil the child" ' (Leo-Rhynie, 1997: 46). The mothers in the study, to varying degrees, grew up experiencing this form of discipline by their parents and they view this as a distinctive Caribbean tradition. While in a very small minority of cases there was little difference between discipline and abuse, for the most part the punishment administered by their parents (usually the mother) was followed by shows of great physical affection and love. The punishment experienced by these mothers, as children, did little to damage close and loving bonds with their parents. Certainly, the majority of mothers still persist in the belief that physical punishment is a culturally accepted method of parental discipline. However, there are class and generational differences in attitudes to and experiences of parental discipline. Generally, the mothers who were raised by parents who had more schooling and were from middle-class backgrounds were less likely to experience physical punishment.

On a more practical note, these middle-class parents had resources that they could threaten to withhold from their children, such as removing toys and other privileges; therefore, they had alternative ways to punish their children that were not options for low-income working-class parents. In discussing their own parenting methods, the first-generation mothers acknowledged that physical punishment was the most common method of disciplining their children. However, the second- and third-generation mothers expressed greater caution about this practice. This is because increased state control and legislation in parenting to safeguard the rights and well-being of children – such as the Children's Act 1989 – and general changes in societal attitudes to parenting have influenced the mothers' views on parental discipline and punishment. For the vast majority of the second- and third-generation mothers any references to physical punishment of their children such as 'beating' represents a symbolic gesture to the Caribbean model of parenting and a re-affirmation of cultural significance rather than actual practice. In reality, the preferred methods of discipline by the mothers was 'grounding' (which is about disallowing recreational activities and privileges outside of the home for an established period of time), stopping pocket money, and restrictions on the use of telephone, television, internet and computer games. The social and historical context in which the mothers situate their own and their parents' disciplinary practices provide a direct challenge to criticism

levelled at disciplinary practices of Caribbean parents by those policymakers that portray their children as 'unfortunate recipients of
repressive regimes' (Callender, 1997: 100). It also re-affirms a Caribbean
cultural identity by focusing on the perceived cultural significance of
this parenting practice.

Food

Food is an important part of cultural identity. However, the obvious-
ness and taken-for-granted nature of food mean that until recently food
has received limited critical attention outside of the anthropology and
health and nutrition research fields. Yet food is a cultural artefact imbued
with meanings and values (Counihan and Esterik, 1997). The type of
food goods chosen, and the preparation and presentation of certain
foods, all re-affirm cultural belonging. The mothers recognise the cultural significance of Caribbean food and they express a commitment
to the preparation of this food as a means through which they can
sustain links to the Caribbean and transmit Caribbean cultural identity inter-generationally. An important mothering practice involves them
cooking Caribbean food for their children and in turn teaching their
children how to prepare this food for themselves.

> My parents brought us up in eating West Indian food. My mother made
> a point of cooking West Indian food and teaching us how to do it. I like
> to cook rice and peas, chicken curry and make guinness punch. I make
> all of these and give it to my daughter . . . so that when she grows
> up she can cook herself these food. I feel it is important that this was
> passed onto me from my Mum and now from me to her. (Michelle, age
> twenty-eight, lone mother, second generation)

Particular foods hold special cultural significance to families and
they are often associated with family celebrations, 'get togethers' and
cultural events. Food also forms part of family ritualising celebrations
and events (Reynolds, 2006a).

> Christmas is our big time. I stick to traditional West Indian food with
> one or two English dishes like potatoes. I start off with garlic pork and
> pepperpot on Christmas morning then I'll make rice and peas, spicy duck
> or lamb and of course a turkey. (Denise, age twenty-two, living with
> partner, third generation)

Caribbean food is also used as cultural signifier by the mothers
to revisit and remember their childhood and construct a collective
memory of cultural belonging. For instance, the mothers commonly
made reference to their experiences of the 'Caribbean Sunday dinner'

consisting of chicken and rice and peas, the 'Caribbean Sunday breakfast' of ackee and saltfish and also the 'dutchpot', a large cooking pot traditionally found in Caribbean homes. Caribbean food, as a cultural signifier, is perhaps one of the clearest manifestations of how notions of a collective Caribbean cultural identity represent an 'imagined spatial collective' (Bakari, 1997) constructed by those residing outside of the region. Particular food types that are specific to individual territories in the region – such as the Jamaican cuisine, ackee and saltfish are amalgamated and redefined as representing Caribbean cuisine.

Celebration of a 'Caribbean' tradition and Black racial identities
Caribbean mothers transmit a positive racial identity to their children in order to establish their children's self-worth, self-esteem and self-confidence, and to challenge and resist racial inequality. These mothers' actions are particularly important because there are limited arenas in mainstream society in which Black racial identities are valued and celebrated, outside of the contexts of sports, music and entertainment (Skellington and Morris, 1996). In my study the mothers looked for methods to help their children celebrate Black racial identity:

> I remember maybe they [children] had been called a name at school –
> I had to explain to them that, yes, they were Black and that Black was
> beautiful. When people try and get brown in the sun they associate it
> with health, well-being and happiness. I had to show them it was truly
> wonderful to be a Black person and not a negative thing, to counteract
> the things children would be telling them at school. (Cara, age 50, widow,
> first generation)

The mothers in their child-rearing transmit to their children cultural identity and notions of cultural belonging that they can draw strength from in times of difficulties. Returning to Caribbean customs, values and traditions also fosters acceptance and belonging in their children's lives. In addition, the mothers encourage their children, at a very young age, to develop 'race' awareness and a racial consciousness within a global diasporic context. This was primarily achieved through the provision of toys, games and books, sculptures and paintings that advance positive self-images of Black identities. Some mothers sent their children to Black supplementary schools and Saturday Schools where subjects such as Afrocentric studies, Black history and cultural studies were taught, which complemented the mainstream teaching curriculum. Increasing globalisation and transcultural links mean that mothers raising children today have more available resources to educate their children about Black racial identities. First-generation mothers bringing up their children thirty or forty years ago who wanted to teach their children similar ideas did not have many of the resources that the mothers have access to today, as these were simply not available. For example, Cara recollects that raising her daughters during the 1970s she was keen to open dialogue with them concerning the historical structural location of Black people in Britain, but resources such as Black dolls and Black books were unavailable to her at that time.

Today, in contrast, the emphasis is very much on Black people fostering transnational links with other Black people and developing Black cultural identities that transcend national borders and notions of national citizenship (Goulbourne and Solomos, 2003; Reynolds, 2006b). This serves to unite Black people globally irrespective of geographical and national boundaries. The mothers actively encouraged their children to learn about the diverse cultures and ethnicities of Black people around the world by utilising diverse cultural resources. Therefore, when I visited the mothers' homes during interviews it was very common for me to see African artwork, photographs, masks, sculptures, paintings and other Black cultural artefacts, representing the 'fusion of influences' hybrid links between past and present, and between the Caribbean, African nations, the UK and the rest of the world. The fact that we are also living in of era of advanced telecommunication, increased travelling and migration also facilitates greater links between Black people worldwide.

Conclusion

In conclusion, this discussion explores the way in which mothering and the family have been used by Caribbean mothers as key sites in which they have engaged in the struggle to establish cultural belonging and challenge racial discrimination faced in their own and their children's lives. Situating these mothers' daily lives within a historical and social context reveals that social constructions of race, ethnicity and gender are integral to understanding their experiences and struggles. Across successive generations and societies Caribbean mothers have demonstrated their resilience and their ability to respond to social change by adapting their family patterns, familial roles and household structures to suit their specific circumstances. This bears strong testimony to the strength of Caribbean mothers, their family networks and family relationships for future generations.

References

Amos, V. and Parmar, P. (1984), 'Challenging imperialist feminism', *Feminist Review*, Special Issue, 17, 3–19

Arnold, E. (1997), 'Issues of reunification of migrant West Indian children in the United Kingdom', in Roopnarine, J. and Brown, J. (eds), *Caribbean Families: Diversity Amongst Groups* (London: JAI Press Ltd.)

Bakari, I. (1997), 'Memory and identity in Caribbean cinema', *Cultural Memory: A Journal of Culture, Theory and Politics*, 30 (Winter), 74–83

Barrow, C. (1996), *Family in the Caribbean: Themes and Perspectives* (London: James Currey Publishing)

Berleant-Schiller, R. and Maurer, W. (1993), 'Women's place is everyplace: merging domains and women's roles in Bermuda and Dominica', in Momsen, J. (ed.), *Women and Change in the Caribbean* (London: James Currey Publishing)

Brodber, E. (1986), 'Afro-Jamaican women at the turn of the century', *Social and Economic Studies Special Issue: Women in the Caribbean*, 35:3, 19–31

Brodber, E. (1974), *The Abandonment of Children in Jamaica* (Jamaica: Institute of Social and Economic Research)

Bryan, B., Dadzie, S. and Scafe, S. (1985), *The Heart of the Race: Black Women's Lives in Britain* (London: Virago)

Callender, C. (1997), *Education for Empowerment: The Practice and Philosophies of Black Teachers* (London: Trentham Books)

Carling, A., Duncan, S. and Edwards, R. (eds) (2002) *Analyzing Families* (London: Routledge)

Clarke, E. (1957), *My Mother Who Fathered Me* (London: George Allen Unwin)

Counihan, C. and Esterik, P. V. (1997), *Food and Culture: A Reader* (New York: Routledge)

Davis, A. (1981), *Women, Race and Class* (London: Women's Press Ltd)

Dench, G. (1996), *The Changing Place of Men in Changing Family Cultures* (London: Institute of Community Studies)

Dodgson, E. (1984), *Motherlands: West Indian Women in Britain in the 1950s* (Oxford: Heinemann)

DuBois, W. E. B. (1908), *The Negro family* (Atlanta: Atlanta University [citations: New America Library edition, New York, 1969])

Fog-Olwig, K. (1999), 'Narratives of children left behind: home and identity in globalised Caribbean families', *Journal of Ethnic and Migration Studies*, 25:2, 252–66

Fog-Olwig, K. (1993), *Global Culture, Island Identity, Continuity and Change in Afro-Caribbean Community of Nevis* (London: James Currey Publishing)

Fortes, M. (1956), 'Foreword', in Smith, R. T. *The Negro Family in British Guiana* (London: RKP, 2nd edn)

Frazier, F. (1948), *The Negro Family in the United States* (Chicago: University of Chicago Press)

Gilroy, P. (1987), *There Ain't No Black in the Union Jack* (London: Hutchinson)

Gonzalez, V. (1982), 'The realm of female familial responsibility', *Woman and the Caribbean Project* (Barbados: University of West Indies, Vol. 2)

Goulbourne, H. (2002), *Caribbean Transnational Experience* (London: Pluto Press)

Goulbourne, H. and Chamberlain, M. (eds) (2001), *Caribbean Families in Britain and the Trans-Atlantic World* (London: Palgrave Macmillan)

Goulbourne, H. and Solomos, J. (2003), 'Families, ethnicity and social capital', *Social Policy and Society*, 2:4, 329–38

Griffin, C. (1996), 'Experiencing power: dimensions of gender, "race" and class, in Charles, N. (ed.), *Practising Feminism: Identity, Difference and Power* (London: Routledge)

Gutman, H. (1976), *The Black Family in Slavery and Freedom 1750–1925* (New York: Vintage)

Herskovits, M. J. (1941), *The Myth of the Negro Past* (New York: Harpers and Brothers)

Hill-Collins, P. (1994), 'Shifting the centre: race, class and feminist theorizing about motherhood', in Glenn, E., Chang, G. and Forcey, L. (eds), *Mothering: Ideology, Experiences and Agency* (California: Routledge)

Hill-Collins, P. (1990), *Black Feminist Thought: Knowledge, Empowerment and the Politics of Consciousness* (Boston and London: Unwin Hyman)

Leo-Rhynie, E. (1997), 'Class, race and gender: issues in childrearing in the Caribbean', in Roopnarine, J. and Brown (eds), *Caribbean Families: Diversity Amongst Groups* (London: J. Ablex Publishing Corporation)

Lowenthal, D. (1972), *West Indian Societies* (Oxford: Oxford University Press)

Mama, A. (1995), *Beyond the Masks: Race, Gender and Subjectivity* (New York: Routledge)

Massiah, J. (1986), *Women in the Caribbean Part I and II* (Jamaica: Institute of Social and Economic Research)

Mirza, H. (1997), *Black British Feminism: A Reader* (London: Routledge)

Modood, T., Berthoud, B. R., Lakey, J., Nazroo, J., Smith, P. and Virdee, S. (1997), *Ethnic Minorities in Britain: Diversity and Disadvantage* (London: Policy Studies Institute)

Naples, N. (1996), 'Activist mothering: cross-generational continuity in the community work of women from low-income urban neighbourhoods', in Chow, E., Wilkinson, D. and Zinn, M. (eds), *Race, Class and Gender: Common Bonds, Different Voices* (California: Sage)

Nnaemeka, O. (1997), *The Politics of (M)othering: Womanhood, Identity and Resistance in African Literature* (London: Routledge)

Owen, D. (1997), *A Demographic Profile of Caribbean Households and Families in Great Britain, Living Arrangements, Family Structure and Social Change of Caribbeans in Britain: ESRC Populations and Household Change Research Programme* (Warwick: University of Warwick, Centre for Research in Ethnic Relations)

Peters-Ferguson, M. (1988), 'Parenting in Black families with young children: a historical perspective, in McAdoo, P. and McAdoo, H. (eds), *Black Families* (California: Sage, 2nd edn)

Powell, D. (1986), 'Caribbean women and their response to familial experience', in Masssiah, J. (ed.), *Women in the Caribbean Part I* (Jamaica: University of the West Indies, Institute of Social and Economic Research)

Pulsipher, L. (1993), 'Changing roles in the traditional West Indian house-yards', in Momsen, J. (ed.), *Women and Change in the Caribbean* (London: James Currey Publishing)

Reynolds, T. (2006a), 'Bonding social capital within the Caribbean family and community, *Journal of Community, Work and Family*, 9:3, 273–90 (special issue: *Ethnicity and Social Capital*)

Reynolds, T. (2006b), 'Caribbean young people, family relationships and social capital', *Journal of Ethnic and Racial Studies*, 29:6, 1087–103 (special issue: *Social Capital, Migration and Transnational Families*)

Reynolds, T. (2005), *Caribbean Mothers: Identity and Experience in the UK* (London: Tufnell Press)

Reynolds, T. (2003), 'The success of our mothers: Caribbean mothering and childrearing in the UK', in McCalla, D. (ed.), *Black Success in the UK: Essays in Racial and Ethnic Studies* (Cambridge: Vision Enterprise/Cambridge University Press)

Reynolds, T. (1999), 'African-Caribbean Mothering: Reconstructing a "New" Identity' (PhD Dissertation, South Bank University)

Reynolds, T. and Zontini, E. (2006), *A Comparative Study of Care and Provision Across Caribbean and Italian Transnational Families, Families and Social Capital ESRC Research Group Working Paper Series, no. 16* (London: South Bank University)

Rhodes, P. J. (1992), 'The emergence of a new policy: racial matching in fostering and adoption', *New Community*, 18:2, 58–70.

Ribbens, J. (1995), *Mothers and their Children: A Feminist Sociology of Childrearing* (London: Sage)

Roopnarine, J. and Brown, J. (eds) (1997), *Caribbean Families: Diversity Among Ethnic Groups* (London: JAI Press Ltd)

Roschelle, A. (1997), *No More Kin: Exploring Class, Race and Gender in Family Networks* (California: Sage)

Russell-Browne, P., Norville, B. and Griffith, C. (1997), 'Childshifting: a survival strategy for teenage mothers', in Roopnarine, J. and Brown, J. (eds), *Caribbean Families: Diversity Amongst Groups* (London: JAI Press Ltd)

Safa, H. (1986), 'Economic autonomy and sexual equality in Caribbean Society', in Massiah, J. (ed.), *Women in the Caribbean Part I* (Jamaica: University of the West Indies, Institute of Social and Economic Research)

Sanford, N. (1976), 'Child lending in Belize', *Belizean Studies*, 4:2, 26–36

Seguera, D. (1994), 'Working at motherhood: Chicana and Mexican immigrant mothers and employment', in Glenn, E., Chang, G. and Forcey, L. (eds), *Mothering: Ideology, Experiences and Agency* (California: Routledge)

Senior, O. (1991), *Working Miracles: Women's Lives in the English Speaking Caribbean* (London: James Currey Publishing)

Shaw, S. (1994), 'Mothering under slavery in the antebellum South', in Glenn, E., Chang, G. and Forcey, L. (eds), *Mothering: Ideology, Experiences and Agency* (California: Routledge)

Skellington, R. and Morris, P. (1996), *Race in Britain Today* (London: Sage Publications)

Smith, R. T. (1996), *The Matrifocal Family: Power, Politics and Pluralism* (London: Routledge)

Smith, R. T. (1962) *West Indian Family Structures* (Seattle: University of Washington Press)

Smith, R. T. (1953), *The Matrifocal Family* (London: Routledge, Kegan and Paul)

Stack, C. (1974), *All Our Kin: Strategies for Survival in the Black Community* (New York: Harper and Row)

Stack, C. and Burton, L. (1994), 'Kinscripts: reflections on family, generation and culture', in Glenn, E., Chang, G. and Forcey, L. (eds), *Mothering: Ideology, Experiences and Agency* (California: Routledge)

Sudakasa, N. (1996), *The Strength of our Mothers: African and African American Women and Families* (New Jersey: African World Press Inc.)

Sudbury, J. (1998), *Other Kinds of Dreams: Black Women's Organisations and the Politics of Transformations* (London: Routledge)

Waters, M. (1999), *Black Identities: West Indian Immigrant Dreams and Realities* (Harvard: Russell Sage Foundation)

Notes

1 In the UK the term 'Caribbean' also referred to as 'Black Caribbean' or 'African Caribbean', is an official racial-ethnic category that is used to classify people originating from Caribbean ethnic backgrounds. For the purpose of this chapter the term 'Caribbean mothers' and 'Caribbean mothering' refers exclusively to African Caribbean mothers and their mothering experiences. African Caribbeans or people of African and Caribbean origin or descent and family heritage, are the largest and most instantly recognisable Caribbean migrant community in the UK (Goulbourne, 2002; Owen, 1997). The (mis)representation of the Caribbbean as a collective and unitary region conflates and disguises the fact that the Caribbean is a diverse and differentiated region with each territory processing its own unique traditions and customs. Further to this, within each specific country divisions of class, caste, 'race', ethnicity and rural/urban living all influence household patterns and family relationships.

2 Throughout the chapter, I continually interchange between describing the mothers as Black and Caribbean. This is deliberate on my part in order to reflect the interactional nature of their Caribbean cultural ethnic origins and Black racial politicised status in the UK in shaping their mothering and female identity (Reynolds, 2005; Sudbury, 1998). In addition, by using the term 'Black' I understand that many issues highlighted in the discussion will

also be relevant and applicable to other Black and minority ethnic mothers because they share the same structural racialised subordinate location.

3 The findings is based on research work from the project entitled, *Caribbean Families, Social Capital and Young Peoples Diasporic Identities*, This study was one of a number of projects within the Ethnicity Strand of the Families and Social Capital, Economic and Social Research Council (ESRC) Research Group at London South Bank University. The research formed part of the Families and Social Capital ESRC Research Group Programme of work (ESRC Award Reference: M570255001).

6

Black UK families and the labour market: a historical review of the continuing difficulties of establishing a firm economic base

Jerome Williams

Introduction

There has been an increasing attention amongst social scientists of the labour inequalities of minority ethnic communities, partly because of their rising proportion within the United Kingdom (UK) population and partly due to issues connected to social exclusion and institutional racism. The so-called inner-city disturbances of the 1980s, from Brixton in the southeast to Toxteth in the northwest of England, have scarred the personalities of the deprived residents who have experienced various rising patterns of unemployment, discrimination and cultural alienation linked to poverty, lack of security and the subsequent breakdown in family life. Alas, it appears that Black people have borne the brunt of the social and economic hardship through various periods of the 1980s, 1990s and now into the new millennium. This chapter examines the labour status and experiences of Black people in the UK; the main focus is geared towards people of African Caribbean descent. Evidence of economic success and achievement enjoyed and experienced by other minority ethnic migrant groups to the UK such as Jews, Greeks, Turkish Cypriots, Italians and South Asians is, indeed, not so apparent amongst the African Caribbean population, who are a significant proportion of the UK community living within deprived inner-city areas.

Historically, many African Caribbean people had hoped when migrating to Britain from their native islands that they would have found ready acceptance for themselves and their children in the 'mother country'. They had been nurtured to view British society as the guardians of the rule of law, the custodians of justice and fairness and a Christian society built upon tolerance and charity towards strangers. They came to a post-war Britain in the 1950s and 1960s in an effort to find work as a means of eradicating the threat of poverty, as Britain had experienced an economic boom with employment supplied mainly from manufacturing industries, the health service, transport and a variety of menial occupations. Such post-war opportunities became available to African Caribbean and other minority ethnic groups. However, the situation changed dramatically during the 1980s and early 1990s, with evidence that the downward employment trend for the African Caribbean community continues. In general, the UK economy has experienced a decline in manufacturing activities and as a result unemployment rose from within that sector. In its wake minority ethnic communities were hit proportionately hardest and this led to an increased level of deprivation and hardship among sections of that group. This view is supported by a Government Equalities Office (2008) report that ethnic minorities are less likely to find and sustain employment than their White counterparts, and this disadvantage has persisted for more than a decade. The waste of employment potential has both economic and social costs, contributing to social exclusion and damaging to community cohesion.

In 1997 Haynes, looking at the economic history of Black UK individuals, commented that their lack of socioeconomic success was mainly due to racial discrimination. According to Haynes (1997), despite successive governments passing legislation to eliminate racial discrimination and promote equality of opportunity, Black Britons continued to show signs of entrenchment at the bottom of the socioeconomic ladder. More recently (Equal Opportunities Review, 2005), the UK Government spending review adopted a public service agreement target of reducing the gap between White and minority ethnic employment rates (which were 75 per cent and 58 per cent respectively), through improvements in educational performance, employment programmes and equal opportunities policies by tackling specific barriers. This led to a slight decrease in the White/minority ethnic gap in employment from 16.9 to 15.9 per cent points between spring 2003 and spring 2005. The Government's objective was to try to reduce this gap, and that in ten years' time no one should be disadvantaged in their employment prospects because of their ethnicity. Nevertheless, labour inequalities persist and are underpinned by structural problems of discrimination and disadvantages; these considerably increase the risks as well as the incidence of poverty among African Caribbean communities. According to Haskey (2002), about one in thirteen low-earner-parent families comes from minority ethnic origins – 85,000 families in all with 140,000 dependent children. Of these about one in two are of African Caribbean origins. Since it has been observed that low-paid workers are highly vulnerable to unemployment and often have limited savings to cope with it, they have less access to fringe benefits and receive less benefit from official schemes where these are related to pay, length of service and contribution record. The employment figures suggest that the risk of living in poverty may be found to be the highest among children living in families with one or more adults unemployed, followed by those in families with low-paid workers. Since African Caribbeans are over-represented in each of these groups, their families stand a significantly higher risk of living in poverty. Unfortunately, there are large gaps in information on the effects of the inequalities in the labour market; it is patchy and unreliable, particularly on access to educational opportunities and work. However, the lack of appropriate data does not invalidate the conclusion that African Caribbean men and other minority ethnic groups are over-represented among the low paid. The available data understate the scale of the problem and the consequent risk of poverty – but what are the answers to the problems of economic and social hardship experienced by Black Britons? The remainder of the chapter will provide a further overview of the labour disadvantages of African Caribbeans and analyse small businesses, including the roles they perform in a capitalist society along with some of the prerequisites for business success. This will be placed in the context of African Caribbean community business strategies as based on the literature and the writer's direct experiences as a business management professional.

Labour inequalities and African Caribbeans

The labour market outcomes for minority ethnic communities are varied: for example, Indian and Chinese communities perform relatively well in terms of occupational attainment, earnings and employment, in comparison with African Caribbean men (Leslie *et al.*, 1998). African Caribbean men are more likely to work in low-paid jobs with poor working conditions than White men (CRE, 2007; Jones, 1993; Vinod, 1993). Evidence also indicates that most men from minority ethnic groups have a high proportion of workers on low weekly wages. They are also more likely to face worse working conditions, such as doing shift work particularly at night with longer hours of work and less access to training and occupational benefits (Model, 1999; Modood *et al.*, 1994).

While some members of the African Caribbean group seem to have escaped the disadvantage of poverty, current employment figures suggest that others are probably worse off in some ways than their equivalents twenty years ago (Clark and Drinkwater, 2007; CRE, 2007;

ONS, 2001). In the UK, there is a high rate of unemployment for Black men specifically and across the Black community in general. Black men are more than twice as likely to be unemployed as compared to White men (Berthoud, 1999; Reynolds, 2001). Young African Caribbean men are disproportionately without qualifications, work and a stable family life, and disproportionately in trouble with the police. They are consistently in lower-level jobs and suffer from higher unemployment rates than men in the White population.

While for most groups the disadvantage may be diminishing across the generations, this is less clearly the case for African Caribbeans. Though African Caribbeans are the longest established of all the major post-1945 settlement groups, their households are as much as a quarter worse off than those of UK Whites. According to the 2001 Census approximately 15 per cent of non-retired White UK men aged twenty-five and over are not in paid work, with similar proportions for 'White Other' and for Indians. By contrast, the equivalent proportions for Black Africans and African Caribbeans are 30–40 per cent (ONS, 2001). Also, African Caribbeans who were born in Britain have not necessarily reached higher in the socioeconomic scale than other ethnic minorities who have recently migrated to Britain. People of African Caribbean descent continue to have an entrenched disadvantage compared to the White UK population and to some groups within the more recently arrived South Asians.

Nonetheless, African Caribbean women, when compared to other minority ethnic groups, are more likely to be working full-time or to be looking for full-time work. The position of African Caribbean women relative to White and 'Other' women is much better than that of African Caribbean men compared with 'Other' men. Many young African Caribbean women are in work, with earnings higher than those of White women. They are much less likely to be in manual work (or part-time work), in fact, of all groups, African Caribbean women are most likely to be in intermediate and junior non-manual posts (CRE, 2007). This, according to Reynolds (2001), reflects the important economic role traditionally played by African Caribbean women, whether they have dependent children or not, but they are disproportionately more likely to be lone parents, with direct implications for household incomes.

Small businesses and African Caribbeans

Social Enterprise (2008), a publication from the Government Equalities Office, revealed from the 2005 Global Enterprise Monitor survey, that

Black Africans are three times as likely and Black Caribbeans twice as likely to be involved in social entrepreneurship activities as their White counterparts. Given the often held belief that business involvement has usually been the traditional means by which migrant groups create employment for themselves and members of their families to overcome social discrimination and levels of deprivation and disadvantage, why have African Caribbeans been so conspicuously absent from the business scene (ONS, 2001)? Indeed, such conventional wisdom has gained support from many distinguished quarters; for example, as far back as the 1970s, the Conservative William Whitelaw, when he was Home Secretary, believed that 'the major solution to the straddling of Blacks in decaying inner cities is the encouragement of small businesses'. Politicians can often make statements on certain issues placing them in a political context, suitable for the making of headline news or in defence of some policy or action. On the other hand, social scientists often adopt the practice of social theory when defending or agreeing to the cause and effect of humanitarian issues. Yet, the Commission for Racial Equality (1984) announced, in very similar terms: 'the Commission considers that the growth of a strong minority ethnic business sector is of crucial importance to the attainment of racial equality' (Employment Report Supplement, September, 1984: 1). In effect, it was Lord Scarman's pronouncement following the 1981 Brixton disorders that has been embraced by many as a panacea for all the ills that affect Black people:

> The encouragement of Black people to secure a real stake in their own community through business and the professions is in my view of great importance if future social stability is to be secured. I do urge the necessity for speedy action if we are to avoid the perpetuation in this country of any economically disposed Black population. A weakness in British society is that there are too few people of West Indian origin in the business entrepreneurial and professional class. (Scarman, 1986: 167–8)

Enterprise was touted and seen as not only desirable but in essence feasible, with the quantitative rise of a new Asian business economy offering itself as an exemplar of what could be achieved by an equally visibly minority ethnic group. The Asian business community was held as an example of 'hard work' even by HRH The Prince of Wales (*The Times*, 20 November 1981). This image of success was further upheld by a steady stream of UK press reports citing that there are more than 300 Asian millionaires in Britain, with eight Asian entrepreneurs taking their place among the country's richest 200 individuals (Day, 1992). For Lord Scarman and other advocates of this policy the destiny of the Black communities could be decided by the embracement of the business ethic. However, whilst small businesses are widely embraced as an important form of activity for minority ethnic communities in the UK, Clark and Drinkwater (2007) have demonstrated how this broad generalisation over space and time disguises considerable variation rates by ethnicity and gender. For men, in both the 1991 and 2001 Census years, there is considerable variation in small-businesses rates. In 1991 these varied from 9.1 per cent for the African Caribbean group to 34.1 per cent for the Chinese. The African and African Caribbean had the lowest rates, with the Asian group having higher rates. Chinese and Pakistani men had the highest, followed by Indian, Bangladeshi and White groups. The ranking of the ethnic groups remained the same in 2001 (ONS, 2001 and 1991). Conversely, it appears that other minority ethnic migrant groups, regarded as more advanced economically than African Caribbeans, have adopted the small business route as a means of recognition, employment practice and social mobility. To fully appreciative the challenges for African Caribbean small business entrepreneurs there is a need for a general exploration of small business to reveal the keys for success and failure.

Small businesses: an overview

Working for oneself may be an option to develop particular skills or motivations and can be rewarding both financially and in terms of life or job satisfaction. This section provides an examination of the importance of small businesses to the UK economy and also identifies the significant distinguishing characteristics of small firms and the roles they play in modern western economics. An examination of small business as a form of activity for African Caribbeans is also presented.

Characteristics of small businesses

An accurate definition of the small firm has been aptly demonstrated by Curran (1986). In economic terms they generally have a small share of the market, although Storey (1982) notes that small businesses or firms:

> could also have a large share of a very small market. Secondly, the small firm is managed by its owners or part owners in a personalized way and not through the medium of a formalized management structure. Thirdly, it is also independent in the sense that it does not form part of

a larger enterprise and that the owner-managers should be free from outside control in taking their principal decisions. (Storey, 1982: 7)

In addition Storey (1994, 1982) notes that the small firm normally produces either a single product or a set of closely related products, generally at a single establishment. Its operations and services are mainly geared to a local market with the obvious exceptions of import/ export firms. At the end of 1989 there were an estimated three million businesses in the UK; of these almost 97 per cent employed fewer than twenty people and they accounted for almost 35 per cent of total employment outside central and local government (Employment Gazette, 1992). At the aggregate level, the expansion rates for small business in the UK were relatively stable during the 1990s, at around 13 per cent of the total employment (Clark and Drinkwater, 2007).

Small firms have become increasingly acclaimed as major creators of new jobs in 'developed countries' since standardised products, which have traditionally been produced in large enterprises, are now increasingly produced by 'developing countries' (Storey, 1994). Today's giant corporations were once back-street enterprises. A historical perspective is used to stress the importance of this assumption, in that the investors and pioneers who began the industrial revolution, the technologists of this century and the founders of many of our great companies started as small family concerns – examples include Marks and Spencer Public Limited Company (PLC), Hanson's Trust PLC, Richard Branson's Virgin empire, and the Johnson Corporation of the United States of America (USA). However, some caution is exercised by Storey (1982). He claimed that, during the economic boom of the 1960s, of all firms employing fewer than ten people in 1965, 26 per cent had gone out of business and 61 per cent continued to employ fewer than ten people by 1976. Hence only 13 per cent of all firms in this size category showed an increase in employment sufficient to push them into a larger size category. During the latter 1980s, the recession of the 1990s and 2007 downturn, all types of firms have experienced economic difficulties to the extent that some have actually ceased trading. No two or more periods show conditions to be exactly the same, thus Storey, deciding to err on the side of caution, has indicated that today's small firm will show virtually no growth and that the next most likely outcome is that it will not exist in ten years' time. Growth and development are based on a number of favourable economic conditions, one being the existence of a buoyant economy. In the absence of these, success cannot be guaranteed.

Nonetheless, small firms make a vital contribution towards a healthy national economy and provide a 'seed bed' of invention and innovation. Being found in industries where technical development is essential for survival the low capital requirements in modern micro-electronics make this industry particularly suited, at present, to new small firms. Small firms tend to possess the capacity to take risks to innovate, whether in product, techniques or service, and can bring about radical changes – for example, the entrepreneur Sir Clive Sinclair with his revolutionary electronic productions during the 1970s and the early 1980s. Equally, they can provide a harmonious working environment where owner and employee work side-by-side for their mutual benefit (Bolton, 1971; Storey, 1994). Usually the size of the workforce is small, thus attracting no external institutional interference or disruption; for example, trade union involvement within the small business. This argument is based on the human side of operation and Schumacher's (1972) view that 'small is beautiful' relative to the observation that industrial strife is lower in small firms.

In addition, small firms play a key role in the regeneration of our inner cities (Bolton, 1971; Storey, 1994). The inner-city areas of the industrialised nations contain heavy concentrations of the social problems of unemployment, low incomes and poor housing. It is argued that small firms can make an important contribution to the regeneration of such areas. For a variety of reasons including planning and environmental control, large firms are restricted from locating within the inner cities; this gives the scope for small businesses, especially those of a non-manufacturing nature, to be established in areas more conducive to government policies. As far back as the 1970s, the White Paper *Policy for Inner Cities* (Department of Environment, 1977) emphasised the need to encourage the expansion of local firms through sympathetic planning policies and practical actions. The Paper argued that the resources and energies of small- and medium-sized firms are essential if real progress is to be made and the diversity and vitality, for so long characteristic of inner cities, is to be restored. Storey (1994) believed that small firms have several major advantages over larger firms because they require relatively small sites to produce their outputs and use relatively labour-intensive production processes. The inner city usually has expensive sites and may be more appropriate for firms that require only small amounts of land. The use of labour-intensive production methods means that it is likely to have the maximum impact upon local employment.

Nevertheless, the percentage of African Caribbeans in small businesses remains relatively marginal. This apparent 'inability' of African

Caribbeans to develop the opportunities and venture into small businesses is now receiving attention, with researchers such as Ram and Deakins (1995), Soar (1991) and Ward (1991) drawing parallels with their Asian counterparts and concluding that African Caribbeans are weak in almost all areas necessary for a successful small business venture. These include motivation, personal wealth and resources, family and community networks, role models, and credibility in the eyes of the controllers of business resources. On examination of this thesis Barrett *et al.* (1996) – whilst agreeing that such arguments concur with the standard expectations, in that Asian business owners perceive themselves to be more successful – have identified a number of issues that offer an explanation for the perceived failure of African Caribbeans in business. Firstly, they argue that evidence demonstrates that successful small businesses are very few in comparison with the total business sector and that the long working hours actually seem to be inter-related with poor returns. They conclude that this is due to the nature of the businesses, such as food retail and confectionery–tobacconist–newsagent, which are by their very nature labour-intensive and competitive as well as low yielding, rather than any cultural predisposition to working long hours. Such business ventures have also been propelled by the collapse of the job sectors in which minority ethnic communities were traditionally concentrated. African Caribbean lack of performance is therefore not as a result of cultural–behavioural differences, but is more a result of external factors that include lack of markets and the persistent discrimination by banks.

Small businesses as a panacea?

In the 1960s small-scale and family-owned businesses were viewed as inefficient and a constraint upon economic growth; however, by the late 1970s they were being touted by UK politicians as a fundamental plank in the programme to bring about regeneration of not only the economy, but society in general (Scase and Goffee, 1980). Small businesses, it seems, offer opportunities for upward mobility for those groups unable to obtain entry into various salaried middle-class occupations – indeed, several writers (e.g. Waldinger *et al.*, 1985) have emphasised the importance of self-employment and small-scale proprietorship as avenues of self-advancement for deprived and disadvantaged groups. If through lack of credentials or because of explicit or implicit discrimination some individuals and groups are unable to compete equally with others for occupational preferment, the market provides an apparently open career alternative – as many converted members of the minority ethnic communities have acknowledged. Bechofer *et al.* (1971), regarded small businesses as fulfilling important ideological functions within contemporary capitalist societies because they are the custodians of certain 'core' capitalist principles. The over-riding value of many small-business owners is 'independence' – the appeal of being 'your own boss' (Scase and Goffee, 1980; Metcalf *et al.*, 1996). The lives of many small-business owners are dominated by the possibility of individual mobility (Barrett *et al.*, 1996; Curran, 1986; Curran and Burrows, 1987; Reeves and Ward, 1984; Waldinger *et al.*, 1985, 1990).

Entrepreneurs have now become popular figures after years of neglect; they are viewed as reliant 'self-made' men and women who are prepared to take risks for a dynamic economy. This ideology portray small businesses as a functional prerequisite for capitalist societies as a whole; it creates employment, facilitates the management of labour, regenerates decaying inner cities and, at the individual level, provides independence for entrepreneurs. The Bolton Committee Report (Bolton, 1971) argued that ideology can also work against the growth of small firms. According to this theory the growing role of the State adversely affects the competitive position of small firms – due to the nationalisation that prevented the entry and growth of private firms in certain sectors. It is not too surprising therefore that the 'small is beautiful' dictum (Schumacher, 1972) re-emerged with the coming to power of Margaret Thatcher's Conservative Government in 1980, which opposed state intervention and idolised entrepreneurship acumen. This analysis was that small businesses should be expected to cure all unemployment ailments, however 'chronic the disease'. Consequently, small-business development must not be seen as the automatic route to employment, wealth and social mobility and prosperity as it also depends on a number of variables such as access to capital, availability of management skills, available markets, favourable economic conditions and perhaps a political environment providing the climate and supporting facilities by way of policies to enhance success. In particular, small businesses among minority ethnic communities remain highly concentrated in certain sectors, often involving long hours working in restaurants and takeaways or driving taxis. Yet the recurring question still requires an answer: why do people of African Caribbean descent in the UK remain underrepresented in business activities? Statistics from 2001 showing self-employment in males linked to ethnicity (Clark and Drinkwater, 2007) indicate Indians at 21 per cent, Pakistanis and Bangladeshis at 26 and 20 per cent respectively, Chinese at 28 per cent, Whites at 17 per cent, African Caribbeans at 13 per cent and all others at 16 per cent.

Theories and characteristics of minority ethnic businesses

Research on businesses operated by Black people in the UK is non-existent when compared with similar work undertaken in the United States of America (USA). Previously, attention had been centred on the apparent success of the early migrant Jews who fled persecution and near genocide in their homelands. It is because of the remarkable success of some people from the Jewish community (Waldinger *et al.*, 1985) – for example, Marks and Spencer – that subsequent migrant groups are expected to emulate them. Presently, the attention has turned to South Asian groups, and their progress has been studiously monitored; in the 1970s, 80s and 90s several researchers such as Aldrich *et al.* (1986) and Nowikowski (1984) concentrated their studies on South Asian businesses. Nevertheless, three main studies during the 1980s attempted to include African Caribbean entrepreneurs. Martin Kazuka (1980), in *Why so Few Black Businessmen?*, attempted to highlight the problems faced by Asian and African Caribbean businesses in Hackney; Reeves and Ward (1984) considered *West Indians in Business in Britain*; and Wilson (1983) surveyed *Afro Caribbeans and Asian Businesses in Brent*. With analysis that is of contemporary relevance Ward and Reeves' (1981) review of the literature proposed a set of models examined below that attempted to encapsulate the different explanations for African Caribbean lack of involvement in business.

Economic opportunity model

Ward and Jenkins' (1984) first explanation proposes an 'economic opportunity model', which assumes that minority ethnic business activities are essentially no different from routine capitalistic entrepreneurial activities, depending for their success or failure on the opportunities presented by the market. Therefore, the first area of opportunity is the market provided by an ethnic group's own consumption patterns. In order for it to be a viable business, sufficient opening must exist in the labour market to create a large enough demand for the provision of minority ethnic products and services. To this, however, a caveat is added: 'the opportunity is typically an "ethnic niche" though this need not be the case'. Indeed, theorists have suggested that entrepreneurs may be more likely to emerge from deprived or marginalised groups in society (Jones *et al.*, 1992). Membership of an ethnic fraternity may act as a competitive advantage for the entrepreneur and a powerful stimulus for business activity.

In their analysis of Chinese businesses in the USA, Light *et al.* (1994) indicated the manner in which a small business sector became larger and more prosperous because of group solidarity. They also provided some indication of the benefits accrued from business activities, both at the individual and group levels. Business activities provided enrichment and social mobility for the self-employed and consider-able employment for non-business people. Bonacich and Modell's (1980) theory of middlemen minorities argues that, by virtue of ethnic membership, minority businessmen are able to draw on certain com-mercial resources unavailable to non-members of the group. Any alien groups isolated from and stigmatised by mainstream society tend to develop a strong sense of internal solidarity.

However, Ward and Reeves (1981) have argued that a clearly defined submarket is most likely where a minority is culturally separate from the host society. 'There are more businesses, therefore among Indian and Pakistani communities than among those from the Caribbean whose lifestyle is less divergent from that found in Britain' (Ward and Reeves, 1981: 15). Research studies have noted that African Caribbean businesses, in particular, tend to be heavily dependent on African Caribbean markets, even those firms not specialising in minority ethnic products and services. Ward and Reeves' (1981) study noted that with the amount of competition in the minority ethnic sector, expan-sion can only occur through servicing the wider market, but moving from heavy reliance on minority ethnic business may not be easy. The researchers 'were given clear examples of racial bias being used to restrict the opportunities of the Black firms trying to expand into the White (mainstream) marketplace (Ward and Reeves, 1981: 23). Further analysis of the problems encountered by African Caribbean businesses was provided by Ward and Jenkins (1984), who describe:

1. how the potential for entry and expansion is limited by the intrinsic boundaries of the labour market;
2. the historical circumstances relating to the political situation where the business cycle or world economy may determine the scope of minority ethnic involvement; and
3. that differences in the level of western business skills, such as accounting or marketing, may be important (Ward and Jenkins, 1984: 232).

In the London Borough of Brent, Wilson (1983) found a heavy depend-ence on ethnic markets, which, while offering advantages at the start-up stage, was likely to inhibit growth and development and to leave businesses vulnerable to adverse changes in the local economy.

Wilson stated that the transition from ethnic to wider markets is the key to business growth and prosperity and further reported that his survey produced no evidence of a successful transition to non-ethnic markets. He concluded that both Asians and African Caribbeans are dependent on their own minority ethnic markets and believed that this is more pronounced among the African Caribbean community. Businesses operating in an 'ethnic niche' depend significantly on ethnic loyalty and solidarity for survival. Wilson found that African Caribbean customers were perceived as being unsupportive of their own ethnic group. This was compounded by White customers' unwillingness to support Black businesses. Ward and Reeves (1981) also found similar evidence. A builder in their sample was adamant that he preferred to do business for and with Whites because there was 'less hassle' involved. Wilson also found that African Caribbean firms receive almost no support from Asian groups (Wilson, 1983: 66).

Barber (1982), in an article entitled 'We are Black and we mean business', commented that 'serving an exclusively ethnic market can be a handicap: there are only 660,000 Caribbeans in Britain, and that means that the market is inevitably restricted' (Barber, 1982: 55). However, Ward and Reeves (1981) found successful European and Asian firms who rely heavily, if not entirely, on the West Indian market operating in sectors where most West Indian firms are concentrated, such as hairdressing and travel agencies. When asked to account for their success, respondents remarked that 'West Indians would not buy from a West Indian' and 'West Indians are very independent – they look for the best buy whoever is selling' (Ward and Reeves, 1981: 23). The inference is that they look for value for money and would buy from the supplier offering best value, regardless of ethnic background.

In line with Ward and Jenkins' 'opportunity model' Kazuka (1980) identified another major problem inhibiting Black business enterprise – a lack of training and experience in necessary management skills such as marketing, financial control, accounting and buying. This arose from a history of restricted educational and employment opportunities and had a greater affect on the West Indian than the Asian community. According to Ward and Reeves (1981: 24), whereas Asian communities in Britain contain many 'professional students' who accumulate degrees and qualifications relevant to the world of business, among the West Indians the reverse is true: largely because they came to Britain from a background of skilled and semi-skilled manual employment; they lack qualifications in management. Barber also concluded that:

West Indians often lack the basic tools for running businesses of their own. Few have management skills, few have any familiarity with marketing, accountancy, sales administration or customer relations, but there is evidence that West Indians start from a position even further back than Asians or white businessmen struggling to get up the economic ladder. (1982: 55)

Cultural model

The second explanation proposed by Ward and Jenkins (1984) is the 'cultural model', which argues that some cultures predisposed their members towards successful pursuit of entrepreneurial goals. The argument is that members of the Jewish community are exemplars of this cultural model, typified by Jewish migrants in New York, who are characterised with 'sobriety, temperance, frugality, willingness to defer gratification and commitment to education' (Pollins, 1984). Light (1972) contrasted the remarkable and occupational achievements of Koreans, Chinese and Japanese North Americans with the experiences of African North Americans. All these groups faced severe discrimination and prejudice, but the three Asian groups were able to achieve considerable business success. Light argues that the forms of cultural organisation and the cohesive character of the communities were critical in facilitating their business achievements. They were able to call on village and traditional ties, supporting and operating in a communal manner. The same theory has been applied to account for the success of the UK Asian community. According to Barrett *et al.* (1996), UK Asians can chart a historical background of an ancient and distinctive cultural tradition that, when transposed to the British context, provides them with a powerful sense of identity and a communal base for the mobilisation of economic resources. In contrast, African Caribbeans have in effect suffered cultural genocide through enslavement and transportation, creating an existential vacuum that has profoundly destructive and lasting implications for sense of identity, individual self-esteem and image of the group in the eyes of non-members. From an entrepreneurial perspective, this history manifests itself in all manner of negative forms such as weak families, community structures without ethnic solidarity, lack of individual motivation and self-confidence, and isolation, with lack of supporting social relations and appropriate institutions for capital generation.

Perhaps it is not surprising that African Caribbean businessmen and -women have identified access to finance as a major obstacle to the start-up and growth of Black businesses. Kazuka (1980) reported that Black people, because of their low economic position and wages, faced difficulties in accumulating capital to start businesses. He also found that they experienced difficulty in obtaining finance from banks partly because of insufficient collateral. There was a perception of discrimination as 25 per cent of businesses questioned believed it was a matter of bank policy not to lend to Black businesses. Kazuka also referred to 'unusually high collateral requirements for which [he] found no satisfactory explanation' (1980: 8). Ward and Reeves' (1981) research indicated the possibility of bank managers holding negative stereotyped attitudes about African Caribbeans seeking business loans. This was confirmed by Wilson (1983), who added that the negative views of African Caribbean entrepreneurs was contrasted with the positive outlook they gave their South Asian customers. Wilson concluded that 'the African Caribbean firms faced problems of access to bank finance which was likely to reduce rates of formation and growth' (Wilson, 1983: 43). Brooks (1983) identified a similar pattern of difficulty with bank loans. Of those seeking loans for start-ups, 74 per cent of African Caribbeans, 13 per cent of South Asians and 6 per cent Whites were unsuccessful. A similar pattern was found in respect of loan facilities for improvements or expansion.

More recent studies have indicated that lack of access to private and public funding for African Caribbean businesses continues to hamper their start-up and development. For example, researchers from Loughborough University Business School (Atkins *et al.*, 2006) concluded that:

> It is our opinion that there is an enormous amount that the banking community have to do to put themselves right with the African Caribbean community. After all, as our research has shown, over 80% of the African Caribbean business start-ups in the new millennium are 'self financed' and if, as our research shows, around 60% of the African Caribbean business community regard their relationship with the bank as 'poor', then there is a massive room for improvement. (Atkins *et al.*, 2006: 268)

Most African Caribbean business start-ups were either out of personal savings or with help from family and friends. Only 5 per cent of these entrepreneurs have obtained bank funding. The researchers concluded of the other 95 per cent that either their bank loan attempt had failed or they were discouraged by negative experiences of friends and family and did not approach the banks.

It appears that these issues are recognised by various government departments with the Labour Government establishing an Ethnic Minorities Business Task Force in 2007 with a mandate to help faster growth among Black and Minority Ethnic (BME) firms and boost economic participation by BME entrepreneurs (DTI, June 2007).

Reaction model

The third explanation proposed by Ward and Jenkins (1984) argues that self-employment by members of minority ethnic groups is a reaction against racism and blocked avenues of occupational mobility; a survival strategy for coping on the margins of the White-dominated mainstream of the economy. This they referred to as the 'reaction model'. Thus Aldrich *et al.* (1984) stressed that a key factor in assessing prospects for Black businesses lies in looking at alternative responses made by Black migrants to White hostility in the labour market and, in particular, at the possibility that associations formed to combat racial discrimination may also serve to galvanise some people into considering business ownership as a possible group response to discrimination (Ward and Reeves, 1981: 20).

Analysis of the models proposed by Ward and Jenkins (1984) highlights similarities between the reasons for the involvement of ethnic minorities and that of the indigenous group. These are no different from those for other typical capitalist activities, with the emphasis on opportunity and the psychological and social predispositions of the participants. However, minority ethnic businesses differ from mainstream capitalist activities in that minority ethnic forms operate in an 'ethnic niche' and are disadvantaged vis-à-vis normal businesses. Similar to other groups, African Caribbean small businesses, particularly in inner-city areas, have difficulty in obtaining access to suitable premises, but the existence of additional disadvantages faced by Black businesses tend to exacerbate their difficulties in this area as well. The kinds of problems that have been identified relate, for example, to the unsatisfactory size, location and condition of premises, which, nonetheless, often have high rates of Council Tax assessment. Kazuka (1980) found that Black businesses were also more likely to have higher insurance premiums because of racial vandalism. Wilson (1983) found that both Asian and African Caribbean groups experienced problems of access to suitable premises, and vandalism and burglary were of particular concern to South Asian firms. There was evidence of greater disadvantage in premises in the case of African Caribbean firms, mainly true in terms of the quality of the premises available to them in inner-city locations.

Despite the negative perceptions of African Caribbean entrepreneurs, Jones *et al.* (1992) have concluded that African Caribbean businesspeople are, in many respects, as well-equipped for business, if not better equipped, than Whites engaged in similar activities. None-theless, even more so than South Asians, African Caribbeans find poor access to markets and capital as major barriers to business success. This of course mirrors earlier research.

Conclusion

The multiple factors that influence the labour status of African Caribbean families in the UK include the employment status of both African Caribbean men and women, the shifting structure of the economy, the decline in manufacturing jobs and the continuing dis-crimination in the participation of African Caribbean men in the employment sector. Although it may be argued that some of the identified problems faced by Black businesspeople are due to normal market pressures that generally beset all small firms, this chapter has argued that, as a result of the seriously disadvantaged socioeconomic position of most minority ethnic communities in UK society, such factors undoubtedly have a greater impact upon African Caribbean businesses. Arguably, if barriers to accessing equal opportunities to employment both in the public and private sectors are removed, then African Caribbeans would have a better chance than at present of accu-mulating savings leading to substantial capital formation within their communities, thus removing one of the major obstacles of entry into business and business development.

The fundamental question is whether African Caribbean communities will find the small business a convenient route into the mainstream of British economic life. A strategy for positive Black ethnic minority enterprise development policies must begin by first accepting that African Caribbeans face special and unique economic problems, which the majority White community does not encounter to the same degree. These include poor access to equal employment opportunities, both in the public and private sectors, and difficulties in obtaining capital for business start-up and development. As a result of the first prob-lem, very little capital formation takes place. As a consequence of this, and arising out of the second problem, very few African Caribbeans go into business and those already in business find it extremely difficult to develop further. This is one of the major reasons why few African Caribbeans are found in manufacturing. In the words of Kazuka (1980: 10), it is in the interest of the nation rather than solely Black ethnic minorities that their latent abilities should be har-nessed to make a positive contribution to the mainstream of the British economy.

Perhaps as a final thought the onus must be on African Caribbeans themselves to develop strategies that will enhance their own communities. This type of action has been taken successfully by other minority ethnic groups, so it seems quite appropriate for African Caribbeans to emulate it.

References

Aldrich, H., Jones, T. and McEvoy, D. (1984), 'Ethnic advantage and minority business development', in Ward, R. and Jenkins, R. (eds), *Ethnic Communities in Business: Strategies for Economic Survival* (Cambridge: Cambridge University Press)

Aldrich, H., Zimmer, C. and Jones, T. (1986), 'Small business still speaks with the same voice: a replication of the voice of small business and the politics of survival', *Sociological Review*, 34, 335–56

Atkins, M., Chapman, R., Cumberpatch, M. and Chivers, G. (2006), *African Caribbean Businesses* (Loughborough: Loughborough University Business School) unpublished report.

Barber, L. (1982), We are Black and we mean business, *Sunday Times* (28 March) (London)

Barrett, G., Jones, T. and McEvoy, D. (1996), 'Ethnic minority business: theoretical discourse in Britain and North America', *Urban Studies*, 33:4–5, 783–809

Bechofer, F., Elliott, B. and Rushford, M. (1971), 'The market situation of small shopkeepers', *Scottish Journal of Political Economy*, 18:2, 161–80

Berthoud, R. (1999), *Young Caribbean Men and the Labour Market: A Comparison with Other Ethnic Groups* (York: Joseph Rowntree Foundation)

Bolton, J. (1971), *Small Firms, Report of the Committee of Enquiry on Small Firms* (London: HMSO)

Bonacich, E. and Modell, E. (1980), *The Economic Solidarity in the Japanese American Community* (Berkeley: University of California Press)

Brooks, A. (1983), 'Black businesses in Lambeth: obstacles to expansion', *New Community*, 19, 441–58

Clark, K. and Drinkwater, S. (2007), *Ethnic Minorities in the Labour Market: Dynamics and Diversity* (London: The Policy Press)

Commission for Racial Equality (CRE) (2007), *Employment and Ethnicity* (London: Commission for Racial Equality)

Curran, J. (1986), *Bolton Fifteen Years on: A Review and Analysis of Small Business Research in Britain, 1971–1986* (London: Small Business Research Trust)

Curran, J. and Burrows, R. (1987), 'The social analysis of small business: some emerging themes', in Goffee, R. and Scase, R. (eds), *Entrepreneurship in Europe* (London: Croom Helm)

Day, T. (1992), 'Minorities and the millionaires', *Mail on Sunday* (5 July) (London)

Department of the Environment (1977), *Policy for the Inner Cities* (London: HMSO)

Department of Trade and Industry (DTI) (2007), *Ethnic Minorities Business Task Force Report* (June)

Employment Gazette (1992), *Small Business Statistics*, February (Milton Keynes: Harrington Kilbride Plc), 47

Employment Report Supplement (1984), *Small Business Statistics*, September, 65 (Milton Keynes: Harrington Kilbride Plc)

Equal Opportunities Review (2005), 'Focusing on Compensation Awards 2004', *Equal Opportunities Review*, 144 (August), 6–25

Haskey, J. (2002), *Population Projections by Ethnic Group: A Feasibility Study* (London: Stationery Office)

Haynes, A. (1997), *The State of Black Britain*, Vol. 2 (Antigua: Hansib)

Jones, T. (1993), *Britain's Ethnic Minorities: An Analysis of the Labour Force Survey* (London: Policy Studies Institute)

Jones, T., McEvoy, D. and Barrett, G. (1992), *Small Business Initiative: Ethnic Minority Business Component* (Swindon: Economic and Social Research Council)

Kazuka, M. (1980), *Why so Few Black Businessmen?* (London: Hackney Ethnic Minority Business Project)

Leslie, D. G., Drinkwater, S. J. and O'Leary, N. (1998), 'Unemployment and earnings among Britain's ethnic minorities: some signs for optimism', *Journal of Ethnic and Migration Studies*, 24, 489–506

Light, I. (1972), *Ethnic Enterprise in America* (Berkeley: University of California Press)

Light, I., Sabagh, G., Bozorgmehr, M. and Dier Martirosian, C. (1994), 'Beyond the ethnic enclave economy', *Social Problems*, 41, 601–16

Metcalfe, H., Modood, T. and Virdee, S. (1996), *Asian Self-Employment: The Interaction of Culture and Economics in England* (London: Policy Studies Institute)

Model, S. (1999), 'Ethnic inequality in England: an analysis based on the 1991 census', *Ethnic and Racial Studies*, 22:6, 966–90

Modood, T., Beishoon, S. and Virdee, S. (1994), *Changing Ethnic Identities* (London: PSI)

Nowikowski, S. (1984), 'Snakes and ladders', in Ward, R. and Jenkins, R. (eds), *Ethnic Communities in Business: Strategies for Economic Survival* (Cambridge: Cambridge University Press)

Pollins, H. (1984), 'The development of Jewish business in the United Kingdom', in Ward, R. and Jenkins, R. (eds), *Ethnic Communities in Business: Strategies for Economic Survival* (Cambridge: Cambridge University Press)

Ram, D. and Deakins, K. (1995), *African Caribbean Entrepreneurship in Britain* (Birmingham: University of Central England)

Reeves, F. and Ward, R. (1984), 'West Indian business in Britain', in Ward, R. and Jenkins, R. (eds), *Ethnic Communities in Business: Strategies for Economic Survival* (Cambridge: Cambridge University Press)

Reynolds, T. (2001), 'Caribbean fathers in family lives in Britain', in Goulbourne, H. and Chamberlain, M. (eds), *Caribbean Families in Britain and the Trans Atlantic World* (London and Oxford: Palgrave Macmillan)

Scarman, Lord (1986), *The Brixton Disorders 10–12 April 1981* (London: HMSO)

Scase, R. and Goffee, R. (1980), *The Real World of the Small Business Owner* (London: Croom Helm)

Schumacher, E. F. (1972), *Small is Beautiful: A Study of Economics as if People Mattered* (London: Abacus Books)

Soar, S. (1991), *Business Development Strategies, TEC and Ethnic Minorities Conference Report, Home Office Ethnic Minority Business Initiative* (Warwick: University of Warwick)

Storey, D. J. (1994), *Understanding the Small Business Sector* (London: Routledge)

Storey, D. J. (1982), *Entrepreneurship and the New Firm* (London: Croom Helm)

Government Equalities Office (2008), *Social Enterprise: Making it Work for Black, Asian and Minority Ethnic Women* (London: Government Equalities Office)

Vinod, K. (1993), *Poverty and Inequality in the UK: the Effects on Children* (London: National Children Bureau)

Waldinger, R., Aldrich, H. and Ward, R. (1990), *Ethnic Entrepreneurs* (London: Sage)

Waldinger, R., Ward, R. and Aldrich, H. (1985), 'Ethnic business and occupational mobility in advanced societies', *Sociology*, 19, 586–97

Ward, R. (1991), 'Economic development and ethnic business', in Curran, J. and Blackburn, R. (eds), *Paths of Enterprise* (London: Routledge)

Ward, R. and Reeves, F. (1981), *Racial Disadvantage: Memorandum on West Indians in Business in Britain: Research Commissioned from the SSRC Research Unit on Ethnic Relations* (London: HMSO)

Ward, R. and Jenkins, R. (1984), *Ethnic Communities in Business: Strategies for Economic Survival* (Cambridge: Cambridge University Press)

Wilson, P. E. B. (1983), *Black Business Enterprise in Britain: A Survey of Afro Caribbean and Asian Small Business in Brent* (London: Runnymede Trust)

Internet sources

Office of National Statistics (ONS), (2001), *Census 2001*: www.statistics.gov.uk

Office of National Statistics (ONS), (1991), *Census 1991*: www.statistics.gov.uk

7

Personal social services and locality: UK Black elders and young carers, health care and housing provision

Alice Sawyerr, Carl Hylton and Valerie Moore

Introduction

This chapter highlights a causal relationship between the sixty-year-old National Health Service and housing provision, and how the intersection of these social services under-serves the Black African Caribbean community in the United Kingdom (UK). Arguments are posed regarding the future care of Black African Caribbean elders as reported by Mirza and Sheridan (2003) and Jones *et al.* (2005). If the wider population of UK-born Black young people of African Caribbean descent believe that it is the State's responsibility to care for their parents and grandparents in old age, the future care of Black African Caribbean elderly may be at risk.

The Association of Black Social Workers and Allied Professions (ABSWAP) argue 'that the experience of being Black in Britain is shaped by institutional and individual racism which permeates all aspects of service offered to the Black community, by statutory and voluntary services alike' (Pennie and Best, 1990). Research reveals that health data are racialised through conscious and unconscious cultural presumptions (Mirza and Sheridan, 2003: 3). However, in spite of the systematic undermining of the Black family by mainstream social service providers, the Black family in the UK has remained 'formidable', with many of its values enshrined in the 1989 Children Act (Pennie and Best, 1990: 1).

Black African Caribbean families' access to and experiences of social welfare and personal services can to some extent be attributed to government policies, such as the 'colour blind' 'Right to Buy' 1960s policies and the 1991 Child Support Act (CSA). The UK Government's attempt to reduce the strain on the public purse via the CSA put pressure on Black African Caribbean women who juggled part-time work along with caring for their children. The impact of this legislation put a strain on Black African Caribbean family relationships. In addition, the needs and experiences of Black young people who care for disabled parents or relatives are not systematically recorded by social-service providers, which gives rise to concerns for future social personal-service provision to Black African Caribbean elders and young people. Social-service professionals appear to lack understanding of African Caribbean Black family issues. This chapter highlights gaps in the provision of a range of social services to Black African Caribbean elders and young people that have serious implications for an ageing society.

In order to provide some context for understanding the current situation for many Black elders who migrated to the UK in the 1940s, 1950s and 1960s, the chapter begins with the ageing Black population in the UK and explores the reasons for migration, and differences in retirement patterns and locality for Black elders and the over-fifties in the 2001 Census. This is followed by key facts about Black elders and social service provision in the UK linked to issues about Black youth who are carers. Housing and homelessness are examined as well as family changes due to migration patterns to the UK. Arguments also focus on the mental-health experiences of migration and how these UK experiences are conceptualised 'back home' in the migrant's countries of birth in the Caribbean – where some Black elders are unable to return for various reasons discussed later.

Welfare State alternative overview

The UK Welfare State was created in 1948 to improve the social condition of 'some of the population' in British society (Open Learn, 2006: 2). The Beveridge Report of 1942 provided the blueprint for implementing his vision, tackling what he called the five giants: want (poverty), disease, ignorance, squalor and idleness (unemployment). During 1945 to 1949 the post-war Labour Government passed nine major pieces of legislation, but Beveridge failed to give consideration to the giants of sexism and racism. His vision did not include consideration of single women or Black families' needs. Instead, it can be argued that he promoted White patriotism to the exclusion of all Black people. His mission message was that: 'Mothers have vital work to do in ensuring the adequate continuance of the British race and of British ideals in the world' (Open Learn, 2006: 1). Beveridge's policies were the foundation for the provision of council housing, free health services, and unemployment benefits and pensions. This state-run compulsory insurance system was dependent on contributions taken at source from workers wages' to support people who were unable to work because of ill-health or industrial injury. In effect, everyone who paid their 'stamps' was entitled to claim, irrespective of whether they were rich or poor. National Assistance, later known as Supplementary Benefit, would be a means-tested benefit paid as a supplement to those in need who were not contributing to the scheme or who had not paid the appropriate level of contributions (Open Learn, 2006: 3). Beveridge's Welfare State, set up to support those in need, serves some sections of British society much better than it does others, and the routes by which social and personal services are accessed and experienced by Black families also differ from majority White ethnic families. The 1940s White British patriotism promoted by the Beveridge vision engendered a sense of national pride through which Black people were viewed as inferior to White people, and (Open Learn, 2006: 8) therefore racism became enshrined in British culture following World War Two.

The post-war era brought as many opportunities as it did difficulties for Black African Caribbean people in the UK. In 1942 the Right Honourable Brendan Bracken indicated that the majority of 'Coloured' people came to Britain from British colonies and were therefore British citizens with (in theory) the same rights as any 'Englishman' (Bousquet and Douglas, 1991: 166). However, Black British citizens were not viewed entirely as complete citizens (Sivanandan, 1983: 103–4). Peach (1968) argued that in the late 1950s, whilst the shortage of labour made migrants economically desirable, the shortage of housing rendered them socially undesirable (Sivanandan, 1983: 104). Black African Caribbean people, therefore, experienced racial discrimination when seeking accommodation.

By 1958, the Black African Caribbean population comprising single men and women, married men, and their wives and children had grown to approximately 125,000 (Fryer, 1984: 372). They worked and paid their 'stamps', which entitled them, as citizens, to all provisions of the UK Welfare State. However, for a number of reasons Black young and elderly African Caribbean people are less likely to access some types of social services because of a lack of awareness of the services available and lack of knowledge about where to find and how to access them (Housing LIN Report, 2006: 7). Lack of mobility and stereotypical perceptions also have an affect (Pennie and Best, 1990); as do institutional and structural racial discrimination (Mirza and Sheridan, 2003: 4).

The Black UK ageing population

Although Black people have lived in England since 1554, a reflection of the trading opportunities between Britain and West Africa at that time (Fryer, 1984), it was during the 1940s, 1950s and 1960s that the majority of the current retiring Black elders migrated to the UK. This chapter will not centre on the detailed migration history of Black Caribbeans and Black Africans to the UK, as this aspect has been covered by Franklin Smith in chapter two of this volume. Instead the focus here will primarily be on the current generation of UK Black elders, including providing a summary of their reasons for migration.

Following World War Two, the majority of the now elderly Black Caribbean men and women who feature prominently in this chapter migrated to the UK. As a result of the human losses incurred during World War Two, the British Government began to encourage migration from the countries of the British Empire and Commonwealth to fill UK labour market shortages (Short History of Immigration, 2002). Many Caribbean men and women were attracted by better prospects in what was often referred to as the 'Mother Country'. There was an abundance of work in post-war Britain's industrial centres, with British Rail, the National Health Service and public transport recruiting almost exclusively from Jamaica and Barbados. The long-term plan for the majority was generally to work and send for their children in the Caribbean to provide them with better educational provision. Their next goal was to save enough money and return 'home' to the Caribbean to resettle before reaching retirement age (Sawyerr, 2007). Many of these Black Caribbean elders for a variety of reasons have been unable to return permanently to their countries of birth before retirement as planned. This issue is explored later in this chapter. In the main, it is this population of Black elders whose numbers are on the increase, and their housing, health and other social-care service provision needs require the attention of policy-makers, researchers and service providers.

In comparison, most Black Africans migrated to the UK during the 1940s to 1960s period mainly 'to further their education', and on completion of this education they returned 'home' where they subsequently took on prominent positions in public services following their countries' independence from colonial western powers (Sawyerr, 2007). Those who permanently made their home in the UK were predominantly African men who either identified with British culture or who were involved in inter-ethnic social relationships and marriages. Some were highly educated professionals, such as medical doctors; others were also educated but unable to find work that reflected their qualifications, skills and experiences. Some Black Africans settled in mixed communities with people from various ethnic groups in Cardiff, Liverpool, Bristol, Manchester and London, where they worked and raised their families (*Black Britons Find their African Roots*, 2003; *Short History of Immigration*, 2002).

There are differences in the retirement patterns and locality within the Black elders' population, with a higher proportion of Black Caribbean elders remaining in the UK following retirement (not always by choice), than Black African elders, especially Black elders from Nigeria and Ghana, who are increasingly choosing to return to their birth countries in Africa following retirement (Elam and Chinouya, 2000). This is a novel and important trend worthy of study.

Dench (1996) found that African Caribbeans clearly identified responsibility for elderly home help as a state obligation rather than a family responsibility. Many younger politically conscious Black British African Caribbeans had greater expectations of their entitlements from the State (Dench, 1996: 52–5). The Policy Research Institute on Ageing and Ethnicity, Minority Elderly Care Research (MEC, 2004), found that Black African Caribbean elders who used social day-care services once or twice per week had higher self-esteem, better general health and enjoyed life more than Chinese/Vietnamese and South Asians. Overall satisfaction with day-care services was highest amongst elders who were more than seventy-five years old (MEC, 2004: 4).

The next section examines the statistical data on the growing Black elderly UK population aged fifty years and over, in comparison with other minority ethnic groups, as well as the general White UK population.

UK ageing population and Black elders aged fifty and over

Data on the number and proportion of Black elders in the UK compared to the general population are crucial because decisions are being made by the current UK Government concerning the 'boom generation' of elders. These data will have health, housing and other social-care policy and practice implications for future generations of elders. According to the Office for National Statistics (2003), there are nearly twenty million people aged fifty years and over in the UK. This was a 24 per cent increase during four decades, from sixteen million in 1961. The number is projected to increase by a further 37 per cent by 2031, when there will be nearly twenty-seven million people aged fifty years old and over in the UK.

Ethnicity

A very small proportion of older people in the UK (4 per cent) are from non-White minority ethnic groups. Statistics from the 2001 Census indicates that 15 per cent (672,000) of people from non-White minority ethnic groups were aged fifty and over. This compares with 33 per cent or a third of the overall population. Black Caribbeans are reported to have the oldest age structure of all the non-White ethnic groups – 24 per cent were aged fifty and over – and the proportion of Black African elders aged fifty and over was 9 per cent. The difference between Black Caribbean and Black African elders is significant as the number of Black Caribbean elders more than doubles the number of Black African elders (Table 7.1). However, with the current increasing numbers of refugees from northern Africa, especially Somalia entering the UK due to ongoing war in the area, it is questionable whether this population of Black Africans will return to their home countries by retirement age. This is likely to lead to a further UK increase in the number of the Black elderly population in the next ten to twenty years, with implications for social care policymakers, planners and service providers. The 'Mixed' ethnic group had the youngest age structure, with fewer than 8 per cent aged fifty and over (National Statistics, 2003).

Key factors about Black elders and personal social service provision in the UK

In 1995, the Department of Health (DoH) Inspection Division reported that there was a lack of information for people whose first language was not English and a low take-up of services by Black and other ethnic minority older people. The DoH Social Care Group commissioned the Racial Equality Unit (REU) to carry out a review of social care for minority ethnic communities. The report, entitled 'Social Care for Black Communities: A Review of Recent Research', found that the stereotype of Black elders living in multi-generational households appeared to still hold true at that time. Sadly, social-care agencies were not in a position to meet the social-care needs of Black elders. There were various barriers ranging from lack of knowledge of services, to racism, or to inappropriate services being provided (Butt and Mirza, 1996). In practice, some twelve years later in 2008, it is questionable whether significant changes have taken place in the stereotypical ideas and beliefs held by health and other social-care professionals or in their service provision to Black elders. In the main, it is still assumed that the younger generation of Black Britons irrespective of

Table 7.1 Older people aged fifty and over in each ethnic group

	50–64 (%)	65–84 (%)	85 and over (%)	All aged 50 and over (%)
White				
British	18.2	14.9	2.1	35.2
Irish	26.7	22.9	1.9	51.5
Other White	13.6	9.5	0.9	24.1
All White	**18.2**	**14.9**	**2.1**	**35.1**
Mixed	**4.7**	**2.7**	**0.3**	**7.6**
Asian or Asian British				
Indian	12.8	6.2	0.3	19.4
Pakistani	7.4	3.9	0.2	11.5
Bangladeshi	6.4	3.1	0.1	9.6
Other Asian	12.5	4.9	0.3	17.6
All Asian or Asian British	**10.3**	**5.0**	**0.3**	**15.5**
Black or Black British				
Black Caribbean	13.4	10.2	0.4	24.0
Black African	6.8	2.2	0.1	9.1
Other Black	5.0	3.0	0.3	8.3
All Black or Black British	**9.9**	**6.2**	**0.3**	**16.4**
Chinese	**11.1**	**4.8**	**0.3**	**16.2**
Other ethnic groups	**11.0**	**2.7**	**0.2**	**13.9**
All non-White minority ethnic population	**9.4**	**4.8**	**0.3**	**14.5**
All population	**17.5**	**14.0**	**1.9**	**33.5**

Source: Office for National Statistics (2003), Census 2001: National Report for England and Wales

their social, financial, employment, health or housing situations would continue to care for their ageing and elderly parents and other relatives. It is considered an intrinsic part of Black African and Black Caribbean cultures and traditions to do so. Consequently, low priority is given to the personal, social-care, housing, mental-health or other ethnic needs of Black elders, as they are generally not considered a population in need of specialist social service provision.

There is also a paucity of research that has specifically examined the housing, health and other social-care needs for Black elders.

Researchers have typically regarded Black and other ethnic-minority elders as a single group – this includes Chinese, Asian, Greek Cypriot and African Caribbean elders – based on the assumption that the population of elders of African descent requiring these services is hardly visible and therefore not worthy of investigation (Livingston *et al.*, 2002). Nevertheless, in reality, as we have previously indicated, the number of Black Caribbean elders requiring social service provision is increasing rapidly as those who migrated to the UK after World War Two reach retirement age (Livingston and Sembhi, 2003).

We now take a short detour to discuss the wider issues of Black family social support to focus on parents and specifically Black young carers, youth in care and their effects on UK Black elders.

Black youth carers

Black parents

Pennie and Best (1990) argue that many White UK social workers do not appreciate the positive cultural dynamics of Black families. Fundamental cultural values of Black families such as multiple mothering, multi-dimensional bonding between parent and child, and the historical symmetry of biological and psychological parenting are pathologised because they do not fit within the UK social services' White middle-class values and the concepts of 'good child-care' enshrined in the Children Act enforced during the early 1980s. However, a change in the Children Act in 1989 reinforced the responsibility of Black parents and their right to be involved in all decisions about their children (Pennie and Best, 1990: 2).

The 1991 Child Support Act (CSA) focussed on reducing the strain on the UK public purse caused by the growth in lone parents claiming state benefits. The CSA was created to calculate and enforce child-maintenance liability from absent parents (Fox-Harding, 1996: 131). During Valerie Blake's interviews with African Caribbean female lone parents, respondents revealed shared experiences of being forced to disclose the whereabouts of their children's absent fathers – irrespective of whether they had made private arrangements with fathers for their children's financial maintenance (Blake, 2006).

Black young carers

The support Black young people provide within Black families is invisible to various social-service providers, including health services and education professionals. Black young people are left unsupported and have to carry out some inappropriate tasks in order to maintain their families. Researchers of a Manchester study found that Black young people were more likely than other young people to be involved in informal caring arrangements in which they provided help with personal medical care, assisted with mobility and carried out domestic roles such as cooking, cleaning, gardening and shopping as well as other tasks. The study revealed that personal social-care agencies did not gather information about Black children and young people providing care to disabled parents or other relatives, and did not acknowledge the support provided, or attempt to identify the young person's needs. Moreover, mainstream and some voluntary personal social-care agencies were reluctant to systematically record and monitor the ethnicity of their service users and service usage. Furthermore, although Black young people had identified services that would help to empower Black families, no family in the study was in receipt any of those services (Jones *et al.*, 2005: 1–3). Parents appreciated the care provided by children and young people and all were aware of the anxiety and stress caused by their circumstances. The young people saw the support they provided as a reciprocal part of family life but did not value concepts such as 'carer' and 'coping', which did not take into consideration specific family perspectives. The young people were also aware of having to work harder at school to maintain their studies, although in some cases their schoolwork suffered. Young Black boys who had caring responsibilities were excluded from school rather than supported to keep up with their schoolwork. Some parents felt that by requesting support from mainstream agencies they risked removal of their children through 'in need' assessments, or use of criteria that excluded members of their family from offering care. Nevertheless, where support was requested from mainstream social agencies it was not always provided or was very poor, and in some cases agencies did not respond. The report found a high level of unmet needs in Black families (Jones *et al.*, 2005: 1–4). Where Black youth are not social carers but become cared for by the State we find this statistic is also disproportionate to their percentage in the UK population.

Black youths in care

Black African and Caribbean young people are over-represented in the residential care population and are more likely to leave care to live independently although unprepared for adult life. According to Beddington and Miles (1989), 'a child of mixed race is two and a half times more likely to enter care than a White child all things being equal' (see Bibini Centre for Young People, 1998–99: 2). Twice as many Black compared to White children are received under 'Voluntary Section', with long-term consequences for the children and their families (Pennie and Best, 1990: 2). Mullender and Miller (1985) and Pennie and Best (1990) challenged the 'colour blind' policies of the 1960s and 1970s through which Black children were placed within White homes (Katz, 1996: 4; Pennie and Best, 1990: 4). Their criticisms led UK local authorities to change their practices, and by the mid-1980s many local authorities had adopted 'same-race' placements (Rhodes, 1992).

We now turn our attention to a short review of the types of accommodation and information access that are available to African Caribbean families in the UK.

Home, housing and location: a short review

Access to shelter is of course one of the most basic human needs; the home acts as a family base and a place to rear children. Several commentators including Balchin (1996), Bousquet and Douglas (1991), Castles and Kosack (1985), Somerville and Steele (2001), Fryer (1989), Race and Housing Inquiry (2001), and Housing Learning and Improvement Network (Housing LIN, 2006) reveal that minority ethnic people in the UK, including Black African Caribbeans, experience 'race' and gender discrimination when trying to access housing provision. Housing is available from statutory, private and voluntary sectors, through local authorities, housing associations, private landlords and specific minority ethnic housing providers offering a range of tenures and types of housing options based on need or ability to pay. Housing associations provide accommodation for many of the poorest families in UK society, with 75 per cent of tenants eligible for Housing Benefit. The 1972 Housing and Finance Act brought housing association rents into the fair rent system (Balchin, 1996: 142), thus enabling people on low income to access their accommodation. However, not all sections of UK society have access to appropriate housing. Black African Caribbean families are more likely than White families to occupy accommodation in the social rented sector (rather than owning their own homes), live in flats and maisonettes in poor neighbourhoods in inner-city conurbations, and reside in properties that are in need of substantial repair (Balchin, 1996; Harrison and Phillips, 2003; Somerville and Steele, 2001).

Obtaining loans to purchase property in good condition is extremely difficult for Black people (Castles and Kosack, 1985; Sivanandan, 1983: 103; Somerville and Steele, 2001). Women are particularly disadvantaged because they earn approximately two-thirds of men's incomes, and building societies prefer to give loans to men (Balchin, 1996: 240).

Despite these hurdles, those Black African Caribbeans who have been able to purchase their own property have often helped to house their migrant compatriots and others (Sivanandan, 1983: 103). The majority of these properties are located in run-down inner-city areas where, in 2000, a Cabinet Office report noted that the forty-four most deprived local authority areas contain proportionally four times as many people from ethnic minority groups as other areas (Cabinet Office, 2000: 7–8).

In Manchester, minority ethnic concentration is defined as a safety issue. During the decade 1991–2001 Manchester and the UK minority ethnic population has increased by more than 50 per cent (MEC, 2004: 3), with the largest concentrations in London, Birmingham and Manchester (which has also seen its minority ethnic population increase by over 50 per cent) (Somerville and Steele, 2001). Research in Manchester by Karn *et al.* (1999) revealed that, despite the serious levels of social and economic deprivation, minority ethnic groups remained concentrated in areas of settlement with strong social attachments to family, friends and faith communities. Fear of racial harassment in majority White areas kept many minority ethnic groups in their areas of 'original' settlement. Karn reported that Black African Caribbean residents of Moss Side felt relatively safe there than in other inner-city areas of Manchester (see Karn *et al.*, 1999, in Chahal and Temple, 2005).

Black elders' housing care

Black-led residential care homes offer a contrast to the provision offered by mainstream institutional care homes. Black care homes are more integrated within local communities and can provide a more positive living experience in relation to resources and level of dependency, whereas mainstream institutional care is viewed as being segregated from local communities and as being places where elders are less likely to live individual independent and autonomous lives (Pearce, 2005: 137).

Recognition of the housing and other social-care needs of minority ethnic elders are acknowledged and given special emphasis in *Quality and Choice for Older People's Housing – A Strategic Framework* (ODPM, 2001); *Preparing Older People's Strategies* (ODPM, 2003: 6) *and Sustainable Communities: Homes for All* (ODPM 2005: chapter seven). Encouraged by the DoH, an increasing number of UK local authorities and health-care providers are moving strategically away from residential care to supported housing models including 'extra care housing' that offers greater independence and control to older people (Housing LIN Report, 2006: 3–4).

Extra care housing

Minority ethnic voluntary providers of 'extra care housing' are usually funded by the DoH or the Housing Corporation Approved Development Grant programme. 'Extra care' has several beneficial functions, including being 'An alternative to residential care, respite and immediate care, and rehabilitative care for people recovering from an illness or operation' (Housing LIN Report, 2006: 3). As well as the usual facilities found in sheltered accommodation, 'extra care housing' may include specifically equipped bathrooms, communal areas and designated staff areas, and are more cost-effective than residential care. It is fast becoming a popular choice among elderly people (Housing LIN Report, 2006: 3), with demand outstripping available provision. Bradley Court in Huddersfield, West Yorkshire, is an example of 'extra care' housing provision to meet the needs of Black elders. The original idea for the scheme came from Kirklees Black Elders, who had identified a large number of Black elders living in unsuitable accommodations (Moore, 2007).

Homelessness and harassment

Racial harassment in the post-war era was prevalent, as sections of the White British population began to view Black African Caribbean settlers as parasites rather than returning heroes and heroines. Connie Mark recalls living in Notting Hill in 1958, when White 'Teddy Boys' led hundreds of Whites in attacks on the West London Black community that caused most Black families to stay indoors. A year later, Kelso Cochrane was murdered by a White youth in North Kensington (Bousquet and Douglas, 1991: 142–3). According to Fryer (1989), in every conurbation of Black settlement, cowardly racist attacks were carried out against Black people's homes (Fryer, 1989: 378–9). In spite of this knowledge, the Commission for Racial Equality (CRE) (1987) argued, it was not until the 1980s that local UK authorities recognised racial harassment as an issue for Black tenants on their council estates (Balchin, 1996: 252).

Whilst rough sleeping has fallen, official homelessness figures increased to more than 100,970 by 2006; this being almost double the 1996 figure. Those 'crashing' in 'squats' or on the floors in the homes of their friends or families, account for a further 380,000 (Mulgan *et al.*, 2006). Compared to their White counterparts, Black African and Caribbean people experience a disproportionate amount of homelessness in terms of their proportion in the wider UK population, but they are less likely to be homeless and on the street (Davies *et al.*, 1996; Kemp, 1997). It follows therefore that young African and Caribbean people leaving care are more prone to becoming homeless (Bibini Centre for Young People, 1998–99). Precise levels of Black African Caribbean homelessness tend to be hidden because individuals sleep on the floors of friends and family (Balchin, 1996: 245). A CRE study of single homeless people revealed that, in 1991, one-third of the young people under twenty-five years old and half of all young women in hostels and in bed-and-breakfast accommodation were from Black and other Minority Ethnic (BME) groups (Somerville and Steele, 2001). Balchin (1996) cites research by Lucy Bonnerjea and Jean Lawton (1987), who found that homeless Black people tended to be offered housing of a poorer standard than White homeless people (Balchin, 1996: 252). The Bibini Centre for Young People (1998–99) found that Black young people were either not considered for good standard housing or offered the lowest-quality accommodation (Bibini Centre for Young People, 1998–99: 3).

The chapter now focuses on significant changes in the migrant population especially from North Africa and the likely increase in the number of Black African elders in the UK. Recognition of this change in migration pattern is important as it will more than likely have major policy and planning implications for housing, health and other personal social-care service provision in the UK.

Significant changes and new trends in the migration patterns of Black Africans to the UK

Although there are Africans in the UK from northern, southern, eastern, western and central Africa, with some becoming well established in the period since the 1950s, only four major African communities were specifically selected for a *Diversity among Black African Communities Study* by the DoH. The chosen groups were from the Nigerian, Ghanaian, Ugandan and Somali communities. In their study, Elam and Chinouya (2000) found that the causes of migration have varied for these four major African communities in the UK since the 1950s. The Nigerian and Ghanaian communities comprised mainly voluntary, planned migrants and students, although more recently there have been instances of political and economic refugees. The Ugandan community has been more diverse, comprising voluntary migrants who settled from the 1960s onwards, following their country's independence, then a wave of asylum-seekers in the 1970s, and a further large wave of people seeking asylum in the 1990s. In contrast, the Somali community were mostly composed of refugees, except a minority described as 'seamen' who settled before the 1950s in port areas, especially

Liverpool, Bristol, and Tiger Bay in Cardiff. The major settlement of the Somali community has mainly been from the 1990s onwards. Somalis are part of the wave of new migrants who have arrived mostly from North Africa. This is likely to lead to significant changes and an increase of the UK Black African elderly population in the near future. Nigerians, Ghanaians and Ugandans who migrated to the UK were fluent in English, and consequently they were able to study, work and settle into UK society. However, the Somali population are reported to vary significantly with regards to their educational, language, cultural, religious and health needs from these other UK African migrants (Elam and Chinouya, 2000).

The effects of acculturation and provision for Black elders

It is important to consider the cultural expectations, values and beliefs that Black elders born outside the UK bring with them in order to develop some understanding and appreciation for how they and the young generation of Black Britons born in the UK conceptualise their roles and responsibilities within their families and communities.

Black African and Black Caribbean elders are traditionally from collectivist cultures (Owusu-Bempah, 2002). Collectivist cultures define 'the self' in terms of group identity and interdependence with the members of one's group. This is in contrast to individualist cultures in western societies such as the UK, mainland Europe and North America, who conceive of 'the self' as autonomous and independent of groups. In collectivist cultures the needs of the family and community take precedence over the needs of the individual, in contrast to western individualist cultures (Markus and Kitayama, 1991; Owusu-Bempah, 2002; Triandis, 1995). The roles and responsibilities of Black elders in collectivist cultures cannot therefore be underestimated as they have a major function in the sociocultural and psychological development of 'the self' in children. Culture becomes an integrated part of the psychological development of the children's values, beliefs, customs, traditions and skills that are transmitted from one generation to the next through social interaction. Children acquire methods of thinking and behaving that develop and continue a community's culture through cooperative dialogues with more knowledgeable society members such as grandparents and other community elders (John-Steiner and Mahn, 1996; Markus and Kitayama, 1991; Owusu-Bempah, 2002; Penuel and Wertsch, 1995; Triandis, 1995). Consequently, when families migrate from collectivist cultures to individualist cultures, it is logical to expect changes and adaptation to aspects of their cultures, traditions, roles and expectations.

For Black elders and their families who migrated to the UK in the 1940s, 1950s and 1960s it is important to find out the aspects of their cultures, traditions, roles and expectations that have changed or been adapted over time. There is a paucity of literature due to a lack of research about the degree to which there has been assimilation, integration, isolation or a combination of some of these by Black elders and the second generation of Black Britons, born and educated in the UK. One such study by Plaza (2000), for example, on the roles and position of grandmothers in African Caribbean families resident in the UK, collected interviews of one hundred and eighty life-histories in 1995–96 from three generations of Caribbean-origin people living in the UK and the Caribbean. Findings from this research suggest that African Caribbean grandmothers resident in the UK play a less active role within their immediate families compared to earlier historical periods. At the same time, however, these grandmothers take on what Plaza refers to as a more 'transnational emissary role' for their families and kin located throughout North America and Europe. Plaza (2000) concludes that Caribbean-born grandmothers appear to be using more 'modern' means for fulfilling certain traditional tasks such as 'child-shifting', 'story telling' or acting as a 'social safety net'. In his conclusion he notes that using their agency these African Caribbean-born grandmothers have been able to carve out new niches for themselves despite changes in family structures brought about by migration and settlement patterns in the UK.

While Black elders have been flexible in adapting some of their 'back home' cultures and traditions to the new environment in the UK they continue to hold on to the area of care and support from extended family members in their old age. This 'back home' perception is not always shared by their children born in the western individualist UK cultures. This trend is noted in a study reported in the Royal College of Psychiatrists Council Report (2001) (CR103). This does not necessarily translate to Black elders being cared for by the State in residential care homes.

More recently, from within the Black community in Birmingham, British Academy of Film and Television Arts (BAFTA) award winning author Mandy Richards confirmed in a *Birmingham Post* newspaper article (5 October 2006) entitled 'Who cares for the pioneers?' that there have been increasing and significant changes in the culture, traditions, expectations and functioning of Black families, especially the younger generation, to the detriment of the personal social care of Black elders in the UK.

> Traditionally, for people of Afro-Caribbean origin, the concept of a 'care home' is alien. For those born 'back home' in the Caribbean the term will conjure images of Alms Houses that were strictly the preserve of the poor. Our mothers, some of whom will have spent their entire working lives as care assistants or domestics in old people's homes or nursing the elderly in British hospitals, wholly resist the prospect. This sentiment is generationally engrained. The effort put in, to raise and educate families with an average of six kids on shift work wages, is the conscious debt Black Brits now benefiting from their parents' struggle owe them.
>
> 'We don't put our people into homes', is a familiar mantra. So what do we do? With communities fragmenting and cultural norms fusing, how are Afro-Caribbean communities managing to care for what is proportionally, the largest non-White elderly population in the UK?
>
> Department of Health statistics reveal over 300,000 older people live in residential care in Britain. Of the 62,000 elderly Black Caribbeans in the UK virtually none are in care homes. The assumption that lack of access to care or financial hardship might be the chief considerations here lacks insight.
>
> Social and economic circumstances may have some part to play but the cultural difference that divides views on the responsibility of care for the elderly is what principally separates Black from White. (Richards, 2006)

With regards to generational differences particularly between people born or educated in the UK and those born or educated in African countries, Elam and Chinouya (2000), in their study, found that the younger generations shared the culture and practices of other London- or UK-born young people. Community views on the impact of this differed. Some respondents believed that young people of continental African descent had minimal interest in their African identity, others were concerned that young people may have conflicting identities, and other respondents believed that younger people became more interested in their African background as they matured, or following visits to Africa.

The next section discusses the current patterns of health and other personal social-care services accessed by UK Black elders.

Health social service utilisation by UK Black elders

Livingston *et al.* (2002), in their study of the health and services utilisation of older migrants, found that the small number of minority ethnic elders aged sixty-five years and over were concentrated in deprived inner-city areas. The researchers reported that the numbers of Black elders were increasing rapidly as those who migrated to the UK after World War Two were reaching retirement age. They contemplated the idea of multiple jeopardy, which postulates that minority ethnic elders – by virtue of age, socioeconomic difficulties and minority status – are at greater risk of illness and thus in greater need of social health-care services.

Similarly, studies of Asian- and African-descent elders have shown that they were more likely to consult their general practitioners (GP) than their UK-born counterparts (Blakemore, 1982; Murray and Williams, 1986) but are referred less to secondary health-care and other social services, particularly psychiatric services (Manthorpe and Hettiaratchy, 1993; Shah and Dighe-Deo, 1997). However, Odutoye and Shah (1999) have been unable to confirm this in a more recent study of Asian referrals to psychiatric services. There are several reasons suggested for the lack of utilisation of psychiatric services by Black elders. These include interpreting symptoms as spiritual problems (Kleinman, 1987) or physical illness (Odell *et al.*, 1997), reluctance of minority ethnic elders to accept referrals to secondary mental-health services (Shah *et al.*, 1998), and perceptions by Black people of racism by health workers (Hutchinson and Gilvarry, 1998). Livingston *et al.* (2002) concluded from their study that medical professionals in the UK are less able to recognise the presentation of psychological distress by people from other cultures. The obvious question to ask is: what steps are being taken to improve the medical professional's recognition levels of the presentation of psychological distress by people from other cultures?

The Royal College of Psychiatrists Council Report (2001) (CR103) suggested that there was minimal apparent evidence of mental illness in minority ethnic elders and that this was reflected in the poor uptake of psychiatric services compared with high admission rates for Black elders with diabetes; this appeared to support their belief in the fallacy that: 'They look after their own kind'. The report suggested that older people from minority ethnic groups have wide experiences of xenophobia and racism, some of the key issues being found in the continuing debate between 'colour blindness' and a tendency to create 'a fetish of ethnicity'. The report argued that a fine balance between being able to access psychiatric services and having a pool of ethnic-sensitive services throws responsibility on both service users and service providers. This 2001 report also reflected strong support among psychiatrists for the idea of identifying lead clinicians with management support in Health Trusts that are responsible for large numbers of ethnic minority elders. This was considered a possible way of increasing awareness for initiating appropriate services. Similarly, the Policy Research Institute on Ageing and Ethnicity (PRIAE) are developing a guide for service providers in Manchester on how to improve health and welfare service provision for Black and other minority ethnic elders. Manchester City Council's 'Agenda 2010' seeks to further improve the situation of minority ethnic elders through planning and developing a strategy on ethnicity and ageing (MEC, 2004: 1–4). What is striking is the lack of recommendations in the (2001) Royal College of Psychiatrists Council CR103 Report and the (2002) Livingston research a year later, for changes or adaptations to the clinical and academic training of doctors and psychiatrists to address these important cultural awareness and poor social-service provision issues.

As we will discuss in the next section, many Black Caribbeans diagnosed with mental stress and mental illness following their arrival in the UK were returned to the Caribbean by the British Government. However, minimal funding has been provided for research to specifically examine mental distress and mental illness in the first generation of Caribbeans who migrated to the UK in the 1940s, 1950s and 1960s.

The experiences of mental stress and mental illness among the 'first generation' of Black Caribbeans in the UK

On the issue of Black elders' mental health, two human geographers, Potter and Phillips (2006) with extensive research experience in the Caribbean, draw attention to the paucity of literature and other information on mental ill-health among the 'first-generation' cohort of Caribbean migrants to the UK in the 1950s and 1960s. They specifically comment on the issues surrounding mental stress, as this area has received relatively little attention in the social-science migration literature. They report that among the few commentators and researchers who have paid attention to this area, Gmelch (1980) has emphasised the particularly stressful impact of migration on individual lives. The 'stress thesis' of migration suggests that planning the move to another country and finding gainful employment along with suitable accommodation, education and social welfare services, together with the challenges involved in establishing new friendship patterns, adjusting to new social and cultural norms and facing racial prejudice, can all be associated with stress that can potentially deteriorate into mental-health issues (Gmelch, 1980; Potter and Phillips, 2006; Western, 1992).

Reid-Galloway (2002) also refers to the organisation 'Mind' as having argued that African Caribbean people, on arrival in the UK, experienced aspects of culture-shock, alienation, unmet social needs and overt racism. Consistent with this line of thinking, Potter and Phillips (2006) indicate further supporting evidence of the stress thesis of migration provided by Mahy (1973) in relation to Caribbean migrants. Mahy interviewed eighty-five Caribbeans who had migrated to the UK from Grenada, Barbados, Trinidad and Jamaica and had been committed as psychiatric patients. The possible etiological factors such as the weather, racial prejudice, job problems and living alone were investigated as part of the research. Of those migrants diagnosed as severely ill, the study found that the great majority had been living alone at the time of their first reported mental illness and had not visited English homes. These factors were considered as evidence of social isolation. Mahy nonetheless concluded that 'these patients would probably have got ill whether they went to Britain or not', but he also noted that 'as expected, a much higher percentage of the severely ill were sent home by the UK government' (Mahy, 1973: 190). For us, what is particularly concerning and disturbing about the UK Government's actions is the absence of supportive mental-health services to this population of Black Caribbean migrants to prevent and address the stressful social issues that had led to their deterioration. Instead, they were shipped out of the UK and replaced by other supposedly 'mentally healthy' migrant workers from the Caribbean. It appears that they were perceived and treated as inanimate objects or 'parts' that were easily replaced.

Negative perceptions of UK Black elder returnees to the Caribbean

In relation to how returnee Black elders are perceived 'back home' in their countries of birth, Potter and Phillips (2006: 586), in their study of second-generation British-Barbadians ('Bajan-Brits') returning to the land of their parents, found that they are frequently accused by indigenous Barbadian nationals of 'being mad'. Narratives of the migrants reflected four major sets of factors:

1. madness as perceived behavioural and cultural differences;
2. explanations that relate to the historical–clinical circumstances surrounding the incidence of mental ill-health among first-generation Caribbean migrants to the UK;
3. madness as a pathology of alienation that is attendant on living in Barbados; and
4. madness as 'othering', 'outing' and 'fixity'.

Potter and Phillips (2006) provide revealing narratives from their second-generation returnee informants interviewed in Barbados. For example, when the informants were asked to explain why returnee Barbadians, referred to by the locals as 'English people', are regarded as 'mad', an informant provided the following detailed historical narrative:

> What I understand was that they sent back people from the 1960s, and the only way that they can get them out of England was to have them certified as insane; so they used to give you a quick certificate that you are mad. And they came back to Barbados and the health service would get the certificate saying that they are mentally disabled. And then people here that work in the health service would tell people that everybody coming back from England is mad. That's what I understood it to be. (Potter and Phillips, 2006: 593)

They also reported that informants appeared to be well aware of the possible roots of 'madness' as the social isolation experienced by Caribbean migrants after their arrival in the UK. An informant provided the following narrative account for the 'away' explanation for the perceived madness:

> when they go away and come back, they tend to come back mad. Why is that . . . ? I think that it is the environment of London and people not talking – you know, not saying 'good morning' – the loneliness – you just go from work to home . . . and you don't have any sort of social life. I think that Bajans think maybe that is why it happens; . . . it is an open environment here, and they go to live in a closed environment – that is what causes the problem to occur. If the pressure is built up for a long time, it seals for a long time and it is harder for them. (Potter and Phillips, 2006: 593)

Other informants confirmed the above analysis, although initially often significantly couching this in terms of the older cohort of retiree return migrants. But it is most noticeable that the condition is squarely linked with migration to the UK, rather than to North America:

> For some reason the madness in English people is particularly concentrated on older returning nationals. A lot of Bajans would say that they knew people here that went to England, led their lives – mainly retired people that have come back here – who are crazy. There are also some people who went to England in the 1960s, and came back pretty quickly crazy, which does not surprise me – obviously, all the challenges that they would have met in England. People would jokingly say it, you know? I think it was the older ones who came back mad. I think that our parents had such a hard time adjusting that two-thirds came back mad. I just think that our expectations are greater than people who live

in the States. The returning nationals from the States don't complain about service in shops, utility companies. The simplest things get us. I am very cautious with people who don't know that I am English. (Potter and Phillips, 2006: 593)

On the other hand, they found that several informants attributed the alleged incidence of madness as much to the stresses and strains caused by being away from Barbados, thereby giving rise to what may be interpreted as the 'home' explanation of returnee madness. This refers to problems that were located or originated in Barbados, while informants were living in the UK or North America. These issues included sending remittances 'back home' and being 'ripped off' by house builders, lawyers and extended family members in Barbados prior to return. An informant explained:

> I don't know where they got that from, but when the early ones came back, they ended up in the mental. You know, if you think about it, you would understand why. They would repatriate money to build a house, and when they came, no house . . . and they would end up in the mental! A lot of people who used to come back to resettle, they would come home to no house – and nobody gives you back that money. They used to send money to relatives, and instead of getting a house started, they would spend the money. For instance, this woman that I know, she used to send money to her mother – and came home to find a small wooden house! And she cried and cried. But what could she do? (Potter and Phillips, 2006: 594)

The overall impression from the informants and local Caribbean narratives was that although there are explanations to account for the reasons why Black returnees from the UK get a mentally ill or 'mad' tag, there is strong stigma attached to mental illness, which is not open for discussion. The UK is therefore perceived as a locality that induces madness in Black Caribbean migrants. They either get sent home as a result of signs of madness soon after arrival during their youth or after many years in the UK when they become elderly. Although it is not possible to resolve it here, the question to pose is: to what extent have these beliefs and perceptions influenced the decision of increasing numbers of Black Caribbean elders to remain in the UK during their retirement years?

Conclusion

The UK Welfare State was created to benefit those who were unable or less able to provide for their families, and it is dependent on the contributions of working people. Beveridge's vision was focussed on ameliorating the social needs of British people, which did not appear to include Black African Caribbean families who also paid 'the stamp'. Whilst in essence it sought to improve the standard of living for the British working classes, Beveridge's Welfare State provision failed to recognise two major factors that have had a lasting impact – these are the giants of sexism and racism.

Research by Jones *et al.* (2005) concerning the needs of young carers and their disabled parents provides an indication that the physical welfare and medical needs of both groups are not being adequately met. What are the implications for young, Black African Caribbean people providing care for the elders in a society with an ageing population? Black and minority ethnic groups have long advocated the need for good-quality culturally appropriate assessment and personal social-care services, but they have been ignored by mainstream care providers (Bibini Centre for Young People, 1998–99; Jones *et al.*, 2005; Pennie and Best, 1990). As recently as 1993, the Wagner Reports were criticised for marginalising the needs of Black people working in or living in social-care settings (Pearce, 2005: 136).

This chapter has raised a number of issues and questions regarding the Welfare State, health services and housing provision and the extent to which the particular specific needs of Black African Caribbean families are being met. To some extent it provides an indication of the general resiliency of Black African Caribbean families in spite of the failures of the National Health Service and housing services to meet their needs. Nevertheless, caution is advised, as we consider the concerns raised by Dench's (1996) research – that there is a danger of over-reliance on the State for personal welfare supports that may lead to the neglect of family structures rather than a belief in the importance of the family (Dench, 1996: 54). We cannot change the past but we can plan for a far better future where Black African Caribbean families benefit from their National Insurance contributions on equal terms with their non-Black ethnic counterparts to enjoy good to adequate housing provision in green suburban areas rather than inner cities.

Further research is strongly recommended, as there is a real dearth of information. It is evident that, in spite of Beveridge's Welfare State, access to mainstream housing, welfare and health-care services remains a key issue for Black African Caribbean families in the UK. At policy level the Policy Research Institute on Ageing and Ethnicity – Minority Elderly Care Research Project (MEC, 2004) has indicated a number of issues that require governmental response to ensure that adequate social services are provided for Black African and Caribbean elders. In addition, future personal social-service provision for Black African Caribbean elders and young people requires a community response. Black African Caribbean communities need to develop a comprehensive strategic plan of action to promote, serve and sustain Black families. Consideration should be given to who is providing care for Black African Caribbean elders, and how their future needs might be met and by whom. This may be an opportunity for more Black churches to become involved to lead appropriate social services.

References

Balchin, P. N. (1996), 'The United Kingdom', in Balchin, P. N. (ed.), *Housing Policy in Europe* (London and New York: Routledge)

Beddington, A. and Miles, J. (1989), 'The background of children who enter local authority care', *British Journal of Social Work*, 19, 349–68

Bibini Centre for Young People (1998–99), *Research Specification for the Leaving Care Home Project: Meeting the Needs of the Young Black Homeless in Manchester* (Manchester: Bibini Centre for Young People)

Blake, V. M. (2006), 'Child Support Interview Transcripts' (unpublished manuscript)

Blakemore, K. (1982), 'Health and illness among the elderly of minority ethnic groups living in Birmingham: some new findings', *Health Trends*, 14, 69–72

Bonnerjea, L. and Lawton, J. (1987), *Homelessness in Brent* (London: Policy Studies Institute)

Bousquet, B. and Douglas, C. (1991), *West Indian Women at War: British Racism in World War Two* (London: Lawrence and Wishart)

Butt, J. and Mirza, K. (1996), *Social Care and Black Communities: A Review of Recent Research* (London: HMSO)

Cabinet Office (2000), *Minority Ethnic Issues in Social Exclusion and Neighbourhood Renewal: A Guide to the Work of the Social Exclusion Unit and the Policy Action Teams so far* (London: Cabinet Office)

Castles, S. and Kosack, G. (1985), *Immigrant Workers and Class Structure in Western Europe* (London: Oxford University Press)

Chahal, K. and Temple, B. (2005), 'A review of research on minority ethnic older people', *Race Relations Abstracts*, 30:4, 3–36

Commission for Racial Equality (CRE) (1987), *Ageing Minorities: Black People as they Grow Old in Britain* (London: Commission for Racial Equality)

Davies, J., Lyle, S., Deacon, A., Law, I., Julienne, L. and Kay, J. (1996), *Discounted Voices: Homelessness Among Young Black and Minority Ethnic People in England* (Leeds: University of Leeds)

Dench, G. (1996), *The Place of Men in Changing Family Cultures* (London: Institute of Community Studies)

Elam, G. and Chinouya, M. (2000), *Feasibility Study of Health Surveys among Black African Populations Living in the UK: Stage 2 – Diversity among Black African Communities* (London: Department of Health)

Fox-Harding, L. (1996), *Family, State and Social Policy* (Basingstoke: Macmillan)

Fryer, P. (1989), *Black People in the British Empire: An Introduction* (London: Pluto)

Fryer, P. (1984), *Staying Power – The History of Black People in Britain* (London: Pluto Press)

Gmelch, G. (1980), 'Return migration', *Annual Review of Anthropology*, 9, 135–59

Harrison, M. and Phillips, D. (2003), 'Housing and Black and Minority Ethnic (BME) communities: review of the evidence base', *Housing Review Summary 180* (London: Housing Support Unit, Office of the Deputy Prime Minister – ODPM)

Housing LIN (Learning and Improvement Network) (2006), *Developing Extra Care Housing for Black and Minority Ethnic Elders: An Overview of the Issues, Examples and Challenges* (London: Department of Health)

Hutchinson, G. and Gilvarry, C. (1998), 'Ethnicity and dissatisfaction with mental health services', *British Journal of Psychiatry*, 172, 95–6

John-Steiner, V. and Mahn, H. (1996), 'Sociocultural approaches to learning and development: A Vygoskian framework', *Educational Psychologist*, 31:3–4, 191–206

Jones, A., Jeyasingham, D. and Rajasooriya, S. (2005), *Invisible Families: The Strengths and Needs of Black Families in which Young People have Caring Responsibilities* (London: Policy Press)

Karn, V., Mian, S., Brown, M. and Dale, A. (1999), *Tradition, Change and Diversity: Understanding the Housing Needs of Minority Ethnic Groups in Manchester* (London: Housing Corporation)

Katz, I. (1996), *The Construction of Racial Identity in Children of Mixed Parentage: Mixed Metaphors* (London: Jessica Kingsley Publishers Ltd)

Kemp, P. (1997), 'The characteristics of single homeless people in England', in Burrows, R., Pleace, N. and Quilgers, D. (eds), *Homelessness and Social Policy* (London: Routledge)

Kleinman, A. (1987), 'Depression, somatisation and the "new cross-cultural psychiatry"', *Social Science and Medicine*, 11, 3–10

Livingston, G. and Sembhi, S. (2003), 'Mental health of the ageing immigrant population', *Advances in Psychiatric Treatment*, 9, 31–7

Livingston, G., Leavey, G., Kitchen, G., Manela, M., Sembhi, S. and Katona, C. (2002), 'Accessibility of health and social services to immigrant elders: the Islington study', *The British Journal of Psychiatry*, 180, 369–73

Mahy, G. (1973), 'The psychotic West Indian returning from Britain', *West Indian Medical Journal*, 22, 189–90

Manthorpe, J. and Hettiaratchy, P. (1993), 'Ethnic minority elders in Britain', *International Review of Psychiatry*, 5, 173–80

Markus, H. and Kitayama, S. (1991), 'Culture and the self: implications for cognition, emotion and motivation', *Psychological Review*, 98:2, 224–53

Minority Elderly Care (MEC) (2004), *Developing a Strategy to Improve Quality of Life of Manchester's Black and Minority Ethnic Elders (MEE)* (Leeds: Policy Research Institute on Ageing and Ethnicity – PRIAE)

Mirza, H. and Sheridan, A. (2003), 'Multiple identity and access to health: the experience of black and minority ethnic women', *Working Paper Series 10* (London: Equality Opportunities Commission)

Moore, V. M. (2007), *Interview with Black Elders Regarding Bradley Court* (Huddersfield, unpublished manuscript)

Mulgan, G., Buonfino, A. and Gelssendorfer, L. (2006), *Mapping Britain's Needs: A Youth Foundation Report for the Commission on Unclaimed Assets* (London: Youth Foundation)

Mullender, A. and Miller, D. (1985), 'The Ebony Group: Black children in white foster homes', *Adoption and Fostering*, 9:1, 33–40

Murray, J. and Williams, P. (1986), 'Self-reported illness and general practice consultations in Asian-born and British-born residents of West London', *Social Psychiatry*, 21, 139–45

Odell, S., Surtees, P., Wainwright, N., Commander, M. and Sashidharan, S. (1997), 'Determinants of general practitioner recognition of psychological problems in a multi-ethnic inner-city health district', *British Journal of Psychiatry*, 171, 537–41

ODPM (Office of the Deputy Prime Minister) (2005), *Sustainable Communities: Homes for All* (London: Department of Health)

ODPM (Office of the Deputy Prime Minister) (2003), *Preparing Older People's Strategies* (London: Department of Health)

ODPM (Office of the Deputy Prime Minister) (2001), *Quality and Choice for Older People's Housing: A Strategic Framework* (London: Department of Health)

Odutoye, K. and Shah, A. (1999), 'The characteristics of Indian subcontinent origin elders newly referred to a psychogeriatric service', *International Journal of Geriatric Psychiatry*, 14, 446–53

Owusu-Bempah, K. (2002), 'Culture, self and cross-ethnic therapy', in Mason, B. and Sawyerr, A. (eds), *Exploring the Unsaid, Creativity, Risks and Dilemmas in Working Cross-culturally* (London: Karnac Books)

Peach, C. (1968), *West Indian Migration to Britain: A Social Geography* (London: Oxford University Press)

Pearce, S. (2005), *People and Places* (Milton Keynes: The Open University)

Pennie, P. and Best, F. (1990), *How the Black Family is Pathologised by Social Services Systems* (London: Association of Black Social Workers and Allied Professions)

Penuel, W. and Wertsch, J. (1995), 'Vygotsky and identity formation: a socio-cultural approach', *Educational Psychologist*, 30:2, 83–92

Plaza, D. (2000), 'Transnational Grannies: The Changing Family Responsibilities of Elderly African Caribbean-Born Women Resident in Britain', *Social Indicators Research*, 51:1, 75–105

Potter, R. and Phillips, J. (2006), 'Mad Dogs and Transnational Migrants: Bajan-Brit Second-Generation Migrants and Accusations of Madness', *Annals of the Association of American Geographers*, 96:3, 586–600

Race and Housing Inquiry (2001), *Challenge Report* (London: Housing Corporation, Commission for Race Equality, National Housing Federation and the Federation for Black Housing Organisations)

Reid-Galloway, C. (2002), *The Mental Health of the African Caribbean Community in Britain* (London: Mind Information Unit)

Rhodes, P. J. (1992), 'The emergence of a new policy: "racial matching" in fostering and adoption', *New Community*, 18:2, 191–208

Richards, M. (2006), 'Who cares for the pioneers?', *Birmingham Post* (5 October)

Royal College of Psychiatrists (2001), *Psychiatric Services for Black and Minority Ethnic Elders* (London: Royal College of Psychiatrists Report CR103)

Sawyerr, A. (2007), 'Identity and Black young People: theoretical and practice considerations', in Sallah, M. and Howson, C. (eds), *Working with Young Black People* (London: Russell House Publishing)

Shah, A. and Dighe-Deo, D. (1997), 'Elderly Gujarat's and psychogeriatrics in a London psychogeriatric service', *Bulletin of the International Psychogeriatrics Association*, 14, 12–13

Shah, A. K., Lindesay, J. and Jaggar, C. (1998), 'Is the diagnosis of dementia stable over time among elderly immigrant Gujarats in the United Kingdom'? *International Journal of Psychiatry*, 13, 440–4

Sivanandan, A. (1983), 'Challenging Racism: Strategies for the 80s', *Race and Class*, 25:2, 1–11

Somerville, P. and Steele, A. (2001), *'Race', Housing and Social Exclusion* (London, Jessica Kingsley)

Triandis, H. (1995), *Individualism and Collectivism* (Oxford: Westview Press)

Western, J. (1992), *Passage to England: Barbadian Londoners Speak of Home* (London: University College London)

Internet sources

Black Britons Find their African Roots (2003), BBC news (14 February), www.news.bbc.co.uk (accessed 30 October 2006)

Office for National Statistics (2003), *Census 2001: National Report for England and Wales*, www.statistics.gov.uk (accessed 28 November 2006)

Open Learn (2006), *The Beveridge Vision*, www.open.ac.uk (accessed 18 November 2006)

Short History of Immigration (2002), BBC news – Race UK: Background, www.news.bbc.co.uk (accessed 30 October 2006)

8

Conceptualisation and effects of social exclusion, racism and discrimination and coping strategies of individuals and families

William (Lez) Henry

Introduction

Many theorists work from the premise that certain problems that affect Black communities are the unwitting consequences of a modern democratic society that naturally legislates against a large number of its citizens. This, however, is not the case and I will argue here that what was done and continues to be done to people of African ancestry is deliberate and necessary to a system that was founded on White supremacist thoughts and actions. As such, there must be a healthy appreciation of the historical forces and circumstances that are largely responsible for 'us' inheriting the racialised world that we now inhabit. In line with this perspective, Welsing offers what she terms a 'functional definition' of racism which is:

> the local and global power system structured and maintained by persons who classify themselves as white, whether consciously or subconsciously determined; this system consists of patterns of perception, logic, symbol formation, thought, speech, action and emotional response, as conducted simultaneously in all areas of people activity (economics, education, entertainment, labor, law, politics, religion, sex and war). (Welsing, 1991: ii)

Welsing makes known how problematic it is to analyse 'racism' and its impact on the lives of Black people, without considering how these 'areas of people activity' are controlled by those who 'classify' themselves as White. Moreover, to overlook the centrality of their role in normalising their privileged position, in this 'global power system', is to deny the reality of their dominant worldview. Of equal importance, Black communities should be mindful when White scholars

– whose 'race' is used as a measurement of what it means to be normal, valued and human – fail to consider that they, or their racial group,
never have to measure up to such ideal types in the way that
Black people do. Although they may classify themselves as White,
their 'Whiteness' is seldom questioned or pathologised in the way
'Blackness' is.

I will, therefore, firstly consider the history of how the Black
presence in the United Kingdom (UK) became the 'object of scrutiny
under the academic gaze', during a time when many theorists tried
to analyse this 'alien' presence. Secondly, I will interrogate the notion
that the shaping effects of science and colonialism are central to understanding our contemporary situation, because both have played a
critical role in how the Black 'other' becomes known to the White
'self'. Finally, I will present an insight into forms of resistance and transcendence, which have become coping and transcendental mechanisms
for Black families and individuals alike. I will then offer my concluding
remarks.

Understanding Black social exclusion: a sociological problem

In our endeavours to determine how the notion of 'race' has become
an integral part of our contemporary social reality, we must consider
the fact that sociologists generally view the issue of 'race' or 'race relations' from between two poles. More importantly, these polemical the-
orisations are often the template for how Black familial relationships
are measured and then presented in the wider public arena as the best
way to understand the behaviour of Black folk. What often happens
is that the social relations of White society, class based or otherwise,
are used as the chief determinants in analysing the behavioural
patterns of Black families and individuals. Black families become the
focus of 'problem-oriented analysis' and therefore 'many behavioural
scientists argued that Black families were no more than simply "sick"
White families' (Nobles and Goddard, 1984: 3). This means that any
sense of autonomy is often denied to Black families, because the 'traditional' ways of being that are used to resist and transcend White racism
are regarded as 'sick', often omitted, or generally glossed over.

The first perspective argues that existing class conflicts within the
social structure are 'racialised' and thus directly relate to the present
organisation of society. Consequently, many Marxist and neo-Marxist
sociologists locate their explanations of 'race' as a social phenomenon
within the economic structure of advanced capitalist countries and suggest that class conflicts shape inter-group conflicts. This perspective

had and still has serious ramifications for the Black communities who came to the UK during the period after World War Two, for in many ways it relegates their immediate concerns to 'the unreal or insubstantial, secondary or peripheral' (Gilroy, 2000: 98). Therefore, whilst it is accepted 'that people do conceive of themselves and others as belonging to "races" and do describe certain sorts of situation and relations as being "race relations"' (Miles, 1982: 42), these are in essence 'false constructions'. An idea that was challenged by Gilroy (1987), who argued:

> Miles therefore attacks black writers who have initiated a dialogue with Marxism over racism in Britain because they use 'race' in spite of its illusory status, to 'encourage' the formation of a particular political force ... Miles describes racism and racialization as having 'autonomous but limited effects' but does not specify how much autonomy his own political strategy will cede to blacks in Britain. (Gilroy, 1987: 22)

Gilroy questions the 'authority' of a form of scholarship that fails to recognise the worth of a 'politics of black autonomy' that would indeed bestow a form of 'insider' ownership to Black writers, thereby enabling them to challenge 'outsider' perspectives on Black reality. This becomes a crucial point for us to grasp because if 'you' have the analytical tools and a sound grasp of the conceptual frameworks that are generally required to present 'our' story from the outside, then why should 'we' not be encouraged to use the same methodology to present an alternative theorisation from the inside? This can be explained by a failure to appreciate that wilful social isolation and its direst consequence, Black structural placement in specific areas in British society, means that avenues of expression, social mobility and meaningful dialogue with the dominant White community are blocked off by forms of social, racial, cultural and political segregation. Moreover, certain non-White groups in a racist society such as Britain are continually subjected to the negative labelling, stereotyping and demeaning social positioning that constitute the everyday exercising of White superiority. Therefore a theory of race formation or 'race relations' must enable the interrogation of how 'unwitting' actions reproduce White privilege, thereby making institutionalised racism seem 'normal'. In fact according to Back (1996):

> I am not suggesting that institutional racism is monolithic or all pervasive. Rather I am concerned to identify the social locations where black people encounter racist ideologies and discourses. (Back, 1996: 162)

Back deals with one of the major concerns of the Marxist scholars who argue that not all White people are in powerful positions, therefore their influence over processes of the 'race relations' that disadvantage Black people will be minimal. Yet what Back does is explain that there are 'social locations where black people encounter', on a daily basis, the barriers that Whiteness constructs for them that do not necessarily impact on normal class relations in the same way. This is because Whiteness is said to 'be everything and nothing' as White people 'colonise the definition of the normal' (Dyer, 1997: 45–6). Moreover, an analysis of the experiences of being racially disadvantaged for being born Black produces knowledge of White dominance and privilege. But experiences of racialised privilege that seek to interrogate what it means to be White discourage knowledge of collective privilege, as White people can choose whether or not to acknowledge racism (Henry, 2007: 28).

There is a difference between having an experience and not having it and more so between having an experience repeatedly, based on the colour of your skin, and never having it at all. This speaks to how 'ethnicities' are racialised: for instance, 'ethnic minorities' are seen as different and inferior, because of ascribed racial differences that are almost always reduced to phenotypic differences. Shared experiences of racialised inclusion or exclusion come from being treated as subordinated or privileged in a systemic sense. Thus it is the relationship between knowledge and power that needs to be considered with regard to racialised social processes, because the effects of 'race' as 'truth' are produced within discourses that are themselves neither 'true' nor 'false'. We therefore need to examine how ideas of 'truth' are historically shaped, mindful that all systems of knowledge, including sociological knowledge, are implicated in relations of power, which is why a solely class-based analysis is unrealistic in this form of sociological inquiry.

The second perspective argues that the issues surrounding 'race' with regard to power and social divisions represent a unique set of sociological problems in their own right, thereby opposing the suggestion that 'race' can be reduced or explained by the class conflicts within the economic structure, as 'race' only arises out of present social conditions. The argument is that the social factors that shape and condition those beliefs about 'race' should be investigated. So, for instance, if you are Black, highly qualified with an impressive track record in your given field and still find that in 2009 you are being discriminated against with regard to promotion or such like, it is pointless you looking solely inward to find answers. Ignoring the manner in which the society you live in is structured along a racial hierarchy, where Whiteness is valued and Blackness is not, is tantamount to committing social suicide. In this type of analysis, where understanding the effects of 'systemic' or 'institutionalised racism' is crucial to the outcome, there must be a focus on the historical particularities of the communities in question, for 'there is nothing simple about being Black in British society' (John, 2006: 279). Doing so will provide an explanatory framework from which we can dismiss matters of coincidence or the 'unwitting' actions of individual racists and ascertain how racialised beliefs have so much currency in contemporary British society. Otherwise we run the risk of reproducing the same line of argument that ignores the voices of those who are the main recipients of racialised discriminatory practices, because 'people are trapped in history and history is trapped in people' (Baldwin, 1985: 81). Consequently, we must recognise that our ideas of history are what inform the present reality and as such we must be mindful that:

> Once people choose to attribute variable social meanings to physical differences and behave as if biology did fix attributes and abilities, then that becomes a part of social reality. What people make of physical differences, the everyday or commonsense notions which influence them, constitutes the social meaning of race. (Richardson and Lambert, 1985: 16)

The suggestion is that by utilising this aspect of 'social reality' a serious challenge can be made to Marxist conceptions of 'race' as class struggles, highlighting various 'sites and mechanisms of power and domination which were not reducible to class and exploitation' (Best and Kellner, 1991: 205). Indeed, it is now commonly accepted within sociology as a discipline that modern theories of racism should begin with the death of the much maligned biological dimension. This argument is generally forwarded as there is no 'scientific' evidence to support any notion of an inherent superiority or inferiority, premised on phenotypic difference, between the 'races'. Nevertheless, it is precisely because the concept of 'race' has no biological foundation, and is therefore a constructed generalised ideal, that it can influence and often determine a group's 'social reality' at a given historical moment.

Crucially, then, the specificity of the historical experiences of the Black communities – whose forefathers and -mothers were brutally exploited as chattel slaves, from which came our present-day exploitation as colonial and post-colonial subjects – needs to be considered. For it is suggested that 'colonialism took over where slavery left off, ensuring that our labour would continue to bolster and maintain the British economy for years to come' (Bryan *et al.*, 1985: 10). Making these palpable historical links known enables us to appreciate why the

Caribbean migrants who sought gainful employment upon their arrival in Britain, during the 1950s and 1960s, found that the kinds of work they were offered soon became known as 'black jobs'. They were the types of employment that would stymie their social mobility and stifle their aspirations, based solely on the colour of their skin and not qualifications because:

> due to racism 'you couldn't get a civil servants job, or any job, in fact, that's commensurate with your education'. Dishwashing, assembly line work, street sweeping, and other manual labouring jobs were taken by individuals trained to be teachers, accountants and administrators. Nursing was the main occupation into which women went; although this provided housing (in largely West Indian-occupied nurses' homes), training and a skilled profession, wages were poor, chances for promotion were minimal, and the duties given to the immigrants were the most undesirable. (Vertovec, 1993: 172)

Vertovec makes known how the system of oppression ensured that Black people inhabited the spaces that were assigned to them in the employment market in Britain, guaranteeing that their structural placement was consistent with how the colonies were organised around the exploitation of Black labour. A factor that makes even more sense when we realise that many of these West Indians ended up in Britain due 'to the pressures placed on people to sell their land' (Campbell, 1986: 86). Hence, whilst it is clear to appreciate that 'race' may not be 'real' with regard to marking biological differences; its consequences certainly are for the Black communities who are left to combat its historical legacy in all aspects of everyday existence. We must therefore be prudent when evaluating the ramifications of a historical legacy that impacts on the manner in which we explain current Black life, because without taking these aspects into consideration the picture will remain biased and incomplete. More importantly, many of the 'experts' on Black life are White researchers who analyse the Black subject/object at a distance, and once the interview is completed, the project is written up, or the computer is shut down for the day they can safely retreat into their private comfort zone. This means that the cloak of Whiteness that insulates many of them from the reality of the condition of the descendants of the African chattel slaves is seldom questioned, except during those moments when they specifically challenge it under the guise of 'white studies'. Therefore, social scientists and other commentators should consider and acknowledge, especially if they are White, how much authority is placed on their accounts of the Black experience in Britain because:

Institutionalised by university seals of approval, such knowledges impact on the life chances of people who find themselves measured, not only by the abuses of overt racism but also by the insidious cultural ortho- doxies of the academic imagination. (Keith, 1992: 551)

Keith suggests that a major concern in these debates are the products of the 'academic imagination' that have a truth-like quality bestowed on them, which is highly problematic when dealing with a thorny issue such as 'race'. This is why 'race' poses so many epistemological pro- blems for disciplines that claim to be 'scientific', because science can- not deal with a variable that promotes an acceptance of an 'imagined' natural 'difference'. Consequently, in their endeavours to address the above epistemological concerns, many social commentators have often, through the debates centred on racism and social exclusion, sought to 'provide' marginalised groups with a platform for debating alterna- tive models of social, economic and political discourse. By recognis- ing plurality through media such as the politics of identity and difference they argue that 'the politics of difference, diversity and identity have given a new edge to demands for equality and social justice' (Meekoosha, 1993: 172).

Marginalised Black groups and individuals who had been ren- dered invisible, or voiceless, during modernity were now seen to be utilising the vehicle of post-modernism to demonstrate the need for 'multiple forms of struggle' in their pursuit of 'social justice'. However, I would argue that even though post-modern discourse gives both indi- viduals and marginalised groups a theoretical model out of which they can articulate and even valorise their differences, its influence on 'race' and racialised thinking has been counter-productive. In fact, this notion of celebrating difference in 'fragmented' western societies 'has normalised a form of ghoulish separateness – a form of segregation which exists simultaneously with cosmopolitanism' (Harris, 1993: 38). This in turn does little to tackle the real issue of how a valorisa- tion of that difference can in fact enhance 'your' subordinated racialised status in a racist society, as real equality between the 'races' gets placed on the back burner. The point is that by celebrating your 'otherness' without addressing the historical circumstances that created that 'other' as an inferior, you run the risk of becoming embroiled in a series of meaningless endeavours. These will serve to further obscure the seminal role you play in your own liberation, because 'the white man has already implanted numerous historical myths in the minds of black peoples; those have to be uprooted' (Rodney, 1969: 51).

One way to deploy Rodney's 'uprooting' process is by realising that the right to be different does not equate to a right to be treated as a social, cultural or political equal, as this reductive redefinition closes off this prospect by promoting cultural diversity. The problem is that whenever 'we' think of 'cultural diversity', 'we' are mostly thinking about the ways of being of the 'ethnics': those marked as non-White by the dominant White society. The irony is that the Whites who are indigenous to the British Isles, especially the English, are seldom thought about as belonging to 'ethnic' groups, which is why we never hear about ethnic majorities in the context of the UK. White people do not really have to consider how their Whiteness is an ever-present non-presence that moulds and shapes a lived reality, bestowing benefits and privileges that have to be earned, in one way or another, by other ethnic groups. The point is that uncritically embracing cultural diversity as the 'right to be different', does little to counter the fact that we are socialised into accepting that 'the whiteness of whiteness is the blindness of wilful innocence' (Lazarre, 1997: 49).

Therefore, this notion of cultural diversity can, rather ironically, be promoted as 'universally' acceptable, because it does little to dispense with the quaint, exotic or even bizarre notion of the inferior 'African/ Black other', who is deemed to be culturally different. These arguments do not deal with the real issue of how 'race' and its highly stratified nature has become the norm in British society, which, when confronted, explains why it is such an ever-present aspect of our contemporary social reality. Nor can they explain the manner in which that sense of distance between the 'races' that was formulated and perpetuated by scientific discourse, presently manifests in various acceptable but distinct cultural forms based on a Black–White dichotomy. The suggestion is that we must be mindful of how the hierarchical 'distance' that was created between the 'races' during modernity's quest for scientific rationality, has been replaced by a 'distance' created by recognising acceptable difference. For its rationale, as we shall discover in the next section, is derived from the most pernicious aspects of scientific racism that manifest as contemporary discriminatory practices.

Science, colonialism and the birth of acceptable distance

Scientific racism received much of its theoretical currency from the likes of Voltaire, who argued 'only a blind man could doubt that the whites, Negroes, albinos, Hottentots, Laplanders, Chinese, are entirely different races' (Malik, 1996: 53). This gives rise to a major concern, which is for us to appreciate how this type of racialised thinking, in the sense of hierarchies with White at the apex, became a constant feature in scientific discourse during the next two centuries. More importantly, 'although white racism affects all "non-white" peoples, Africans and people of African ancestry are the particular targets of the resurgence of a neo-scientistic racism' (Rigby, 1996: 2–3). A mindset that impacts on our present social reality as exemplified in the work of the 'bell curve' theorists (Herrnstein and Murray, 1996) who still hold fast to Enlightenment principles such as: 'The moment in which Kant compromised himself by associating the figure of the "Negro" with stupidity and connecting differences in color to differences in mental capacity' (Gilroy, 2004: 9).

We may be of a mind to believe that the days of using this type of irrational 'rationality' for explaining human variation is no longer relevant, but it was in 2006 that a university professor in Leeds, who is an advocate of the 'bell curve' theory, suggested that 'on average, black people are less intelligent than white people' (Gabriel, 2006). Regardless of how incredibly racist and scientifically untenable we may find such a suggestion, it speaks to the persistence of 'race' as a tool that is constantly being reinvented and reworked by the arbiters of scientific reason. The suggestion being that:

> The neutrality and distantiation of the rational scientist created the theoretical space for a view to develop subjectless bodies. Once subjectified these bodies could be analysed, categorised, classified, and ordered with the cold gaze of scientific distance. (Goldberg cited in Young, 1996: 41)

It is this notion of 'scientific distance' we must unpack here, as the distance between Europeans and Africans has been maintained through a discourse that subsumes the social, cultural and political dimensions of 'race' and subsequently offers solutions that appeal to a common-sense understanding of difference. These appeals to common sense do little to dispel the inherently stratified nature of racial thinking, and many post-modern theorists, inadvertently, give this viewpoint credibility as they argue for a celebration of the right to be different. Advocating the right to be different has created a tension in sociological thinking, a veritable 'crisis of modernity' as modernist equations of 'reason' with 'freedom' are rejected. Furthermore, modernist forms of rationality are deemed to be 'reductive' and 'oppressive' as they are nothing more than ideological 'constructs of domination' (Best and Kellner, 1991: 237) that appeal to a common-sense idea of living in a 'plural society', without recognising the seminal role colonisation played in the creation and maintenance of these constructs.

Fanon's writings on such constructs are replete with examples of how the 'plural' nature of 'colonial societies' manifest in real-life situations and how 'racial pluralism' determines the rules for both 'oppression' and 'resistance'. It is crucial that we understand this relationship because it helps to explain why the struggles of Black communities, economic or otherwise, cannot be reduced to the historical experiences of White families or individuals. Our right to be different is a necessary consequence of wilful segregation, because what often separates 'us' from 'them' is generally what unites 'them' against 'us'. The crucial factor is that the Enlightenment fuelled ideological visions of 'rationality' and 'progress' that depended upon and were determined by, the notions of major 'racial' and 'cultural' differences between Europeans and the indigenous 'others' they globally encountered. Consequently, part of the way we arguably socialise ourselves and our children, as former colonial subjects in the mother country, is to make known that being Black is being a 'problem' in a racist society. Furthermore 'racial socialization is the process whereby we come to know our strengths, understand the world in which we live, and position ourselves to strive' (Leary, 2005: 200). In attempting to explain why this is so, Fanon states that, in the 'colonial' context, the 'cause is the consequence; you are rich because you are white, you are white because you are rich' (Fanon, 1986: 31). Following this line of argument, Fanon suggests that because the 'whites' became rich through a 'colonialism' premised on 'violence'; the 'moral justification' of 'violence' derives from 'the good fortune of those who rule, and the misery of those who are ruled' (Kuper, 1974: 67). Unsurprisingly then:

> It seems uncontroversial to claim that the roots of the racialized postmodern city can be traced to the end of the colonial era. Not until this conjuncture did the metropolises of the West have to confront directly the 'problem of the racially marginalized', of reproducing racial marginalization in their own spaces'. Throughout the colonial era, racialized others were defined in terms of a different biology and a different history, where they were actually considered to have a history at all. (Goldberg, 1995: 46)

Goldberg suggests that in order to understand the roots of contemporary forms of racialisation that underpin the most pernicious and blatant forms of Black social exclusion, we must consider how spaces are reconfigured both in the physical and psychological senses. I am claiming that, in order to comprehend the sites of resistance and transcendence that have enabled the Black communities to be here in this place and at this time, we need to appreciate what is often regarded by many Whites as unsociable or deviant behaviour. This involves the utilisation of identifiably Black cultural forms that were there to galvanise Black people through the recognition of the commonality of their condition; the shared experiences of racist discriminatory practices at the hands of the dominant White community. Indeed, it is the overlooking of these factors that has led to many of the current misunderstandings of what constitutes Black family life and the role and purpose of retaining a sense of difference, as a coping and transcendental mechanism in a hostile environment. For it is the distinct phenotypic variations found within the human family that are the most obvious determinants of inequality between the 'races', even though the biological aspect has been exposed as being literally 'skin deep'. Thus:

> The elaboration of inequality is most marked in the economy and education . . . Inequalities in political rights, in economic participation, in education, ramify throughout the society. They combine with ideologies of cultural difference, contemptuous stereotypes, segregation and other discriminatory devices to give rise to a many-faceted general status of ruling race and subject race. (Kuper, 1974: 269–70)

In line with Kuper's argument I want to suggest that we must appreciate how certain members of the Black communities in the UK recognise 'cultural difference' and use it to strengthen and empower themselves. Furthermore, comprehending how the racial element becomes a liberatory tool for those who are at the far end of the racialised scale for measuring normality is crucial to this argument. Because the history of the African's structural placement in Europe's New World as the 'uncivilised other' only makes sense when it is understood to be a controlling practice that renders the Black 'uncivilised' African as the antithesis of the White 'civilised' European. To make the point clearer, in the final section I will present an example of how such practices were resisted and transcended by the Black communities in Britain.

Strategic avoidance and the embracing of difference

Much has been written on the impact that the arrival of the 'Windrush generation' had on the dominant White communities in the UK from the late 1940s. Particularly in the context of the cultural misunderstandings that took place on both sides, there was an assumption that both parties had an idea of what to expect from each other. However, the truth is that these Caribbean migrants were really an unknown quantity in the UK because the majority of the indigenous White population had very little contact with Black people. That is why the particularities of the lifestyles they knew and obviously transported with them when they came to the 'mother country' for a short term 'visit' became highly problematic. This meant that the cultural, religious, political and social sensibilities that they took for granted, which all members of the human family use as a template for existence in a rudimentary sense, were deemed to be strange, bizarre and more importantly threatening too many of the ordinary White citizens they came in contact with on a daily basis. One possible way to understand this occurrence was that the White working-class people, who Blacks invariably ended up living tooth to jowl with, had little if any practical experience of the lifestyles of these 'dark strangers' (Patterson, 1964). Having very little meaningful contact with Blacks meant that their ideas of Black life were based on a common-sense understanding of what they 'knew' about these 'others'. This is also more often than not the case for the Blacks who came to Britain, so a really important point for us to consider here is where did their knowledge of each other come from? One way I will suggest is through popular cultural forms such as films that glorified the British Empire and the correctness of 'civilised' White domination of 'uncivilised' non-White others. A factor that Young suggests occurred when:

> During the 1920s, Britain's Colonial Office decided to exploit the propaganda qualities of film as it set out to explore how best to capitalize on cinema's potential for disseminating imperial ideology. There was a concern that some of the images of white people could be interpreted as deriding European or British culture . . . and eventually such texts were censored for screenings in the colonies. (Young, 1996: 66)

Young's observation allows us to think about how this form of colonial propaganda impacted on the Black and White communities who would be exposed to these forms of racist propaganda. Firstly, it provided a template for many White people to 'know' these colonised others and firmly appreciate where their placement in the world should be, which is 'out there', somewhere in the colonies as the subjects of 'our' rule. Secondly, it deluded many White people into believing they knew what to expect when those who were ruled 'out there' were 'invited' to come over here to assist in the rebuilding of the mother country after World War Two. What then became problematic for the White majority was when these Blacks, more often than not, failed to act out the stereotypical roles that myriad forms of media propaganda had readied them to expect. In fact, members of the Black communities often found themselves faced with difficult situations that were the result of cultural misunderstandings with the dominant White community, where their ordinary behaviour was often interpreted as bizarre and unwelcome. For instance, Patterson (1964) identified a cultural gap between the newcomers and hosts, in spite of superficial similarities of language and religion. In Brixton, the White population largely upheld 'respectable' norms that stressed privacy, 'keeping themselves to themselves', cleanliness and tidiness, quietness and family propriety. But, she pointed out that, no migrant group has in the mass so signally failed to conform to these expectations and patterns as have the West Indians. The newcomers tended to be noisy and gregarious, and less fastidious about housekeeping standards, and they had a higher proportion of common-law marriages. These departures from 'normal' expectations inevitably caused tensions between the two communities (Richardson and Lambert, 1985: 33).

This is not the place for me to discuss the obvious cultural distortions and myopia that underpin Patterson's account of Black family life (Henry, 2007: 20), where 'the onus is upon black "immigrants" to assimilate' (Graham, 2002: 38). Rather, I wish to focus on what she describes as 'superficial similarities of language and religion', because one thing that many from the Caribbean thought they had in common with White society was indeed the English language and religious practices. Yet the reality was different as even an innocuously simple activity such as worshipping in the local church caused consternation amongst the White masses who were often perplexed by the actions of the Black members of the congregation. Blacks would fail to sit passively and wait for the given moment when they were 'allowed' to participate, as there was an expectance to be 'moved' by the 'word' throughout the service. This meant that Blacks would often engage in impromptu antiphonic exchanges with the preacher because being an active part of the service is the norm in African-derived forms of worship. Hence the resultant clash of cultures occurred as:

> inside white mainstream churches, African Caribbean British people are asked to engage in liturgies which negatively evaluate blackness, black people and black culture. Nowhere is this more telling than in the songs and hymnody of the Anglican and Methodist churches. In these churches 'real' music is generally 'white church music'. Cultural racism is the prime cause of this historical trend. Let me explain. Black liturgies are fixed and essentialised in the mainstream psyche as 'loud', 'crude' and far too 'emotional'. (Beckford, 1998: 35)

Beckford's comments reveal how the pejorative language that is used to describe Black forms of Christian worship is the same as used in other White explanations of Black 'deviant' and 'unsociable' behaviour.

Indeed the underlying assumption is that whatever White people do is 'right' as their way of doing things is the yardstick that is used to measure normal behaviour, juxtaposed against the 'fixed' and 'essentialised' behaviour of Black people. The fact is that these are products of a White racist imagination that placed being godlike – Christian – as the sole purview of being White, and therefore 'correct' forms of worship were also measured by being White. This takes on a serious dimension for us here because the majority of Africans and people of African ancestry, as has been extensively argued in various places (Barrett, 1977; Beckford, 2001, 2006; Campbell, 1986; Cruz, 1999), largely embraced Christianity during the chattel slave era. Many would therefore use Christianity as a coping mechanism to deal with real earthly concerns that on the surface appeared insurmountable; for them salvation from the oppression they faced in the UK was found in the forms of worship and prayer that enabled their ancestors to overcome the horrors of chattel enslavement. This in turn explains how coping and transcendental mechanisms that are part and parcel of expressive cultures, sacred or secular, are transmitted through the generations across time and space.

It was this form of worship and prayer that was the cause of fear and consternation amongst the Whites in attendance who had no experience of praising God in this way. What then become apparent are the distinct differences in what was expected from the service by the White and Black members of the congregation. The Whites were generally expected to sit passively and receive whatever they were given by the preacher and vocally participate during the singing of hymns or saying of prayers. Whereas Blacks saw the sermon as a space within which they could purge themselves of traumatic experiences through ritualised drama, as the Black church creates an environment that encourages individual and collective emotional involvement. Thus what for them is being communicated is based on eliciting a collective response from the preacher's individual call, for the medium does not restrict that which is being communicated and is there to promote both incitement and catharsis. Therefore the cultural conflict that arose from the encroachment of Black forms of worship into the White Christian space of worship can be explained as a form of historical, cultural continuity. Of even more importance, these Black forms of worship contain the types of defiance and resistance that enabled families and communities to recognise the commonality of their condition during the chattel slave era.

Alleyne suggests that during this period there was a merging of African and European religious forms with music and dance: that which became a key factor in unifying the chattel slaves, 'because they were major instruments of both cohesion and revolt' (Alleyne, 1988: 118). This type of merging is, according to Spencer, not unusual for people of African ancestry as it is akin to an African notion of spreading or transmitting a 'social gospel', which dealt with real earthly problems (Spencer, 1995: 68). This means the religious message had to be conveyed in a manner in which the people could truly recognise their own social position and more importantly actively participate as part of a recognised collective to remedy this position. Moreover, Africans on the continent and their descendants within the diaspora were, and still mainly are, expected to partake in religious ceremonies through orality and rhythmic movement, because 'African religious traditions take into consideration not only one's intellect, but also one's emotions, the mental and the visceral' (Barrett, 1988: 27). Hence, unlike the European missionaries, the African did not condemn rhythmic movement of the body and spontaneity of the voice as they regarded them as intrinsic aspects of worship. Far more importantly, they realized that they could use 'Christianity as a shield against a social system that aimed at nothing less than pulverizing them into docile, compliant bodies' (Cruz, 1999: 87). The sentiments behind recognising the reality of racist oppression and using your counter-cultural forms as 'ideological weaponry' (Cooper, 2000) to combat it have remained a constant in Black life. Because this 'releases within the people a feeling of power over everyday suffering and poverty and oppression, as well as a physical closeness or even oneness with the great gods and spirits of their religion' (Barrett, 1988: 118–19).

It is the idea of self-empowerment, resistance and transcendence that comes from embracing identifiably Black cultural forms that has enabled Blacks to rebuild family and community within the confines of the White world. For this reason when the Windrush generation came to these shores and were faced with all forms of oppression, both individually and collectively, they already had tried and trusted methods in place to counter White racism and largely understood that:

> For many white people who believe themselves to be tolerant, understanding, accepting and so on it is often very difficult to appreciate the multiplicity of mechanisms that exist in a society which perpetuates systems of disadvantage among black people ... the ideology of racism is an immensely complex and changing phenomenon, and consequently racist practices become less visible, less specific and are therefore more difficult to notice and comprehend. (Lago and Thompson, 1996: 21)

Appreciating this reality led many Blacks to distance themselves from points of potential conflict with Whites and create their own places of worship and other sites of socialisation. Because 'the over-determining salience of race in Britain led many migrants to close ranks regardless of class . . . as many . . . felt that all Jamaicans were in the same social class' (Harris, 1993: 244). Harris' observation is also true for non-Jamaican migrants, as many White Britons believed that if you were Black and spoke with an accent you were Jamaican, due to the obvious numerical advantage that Jamaicans had at that time. The suggestion is 'that in Britain, it is evident that Jamaican culture is hegemonic in the Gramscian sense of leadership and influence among Caribbean heritage communities as a whole' (Tate, 2002: 198). Therefore, it is crucial for us to appreciate the significance of this occurrence as it is a doorway to understanding how the various peoples from the Caribbean pulled together to ensure their continued survival in a hostile, racist environment.

Conclusion

Many who have endeavoured to theorise the impact of White racism on the Black communities in the UK have failed to regard this relationship as one of ongoing European aggression against people of African ancestry. Failing to perceive it as such ensures that the immediate concerns of people of African ancestry have either been viewed through the lens of wider social concerns, or have been dismissed entirely as matters of re-education. Such re-education generally entails stripping away the worldviews and cultural forms that the migrants brought with them, along with their suitcases, when they came to these shores as the Windrush generation. In other words, that which prevents their full assimilation as British citizens is in essence the tried and trusted modes of resistance and transcendence that were a constant source of re-linking with their humanity during the Maafa of the African holocaust: the chattel slave experience. For this reason any explanation of contemporary Black life must interrogate the critical role that notions of Whiteness play in all aspects of Black socialisation, in an inherently racist society such as Britain. By doing so we will be better placed to unshackle the African mind and mount a meaningful challenge to White supremacist 'thoughts and actions' (Henry, 2006) that offers an alternative epistemological and ontological take on what it means to be Black from an 'insider' perspective. A failure to do so is to remain complicit in our own self-destruction, for the mainstay of the Black communities have been and still are the identifiably Black cultural forms that provide us with the tools to combat racism and other forms of exclusionary practices across a range of social, cultural and political contexts. For it was such practices that the Windrush generation utilised when they arrived in Britain to ensure their and our survival, and to overlook the significance of the building blocks they left for future generations is to do them and our ancestors a gross injustice. This is what needs to be understood in any endeavour to better our current racialised predicament in meaningful and practical ways.

References

Alleyne, M. (1988), *Roots of Jamaican Culture* (London: Pluto Press)

Back, L. (1996), *New Ethnicities and Urban Culture* (London: UCL Press)

Barrett, L. E. (1988), *The Rastafarians: Sounds of Cultural Dissonance* (Boston: Beacon Press)

Barrett, L. E. (1977), *The Rastafarians: The Dreadlocks of Jamaica* (Boston: Beacon Press)

Baldwin, J. (1985), *The Price of a Ticket* (New York: St Martins)

Beckford, R. (2006), *Jesus Dub: Theology, Music and Social Change* (London: Routledge)

Beckford, R. (2001), *God of The Rahtid; Redeeming Rage* (London: Darton, Longman and Todd Ltd)

Beckford, R. (1998), *Jesus is Dread Black theology and Black Culture in Britain* (London: Longman and Todd)

Best, S. and Kellner, D. (1991), *Postmodern Theory* (London: Palgrave Macmillan)

Bryan, B., Dadzie, S. and Scafe, S. (1985), *Heart of the Race: Black Women's Lives in Britain* (London: Virago Press)

Campbell, H. (1986), *Rasta and Resistance* (London: Hansib Publishing)

Cooper, C. (2000), 'Rhythms of resistance: Jamaican dancehall culture and the politics of survival' (Paper received via email to author of chapter, May 2000)

Cruz, J. (1999), *Culture on The Margins: The Black Spiritual and the Rise of American Cultural Interpretation* (Princeton, NJ: Princeton Press)

Dyer, R. (1997), *White* (London: Routledge)

Fanon, F. (1986), *Black Skin, White Masks* (London, Pluto Press)

Gilroy, P. (2004), *After Empire: Melancholia or Convivial Culture* (Oxford: Routledge)

Gilroy, P. (2000), *Between Camps: Nations, Cultures and the Allure of Race* (London: Penguin Books)

Gilroy, P. (1987), *There Ain't No Black in the Union Jack* (London: Hutchinson)

Goldberg, D. T. (1995), 'Polluting the body politic: Racist discourse and urban location', in Cross, M. and Keith, M. (eds), *Racism, the City and the State* (London: Routledge)

Graham, M. (2002), *Social Work and African-Centred World Views* (Birmingham: Venture Press)

Harris, C. (1993), 'Post-war migration and the industrial reserve army', in James, W. and Harris, C. (eds), *Inside Babylon: The Caribbean Diaspora In Britain* (London: Verso)

Henry, W. (2007), *Whiteness Made Simple: Stepping Into the GREY zone* (London: Learning By Choice Publications)

Henry, W. (2006), *What The Deejay Said: A Critique From The Street* (London: Learning By Choice Publications)

Herrnstein, R. J. and Murray, C. (1996), *Bell Curve: Intelligence and Class Structure in American Life* (New York: Free Press Paperbacks)

John, G. (2006), *Taking A Stand: Gus John Speaks on Education, Race, Social Action and Civil Unrest 1980–2005* (Manchester: Gus John Partnership)

Keith, M. (1992), 'Angry writing: (re)presenting the unethical world of the ethnographer', *Society and Space*, 10, 551–68

Kuper, L. (1974), *Race Class and Power* (London: G. Duckworth and Company)

Lago, C. and Thompson, J. (1996), *Race, Culture, and Counselling* (London: Open University Press)

Lazarre, J. (1997), *Beyond the Whiteness of Whiteness* (Durham, NC, and London: Duke University Press)

Leary, J. D. (2005), *Post Traumatic Slave Syndrome: America's Legacy of Enduring Injury and Healing* (Milwaukee, WI: Uptown Press)

Malik, K. (1996), *The Meaning of Race* (London: Palgrave Macmillan)

Meekoosha, M. (1993), 'The bodies politic – equality, difference and community practice', in Butcher, H. A., Glen, P., Henderson, J. and Smith, J. (eds), *Community and Public Policy* (London: Pluto Press)

Miles, R. (1982), *Racism and Migrant Labour* (London: Routledge and Kegan Paul)

Nobles, W. and Goddard, L. L. (1984), *Understanding Black Family: A Guide for Scholarship And Research* (Oakland, CA: Black Family Institute)

Patterson, S. (1964), *Dark Strangers* (Bloomington: Indiana University Press)

Richardson, J. and Lambert, J. (1985), 'The sociology of race', in Haralambos, M. (ed.), *Sociology New Directions* (Ormskirk: Causeway Press)

Rigby, P. (1996), *African Images: Racism and the End of Anthropology* (Oxford: Berg)

Rodney, W. (1969), *Groundings with My Brothers* (London: Bogle-L'Overture)

Spencer, J. M. (1995), *The Rhythms of Black Folk: Race, Religion and Pan-Africanism* (Trenton, NJ: Africa World Press Inc.)

Tate, S. (2002), 'Colour matters, "race" matters: Afrikan Caribbean identity in the 21st Century', in Christian, M. (ed.), *Black Identity in the 20th Century: Expressions of the US and UK Afrikan Diaspora* (London: Hansib)

Vertovec, S. (1993), 'Indo-Caribbean experience in Britain: overlooked', in James, W. and Harris, C. (eds), *Inside Babylon: The Caribbean Diaspora In Britain* (London: Verso)

Welsing, F. C. (1991), *The Isis Papers: The Keys to the Colors* (Chicago: Third World Press)

Young, L. (1996), *Fear of the Dark* (London: Routledge)

Internet source

Gabriel, D. (2006), 'Bell Curve Theory spouted by Ellis widely discredited' www.blackbritain.co.uk

9

The cultural politics of African Caribbean and West African families in the UK

Perry Stanislas

This chapter explores the experiences and challenges facing African Caribbean and West African families in Britain. Specifically, it addresses the experience of migration and settlement, and the role of racism in structuring the latter process. Secondly, it addresses how this shapes the cultural and political orientation of these families and the strategies relied on in pursuit of individual and collective goals and their contribution to familial problems. Thirdly, it identifies the factors that bring these communities into contact with the criminal justice system. Finally, the chapter explores the relationship of these ethnic groups to the political system in efforts to influence key issues affecting family life.

Introduction

This paper has its origins in the Fourth National Survey of Ethnic Minorities in Britain by Berthould *et al.* (1997), specifically in response to a number of important changes within the African Caribbean community and their implications for family formation. An interesting omission in this study is Black Africans, which is particularly revealing given their long history with Britain (Fryer, 1984).

Of special interest is how these communities have responded to challenges that characterise the experiences of Black ethnic groups given the importance of colour, class and culture in determining life-chances (Rattansi and Westwood, 1994; Stanislas, 2009). These issues are also critical to discussions about social capital, family structures and ethnicity (Goulbourne, 2006; Reynolds, 2004). Social capital seeks to describe practices that facilitate power and social inclusion. Critical to this process is the maintenance of ethnic group consciousness that may conflict with prevailing notions of integration.

Inter-racial relationships and family formation

Many of the contemporary changes that have weakened the African Caribbean family – such as the increase in lone-parent families, the significant decline in marriage, high divorce rates and increasing numbers living alone – have all been noted (Berthould *et al.*, 1997). An area that has not received adequate attention is the issue of inter-racial relationships. The picture of increasing numbers of African Caribbeans entering relationships with others outside of their ethnic group, predominantly Whites, along with the aforementioned factors, reinforces concern about the impact of cultural changes on this minority ethnic group and how this constrains the ability of its leadership to address problems (Dench, 1996; Stanislas, 2006).

The social significance of inter-racial relationships has been of critical importance as an indicator of White racial tolerance in the context of migration and settlement (Banton, 1985; Patterson, 1963). Berrington (1994) maintains that assimilation of ethnic minority communities has long been a governmental goal in responding to new minorities. Fortier (2005) and Holmes (1991: 91) indicate that the notion of racial tolerance as popularly articulated is often racist, especially regarding notions of assimilation. Berrington (1994) highlights the difficulties with this goal given the discrimination experienced by minority ethnic communities. Beishoon *et al.* (1998) and Modood *et al.* (1997) cite the resistance to assimilation in familial matters, particularly amongst Asian communities, on cultural grounds. In the case of African Caribbeans, while sharing Asian cultural anxieties, they also expressed resistance to this practice based on political terms (Stanislas, 2006: 27–49).

These concerns have taken the form of sharp criticism from sections of the African Caribbean community of the disproportionate number of high-profile group members who have White partners (Hare, 1989: 86; Song and Edwards, 1997: 236; *Sunday Times*, 1997). Of particular salience is the portrayal of inter-racial relations as the predominant representation of African Caribbean preferences on television programmes such as 'EastEnders' and the racism that underpins this (Williamson, 2005: 15–17). This is seen as having a negative impact on African Caribbeans' self-esteem and their perceptions by denying them a positive cultural identity, which is part of the process of dehumanisation (Fanon, 1967). The role of dominant institutions in this context applies pressure on African Caribbean group boundaries in attempts to breach it (Wallman, 1986), or 'culturally invade' (Freire, 1970).

An important issue raised by the high rates of inter-racial marriages is the implications for the development, if not long-term survival, of the African Caribbean community, given its size of just more than 1 per cent of the UK population and its zero growth rate (Berthould, 2000: 13; Modood *et al.*, 1997: 342), especially as inter-racial marriages have a marginal effect on the White dominant group, while having an adverse effect on the former (Hare, 1989: 161–2; Office for National Statistics, 2001). This is reinforced by the fact that mixed-race people have the highest rates of inter-ethnic marriages and are more likely to marry Whites, further reducing the African Caribbean community (Berrington, 1994; Office for National Statistics, 2001). Interestingly, Dual Heritage individuals sometimes hold racist views towards Blacks (Gilbert, 2005: 56; Stanislas, 2006: 48). This is against a background of Britain having completely assimilated several settlements of Blacks since the fifteenth century, which is an important factor, along with migration controls, for the small size of the Black population in the country (Chamberlain and Goulbourne, 2001). These anxieties differ from those of previous generations, where concern was about low numbers of African Caribbean women (Selvon, 1956; Patterson, 1963), or the novelty value of Black males having access to White women given the historic availability of subordinate Black women to dominant White men (Fanon, 1967; Song and Edwards, 1997: 238). These worries also diverge from the traditional pattern of inter-racial relationships being restricted to minority males (Berrington, 1994: 534; Dench, 1996).

The disproportionate amount of African Caribbeans engaged in inter-racial relationships (approximately 50 per cent: Berthoud *et al.*, 1997: 342) has been explained as an indicator of other social factors, such as a 'propelled desire to escape from the ethnic group and its problems' (Dench, 1996: 51) or what Banton (1985) terms an 'exit strategy', and complements the charges of 'self-hate' levelled at celebrities and witnessed amongst other communities such as Jews (Allport, 1987: 152–3; Fanon, 1967: 18–24).

For Wallman (1986: 230) the high rates of African Caribbeans in mixed relationships are indicative of the greater transparency and penetrability of the community's cultural boundaries (compared to Asians), distinguished by the relative ease by which 'outsiders' can cross them, and the weak normative constraints limiting its members from reciprocating. This complements Banton's (1985) description of the 'push' and 'pull' factors at work in minority ethnic communities. In this instance, the push factors are represented by the dissatisfaction of African Caribbeans with the partners available within its ethnic boundaries compared to the opportunities outside of it.

West African families

There is a dearth of research on West African families and how they have adapted to British life. Craven's (1968) study of West African students provides the broad contours of much of what is known about aspects of their social life. Equally, Craven makes many important observations that subsequent generations of scholars have failed to develop. One area is the familial complexities of West Africans, often with wives back home and in Britain, given that a significant number were mature students. In many cases this contributed to wives and family being abandoned, while new relationships were formed and in others dual relationships operating simultaneously (Craven, 1968: 50). On the other hand, this could lead to new girlfriends or children being abandoned when the student returned home.

While the importance of White female partners to African Caribbean males has been noted, the status attached to them for significant numbers of West African males is described by Craven (1968: 13). The gendered nature of migration led to many West African males forming relations with White women. Craven notes that relationships with White women were not only crucial in providing much important support for struggling students, as well as opportunities for exploitation, but were liberating for many who were removed from the weight of familial expectations and obligations common to West Africans, given their relative anonymity in a foreign country. The pressures on West African students to perform cannot be underestimated and can be seen in the most extreme cases of suicide and mental illness (Chinouya and Elam, 2001; Craven, 1968).

For many Africans, relationships with White women were seen as a symbol of prestige (Fanon, 1967). Craven (1968) notes that many students left home countries with the expressed intention of obtaining a White wife or girlfriend. The outcome of these relationships can be seen in the disproportionate number of Dual Heritage children of West African fathers in foster-care. The athlete Daley Thompson is an example (Cashmore, 1982). Some of these relationships developed into successful marriages, as evidenced by the parents of Paul Boateng, former Member of Parliament and then, from 2005, British High Commissioner to South Africa (Craven, 1968: 50; Stanislas, 2006). In other instances, West African parents back home encouraged potential wives to go to Britain to marry their sons, given their fears of them forming relations with White women, which had adverse consequences for them economically and culturally, weakening their social capital (Emecheta, 1974; Ogbobode Abidde, 2005).

One of the few studies on familial organisations and cultural practices amongst West Africans in Britain is Goody and Groothues (1979). Their work on gender role segregation amongst patrilineal and matrilineal West Africans found, contrary to prevailing expectations, that there was a large degree of sharing roles and responsibilities, particularly amongst the patrilineal Igbos from Nigeria. Furthermore, families who conformed to traditional role segregation were more likely to experience domestic problems.

A major area of difficulty within many West African families was the issue of money, particularly that earned by wives, and the greater autonomy experienced by women in Britain (Craven, 1968: 21). This is likely to have been even more pressing for failing or frustrated males (Craven, 1968; Emecheta, 1974: 64). The issue of women not meeting traditional expectations was often used to justify male concerns, which masks the fact that this equally applied to males given their new environment and the challenges it entailed (Chinouya and Elam, 2001).

An interesting observation within the literature is evidence of domestic violence against women by West African men or a positive predisposition in this direction (Emecheta, 1974: 64). Stapleton (1978: 23) describes prevalent male attitudes: 'A man should not be cruel to his wife and, although he may beat her, relatives or neighbours will intervene if he takes this too far'.

What is particularly interesting about these findings – despite the dearth of studies on West African families, compared to their African Caribbean counterparts – is the weight given to domestic violence by Nigerian Emecheta and White author Stapleton. Very little regarding domestic violence is found in the work of early commentators on the African Caribbean community, for example Patterson (1963), until Bryant *et al.* (1985), in what can be viewed as a mandatory statement against domestic violence from a Black feminist perspective. These concerns are reinforced by research indicating the high levels of domestic violence in West Africa (Ezechi *et al.*, 2004). This is not to suggest that domestic violence is not an issue of concern within the African Caribbean family (Mama, 1995); its structural characteristics may have some import for its lack of prevalence in Britain, unlike in the Caribbean itself (Bailey and Nain, 2003).

Another area where significant amounts of stress was found in the West African family, and was particularly pronounced in the matrilineal Ashantis from Ghana, was the cultural expectations of men to financially support their sister's children (Emecheta, 1974). Goody and Groothues (1979) found the most dissatisfaction within marriages was amongst the Ashanti, providing some important indications of the potential for change of these practices (Little and Price, 1967).

One area of West African family practice that has probably drawn most attention has been around the issue of childcare and fostering practices. A characteristic of many West African students was that a significant number of them were married with children (Craven, 1968; Stapleton, 1978: 58). Common to most West African cultures children are highly valued (Craven, 1968: 46) and in many cases a marriage is not viewed as binding until a child is born (Little and Price, 1967: 409). While males constituted the majority of students, they were joined by increasing numbers of female students and female economic migrants. West African women, similar to their Caribbean counterparts, are important economic actors in their own right (Hakim, 2003; Stapleton, 1978: 60). This explains the highly instrumental attitudes amongst West Africans in focusing primarily on education and work to earn money, where finding childcare, as in the case of African Caribbean women, was seen as a short-term obstacle. Childcare issues were overcome by the reliance on the African practice of 'fostering' where children were raised by members of the extended family, in common with Caribbean practice (Pryce, 1986: 109–11), or close friends (Caldwell, 1996: 339; Craven, 1968: 80). This led to great demands for White foster-families, often involving placing children in homes a significant distance from the parents' place of residence. This practice led to difficulties with White social-service agencies who interpreted it as uncaring and irresponsible (Craven, 1968: 81).

This concern of social agencies was not unfounded, insofar as the predominant view of those supporting this practice tended to be based on economic concerns with little consideration of its adverse impact on children's welfare. It was not uncommon for babies who were barely months old to be fostered or left in care indefinitely, with little contact with their parents, as in the case of marriage breakdown (Craven, 1968: 25). For example, footballers John and Justin Fashanu, of Nigerian and Guyanese parents, were brought up by foster-parents after the collapse of their parents' marriage (Cashmore, 1982). Evidence of ill-treatment of children (Emecheta, 1974: 49–53) or problems associated with the identity formation *inter alia* of Black children being brought up in an alien White environment, along with changing parental priorities, contributed to the demise of this practice (Craven, 1968: 25).

The problems associated with African fostering practices has drawn the attention of Caldwell (1996), who cites how it leads to disadvantage and ill-treatment in a wide range of areas, such as access to healthcare. He maintains that despite well-established traditions of fostering, there exists a hierarchy of treatment within African family systems based on biological relationships. While it is unknown how prevalent these practices are amongst West Africans in Britain, or African Caribbeans for that matter, the appalling circumstances surrounding the death of Victoria Climbie in 2000 and murder of Toni-Ann Byfield in 2004 gave a chilling reminder of some of the worst outcomes of these customs.

Educational and economic success has been a major stimulus for West African migration and these issues are important in the organisation of crucial areas of family life. Consequently, an important theme in the literature is the educational and economic performance of West Africans and the various ramifications of this for family life. Emecheta (1974) describes how the expectations in coming to Britain for many soon begun to be displaced with bitter experience. Key amongst these was their experiences in employment, which was critical in supporting their education. Central to this was the racial discrimination faced by Black people in the workplace, which had an immediate impact on aspirations. Despite relatively high levels of educational qualifications West Africans found great difficulties obtaining commensurate work. Moreover, they were often disadvantaged by their foreign accents, particularly in terms of how such accents are perceived when possessed by non-Whites (Craven, 1968: 42). This discrepancy between educational qualifications and employment is a characteristic of West Africans, particularly in regards to their under-employment and high levels of unemployment, especially amongst males (Daley, 1996; Dustmann *et al.*, 2003).

Disproportionate concentration in poorer housing and low incomes have been the key factors shaping many social problems experienced by West Africans, some of which have been outlined by Chinouya and Elam (2001). Also identified are the tensions within many families between males and females shaped by the superior opportunities and welfare support available to women, compared to the employment options of many men. There is some indication that many middle-class West Africans use cheaper public housing as a means to accumulate capital for business ventures, while others may seek particular types of employment allowing themselves to do more than one job or possess sufficient flexibility to achieve other things (Daley, 1996).

Characteristics of African Caribbean and West African families

Any discussion about African Caribbean family patterns has to recognise the importance of historical experience in creating a diversity of family types. A critical element in the enslavement of Africans taken to the west was the deliberate destruction of tribal social organisations with its supporting practices (Blauner, 1976). The absence of many of the traditional norms around kinship and tribal practices is one important difference between African Caribbean and West African families. The demands of trans-Atlantic African enslavement in terms of the reproduction of children for labour, plus the flexibility and movement of enslaved Africans, led to the creation of African Caribbean family-types from male-headed married units, to those headed by women raising children independently (Patterson, 1963: 299–300). Also, there is what has been called 'visiting unions' (Berrington, 1994: 528; Smith and Smith, 1986) whereby males live separately, but contribute to the maintenance of the family. Beckford (2005) identifies six types of African Caribbean families in Britain reflecting this adaptive capacity (Patterson, 1963; Pryce, 1986). One family type not reflected in the British literature is multiple partnerships consisting of men and women with more than one permanent sexual partner and similar to polygamous relations (Chevannes, 2001: 217).

Adaptive theories suggest that African Caribbean families should be understood as fluid structures shaped primarily by economic security as opposed to fixed social responses (Beckford, 2005). Despite the cultural relativism of this approach, the tendency to focus primarily on positive features can be seen by its valorisation of the African Caribbean family: in particular, its ability to meet numerous exigencies and, especially, the wide range of roles afforded to women (Berthould *et al.*, 1997; Chamberlain and Goulbourne, 2001).

The other major perspective in explaining the African Caribbean family comes from disorganisation theories, predicated on the assumption that the 'weak' nature of social and familial structures contributes to cultures of pathology and maladaption (Cashmore, 1982; Stinchcombe, 1965). Specific examples of the assumed outcomes of such cultures are high levels of illegitimacy, social dislocation and crime (Gilroy, 1990; Seidel, 1986). Given the oppression Black family structures have experienced it is inconceivable that some degree of pathology does not exist (Fanon, 1967; Leary, 2005), even if it is usually overstated (Hare, 1989: 164).

One of the advantages of this perspective is elucidating the relationship between family forms, internal processes and social structures in integrating individuals and regulating social behaviour. Implicit in these theories is the assumed relationship between structure, culture, ideology and masculine dominance, even though these may be related in complex ways (Chevannes, 2001: 205–6). This cultural antecedence explains the greater number of African Caribbean family-types compared to mainstream society (Berrington, 1994; Berthoud *et al.*, 1997). This is challenged by Dench (1996: 34), who argues that African Caribbean family practices have changed in important ways due to the impact of British society. This is evidenced in the attitudes towards family formation amongst second-generation African Caribbeans compared to their parents. The effects of British society on Caribbean family formation can be seen in a variety of ways that are rooted in the migration experience (Patterson, 1963: 304–6): for instance, the impact of a large urban society and priorities of early migrants in weakening social sanctions on males in meeting social obligations to women and families. The effects are also seen in how access to wider employment opportunities created greater independence amongst African Caribbean women supported by the role of the welfare state, as in the National Assistance Board, which provided a stop-gap in between work, or assistance with children (Berthould, 2000: 14; Patterson, 1963). For Dench one of the consequences of these rapid changes has been important signs of cultural dislocation as seen in the disproportionate decline in marriage and the significant increase of lone-parent families and divorces.

Interestingly, Chamberlain and Goulbourne (2001) suggest that Caribbean family-types are symptomatic of a modernity that demarcates change from traditional societies to an era represented by choice, and that Caribbean families are in the vanguard of this transition. These post-modern attitudes are a source of anxiety for many people and in the writer's view are central in making this ethnic community one of the weakest and structurally fragile in Britain (Berthould *et al.*, 1997; Office for National Statistics, 2001).

Any examination of West African family structures recognises the importance of patrilineal and matrilineal systems in shaping family practices. These practices seek to privilege the male line of descent in terms of inheritance, social power and traditional rights and are well illustrated by the Yoruba of Nigeria, compared to the matrilineal practices of the Ashanti, where the female line of descent enjoys higher status (Goody and Groothues, 1979). Matters of descent and social power are central in understanding West African family systems. Marriage is seen primarily as a union between extended kinship systems that are crucial in shaping the characters of these families, the roles of spouses and decision-making. Accordingly, African family systems can be seen as social systems rooted in matters of descent and places of origins (Caldwell, 1996; Vellenga, 1983). Central concerns within this context are matters relating to fertility and decision-making, which have provided an important organising principle in studies of the African family (Adeokun, 1983; Isiugo-Abanihe *et al.*, 2006).

Marriage constitutes the basic unit of family organisation in West African societies, of which there are two general forms: monogamy and polygamy (Craven, 1968; Little and Price, 1967). While the former is based on the Christian church and legal considerations, the latter is a product of custom. Monogamy has become increasingly more popular due to a number of factors, which include economic constraints or the desire by both males and females to weaken familial obligations. The impact of education and westernisation has also had a considerable effect on reducing the popularity of polygamy (Little and Price, 1967).

Marriage is a normal expectation within African societies given its importance for producing children within the broader social kinship structure and organisation of society; most individuals, particularly women, will spend a significant period of their lives within this institution (Ware, 1983). Daley (1996) notes that 33 per cent of West Africans in Britain were married at the time of his study.

One of the interesting things about the West African marriage systems is their complexity and functionality (Ware, 1983: 15–16). While polygamy is one of the most well-known practices that distinguish Africa from the west (Stapleton, 1978: 24), Vellenga (1983) illustrates the various notions of what constitutes a wife and the advantages and disadvantages that these cultural definitions and practices entail. An important feature of Vellenga's study is how married men are allowed to pursue relationships with unmarried women and the various ramifications of this. Accordingly, what determines the status of the 'other woman' is her relationship with the wider family in question. For example, whether she is a passing attraction or more permanent, especially if children are produced, can improve her status to that of the 'informal wife'. An important qualification made by Vellenga (1983: 147) is while polygamy has decreased in popularity, the move to monogamy should not be confused with the assumption that married men are prohibited from having outside relationships. These practices have important consequences on the types of families to be found in West Africa. For while lone-parent families, as they are popularly represented, are not encouraged (Craven, 1968: 22), they are inevitable and found in these societies as they are amongst contemporary British West Africans, and indeed they are a growing family-type (Craven, 1968; Hunt and Lightly, 2001). Dinan (1983) shows, and in common with Caribbean practice (Kincaid, 1988), how many women unable to meet men of their choice pursue a lone-parent strategy, as mistresses, rather than marry poorer and less-educated men.

Another distinguishing feature of West African family life that contrasts significantly with western practice is the assumption that marriage does not require both parties to share similar residence. While wives may live with their husbands at various periods of their marriage, they often spend significant time apart maintaining their own homes, but sharing resources. This practice helps to foster both autonomy and interdependency (Abu, 1983). Daley (1996) demonstrates how this practice, and conflicting assumptions, creates problems in studying the demographics of West Africans, insofar as women define themselves as being married, even when their husbands are 'back home' or elsewhere, either on a temporary basis consisting of many years, or permanently. The absence of a husband cannot be seen as being indicative of marriage breakdown. This can be seen in the instance of male students completing their studies and returning home, leaving their wives in England working and caring for children (Goody and Groothues, 1979: 69).

The African Caribbean and West African community in Britain

The history of Caribbean and West African settlement in Britain is related to the colonial status of these territories. As early as the sixteenth century people from these regions resided in Britain due to slavery and maritime trade, forming communities around ports such as Liverpool and Bristol (Fryer, 1984: 58–66). Large-scale migration from the Caribbean started in 1948, reaching its peak by the early 1960s.

Prior to the 1950s, West Africans in Britain were estimated to be approximately ten thousand (Daley, 1996: 44). The coming of independence for African countries witnessed increasing numbers of West African students coming to Britain. This group consisted overwhelmingly of part-time students and a minority sponsored by home governments or British agencies. The lack of records makes it difficult to ascertain the present numbers of West Africans in Britain, until the inclusion of the Black-African category in the 1991 Census (Craven, 1968; Daley, 1996). Craven noted in 1968, which was borne out later, the majority of West Africans came from Nigeria, Ghana and Sierra Leone. The most recent figures put the size of the Black-African population as under 1 per cent (0.8 per cent) of the British population (Office for National Statistics, 2001). The official figures do not reflect their actual numbers (Chinouya and Elam, 2001: 7). Daley (1996: 58) has described an 'invisible' community who entered the country as students, or for other short-term purposes, who are illegal residents (*Hackney Gazette*, 11 January 2007). The numbers of West Africans increased during the 1980s with economic and political problems in Nigeria and Ghana, which led to the influx of students, often from the middle classes who were able to afford to study abroad, along with those claiming political asylum (Daley, 1996; Hunt and Lightly, 2001). The factors shaping West African residential patterns were the presence of family members or friends, the availability of cheap accommodation, and work and its proximity to places of study (Craven, 1968).

Employment

The socioeconomic problems experienced by African Caribbeans are historic in character and shaped by racial discrimination and marginalisation although buttressed for earlier generations by a growing economy. According to Berthould *et al.* (1997: 89) unemployment amongst African Caribbeans stood at 31 per cent compared to 15 per cent for White males. Amongst African Caribbean males in the age group most likely to be starting a family, the under 35s, unemployment for men with no qualifications stood at 61 per cent and, moreover, males of this group were more likely to be unemployed at each level of education (Dustmann *et al.*, 2003).

One of the immediate problems experienced by West African students was finding employment commensurate with their experience or education given the racism experienced. This can be seen in the popular desire for administrative work and the frustrations experienced in obtaining such positions. This was not assisted by the circular problem experienced by Black people, of having qualifications but lacking practical experience (Daley, 1996: 56). The experiences of West African women was not much different and can be seen by the concentration of those educated in the areas of nursing and secretarial work, with the majority forced into industries such as factory work (Emecheta, 1974). West African employment patterns in contrast to their educational performance, as one of the most qualified ethnic groups, continue to represent a major issue of concern (Dustmann *et al.*, 2003). They remain the social group who are most likely to be unemployed and the lowest paid (Daley, 1996: 61; Dustmann *et al.*, 2003). The discrepancies between education and employment of West Africans can be seen by the facts that 20 per cent of those with degrees are unemployed and that it is not uncommon to find Masters degree graduates driving mini-cabs or working as security guards (Daley, 1996).

As with the African Caribbean community, unemployment is much more significant for males (Dustmann *et al.*, 2003: 61). However, it is important to balance these findings with the successes of both

communities, seen for example by West Africans in the medical profession (Daley, 1996) and increasingly working within the media. For
example, successful West Africans in the public eye include June
Sarpong, who in 2007 was awarded an MBE (Member of the British
Empire) (*Sun*, 17 June 2007), and fashion designer Ozwald Boateng,
who have joined their African Caribbean counterparts, albeit small in
number, in changing the external image of British life (Donnell, 2002).

Social problems and African Caribbean and
West African families in Britain

The issue of low income and high levels of male unemployment among
African Caribbeans coincides with the decline in the popularity of marriage within this ethnic group (Berthould, 2000: 12; Winslow, 2001: 64).
What is revealing in the representation of issues concerning African
Caribbean families is the multiplicity of matters raised by women
of all ethnic communities from domestic violence or male resistance
to the presence of women in employment (Berthould, 2000). The core
concerns, it would appear, for African Caribbean women pivot mainly
around economic-related matters (Dench, 1996; Pryce, 1986).

The predominant representation of African Caribbean males culturally with serious import for family formation was illustrated in
a BBC (British Broadcasting Corporation) documentary entitled *The
Problem with Black Men*, where many views and images articulated
in popular media (Appleyard and White, 2004; Pryce, 2005) were crys-
tallised. The programme created outrage in the African Caribbean
community because of its racist depiction of males being essentially
'irresponsible', 'lacking ambition', or 'absent fathers' and responsible,
by inference, for the increase in lone-parent families (Holloway, 2004).
Why women would want to bear children by such males was not
seen as worthy of consideration by the programme (see Reynolds, 2001
for an alternative view). The notions of African Caribbean males as
errant fathers has become one of the most prominent themes in contemporary concerns, following on the heels of government campaigns
on 'feckless fathers' and the introduction of the controversial Child
Support Agency (Augustine, 1998; Bradshaw *et al.*, 1999). Lone-parent
families make up 51 per cent of African Caribbean households
(Reynolds, 2001) and according to Berthould (2005) and Bradshaw
et al. (1999: 26–7) a significant percentage of them are a product of
relatively unstable or short-term relationships. What is revealing in
these accounts is the lack of critical enquiry involved. In the first instance,
the numerous routes into lone-parenthood or types of families contained

within the generic term are rarely examined (Crow and Hardey, 1999), and there is a natural presumption that males are responsible for important decision-making leading to children being born in such circumstances, which leads to women being perceived as victims. Thus this attitude fails to recognise that women often consciously decide for numerous reasons that they have a need to conceive, relegating the decisions or wishes of male partners as secondary (Aldous and Ganey, 1999: 159; Chevannes, 2001: 216; Dench, 1996: 59; Draper and MacCormack, 1987). For example, Draper and MacCormack, along with Chevannes, argue that pregnancy is often welcomed amongst Jamaican adolescent girls as symbolising adult status, while for Renvoize (1985) many women have deep desires to give birth and become mothers to provide personal fulfilment.

Bradshaw *et al.* (1999: 29) found disagreements and lack of communication to be an important factor in relationship breakdown resulting in lone-parent families, while consultant psychologist Guishard-Pine cites the attitudes and behaviour of many African Caribbean women as a contributing factor leading to lone-parent families, with an adverse impact on children and fathers (Pryce, 1986). One example is the prevailing view amongst many women that fathers are dispensable (Berthould, 2000: 14), which is often associated with a quasi-feminist rhetoric (hooks, 1995: 73–5). This is reinforced by the role of the State in the provision of housing, which is a critical factor in shaping interpersonal dynamics in the context of relationship breakdown (Bradshaw *et al.*, 1999: 70–1; Crow and Hardey, 1999; Julien and Mercer, 1988: 94–5) along with other benefits that are important in assisting women to become independent and in exacerbating this trend (Berthould, 2000; Bradshaw *et al.*, 1999: 7; Dench, 1996: 21; Hare, 1989: 164–5). As Renvoize (1985: 94–5) suggests, the low expectation of meeting 'Mr Right' can influence women to make the decision to become lone mothers (see Winslow, 2001). By the same token, the State has weakened traditional Caribbean norms around fatherhood and its obligations and entitlements (Chevannes, 2001: 222–4).

An issue that has been identified in the scant literature as a source of problems in West African conjugal relations is the employment difficulties of males and the impact of this on their power in the family (Chinouya and Elam, 2001: 4). While the challenge to notions of masculinity is one issue, another is how westernisation has led to attitudinal changes of many West African men regarding matters of gender equality (Chinouya and Elam, 2000: 42) or in facilitating inter-ethnic or racial marriages and relationships, both with Black women not from a West African background and with White women. According to Dustmann *et al.* (2003) approximately 10 per cent of Black Africans marry outside their ethnic group. These changes have been seen as anathema to many traditionalists (Ogbobode Abidde, 2005), but, regardless, their impacts can be seen in the growing numbers of Anglo-Nigerians *inter alia* (Chinouya and Elam, 2001: 29). The various outcomes of these changes within the contemporary West African family and responses to them are unknown, whether in terms of domestic violence (Emecheta, 1974; Mama, 1989; Stapleton, 1978) or in terms of family breakdown. Another set of issues is in the area of health, where stress and mental health matters contribute to crime (Chinouya and Elam, 2001; *Hackney Gazette*, 2007). Another area of interest that can be drawn from the African Caribbean experience is whether marriage to Whites leads to weakening of ethnic links and networks or strengthens them in terms of access to social capital (Goulbourne, 2006). A related development is the increasing numbers of low-income West African lone-parent families who are an important constituent of the churches springing up throughout the country (Hunt and Lightly, 2001).

Crime

One of the most pressing problems facing the African Caribbean family is the relationship between low-income, 'weak' families and the exposure of young people to crime and victimisation (Reynolds, 2004: 7). Fitzgerald *et al.* (2003) describe how the materialist socialisation of many African Caribbean youth in terms of their possession of fashion items makes them particularly prone to being victims of crime and especially violent crime (Stanislas, 2009). Lack of income was also found to be an important factor in the offending behaviour of many African Caribbean youth who came from poor households. The limited nature of resource structures has been critical in limiting the opportunities available to this group, and the situation seems not to be assisted where significant numbers are in relationships with Whites.

West Africans experience similarly negative responses from the police to their presence as African Caribbeans; in many cases this is more negative, given the perception of them as potentially illegal immigrants (Daley, 1996). This can be seen by the terrible circumstances leading to the killing of failed student David Oluwale by the police, which sparked a successful campaign led by the African Caribbean community in the 1970s and an important illustration of early African/African Caribbean political solidarity (Stanislas, 2006). West African youth are subject to similar treatment from the police resulting in disproportionate deaths in custody (Bowling and Phillips, 2003). The concentration of West Africans in poor areas makes them vulnerable to violent crime, as illustrated by the death of Damilola Taylor and the shooting and killing of Zainab Kalokoh in a bungled robbery at her godchild's christening (Black, 2006).

Little attention has been given to West Africans and their participation in crime; however, the role of the young Nigerian gang involved in the death of Mrs Kalokoh has brought this to public attention (BBC, 2007). While they are not usually associated with violent crime, there is evidence of West African involvement in drug trafficking (Chigwada-Bailey, 1991). The role of West Africans in crime has been traditionally small and restricted to matters of minor fraud and welfare benefit abuse (Craven, 1968: 34). In recent decades, however, West Africans have been implicated in fraud rackets involving housing allocations (Daley, 1996) and more recently have been the centre of multi-million pound international fraud rackets often involving identity theft and similar offences (BBC News, 2006b).

Black politics and African Caribbean and West African families

The origins of a common UK Black politics encompassing African Caribbeans and West Africans has its origins in older communities such as Liverpool. For example, the 'Colonial People's Defence Association', formed in 1951, had an explicit 'race'-based outlook. This followed similar cooperation that had led to the Fifth Pan African Congress in Manchester in 1945 (Adi, 1994). Such an orientation emphasises the commonalities between continental Africans and their diasporan counterparts, thus increasing social capital, which was viewed as outweighing their differences.

These sentiments are not reflected in the early sociological literature. The relationship between these communities painted by early White academic observers often seems distorted by their own prejudices, if taken at face value. Craven (1968) cites extreme mutual prejudices, almost far surpassing those held by Whites towards either group; to the extent that employers, it is suggested, were forced to not employ Africans and African Caribbeans simultaneously. Emecheta (1974: 70) describes the petty prejudices within sections of the West African and Caribbean communities that are balanced by the cooperation and solidarity that existed, or the aspirations in that direction. An interesting observation is how intra-group class and caste snobbery amongst West Africans had to accommodate itself with the downgrading effects of racism – a process similar to that experienced within the Caribbean community (Hall, 2000).

The existence of a unique ethnic cultural outlook, alongside a shared Black perspective and the tensions between them, has constituted an important feature of the political relations between West Africans and African Caribbeans (Goulbourne, 1990: 11). An illustration of this was seen in the mutual displeasure to the crass efforts at one-upmanship by Diane Abbott, Member of Parliament (MP), in remarks comparing Nigeria with Jamaica regarding corruption (Temko, 2006). The dominant faction ideologically within the West African and African Caribbean communities, in terms of profile, has been those who share a common Black political outlook that has been dominated historically by the more active African Caribbeans, with the support of small, but important, numbers of West Africans. This can be seen by the role of Nigerian Black Power radicals Obi Egbuna and Franklin Davies, who was a key figure in the Spaghetti House siege in 1975 (Stanislas, 2006: 83). African women also played a vital role in the development of a British Black politics, illustrated by Martha Ousma, from Ghana, who was a trusted stalwart of Bernie Grant (Bryant *et al.*, 1985; Holloway, 2006).

The 1981 national street disturbances across Britain illustrated the widespread discontent that existed within Black communities, sparked by the physical resistance of African Caribbean males to racist policing (Stanislas, 2006). The events that followed saw the publishing of the Scarman Report, the formation of Black sections within the Labour Party and the spread of equal opportunities initiatives throughout UK local authorities. Two years after the Broadwater Farm disturbances in 1987, three Black MPs, two African Caribbeans and one of West African origin, were elected, marking a watershed in decades of grassroots struggles (Goulbourne, 1990). The grassroots activities of Black communities may have had more significance in the election of Black representatives than electoral activities (Goulbourne, 1990). Fieldhouse and Purdam (2001) show how only 36.3 per cent of African Caribbeans voted in the 1987 elections – compared to 63.8 per cent of Asians – and Black Africans and African Caribbeans have consistently the lowest rates of political participation. One important factor in this finding is Black people's mistrust of the political system and its racism, often seen by the behaviour of local ruling parties. A good example concerns Brent Labour Party's selection of two African women, Nkechi Amalu-Johnson and Pauline Ngaya, neither of whom had any political credibility; shortly afterwards they were arrested in the midst of a housing fraud scandal, and they later defected to the Conservatives, which gave them control of the Council (Guardian, 1994; Hansard, 27 July 1993; Hognigsbaum, 1994; Small, 1994).

Back and Solomos (1995) have identified the constraints working against the development of a Black political agenda capable of addressing many of the issues affecting Black families. Key among these is the power and control of local political parties by the White party hierarchy, the result of which is their ability to silence Black dissent or co-opt it through patronage and funding. This can be seen in Brent, London, which has the largest number of Black councillors in the country, who sat silently while the Council, in the midst of Thatcher's war against public spending (with its racist overtones), dismantled the Black voluntary sector through disproportionate funding cuts (Stanislas, 2006: 228). These actions wiped out a crucial sector of service provision and an important factor in community cohesion (Stanislas, 2006). In many cases local authorities manufactured grounds relying on crude racism to close down very important Black service providers and community organisations, thus increasing unemployment and losing crucial human resources and other social capital required by disadvantaged communities (Stanislas, 2006: 221–5). The attack on the equal opportunities agenda and Black people can also be seen by the victimisation and eventual removal of many important bureaucratic leaders in this area. Hackney Council engaged in a protracted campaign to remove its senior executive, Sam Yeboah, previously its 'Race Unit' chief, including efforts to link him to a West African housing fraud scandal (CRE, 1998).

In some instances important Black organisations failed for 'other' reasons. An example of this is the Moyenda Black Family Project, a very innovative initiative carrying out groundbreaking work in the areas of parenting, family support and crime diversion (Beckles *et al.*, 1999), which collapsed in the late 1990s after the resignation of its founder Lynthia Grant (Odih, 2002: 94). The loss to the Black community with the demise of Moyenda and the departure of its leader was immediate, with Grant taking up employment as the Director of 'Mentoring Plus Brent', a government-run bureaucrating programme targeted at Black boys and less responsive to community needs (Odih, 2002), after falling out with her previous employer. Efforts to save the nationally recognised Moyenda Project by bringing it under the umbrella of Coram Family (a children and family support charity established in 1739), and following the appointment of development worker Dr Carl Hylton, was short lived. Coram's concerns over income generation led to the dissolution of the 'Coram Family Moyenda Project' (as it became known) in 1999 (Hylton, 2001). The writer was the founder of the male social fraternity 'Utani', which specialised in the needs of Black men, and worked as a trainer and consultant for the Moyenda Project during Grant's leadership.

The Blair Government's colour-blind approach to socioeconomic policies (Johnson, 2002) compounded the problems experienced by Black communities and their families across the UK and if anything one of the most distinguishing features of his administration was its aggressive use of patronage with regards to ethnic minority politicians or high-profile figures, such as Trevor Phillips, OBE (Order of the British Empire). Phillips was key in Blair's vicarious media communication with the Black community, which was the target of his personal responsibility agenda in the area of social policy, even though it was directed primarily to the White mainstream. For example, Phillips' response to the increasing number of Black lone-parent families consisted of little else than to blame Black men (Appleyard and White, 2004). The fact that Black men benefit the least from this trend, or the fact that the problems experienced by families have far more complex roots, does not fit well with the White populist avarice of Phillips and similar figures. It is this indifference in policy terms that shapes Appleyard and White's (2004) views that Black and poor communities have been abandoned by the Government and Black politicians, further illustrated by their silence to the protests of predominantly West African cleaning workers about their appalling wages and conditions (BBC News, 2006a). Fortunately, politics is not reducible to government, and despite the reduction in voluntary organisations and resources, and increasing social problems, sections within Black communities continue to carry out work that provides support and services to families (see Chinouya and Elam, 2001; Reynolds, 2004: 8). One obvious example has been the growing West African churches, which replicate some of the characteristics of their African Caribbean counterparts (Hunt and Lightly, 2001).

An important illustration of Black political leadership can be seen by individuals and organisations such as Bini Brown of the African-Caribbean Self Help Organisation (ACSHO) in Birmingham. Brown and his organisation are veterans in the struggle of Black communities in their area, with roots in the Black Power/Pan Africanist Movement of the early 1970s (Stanislas, 2006: 87). ACSHO illustrates the importance of independence in the ability to preserve autonomous leadership structures and organisations capable of meeting community needs. The importance of this type of organisation cannot be understated. Such organisations are crucial in promoting and maintaining ethnic group solidarity (Hylton, 1999; Stanislas, 2006) alongside the importance of the Black family. The significance of Brown and ACSHO in their articulation of a non-establishment-defined Black agenda can be seen by the animosity they draw from sections of the Asian community in the bitter ethnic politics that characterises an aspect of the city's history (Brown, 1982; John, 2005). These tensions are also shaped by the close relationship of Asian cliques with the Labour Party hierarchy (Back and Solomos, 1995; Stanislas, 2006: 251–3), which cast further shadows over the latter, given the numerous efforts to silence Brown, an ancient thorn in the side of the status quo (Adumekwe and Holloway, 2005; John, 2005). These tensions were exploited during disturbances in 2005 that led to the racist killing of an African Caribbean male by a group of Asians, in the wake of allegations of the rape of a Jamaican female migrant by another group of Asian males (John, 2005).

While there are very few organisations with the historical longevity of ACSHO in London, given the impact of funding cuts, there are greater opportunities in the capital to coopt Black leadership talent (Goulbourne, 1990: 11; Stanislas, 2006) and emerging organisations include 100 Black Men of London, who run education, social and cultural support programmes for young Black men. Other organisations, such as *New Initiatives* in South London, run similar programmes for both genders. Organisations that meet important economic and other social needs of low-income Black families can be seen in the Tehuti Investment Club, based in North London. The organisation seeks to build human capital, which is a fundamental ingredient for success. An obvious example is the development of wealth-creation strategies, and personal development and life-planning skills. In the area of media campaigning the organisation Ligali, led by its British Nigerian Toyin Agbetu, has emerged as a widely respected force of highly informed Black opinion. These efforts seek to fill the vacuum left by the demise of many key local and national Black organisations. They also serve as important models of good practice that need to be replicated many times over in Black communities throughout the UK.

Conclusion

Following the exploration of many of the features of the African Caribbean family in Britain several conclusions can be drawn. The first issue is that this is an institution under attack due to systemic racism and the weakness of cultural attachments resulting in the dangerous levels of racial inter-marriage *inter alia*. Secondly, the economic marginalisation of African Caribbean males has contributed to forms of families that are highly problematic in their ability to meet the needs of children and a principle mechanism in the reproduction of poverty and other social problems. In this context, issues such as the rights of women and notions of individual choice regarding the birth of children have to be reconciled with issues of responsibilities, particularly given the victim status adopted by Black women in these discussions.

In the case of West Africans, one of the pressing needs is for their recognition as a well-established presence within Britain and for this to be reflected in the academic and popularist literature. One of the starting points of such a change is research on family patterns and greater detail in the types of problems being experienced, particularly in regards to income and gender relations. How matters of kinship and cultural or social capital alleviate many of these strains or exacerbate them are issues for further study. The relationship of West Africans to the criminal justice system as victims or offenders is also an important area of inquiry.

The creation and maintenance of independent Black institutions is a critical structural precondition for meeting Black needs, particularly in providing education and support to families, and especially the young, around matters affecting family formation. They are also important in institutionalising the crucial values and aspects of ethnic identity and pride that this can entail, and in so doing they contribute to increasing social capital.

These organisations play a crucial role in the development of a social policy agenda that meets the needs of Black and poor families. However, a prerequisite for mainstream political engagement must be the existence of strong independent structures that can hold those who speak in the name of Black people to account and ensure 'White' government takes their concerns seriously.

References

Abu, K. (1983), 'The Separateness of Spouses: Conjugal Resources in an Ashanti town', in Oppong, C. (ed.), *Female and Male in West Africa* (London: Allen and Unwin)

Adeokun, L. (1983), 'Martial sexuality and birthing space among the Yoruba', in Oppong, C. (ed.), *Females and Male in West Africa* (London: Allen and Unwin)

Adi, H. (1994), 'West African students in Britain 1900–1960: The politics of exile', in Killingray, D. (ed.), *Africans in Britain* (London: Frank Cass)

Aldous, J. and Ganey, R. (1999), 'Family life and the pursuit of happiness: the influence of gender and race', *Journal of Family Issues*, 20:2, 155–80

Allport, W. G. (1987), *The Nature of Prejudice* (Indiana: Addison Wesley)

Appleyard, B. and White, L. (2004), 'The Ghettos in the Mind', *Sunday Times Special Report* (10 October)

Augustine, P. (1998), *Baby Father* (London: X Press)

Chigwada-Bailey, R. (1991), *Black Women's Experience of Criminal Justice* (London: Waterside Press)

Back, L. and Solomos, J. (1995), *Race, Politics and Social Change* (London: Routledge)

Bailey, B. and Nain, T. G. (2003), *Gender Equality in the Caribbean: Reality or Illusion* (Kingston: Ian Randle Publishers)

Banton, M. (1985), *Promoting Racial Harmony* (Cambridge: Cambridge University Press)

Beckford, R. (2005), 'From West Africa to the West Midlands: African-Caribbean Household Types' (Paper received via email to author of chapter, May 2005)

Beckles, Y., Grant, L., Stanislas, P. and Weekes, D. (1999), *Black Parents and Their Children's Education: 20 Action Points* (London, Runnymede Trust)

Beishoon, S., Modood, T. and Virdee, S. (1998), *Ethnic Minority Families* (London: Policy Studies Institute)

Berrington, A. (1994), 'Marriage and family formation among White and ethnic minority population in Britain', *Ethnic and Racial Studies*, 17:3, 517–44

Berthould, R. (2000), *Family Formation in Multi-cultural Britain: Three Patterns of Diversity* (Essex: lser Essex)

Berthould, R., Modood, T. and Lakey, J. (1997), *Ethnic Minorities in Britain: Diversity and Disadvantage* (London: Policy Studies Institute)

Black, C. (2006), 'We need tighter borders says Met chief', *Daily Mail* (22 December)

Blauner, R. (1976), 'Colonized and immigrant minorities', in Bowker, G. and Carrier, J. (eds), *Race and Ethnic Relations* (London: Hutchinson)

Bowling, B. and Phillips, C. (2003), *Race and Crime in Britain* (London: Longman)

Bradshaw, J., Skinner, C. and Stimson, C. (1999), *Absent Fathers* (London and New York: Routledge)

British Broadcasting Corporation (BBC) (2007), *Panorama, On the Knife's Edge* (13 August)

Brown, J. (1982), *Policing by Multi Racial Consent* (London: NVCO)

Bryant, B., Dadzie, S. and Scafe, S. (1985), *The Heart of the Race: Black Women's Lives in Britain* (London: Virago)

Caldwell, C. J. (1996), 'The demographic implications of the West African family systems', *The Journal of Comparative Family Studies*, 27:2, 331–52

Cashmore, E. (1982), *Black Sportsmen* (London: Routledge, Kegan and Paul)

Chamberlain, M. and Goulbourne, H. (ed.) (2001), *Caribbean Families in Britain and the Trans-Atlantic World* (Warwick: Palgrave Macmillan)

Chevannes, B. (2001), *Learning to be a Man: Socialization and Gender Identity in Five Caribbean Communities* (Barbados: University of West Indies Press)

Chinouya, M. and Elam, G. (2001), *Final Report on Feasibility Study of Health Surveys Amongst Black African Populations Living in the UK* (London: Department of Health)

Craven, A. (1968), *West Africans in London* (London: Institute of Race Relations)

CRE (Commission for Racial Equality) (1998), *7th September News Brief* (London: Commission for Racial Equality)

Crow, G. and Hardey, M. (1999), 'Diversity and ambiguity among lone-parents families in Britain', in Allen, G. (ed.), *The Sociology of the Family: A Reader* (London and New York: Routledge)

Daley, P. (1996), 'Black-Africans: Students who stayed', in Peach, C. (ed.), *The Ethnic Minority Population of Britain* (Newport: Office for National Statistics)

Dench, G. (1996), *The Place of Men in Changing Family Cultures* (London: Institute of Community Studies)

Dinan, C. (1983), 'Sugar daddies and gold-diggers: single women in Accra', in Oppong, C. (ed.), *Females and Males in West Africa* (London: Allen and Unwin)

Donnell, A. (ed.) (2002), *Companion to Contemporary Black British Culture* (London and New York: Routledge)

Draper, A. and MacCormack, P. C. (1987), 'Social and cognitive aspects of female sexuality in Jamaica', in Caplan, P. (ed.), *The Cultural Construction of Sexuality* (London: Tavistock)

Emecheta, B. (1974), *Second-Class Citizen* (London: Heinemann)

Ezechi, O. C., Kalu, B. K., Ezechi, L. O., Nwokoro, C. A., Ndububa, V. I. and Okeke, G. C. E. (2004), 'The prevalence and pattern of domestic violence against pregnant Nigerian women', *Journal of Obstetrics and Gynaecology*, 24:6, 652–6

Fanon, F. (1967), *Black Skin White Mask* (New York: Grove Press)

Fieldhouse, E. and Purdam, K. (2001), *Voter Engagement Among Black and Ethnic Minority Communities* (London: The Electoral Commission)

Fitzgerald, M., Hales, C. and Stockdale, J. (2003), *Young People and Street Crime: Research into Young People's Involvement in Street Crime* (London: Youth Justice Board for England and Wales)

Fortier, M. A. (2005), 'Pride, politics and multiculturalist citizenship', *Ethnic and Racial Studies*, 28:3, 559–78

Freire, P. (1970), *The Pedagogy of the Oppressed* (London: Penguin)

Fryer, P. (1984), *Staying Power: The History of Black People in Britain* (London: Pluto Press)

Gilbert, D. (2005), 'Interrogating mixed-race: a crisis of ambiguity', *Social Identities*, 11:1, 55–74

Gilroy, P. (1990), 'One nation under a groove: the cultural politics of race', in Goldberg, T. D. (ed.), *Anatomy of Racism* (Minneapolis and London: University of Minnesota Press)

Goody, E. and Groothues, M. (1979), 'Stress in marriage: West African couples in London', in Khan S. V. (ed.), *Minority Families in Britain: Support and Stress* (London: Palgrave Macmillan)

Goulbourne, H. (2006), 'Families, communities and social capital', *Community Work and Family*, 9, 235–50

Goulbourne, H. (1990), *Black Politics in Britain* (London: Avebury)

Guardian (1994), 'Ex Councillor on Fraud Charges' (18 October)

Hackney Gazette (2007), 'Illegal Traffic Wardens Sacked' (11 January)

Hakim, C. (2003), *Models of the Family in Modern Society* (London: Ashgate Publications)

Hall, S. (2000), 'Old and new ethnicities, old and new identities', in Back, L. and Solomos, J. (eds), *Theories of Race and Racism* (London and New York: Routledge)

Hansard (1993), *Parliamentary Opposition Day Debate, District Auditor* (27 July), Column 149, 1053 (London: House of Lord Publications)

Hare, N. (1989), 'A complete theory of the Black family', in Hare, N. and Hare, J. (eds), *Crisis in Black Sexual Politics* (San Francisco: Black Think Tank)

Hognigsbaum, M. (1994), 'Whatever Happened to Barmy Brent', *Evening Standard* (25 April)

Holmes, C. (1991), *Immigrants, Refugees and Minorities in Britain* (London and Boston: Faber and Faber)

hooks, b. (1995), *Killing Rage: Ending Racism* (London: Penguin Books)

Hunt, S. and Lightly, N. (2001), 'The Black British pentecostal revival: identity and belief in the "New" Nigerian churches', *Ethnic and Racial Studies*, 24:1, 104–24

Hylton, C. (2001), 'Report Audit: Coram Family Moyenda Project, January 1999–December 2000', unpublished report (26 March)

Hylton, C. (1999), *African-Caribbean Community Organisation: the search for individual and group identity* (London: Trentham Books)

Isiugo-Abanihe, U. C., Oyediran, K. and Bankole, A. (2006), 'Correlates of spousal communication on fertility and family planning among the Yoruba of Nigeria', *Journal of Comparative Family Studies*, 37:2 (Spring), 441–60

John, G. (2005), 'This conflict has been 30 years in the making', *Guardian* (26 October)

Johnson, C. (2002), 'The dilemma of ethnic privilege: a comparison of constructions of British, English and Anglo-Celtic identity in contemporary British and Australian political discourse', *Ethnicities*, 2:2, 163–88

Julien, I. and Mercer, K. (1988), 'Race, sexual politics and Black masculinity', in Chapman, R. and Rutherford, J. (eds), *Male Order: Unwrapping Masculinity* (London: Lawrence Wishart)

Kincaid, J. (1988), *A Small Place* (New York: Farrrar, Straus and Giroux)

Leary, J. D. (2005), *Post Traumatic Slave Syndrome* (Portland, OR: Uptone Press)

Little, K. and Price, A. (1967), 'Some trends in modern marriage among West Africans', *Journal of the International African Institute*, 37:4, 407–24

Mama, A. (1989), *The Hidden Struggle: Statutory and Voluntary Responses to Violence Against Black Women in the Home* (London: Whiting and Birch Ltd)

Modood, T., Berthoud, B. R., Lakey, J., Nazroo, J., Smith, P. and Virdee, S. (1997), *Ethnic Minorities in Britain: Diversity and Disadvantage* (London: Policy Studies Institute)

Odih, P. (2002), 'Mentors and role models: masculinity and the educational "underachievement" of young Afro-Caribbean males', *Race, Ethnicity and Education*, 5:1, 91–105

Patterson, S. (1963), *Dark Strangers* (London: Tavistock Publications)

Pryce, K. (1986), *Endless Pressure: A Study of West Indian Lifestyles in Bristol* (Bristol: Bristol Classic Press)

Rattansi, A. and Westwood, S. (1994), *Racism, Modernity and the Western Front* (London: Polity Press)

Renvoize, J. (1985), *Going Solo: Single Mothers by Choice* (London: Routledge, Keagan and Paul)

Reynolds, T. (2004), *Caribbean Families, Social Capital and Young People's Diasporic Identities* (London: South Bank University)

Reynolds, T. (2001), 'Caribbean fathers in family lives in Britain', in Goulbourne, H. and Chamberlain, M. (eds), *Caribbean Families in Britain and the Trans-Atlantic World* (London: Palgrave)

Selvon, S. (1956), *The Lonely Londoners* (London: Longman Caribbean Writers Series)

Seidel, G. (1986), 'The family in the new right', in Levitas, R. (ed.), *The Ideology of the New Right* (London: Polity Press)

Small, S. (1994), *Racialised Barriers: The Black Experience in the United States and England in the 1990s* (London and New York: Routledge)

Smith, J. D. and Smith, C. F. (1986), *To Shoot Hard Labour: The Life and Times of Samuel Smith, An Antiguan Working Man 1877–1982* (Scarborough, ON: Eden Publishers)

Song, M. and Edwards, R. (1997), 'Comment: raising questions about perspectives on Black lone-mothers, *British Journal of Social Policy*, 26:2, 233–44

Stanislas, P. (2009), 'The policing experiences and perceptions of new communities in Britain', in Salah, M. (ed.) *Europe and its Established and Emerging Communities: Assimilation, Multiculturalism, or Integration* (London: Trentham Press)

Stanislas, P. (2006), *Models of Organisation and Leadership Behaviour Amongst Ethnic Minorities and Policing in Britain* (PhD Dissertation, University of London)

Stapleton, P. (1978), 'Living in Britain', in Ellis, J. (ed.), *West African Families in Britain* (London: Routledge, Keagan and Paul)

Stinchcombe, A. (1965), 'Social structure and organizations', in March, G. J. (ed.), *Handbook of Organizations* (Chicago: Rand McNally and Company)

Sun (2007), 'A result as Star gets CBE' (17 June)

Sunday Times (1997), 'Mixed marriages put celebrities on trial' (6 March)

Temko, N. (2006), 'If you think Jamaica is bad try Nigeria: how Diane Abbot enraged a community', *Observer* (14 May)

Vellenga, D. D. (1983), 'Who is a wife? Legal expressions of heterosexual conflict in Ghana', in Oppong, C. (ed.), *Female and Male in West Africa* (London: George, Allen and Unwin)

Wallman, S. (1986), 'Ethnicity and the boundary process in context', in Rex, J. and Mason, D. (eds), *Theories of Race and Ethnic Relations* (Cambridge: Cambridge University Press)

Ware, H. (1983), 'Female and male life-cycles', in Oppong, C. (ed.), *Female and Male in West Africa* (London: Allen and Unwin)

Williamson, J. (2005), 'Celebrity Culture, Consumerism and Black Girls: A Womanist Perspective on Negotiating Sex and the City' (Paper received via email to author of chapter, June 2005)

Winslow, S. (2001), *Badfellas: Crime, Tradition and New Masculinities* (Oxford and New York: Berg)

Internet sources

Adumekwe, O. and Holloway, L. (2005), *Wall of Silence? The Cops are the Bricks,* Black Information Link, www.blink.org.uk (accessed 25 February 2007)

BBC (British Broadcasting Corporation) News (2006a), *City Cleaners Protest in Pay Row,* 22 November, www.bbc.co.uk (accessed 22 November 2007)

BBC (British Broadcasting Corporation) News (2006b), *Nigerians Scams Cost UK Billions,* 20 November, www.bbc.co.uk (accessed 21 March 2007)

Dustmann, C., Fabbri, C. F. and Preston, I. (2003), *Labour Market Performance of Immigrants in the UK Labour Market,* www.homeoffice.gov.uk (accessed 3 November 2006)

Holloway, L. (2006), *Why No Black MP for Brixton?* Black Information Link, www.blink.org.uk (accessed 12 September 2007)

Holloway, L. (2004), *BBC Promoting Stereotypes with TV Attacks on Black Men,* Black Information Link, www.blink.org.uk (accessed 26 August 2005)

Mama, A. (1995), *The Hidden Struggle: Statutory and Voluntary Responses to Violence Against Black Women in the Home* (London: Whiting & Birch)

Office for National Statistics (2001), *The 2001 Census,* www.statistics.gov.uk (accessed November 2006)

Ogbobode Abidde, S. (2005), *Nigerians and their Foreign Wives,* Nigerians in America website, www.nigeriansinamerica.com (accessed 11 December 2006)

Pryce, S. (2005), *African-Caribbean Baby Fathers – A Myth or Reality, Experts Ask,* Black Britain, www.blackbritain.co.uk (accessed 16 August 2005)

10

Rites of passage and family bonds

Trevor Gordon

Introduction

This chapter calls for more scientifically rigorous and African-centred (Black academic) methodologies and approaches to the use and understanding of rites of passage. It will begin by examining the historical development of the Black family from trans-Atlantic enslavement and colonialism to the recent arrival in the 'Mother Country' and our subsequent treatment and assimilation into the 'host' or 'Mother' culture in the United Kingdom (UK). It will argue that historically the notion of a Black family never really existed in the psyche of the British until late into the twentieth century due to the dehumanisation and demonisation of enslaved Africans that lasted more than four hundred years. This process of trans-Atlantic enslavement commenced with the separation of African families followed by a period of forced transition from a matriarchal to patriarchal family structure, and this was then followed by the forced assimilation and incorporation of British cultural values and norms. The right to housing, education and employment are examined, as these are the three main areas of the host society that Black families have to successfully navigate if they are to survive, successfully develop and make a meaningful contribution while in the host society. In particular, the chapter focusses on the socioeconomic factors that impact on Black family life, and which control and in many cases determine the socioeconomic outcomes and social structures for Black families and their lives in Britain. In many instances, it is argued, these structures are under-pinned by historical and contemporary institutional and individual racism. The denial of fair, just and equitable structures, which has deliberately prevented equal rites of progress or rites of passage in the host culture, in addition to deficit-oriented research models, have inevitably resulted in Black families being judged as dysfunctional and pathological.

The Black family, its treatment and progress in the UK is an under-researched area, but one that causes much debate and conjecture. This present work will contribute to the process of understanding the socioeconomic plight of these family units. The Black family in this context is taken to mean those families of African and African Caribbean origin residing in the UK. These family cohorts now include a very large Dual Heritage or 'mixed' community that is also included in the population group. Between 1992 and 1998 the 'mixed' category population has doubled in the UK and scholars, academics and researchers, I would argue, should include this minority community in all future research about the Black family in the UK (Madge, 2001; Phoenix and Tizard, 2002; Root, 2002).

I share the view voiced by Harriette Piper McAdoo that 'demythologising' the Black family is also a major academic task and as:

> interdisciplinary researchers we have been able to go beyond the negative or stereotypical views that had been held as the position of black families. Unfortunately the wider society has not yet made this journey and many of us are constantly called upon to speak against the negative images that are held about black families. (McAdoo, 1981: 10)

She went on to conclude that 'demythologising of the negative images of the black family is an on-going process that will probably continue for generations to come' (McAdoo, 1981: 10). More recent writers still argue that there is a requirement for researchers and academics to 'demythologise' the Black family (Browder, 2004; Person-Lynn, 1996: 25–6, 48, 64–5, 87–9, 129).

I will argue that the socioeconomic progress or the passage of the Black family is determined and driven by the status inferred upon it by the host society or ruling elite. In a society where 'all men are equal' but class and social status determine to a greater extent your life chances and outcomes, I argue that your passage through life or your life cycle is already predetermined in many respects by the values and expectations of the host society, in this case the UK (Sowell, 1983). Sir Edward Cust's 1839 address to the London Colonial Office, best articulates the issues:

> It is out of season to question at this time of day, the original policy of conferring on every colony of the British Empire a mimic representation of the British Constitution. But if the creature so endowed has sometimes forgotten its real significance and under the fancied importance of speakers and maces, and all the paraphernalia and ceremonies of the imperial legislature, has dared to defy the mother country, she has to thank herself for the folly of conferring such privileges on a condition of society that has no earthly claim to so exalted a position. (Bhabha, 1986: 198)

All societies and cultures operate systems that have incorporated historical 'rites' by embedding them over time into that society's cultural rules, regulations and ultimately legislation. Many 'rites' eventually become codified into more formalised 'rights' and this generally includes all economic, political and social outcomes. Before we examine the Black family we need first to establish what are historically based 'rites of passage'. At the beginning of the last century European scholars such as Arnold Van Gennep (1909) believed that they had now amassed enough data to begin to classify these acts or rites in the pursuit of science. He acknowledged, as I do now, the vastness of material, as all elements of humanity have rites or rituals and these can be found in many ceremonies around the world today. Van Gennep argues that all societies contain distinct social groupings but that one thing remains constant throughout all cultures: the division between the secular and religious worlds. To move from one state of being or existing to another requires a journey, or 'passage'. In the secular sense, for families and individuals this will mean that in order to move from class to class, position to position, job to job or home to home they must fulfil certain conditions and expectations. In European societies, Van Gennep asserts that all these conditions and expectations have one common basis: economic or intellectual outcomes. He noted that in the 'least advanced societies', and this must have included African and Caribbean societies at his time of writing, the holy or spiritual is evident in nearly every phase of individual or family development (Ephirim-Donker, 1997). Spirit, or the sacred, to these 'primitive' societies, he argued, is central to successful progress and growth. It functions on a belief or faith that cannot be scientifically qualified and quantified (Asante, 1992).

Two schools of thought developed and rites were separated into two distinct kinds:

(a)   'Sympathetic rites', some with an animistic basis. These rites are based on reciprocity, like-for-like, on word and deed.
(b)   'Dynamistic and contagious rites', it is argued, are based on the concept of a power that is not individual or personalised. These rites are rooted in the belief that natural or acquired characteristics are material and transmissible.

It was felt appropriate at that time to single out and legitimise rites of passage as a special single category that was then sub-divided into rites of separation, transition rites and rites of incorporation. In looking at the rites of passage for Black families in the UK we shall focus on these three areas; rites of separation, transition and incorporation.

Historically, prior to trans-Atlantic enslavement and colonialism, African people throughout the continent had practised rites of passage for a millennium (Chandler, 1999; Diop, 1987; Ephirim-Donker, 1997; Some, 1994). In African societies, then and now, ritual was and continues to be the most important method of binding a community together in close relationship with the material, physical and spirit worlds. Ritual is a way of life for the spiritual person because it is a tool to maintain the delicate balance between body and soul (Some, 1999). Some goes on to argue that it is important to note that ritual is not compulsive or repetitive behaviour such as smoking or using the toilet – nor is it everyday formalities such as shaking hands or a kiss or hug. It is important to distinguish between ritual and ceremony. A wedding is a good example of this. A wedding is a formal ceremony of marriage but it takes on many spiritual or ritualistic elements depending on your culture, faith, history and background.

More recently much work has been done on the underachievement of Black boys and young men in the education sector (Majors, 2001; Sewell, 1997). Many now argue that these young men require some sort of rites of passage to ensure they do not end up in jail or on a mortuary slab, or ultimately in some other manner become not very useful members of society. Jawanza Kunjufu affirms this thus:

> Traditional cultures throughout the world have often devised ways of dramatising or ritualising the passage into manhood and of transferring that passage to a community event. Throughout the use of structured initiation rites, these societies have been able to help and guide the youths through there period of developmental crisis. By formalising the transition process, complex problems of identity formation are translated into concrete and straightforward tasks. Often, the trials a youth endured were extreme. (Kunjufu, 1992: 33)

Today in the west we see young people joining gangs and going through their own forms of initiation ceremonies or rites of passage. One major gang leader stated that we 'will always have youth because we make them feel important' (Kunjufu, 1992: 33). Many street gangs spend time with new recruits making them feel important. I call it the psychology of respect. This is where crime, drugs and many illegitimate activities are 'legalised' or accepted as part of the power inferred by gang membership. One young man in the Pupil Referral Unit that I work with in a voluntary capacity stated recently: 'I joined the Muslim gang because they can protect me. They have the weapons and the unity. They are my family'.

I hope that the development of systems of rites of passage will be forthcoming to assist Black males and increasingly Black females in the UK not only to realise their own potential but to realise that success of the Black individual is also linked to the success of the Black family and community. There are many successful Black individuals in the world, past and present, but as a collective we are generally not considered to be economically or politically successful (Santley School, 1993: 4a–10a; Van Sertima, 1985: 5, 14–15, 65–6, 87, 127–8). In more concrete terms the success or successful passage of the Black family through rites of separation, transition and incorporation into the host society is not determined by the Black family but by the rules of the host community. These rules have been set and I argue that the expectation of success of the Black family has never been part of the host psyche (Dawson and Tajfel, 1965).

The Black family: separation, transition and incorporation

The Black family and community in the UK today have a long and established historical and colonial past with the 'Mother Country'. There has been a Black presence in Britain prior to Roman settlement (MacRitchie, 1884; Storkey *et al.*, 1997). Indeed, by the end of the nineteenth century there was already a major presence of Black people in the port cities of London, Liverpool, Cardiff and Bristol (Solomos, 2003).

Rites of separation

Enslavement has been practised by human kind for what seems like our entire existence. Paterson (1993) defines enslavement as an extreme form of domination by one person over another that is a form of social parasitism. He goes on to argue that 'It originated as a substitute for certain death, such as spearing condemned prisoners of war, and was maintained through brutality'. He asserts that slavery 'is the permanent violation and domination of natally alienated and generally dishonoured persons'. He uses the term 'natal alienation' to describe the slave's loss of a birth-right to his or her own cultural existence beyond that which the 'master' permits, which thus forces them to experience a form of social death (Paterson, 1993: 3). Beginning towards the end of the sixteenth century, the destruction, separation and ultimately the control of the new 'black Gold' – namely trans-Atlantic enslavement, colonialism and empire for economic gain – required the complete and systematic separation and destruction of the African family and African community unit. Enslaved Africans were brutally and forcefully removed from Africa in their millions and shipped to every corner of the globe (Duignan and Gann, 1975). In the early eighteenth century enslaved Africans became Africa's largest export. There is no doubt in the mind of Klein that 'this forced migration was one of the great crimes against humanity in all world history' (Klein, 1986). When Christopher Columbus 'ran into' the 'New World' in 1492 he praised God and enquired after gold. Dr Theophilus E. S. Scholes, an early Jamaican scholar and traveller of the late nineteenth century, emphatically stated that racial domination supplemented class domination. He argued that as competition from other European colonialists and industrial rivals increased it was necessary for England to increase the 'exploitation of coloured communities' in its colonies (Bryan, 1998).

Capitalism and trans-Atlantic enslavement are inextricably tied to each other, and Williams (1964) successfully captures this in his work *Capitalism and Slavery*. He states:

> In June 1783 Prime Minister Lord North complemented the Quaker opponents of the slave trade on their humanity, but regretted that its abolition was an impossibility as the trade has become necessary to almost every nation in Europe. Slave traders and sugar planters rubbed their hands with glee. The West Indian colonies were still the darlings of the Empire, the most prestigious jewels in the British diadem. (Williams, 1964: 126)

He goes on to quote Adam Smith as writing that 'the sugar planter ranked amongst the highest capitalists of the mercantilist epoch'. The same can also be assumed of the cotton planters.

All aspects of the enslaved Africans' original cultures were, in the main, denied to them. This included not being able to speak your mother-tongue language and practise any religious rites or rituals other than those given to you by your 'owner' or 'master'. You could no longer eat or drink your traditional diet and ultimately you were not part of a family unit or community (Anderson, 1995: 64–5, 69, 72). Africans in their millions were reduced to a status a little lower than a horse. Indeed, this is how many plantation owners were encouraged to see their new stock. In keeping with good rearing practices all horses must be 'broken' or brought under the complete mental subjection of the 'rider' or owner. The breeding of enslaved Africans also followed this principle, namely that you only allowed your best stallions to mate with your mares. This also effectively divided enslaved African males into two distinct groups. The psychological breaking of millions of enslaved Africans was planned and executed during a period of four hundred years (Hassan-El, 1999). The speeches of 1712 and early racist doctrines of Lynch are a must-read in order to focus on the mind-set of the oppressor or slave master during the early 1700s. Lynch has the dubious honour of having the act of hanging rebellious enslaved African named after him. The practice of 'lynching', burning and killing African Americans, remained a practice in the United States of America (USA) up until the late 1960s (Ginzburg, 1988). The 1967 Pulitzer Prize winner David Brion Davis states that the 'inherent contradiction of slavery lay not in its cruelty or economic exploitation, but an underlying conception of a man as a conveyable possession with no more autonomy of will and consciousness as that of a domestic animal' (Davis, 1988).

The men were separated from the women, except for the purposes of breeding, the children from their mothers, house slaves from field slaves and ultimately light skinned from dark skinned. The children of slave owners' rape of Black females, and resulting from the lust of White female family members for enslaved Africans, were inevitably given a higher status than their African ancestors, as they were now classified as 'half caste'. The UK athlete Colin Jackson recently traced his genealogy in the television documentary *Who Do You Think You Are?*. This led to him visiting Jamaica in the Caribbean, where he discovered at first hand – through the work of Black scholars and academics and the historical passing-down of information from generation to generation – the mind-set of both sets of ancestors, enslaved Africans and 'owners'. For Colin and many others this realisation can be emotionally and psychologically painful (Jackson, 2006). Caste comes from a Portuguese word, and was originally used to define impure sugar as in 'caste' sugar or unrefined impure sugar. The use of the descriptor 'caste' would remain in the language and psyche of Europe until the late 1980s. The Portuguese in the early fifteenth century were the first Europeans to send agents to Africa, to oversee the interests of the Portuguese crown (Berlin, 1998). The remaining European powers, including England, were not far behind them. Portugal and England would eventually remain the dominant enslavers of Africans right up until abolition in the 1860s (Klein, 1986: 140).

Defined in law as legal chattel, enslaved Africans were advertised as commodities and any marriages between them were not legally binding. This ensured that the Black family did not have a shape or indeed exist in the eyes of the 'masters' (Brown *et al.*, 1993). The plantation system for enslaved Africans in both South and North America was completely without any compromise or mercy. Thompson (1987) argues that no semblance of their original language remained and virtually all aspects of African culture were obliterated from the mind-set of millions of 'former Africans'. The system of trans-Atlantic enslavement in the Caribbean was equally repressive, but economic necessity required a different approach to the keeping and 'rearing' of enslaved African 'stock'. The 'Pen System' utilised in Jamaica allowed many enslaved Africans to leave the plantation and fend for themselves in controlled areas or pens. This meant, for many, times of free association with fellow enslaved Africans. Many trades developed in the pens as did a retained sense of an African past (Robotham, 1998: 30). Some owners of enslaved Africans allowed women and men to conceive children in the pens and many had to accept the offspring of these pen-based relationships. After all, they were still the property of the 'masters'. An extended family system or welfare state developed where sisters, aunts, brothers, grandparents and the children themselves would be involved in supporting, feeding and rearing any offspring. Education also prevailed and many educated themselves in the pens: William Gordon, Paul Bogle and Marcus Garvey, to name but a few. An informal economy also developed and enslaved Africans actually saved resources collectively. 'Partner' money is still the main form of savings for many Caribbean and African families in the UK today.

The Jamaican and Caribbean extended family of today was then in its infancy. I believe this view is supported by the retention in Jamaican language use to this day of African words, and the underpinning dialect or patois, which is in essence African. The use of patois is still very important in the social and cultural binding of the African and Caribbean family unit and community in the UK today. Craton states that:

> Perhaps the most important question is how long and how deep ran the influence of Africa. African legacies were far more covert than European borrowings. But because of folklore and proverbs identical with African originals, along with songs, dances, games, recipes, and some 10% of African words in the different Creole languages, the African influence in the slave quarters must have been extremely strong, even after the African-born became a minority. (Craton, 1982: 47)

A sense of family and community developed in the pens and also on some plantations. The wonderful cuisine of the Caribbean was also developed in the pens, where enslaved Africans were expected to feed and clothe themselves once they were given the basic raw materials to do so. Spiritual or religious practices also occurred in the pens, and 'Obia' and 'Voodoo' are still widely practised in the Caribbean and the UK today; however, many enslaved Africans adopted the new religion of Christianity as a means of further legitimising themselves by taking on the religion of the 'master' (Craton, 1982: 46–7, 248–50).

Trans-Atlantic slavery was eventually 'abolished' in 1863, though there is ample evidence to suggest that the trade continued for many years after this date. The industrial revolution made enslaved Africans obsolete as a mode of production, and the cost of keeping 'slave stock' was no longer economically viable (Ellis and Walvin, 1981; Midgley, 1992). Four-hundred and twenty-three years of 'rites or the rituals of separation' from your history, culture, language, sexuality and ultimately your reliance on self will ultimately lead to your assimilation and acculturation within the host or ruling society or to your extinction. Indeed, Watson (1977) expresses the view, under the heading: 'Immigration and Class: The Marxist Approach', that the assimilation approach dominated the field of ethnic studies in the 1960s. Many writers at this time argued that Black migrants from Africa and the Caribbean would eventually be absorbed into the indigenous working classes, much like the Irish and the Jewish communities before them. In May 1976 the London Borough of Hackney attempted to recruit an 'Immigrant Assimilation Officer' (Watson, 1977).

The first hundred years following trans-Atlantic African enslavement were characterised by exploitation based now purely on 'race' or social status. The African American was already established, for better or worse, in the host culture and country; not so the Caribbean, who had still to experience the 'Mother Country' first hand (Cooper *et al.*, 2000). The same could be said for Africans under colonial rule, who similarly had worked for empire but not in the 'Mother Country' (Duignan and Gann, 1978).

Rites of transition and incorporation

The end of empire and the need for labour following World War Two saw many Black Commonwealth citizens arrive in Britain (Torrington, 1996). Between the mid-1950s and 1978 Black Britain increased from approximately half a million to two million people; from 1 to 3 per cent of the population at that time (Haynes, 1983). These new arrivals posed a number of social, political and economic questions that needed careful examination, most pressingly from the viewpoint of the Black family itself. Other European nations did take many White migrants after the Second World War but it is easy to see how the label 'immigrant' came to mean Black. Many of these newly arrived citizens (I use citizen here to imply a legal right of abode), were coming to the 'Mother Country' and the vast majority felt that they and their children and families would be equally accepted. These new arrivals from the Caribbean and other Commonwealth areas did not meet any restrictions on entry to the UK. The 1948 British Nationality Act guaranteed an open door policy towards migration from the Commonwealth. Many now argue that the Act, passed by a Labour Government, was a cynical measure aimed at facilitating the supply of much-needed cheap labour. Solomos writes: 'British subjects from the colonies did arrive during this period, particularly from the West Indies, but almost as soon as they began to arrive they were seen as a problem' (Solomos, 2003: 52).

Many Africans and Caribbeans had been raised and educated to view British society as guardians of the law, the custodians of justice and a fair 'Christian' society, built on tolerance and charity towards others (Haynes, 1983). Four hundred years of slavery and colonialism had left these Black 'subjects' with a diminished, polluted and misconceived understanding of the rites of passage required to succeed in the mother culture or host country. Never in their wildest dreams did they expect to find a society hostile to their presence or a deep-rooted resentment that was, and is, fuelled in the main by racism and racial discrimination.

It is important at this stage to understand the pattern of Black migration into the UK. The bulk of Caribbeans arrived in the 1950s and migration from the Caribbean has been a very slow trickle ever since, unlike African migration, which has been fairly constant. The Caribbean population was by far the largest group within the UK Black population in 1965, but the 1991 and 2001 Census data reveals that this position has now been taken by the African community (Storkey, 2001). In the 1950s these new 'Black immigrants' faced opposition from the moment they arrived. Some of this opposition can be related to the process of individual personality. But as Holmes (1991) goes on to argue: 'this form of enmity can be defined as prejudice. But the majority of opposition is socially and culturally generated, rather than organically related to the individual psyche. This latter form of hostility can be described as antipathy' (Holmes, 1991). Many newspaper articles in the 1980s contained antipathetic sentiment towards Caribbeans, Asians and Africans. The gratuitous use of adjectives such as 'Black' or 'Coloured' were employed particularly when reporting criminal activities. Hostile comments and words such as 'contaminating', 'wog' and 'Paki' became the currency of everyday talk in society, much of it fuelled by the new and emerging post-war media industry (Troyna, 1981; Twitchin, 1988).

The Black family found many obstacles deliberately placed in its way that hindered its progress or rites of passage. In the early 1950s

Halsey commented on the automatic assimilation of minorities and new arrivals into the working classes irrespective of what education the 'minority' had received in the colonies or elsewhere (Halsey, 1986). Hence qualified engineers, doctors, nurses, teachers and other professionals were not recognised and many had to take jobs lower down the economic ladder. For example, my mother arrived in the UK in 1961 as a qualified nurse but had to work for nine years as an 'Auxiliary Assistant' (one rung above bedpan cleaner), before being allowed to fully use her skills, abilities and expertise.

The Black family: rights to housing, education and employment

The three main areas that require a greater degree of success for any family unit or community to successfully survive, grow and develop positively are successful rites of passage to reasonable and affordable housing, access to and a good standard of education, and access to economic success through employment and entrepreneurial endeavour. (I also acknowledge that access to health care is also a major factor.) I will now briefly examine these three key areas not only from the perspective of blockages to the right of fair passage and ultimately, in many cases, the absolute denial to the rite of passage but also from the perspective of finding alternatives and other ways of securing a fair and reasonable outcome. Simply put, what mechanisms have Black families and the Black community developed to overcome racism, whether institutional or day-to-day racism? What 'rites of passage' have the Black family and community developed for its survival in what some observers would view as an increasingly negative and hostile environment (Cork, 2005; Hare and Hare, 1993)?

The right to housing

The need for safe, affordable good-quality housing seems to have been the main concern upon arrival for many African, Caribbean and Asian families. Historically, among the general population in the UK owner-occupation and good-quality housing are strongly associated. The more affluent people are, the higher their standard of housing and the more likely they are to be owner-occupiers. However, research clearly shows that for the first generation of minority ethnic arrivals none of these traditional patterns holds good. It would seem that owner-occupation performs a completely different function for this community. The 1971 Census figures show that 50 per cent of West Indians and 50 per cent of the general population were owner-occupiers. This figure rises to 76 per cent in the Asian population at that time. What this clearly shows is that during a very short space of time in England – and in spite of the fact that they tended to be doing inferior, lower-paid jobs and having much larger extended families to support – West Indians achieved the same level of owner-occupation as the White population (Smith, 1977). At that time, 26 per cent of West Indians received council accommodation, compared to 28 per cent in the general population. However, West Indians also occupied 28 per cent of the private rented sector, compared to 22 per cent of the general population.

The need for housing was an absolute priority for the new arrivals. The same is true for many new arrivals today. Shelter is the first basic requirement for a human being to function. The majority of these new arrivals had never owned the homes, tenement yards, villages and compounds that they once lived in. They already had first-hand experience of exploitative and dishonest landlords 'back home'. They saw acquiring and owning your own shelter as the absolute priority, not only in relation to having a secure roof over your head but also to remove the possibility of extortion, exploitation and racism that riddled the privately rented sector at that time. Racism has a long history in the private rented sector. Investigations by the Commission for Racial Equality (CRE) in the 1980s revealed that estate agents had discriminated against minority ethnic communities. The signs of my childhood that used to read: 'No Blacks, No Irish, No Dogs', are no longer displayed since the introduction of the Race Relations Act in 1976. However, there is evidence today that racial bias and institutional racism still exists in the private rented sector, although this discrimination is slightly more subtle (Skellington and Morris, 1996). Racial harassment in the housing sector, along with most racially motivated incidents, has traditionally always been under-reported. The 1987 CRE report into racism in people's homes confirms this under-reporting (CRE, 1987).

Many Caribbean, African and Asian Commonwealth members saved literally every last penny at great sacrifice to their own personal comfort to purchase their own home. Once purchased, these homes formed the first line of safe arrival for the many family members and siblings who were initially left behind in the Caribbean. Many new arrivals were single and had left family behind in the Commonwealth while they attempted to set up a 'bridgehead of safe passage' in the 'Mother Country'. Without a large enough home you could not send for your family. The acquisition of a house, for many, was the only reasonable way or passage forward. This did lead to overcrowding, by British standards, in many homes. However, under empire and in the colonies this type of overcrowding was an accepted part of colonialism and capitalism. For Black families there was no sense of 'overcrowded', just a realisation that one must endure hardship for a time while establishing one's own bridgehead or passage. The community was happy to see, help and embrace its own. Reciprocity truly existed and any help that you and your family were given was given back once you and your family were in a position to do so. For example, my mother, father and I lived in a single rented room, sharing an outside toilet and bathroom, when we first arrived in London in 1961. By 1969 my parents had purchased a small terraced house and we were now renting a small room to family and friends who had recently arrived. This pattern was reproduced across the country in Chapletown, Leeds; Moss Side, Manchester; Brixton, London; and St Paul's, Bristol. The Black community still has considerable investments in property in these areas today and we have now purchased in more desirable areas, and many Black families have 'moved to the suburbs'. This property portfolio or property legacy has also ensured that, irrespective of a lack of economic and political power, Black communities did build a solid financial base that was funded and underpinned by property purchases and transactions. This property base was vital for Black communities in establishing a bridgehead for the successful 'rites or transition and incorporation' into the host society or 'Mother Country'. There are no reported cases of disease or epidemics connected to these new arrivals and within their tightly knit communities. Many previous epidemics in the UK were generally associated with overcrowding and poor hygiene. Overcrowded did not mean unclean for these new arrivals, and as racism was also about the 'dirty' appearance of Black people – or 'dark', 'dirty' skin – personal hygiene was very high on the list for Caribbeans and Africans at that time.

The right to education and employment

The right to education in European cultures is inextricably linked to the right to decent employment, pay and entrepreneurial endeavour. The right to education for any community or group is a fundamental necessity if that community or group is to survive, develop positively and grow successfully. Other than people of African descent I can find no group historically or in the present day that has been systematically denied education on such a vast and politically organised scale. The mis-education of the African commenced with first denying the African any access or right of passage whatsoever to becoming literate. During the more than four hundred years of trans-Atlantic enslavement it was punishable by death by hanging to teach an enslaved African to read anything but the Bible, responsible for bringing literacy to millions of Africans during this time. Ironically, it was the only available 'right of passage' to literacy. It is only through literacy that one can access knowledge. Without the ability to access knowledge you will never, in the main, attempt to access power. For more than two hundred years, enslaved Africans massively outnumbered plantation owners and White workers in North America and the Caribbean. If they had knowledge of this numerical and statistical fact, as the plantation owners did, then trans-Atlantic slavery may well have ended a lot sooner. Knowledge is power.

The denial of education and in many cases the mis-education of Black children, pupils and adults is an area that has been investigated extensively by researchers, academics and community groups in Britain since the mid-1980s. A massive amount of research exists qualifying the constant failure of the British education sector to successfully educate Black children. I can find very few areas of academia and research effort in recent years that have produced so much data, yet the vast majority of these data and subsequent findings appear to have been systematically ignored. This denial and exclusion from formal education, particularly academic education as apposed to vocational education, is well documented (see Gordon 1994 for recent examples of this area of study).

The denial of a 'right of passage' to quality education and the continued high level of exclusion of Black pupils are valid indicators as to the academic progress of Black males and more recently Black females: in 1994 one in six Black exclusions involved a female student but in 2006 the number was one in three. Increasingly, Black children and young people are at risk of permanent exclusion and the discriminatory pattern of exclusions persists. A 'statemented' Black child in care is between 96 and 128 times more likely to be excluded from school than a White pupil (CEN, 2006; Harris, 2006). Community Empowerment Network (CEN) (2006), goes on to ask the question: 'Is what is happening to our children and young people still a result of the crippling combination of negative prejudice, destructive stereotyping and low expectations, in short Institutional racism'?

Black and minority ethnic girls are doing well in school, asserts the Equal Opportunities Commission (EOC), but they face very poor prospects when they start work (Metro, 2006). The 2006 report goes on to say: 'Black Caribbean girls are more ambitious than White girls about their education and their future careers'. However, they face heavy penalties at work, including low pay, poor prospects and fewer job opportunities. The head of the EOC added: 'not enough employers are tapping into this pool of talent. More must be done before another generation fall prey to the same negative cycle of poor pay, poor prospects and occupational segregation' (Simpson, 2006).

The irony of institutional racism in education is that between the 1991 and 2001 Census qualification levels have improved for Black and minority ethnic communities, but not for the White population (Equal Opportunities Review, 2006). However, the difficulties for those from minority ethnic communities in obtaining employment are not restricted to those with lower levels of education and training. The Department for Works and Pensions carried out an analysis of inequalities in the national and local labour markets during the ten-year period 1991–2001. It traced the impact of human and social capital, the contrast from generation to generation, any improvements over time and the 'geography of disadvantage' (Equal Oppotunities Review, 2006). Black and minority ethnic communities continue to have higher unemployment rates and greater concentrations in routine or semi-routine work, with lower hourly earnings than White people. These differentials cannot be explained by age, education or the foreign birth of Black and minority ethnic workers. Even the second generation, who were born and educated in the UK, experience significant disadvantages in relation to unemployment, earnings and occupational attainment. I would argue that this is mainly due to continued poor-quality education, and institutional racism. The research goes on to conclude that these disadvantages, or 'ethnic penalties', are smaller for women than for men, and sexism is thought to be responsible for this as White women also face this disadvantage in the labour market. 'Ethnic penalties' are greater in the private sector in respect to occupational attainment and earnings. Access to education has traditionally been tightly controlled and, unlike housing, money alone cannot secure a reasonable outcome, as many Black families today are finding out in the public or fee-paying sector. Education is the 'gateway' the 'elitist passage' through which the select (Oxford and Cambridge) are allowed to enter. Of all the positions of power and authority in the UK, 83 per cent are occupied by an Oxford or Cambridge graduate, including the Labour Party. This figure has not changed for more than a century.

Many Black and minority ethnic people in today's society view education as paramount if they are to survive in 'their own country'. Many pursue education 'by any means necessary' and give up literally every luxury to study and qualify, and end up with large debts. I returned to education at the age of 26 after I vowed that a White boss would never again utter the statement to me: 'Gordon you are not qualified to speak or give a meaningful or educated opinion'. I created my own 'rights of passage' and educated 'myself' – my inner self. I read all I could find and purchased what was written by Black scholars, academics and historians. I found my 'self' and for the first time I found a meaning behind the creation, existence and ultimately the purpose of the Black family, the African family and all humanity.

Conclusion

A logical and rigorous scientific approach is urgently required to understand the immense value of 'rites of passage'. As we embrace the new millennium it is time to take the paradigms and boundaries of European scholastic practice and build new 'schools' or scientific approaches to understanding Black people and ultimately the Black family. As Black scholars we no longer need to seek the approval of White academics for the use of these 'new' methodologies (some of which are as old as humankind).

I argue that these methodologies are required not only to gain a deeper and more accurate understanding of the Black experience but also to help humanity reach its pinnacle, its zenith and its ultimate purpose. We need to explore how rites of passage influence the individual sociopolitically, economically and spiritually. Ephirim-Donker asserts:

> This Structural model utilizes myths and concepts, rites, dreams and symbolic elements that form the basis for human development ... Areas of our research should include the conceptual theory of personality; reincarnation, conception, birth, post-partum care and early childhood; orality and the cognitive operational patterns of knowing and reasoning; meaning making and patterns of interpreting existence and generativity; eldership; death and ancestorhood. We examined the pedagogical apparatus of cognitive development and the epigenetic basis of orality. Since orality is the foundation for social, economic, political, and spiritual life. (Ephirim-Donker, 1997: 6)

I argue that the Black family in the UK survives partly through the passing down of the 'apparatus of survival' or the 'rites of passage' from one generation to another.

Ironically more and more White men are now involved in a deeper search for their 'lost masculinity'. John Eldridge in his superb work *Wild at Heart* quotes Robert Bly: 'We know that our society produces a plentiful supply of boys, but seems to produce fewer and fewer men.

There are two simple reasons; we don't know how to initiate boys to men and second we are not sure we really want to' (Eldridge, 2001: 83). He goes on to assert:

> Where does a man go to learn his true name, a name that can never be taken from him? That deep heart knowledge comes only through the process of initiation. You have to know where you are coming from, you have to have faced a series of trials that test you; you have to have taken a journey, and you have to have faced your enemy ... A friend tells me that in the Masai tribe in Africa, a young man cannot court a women until he has killed a Lion. That's their way of saying until he has been initiated. Remember – masculinity is bestowed by masculinity. (Eldridge, 2001: 101 and 114)

Eldridge's view supports a theory that I call 'triangulation of self'. Put simply: in order to know your future you must know your past, as your past gives you meaning and direction in your present. Past, present and future – triangulation. This is not a contentious issue as European society fully exploits its knowledge of things past to reinforce things present and future. Many of the second and third generations of Black people in the UK today operate only in the present and future – a linear progression. The original arrivals (first generation) had a triangulated approach to life and survival. The Black family truly existed; few lone-parent families existed at that time and a real community or extended family existed. This is not the case today.

The past for many 'British Blacks' seems negative, when studied from a European perspective. Black people do not wish to embrace 'their' past, when the 'story' is told by Europeans. We need to encourage 'an authentic anthropology' such as that presented by Cheikh Anta Diop to be studied by all scholars, Black and White (Diop, 1987). Diop enables a fuller, richer, more accurate and sympathetic approach to the subject matter.

I close by quoting the 'Song of the Return' in (Some, 1994) *Of Water and the Spirit*:

> I had to go away and learn
> How to know
> I had to go away to learn
> How to grow
> I had to go away to learn
> How to stay there
>
> So I went and knocked at doors
> Locked in front of me
> I craved to enter

Oh, little did I know
The doors did not lead outside

It was all in me
I was the room and the door
It was all in me
I just had to remember

References

Anderson, S. E. (1995), *The Black Holocaust for Beginners* (Danbury, CT: Writers and Readers Publishing Inc.)

Asante, M. K. (1992), *Kemet, Afrocentricity and Knowledge* (Trenton, NJ: Africa World Press)

Berlin, I. (1998), *Many Thousands Gone: The First Two Centuries of Slavery in North America* (Cambridge, MA: Harvard University Press)

Bhabha, H. (1986), 'Of mimicry and man: the ambivalence of colonial discourse', in Donald, J. and Hall S. (eds), *Politics and Ideology* (Milton Keynes: Open University Press)

Browder, A. T. (2004), *Nile Valleys Contributions to Civilization: Exploding the Myth Vol. 1* (Washington, DC: Institute of Karmic Guidance)

Brown, R., Goodheart, L. and Rabe, S. (1993), *In Slavery in American Society* (Washington, DC: Heath and Company, 3rd edn)

Bryan, P. (1998), 'Black perspectives in late nineteenth century Jamaica: the case of Dr Theophilus E.S. Scoles', in Bryan, P. and Lewis, R. (eds), *Garvey, His Work, His Impact* (Mona: University of the West Indies)

CEN (Community Empower Network) (2006), *Annual Report 2006* (London: Community Empower Network)

Chandler, W. B. (1999), *Ancient Future: The Teachings and Prophetic Wisdom of the Seven Hermetic Laws of Ancient Egypt* (Baltimore, MD: Black Classic Press)

Cooper, F., Holt, T. and Scott, R. (2000), *Beyond Slavery, Explorations of Race, Labour and Citizenship in Post Emancipation Societies* (Chapter Hill, NC: The University of North Carolina Press)

Cork, L. (2005), *Supporting Black Pupils and Parents: Understanding and Improving Home-School Relations* (Oxford: Routledge)

Craton, M. (1982), *Testing the Chains, Resistance to Slavery in the British West Indies* (New York: Cornell University Press)

CRE (Commission for Racial Equality) (1987), *Living in Terror: A Report on Racial Violence and Harassment in Housing* (London: Commission for Racial Equality)

Davis, D. B. (1988), *The Problem of Slavery in Western Culture* (Oxford: Oxford University Press)

Dawson, J. and Tajfel, H. (1965), *Disappointed Guests* (Oxford: Oxford University Press)

Diop, C. A. (1987), *Pre-Colonial Africa* (New York: Lawrence Hill Books)

Duignan, P. and Gann, L. H. (1978), *The Rulers of British Africa 1870–1914* (London: Croom Helm)

Duignan, P. and Gann, L. H. (1975), *Colonialism in Africa 1870–1960: The Economics of Colonialism*, Vol. 4 (Cambridge: Cambridge University Press)

Eldridge, J. (2001), *Wild at Heart, Discovering the Secret of a Man's Soul* (Nashville, TN: Nelson Books)

Ellis, D. and Walvin, J. (1981), *The Abolition of the Atlantic Slave Trade* (Madison: The University of Wisconsin Press)

Ephirim-Donker, A. (1997), *African Spirituality, On Becoming Ancestors* (Trenton, NJ: Africa World Press)

Equal Opportunities Review (2006), *Policies are Needed to Counter Racial Discrimination: Equal Opportunities Review*, 154 (July) (London: IRS Publications)

Ginzburg, R. (1988), *100 Years of Lynching* (Baltimore, MD: Black Classic Press)

Gordon, T. (1994), *The Exclusion of Black Children* (MSc dissertation, South Bank University)

Halsey, A. H. (1986), *Change in British Society* (Oxford: Oxford University Press)

Hare, N. and Hare, J. (1993), *The Endangered Black Family* (San Francisco: Black Think Thank)

Harris, P. (2006), *In Search of Belonging: Reflections by Transracially Adopted People* (London: British Association for Adoption and Fostering)

Hassan-El, K. M. (1999), *The Willie Lynch Letter and the Making of a Slave* (Chicago: Lushena Books)

Haynes, A. (1983), *The State of Black Britain* (London: Root Publishing Company)

Holmes, C. (1991), *A Tolerant Country* (London: Faber and Faber)

Jackson, C. (2006), *Who Do You Think You Are?* British Broadcasting Corporation (BBC 1), 20 September (London)

Klein, H. (1986), *African Slavery in Latin American and the Caribbean* (Oxford: Oxford University Press)

Kunjufu, J. (1992), *Countering the Conspiracy to Destroy Black Boys: Vol. 2* (Chicago: Illinois African American Images)

MacRitchie, D. (1884), *Ancient and Modern Britons*, Vol. 1 (London: British Library)

Madge, N. (2001), *Understanding Difference: The Meaning of Ethnicity in Young Lives* (London: National Children's Bureau)

Majors, R. (2001), *Educating our Black Children* (Oxford: Routledge)

McAdoo, H. P. (ed.) (1981), *Black Families* (London: Sage)

Metro (2006), 'Bosses fail Black and Asian Girls', *Metro* (7 September)

Midgley, C. (1992), *Women against Slavery, The British Campaign 1780–1870* (Oxford: Routledge)

Paterson, O. (1993), 'Slavery and social death', in Brown, R., Goodheart, L. and Rabe, S. (eds), *In Slavery in American Society* (Washington, DC: Heath and Company, 3rd edn)

Person-Lynn, K. (ed.) (1996), *First Word, Black Scholars, Thinkers and Warriors: Knowledge, Wisdom, Mental Liberation* (New York and London: Harlem River Press)

Phoenix, A. and Tizard, B. (2002), *Black, White or Mixed Race?* (Oxford: Routledge)

Robotham, D. (1998), 'The development of Black ethnicity in Jamaica', in Bryan, P. and Lewis, R. (eds), *Garvey, His Work, His Impact* (Mona: University of the West Indies)

Root, M. (2002), 'A bill of rights for racially mixed people', in Essed, P. and Goldberg, D. (eds), *Race Critical Theories* (Oxford: Blackwell Publishing Publishers)

Santley School Black History Researchers (1993), *Famous Black Victorians* (UK, Santley School Raising Achievement Project)

Sewell, T. (1997), *Black Masculinities in Schooling* (Stoke on Trent: Trentham Books)

Simpson, T. (2006), 'Bleak prospects for women', *Voice Newspaper* (11 September)

Skellington, R. and Morris P. (1996), *Race in Britain Today* (London: Sage Publications)

Smith, D. J. (1977), *Racial Disadvantage in Britain* (London: Pelican Books)

Solomos, J. (2003), *Race and Racism In Britain* (London: Palgrave Macmillan)

Some, M. P. (1999), *The Healing Wisdom of Africa* (New York: Tarcher Penguin)

Some, M. P. (1994), *Of Water and the Spirit, Ritual, Magic and Initiation in the Life of an African Shaman* (New York: Tarcher Putnam Books)

Sowell, T. (1983), *The Economics and Politics of Race* (New York: Quill)

Storkey, M. (2001), *London's Ethnic Minorities: One City Many Communities* (London: London Research Centre)

Storkey, M., Maquire, J. and Lewis, R. (1997), *Cosmopolitan London, Past, Present and Future* (London: London Research Centre)

Thompson, V. B. (1987), *The Making of the African Diaspora in the Americas 1440–1900* (New York: Longman)

Torrington, A. (1996), *Windrush 98 Overview* (London: Windrush Committee)

Troyna, B. (1981), *Public Awareness and the Media: A Study of the Reporting on Race* (London: Commission for Racial Equality)

Twitchin, J. (1988), *The Black and White Media Show* (Stoke on Trent: Trentham Books)

Van Gennep, A. (1909), *The Rites of Passage* (Oxford: Routledge and Kegan Paul)

Van Sertima, I. (ed.) (1985), *Blacks in Science Ancient and Modern* (Somerset, NJ: Transaction Books), pp. 5, 14–15, 65–6, 87, 127–8

Watson, J. (1977), *Between Two Cultures: Migrants and Minorities in Britain* (London: Blackwell Publishing)

Williams, E. (1964), *Capitalism and Slavery* (London: Andre Deutsch)

11

The Black family and sport: it's all good . . . right?

Kevin Hylton

Introduction

It has been suggested that sport, unlike other key arenas in society, has been viewed as a vehicle for Black people in the United Kingdom (UK) to become integrated or even assimilated into 'British culture' (Polley, 1998; Whannel, 1992). Polley's (1998) argument that sport has delivered a level of recognition and respect to Black people that perhaps they would not have achieved so readily offers food for thought, especially where sport consistently delivers good news about Black people more often than most other areas of social life. The success of Black people in high-profile sport has led to a 'quickening' in the establishment of a, albeit diverse, Black cultural identity (Whannel, 1992). Sport is symbolic in highlighting a regular mutual experiencing of togetherness in Black communities that it is perhaps much harder to see elsewhere, even in politics. Where we can agree on the transitory nature of identities, whether real or imagined, we can also accept that sport has the capacity to bring Black people together in a most profound way. Whannel (1992: 130) has spoken of the 'Black cultural resonances' of the 'Blackwash'! banners held up in celebration of a West Indies Test victory against England. Also sport can bring disparate people together in ways unimagined. For example, Member of Parliament Diane Abbot, who was brought up in a White suburb in Harrow and was schooled in a girls' grammar school where she was the only Black girl, was inspired by Tommie Smith and John Carlos on the podium in the Munich Olympic Games in 1968 and motivated into joining a Black liberation movement that 'made me proud of my race [sic]' (Abbott, 2006: 94).

This chapter considers a number of issues in sport, presenting it as a double-edged sword that concerns the African Caribbean family in its widest sense. It could be said that an ambiguous arena has never been so conspicuous in a society that has historically presented mixed messages about the Black presence in its towns and cities. We will see how the *yin* and *yang* of sport are evident in the plethora of images that African Caribbeans see of themselves, and how sport contributes to our sense of self and others in how we construct our identities. Further, a focus on other areas of sport demonstrates how a sense of contrariness and ambivalence towards Blackness and Black Britishness are played out in the media (Gilroy, 1987; Hylton, 2009; Whannel, 1992). Consequently a critical reading of 'race' and ethnicity in sport requires recognition of 'socially produced, heterogeneous and dynamic processes of being and becoming' (Gunaratnam, 2003: 4). The 'being and becoming' that Gunaratnam refers to involves an ongoing process of visioning and re-visioning self and others over time and space. That is, African Caribbeanness, Blackness and Black Britishness are constantly being transformed and are not fixed, to the extent that when we consider them in sport then our dynamic identity construction will draw upon events, politics, economics, history, location and a multitude of other variables, including imaginations, as part of a constant imaging/imagining process. Williams (1994) adds a caveat to this in stressing the need to embed Black identities into their social context, as the result of detaching the social backdrop to Black identities and Black Britishness is a risk of a reductionist biological explanation of behaviours and African Caribbeanness that we will see is evident in sport discourses. However, even this analysis only begins to scratch the surface of sport's function in our collective consciousness.

Sport and the State

The necessity for governing bodies of sport to focus on 'race' and ethnicity in their daily work can be demonstrated through research by the Government's sport development body, Sport England (Sport England, 2000: 4), which showed clearly for the first time that there are more unmet needs amongst minority ethnic groups in comparison to their White peers. For instance, from 54 per cent of Pakistanis to 81 per cent of the 'Black Other' categories wished to take up a sport that they did not currently participate in, and many of these sports such as swimming defied many of the stereotypes that prevail about Black people and the sports that they like and are 'best suited to'. Curiously the survey only 'touched upon' experiences of racial discrimination or the social factors of opportunities or motivations even though in some categories one in five experienced racism (Sport England, 2000: 6). This 'silence' on racism is symptomatic of the institutional response to such issues. Even in the midst of such ground-breaking research on ethnicity the hegemonic values and assumptions underpinning public-sector sport, where most of us experience our leisure, should be unpacked and criticised. Similarly, in 1999 Sport England's research into its own activities and products found that minority ethnic communities in Derby, Leicester and Nottingham did not have equal access to them. To counter this problem they identified a need for a greater coordination of sports opportunities, a need for community groups to work together and a need for racial equality support for local governing bodies of sports clubs (Wheeler, 2000). This recognition of race equality in these recent experimental 'Active Communities' projects is an indicator of emergent ideas on the need to oppose racism and to recognise racial inequality in sport. What is clear in sport for Black people in the UK is that they have the same chance to win when on the pitch, court or poolside as anyone else, but the political, economic and cultural resources available to them are invariably unequal (Carrington and McDonald, 2003; Hylton/ ILAM, 1999; Jarvie, 1991a, 1991b; Spracklen *et al.*, 2006).

Social commentators such as Goldberg (1993, 2002), Solomos and Back (1995) and Skellington and Morris (1996) are critical of the well-known disparities between those who have the blend of social, cultural and economic capital that keep some on the inside of sport that those outside of the system clearly do not. Thus sport has a role enhancing social inclusion even if its role in this task is perhaps not as clear as the Government's. However, a cursory reading of the related sports literature in the UK identifies an institution repeatedly accused of advantaging White people as players, spectators and employees over those from African Caribbean and Asian backgrounds, even in those sports where success amongst these groups is more conspicuous (Back *et al.*, 2001; Carrington and McDonald, 2001; Jarvie, 1991a; Long and Hylton, 2002; Swinney and Horne, 2005).

Race logic

Due to the innate physicality of sport it has been incumbent upon its policy-makers and commentators to explore, examine and explain this symbolic cultural phenomenon in an instrumental fashion. That is, sport has been deemed by policy-makers, practitioners and the general public to have certain qualities that make it possible to act as a 'cultural glue' due to its many social benefits (Hylton and Totten, 2008; Polley, 1998). Social benefits attributed to sport have included regeneration, social inclusion, integration, social cohesion, character building and positive diversion. Further, our capabilities in sport are often described in physical or psychological terms – as 'natural' differences. These differences in sport are often identified as the difference between those who are likely to succeed in a given sport and those who are not. This discourse of superiority and inferiority in sport is not dissimilar to other debates outside of sport that revolve around genetics, intelligence and ultimately underpin imperialist ideologies (Essed and Goldberg, 2002; Goldberg, 1993). There is a popular perception in sport that our genes and to a degree our cultural background dictate the prowess of an individual sportsman or -woman. This discourse of advantage and of course disadvantage in sport are invariably reduced to 'harmless' racial differences that suggest a more sinister undercurrent or 'race' logic (Coakley, 2001). There is no one interpretation of how these racialised processes work as the intricacies of these issues exercise the minds of many committed to the furthering of our understanding of 'race', sport and the African Caribbean family. Carrington and McDonald (2001: 2) go on to state that it 'is too simplistic to argue that sport improves "race relations", just as it is to say that sport can only reproduce racist ideologies'.

St Louis (2004) accepts that this racist orthodoxy exists while positing that the perception that Black people are particularly strong in motor rather than psychological terms, and that evidence of conspicuous success in high-profile sport is evidence of this, provides for many a *prima facie* case for the existence of racial physical propensities. These racial differences that emerge from a flawed social Darwinism begin and end in a biological reductionist morass. They give support to Younge's (2000: 24) contention that these views suggest that if Black people are naturally talented at sport then they are naturally less equipped intellectually. The ability to generate knowledge of this kind in itself points towards the biases and social positioning of the dominant actors within sport and academia. There are various examples of this in popular culture. The film *Cool Runnings*, the story of the Jamaican bobsleigh team competing in the Olympic Games, was written as a comedy that was underpinned by the conception and stereotype that Black people cannot do winter sports: the somewhat superficial characters portrayed in the film do not like the cold. Similarly, in *White Men Can't Jump*, where the narrative is even more obvious, the film carries still a benign subtext that not only is the White man who couldn't jump, jumping, but he only manages it when he needs to and only after a lot of hard work! Here racial stereotypes prevail again with many racialised ideologies, concepts and stereotypes remaining intact and unchallenged. What is not considered in any respect in these accounts is the corollary of these arguments that Coakley (2001) alludes to in his critical exploration of 'race logic' in sport. He points to the unlikelihood of commentators explaining the achievements of Swiss skiing from a biological viewpoint.

This racial thinking in sport is perpetuated by four weak theoretical propositions, according to St Louis (2004: 32):

1. sports are based on theoretical principles of equality
2. the results of sporting competition are unequal
3. this inequality of results has a racial bias
4. therefore given the equality of access and opportunity, the explanation of the unequal results lies in racial physicality.

This 'race logic' can be propagated by Black or White people. According to Williams (1977), Hargreaves (1986) and Sugden and Tomlinson (2002), the pressures and limits of a given domination or subordination are experienced and internalised by individuals and groups; this process is often described as hegemony, and describes how individuals or groups in society reinforce or challenge their own subordination in a system that can alienate and disenfranchise them. A lived hegemony is always an ongoing process, it is not a passive form of dominance as it has to be continually renewed, recreated, defended and modified. Goldberg (1993: 94) would argue that biology is not the only predicate of racial constructions. Cultural racism, xenophobia and Whiteness processes are other mechanisms to impact upon how we play and experience sport. Even in Carrington and Wood's (1983) classic study, evidence of the internalisation of racial thinking was apparent amongst Black school children to the degree that, in a Gramscian sense, they were reinforcing their own subordination and oppression through discourse and practice. For in addition to the stereotypes of their liberal-minded teachers some of the pupils were readily able to reproduce these racial stereotypes as part of a rationale for their own achievements. This process of thinking, acting and reinforcement is so subtle that even in adults these common assumptions remain unchallenged. In the study for 'Kick it Out' on the nature and extent of racism in grassroots and amateur football, Long *et al.* (2000) found similar processes at work. In this study players were asked to identify stereotypes about themselves, and here there were further examples of the hegemony of racial ideologies permeating the way Black players think and act. Although the African Caribbean and Asian players were aware of views held about them some of the players saw these perceptions in a positive way. Where 'positive' comments about talent, fitness, strength, speed and emotional qualities were identified then a number of these players accepted the views redolent of Carrington and Wood's (1983) school children eighteen years previously. Curiously few stereotypes were posited about White players by the African Caribbean and Asian players or even the White players themselves. Comments about White players were restricted to the national team and the organisation of clubs. This inability to see Whiteness (Roediger, 2002) was a significant issue within the report and subsequent studies, and consequently an issue to be considered later in this chapter.

Race logic in action

Polley's (1998) observation of Kenny Dalglish, the then Liverpool manager, trying to quell the media fervour behind John Barnes' transfer into the Liverpool team in 1989 is an interesting issue for this section to consider. In defence of the signing of Barnes, who at that point became the most significant Black player ever to play at Liverpool, the manager Dalglish, who had played with and against some of the best Black players in the world, offered a response to the media that has become familiar in liberal-minded political discourses, a statement that we can only guess he had heard before and whose sentiments he honestly believes in, when he stated that: 'He [Barnes] is not a Black player, he's a player' (Polley, 1998: 135). There is a parallel here with Gilroy's assertion in the classic *There Ain't no Black in the Union Jack* (1987) that being Black and British is often too much for politicians to reconcile; in fact the couplet becomes naturally separated, as oil and water. In Henderson's (1995) *Wisden* cricket article an England cricket team is weakened by having Black faces in the changing room. In Dalglish's case, Barnes being Black and a footballer was an awkward coupling, causing Dalglish to trivialise Barnes' African Caribbean heritage. At this point in the 1980s, monkey chants in UK stadia along with banana-throwing were commonplace. In fact, one of the iconic images of football in this period was John Barnes back-heeling a banana skin off the pitch whilst playing for Liverpool. Dalglish's comments need to be considered with this backdrop and also need to be understood as reflective of the experience of Black sports people over the years in the UK. This racialised marking of difference through sport has become constitutive of a national discourse of difference and othering due to racial and ethnic background. I would concur with Song (2004) and Omi and Winant (2002) in arguing that what these processes then reinforce are racial hierarchies that can be seen played out on the fields of Eton, East Ham and East Leeds just as they play out in the corridors and classrooms.

Further, sport has been seen by many as an arena where the meanings attached to 'African Caribbean or Asian-ness' are socially constructed, reified, fixed and sharpened (Campbell, 1995; Carrington, 1999; Carrington and McDonald, 2001; Hall, 1990; Ismond, 2003; Polley, 1998). To extend this analysis, inclusions in sport discourses are as important as absences in gauging the perceptions of social groups in the UK. The inclusion of those from an African Caribbean background is as conspicuous as the marginalisation of those from a South Asian heritage. Fleming's (1991: 53) critical analysis of Asians in sport and education presented a view that 'sport is a vehicle for the expression of antagonism and racial tension' is further emphasised by a number of authors (Bains and Patel, 1996; Carrington and McDonald, 2001; Coakley, 2001) not least Jas Bains (2005; Bains and Patel, 1996). Bains and Patel's (1996) ironically titled work *Asians Can't Play Football* was a critical attack on the football authorities for their lack of commitment to including Asians in their infrastructure. The professional and amateur game was a target for Bains, who pointed out the institutional barriers that precluded the development of Asian players and coaches. Nearly ten years on an even more critical Bains (2005) has seen little change in the work of the Football Association even after a number of further events have highlighted this problem in rigorous and robust ways (Long *et al.*, 2000).

The absence of some social groups in the writing of sport literature is not only raced but also gendered as sports writers have failed to include Black women in their analyses. Writers such as Birrell (1989), Hargreaves (1994), Scraton (2001) and Watson and Scraton (2001) have been critical of social science's reluctance in this area. In particular, sports feminists have been reticent about engaging with the leisure lifestyles and sporting experiences of Black women and as a result we know far less about Black women than we do about Black men in sport. Black women are invisible in sports writing in academic and everyday contexts. Where women are given attention in either academic writing, or even sports feminist writing, then the focus is mainly reflective of a White perspective about White women in general (Mirza, 1997). Writing on 'race' and ethnicity has made the Black male as conspicuous in sport as the White woman in mainstream gender theorising, therefore making our understanding of the Black woman's leisure and sporting lifestyles a mystery (Birrell, 1989; Scraton, 2001). These hierarchies in our epistemologies are reflective of wider raced, classed and gendered power processes that seek to structure our knowledge and intellectual development (Goldberg, 1993). Goldberg (1993) recognises the bias of discourses and their ability to normalise vocabularies, thus privileging some whilst marginalising others. The view that sports feminists have regularly dealt in stereotypes of women in sport as White, middle class and heterosexual is further emphasised in Mirza's (1997) work on Black feminism, which alerts us to this marginalising process in sport theorising:

> The invisibility of Black women speaks of the separate narrative constructions of race, gender and class: it is a racial discourse, where the subject is male; in a gendered discourse, where the subject is White; and a class discourse where race has no place. (Mirza, 1997: 4)

Exceptions to this become evident when superstars already famous in the media become a fair topic for a critical lens. The high profiles of Serena and Venus Williams in tennis and Marian Jones and Denise Lewis in athletics have been the focus of work recently that has generated some critical writing in this area (Billings and Eastman, 2002; Schultz, 2005; Spencer, 2004). However, these women cannot be seen as typical of the majority of Black women, of whom we struggle to gather a coherent picture. Hargreaves (1994) argues that what is written about Black women still conforms to stereotypes, as the esteemed athletes above are testimony to, in that they are often described as natural, flamboyant, quick, strong and powerful.

Birrell (1989) argues that what is needed in sports writing is a Black ontology that centres the experiences of heterogeneous Black people, where before it had been at the margins of such work in sport and leisure. Others have led calls to writers in sport and leisure studies to locate the Black presence so that members of the community are viewed as purposive actors in their own 'real worlds' as opposed to passive victims in increasingly pathologised stories (Hylton, 2005, 2009; Singer, 2005). For example, Cashmore's (1982) seminal text on Black sportsmen vilified the Black family of the 1970s in that it was interpreted as being dysfunctional, regularly 'broken' and without support networks. This, Cashmore (1982: 79) went on to argue, was reflective of 'many Black sportsmen growing up in broken homes'. A reading of this influential text would result in a view of the Black family through sport that not only gave the impression that it was careless in respect to its young people but also painted a harrowing picture of many young people in search of adult role models that could only be found outside the family through coaching and other sport networks. The ambivalent picture of the Black family is captured in discussions around their cynical behaviour when their inertia is broken after the child demonstrates that he or she can succeed in the chosen pursuit. Of course, the Black child is described by Cashmore as needing sport as a vehicle for social mobility and career progression. So the centrality of sport to the Black child makes it a doubly hard journey on which to embark as racism and the family militates against him or her. In comparison, Ismond's (2003) more recent ethnographic study, which reflected upon elite sportspeople from Cashmore's (1982) era, generated a counter-story that adopts a more critical Black perspective. On Viv Anderson and Cyrille Regis, Ismond gathers information about their childhoods that sketches a completely different story of familial support and love, and two intelligent young sportsmen putting great store in career planning and education. What we do get from Ismond is an image of a diverse Black community that is raced, classed and gendered and therefore not a narrow homogenous experience about sport and those wishing to pursue it.

African Caribbeans and Whiteness in UK sport

Some of the issues concerning the 'race logic' of teachers and their subsequent impact upon African Caribbeans in education as identified by Carrington and Wood (1983), can be explained with recourse to a focus on higher education. Education is viewed as problematic in being colour-blind and reproducing the inequalities that we experience in wider society due to the academy's apparent inability to systematically adopt an inclusive, global–local, political stance to the way we teach. Harrison *et al.* (2004) are clear that 'race' and diversity are neglected in physical education and sport, and they query the relative absence of 'race' in this academic arena. What in effect we do get are versions of conceptual Whiteness or Blackness that themselves signify notions of 'achievement', 'middle classness', 'intelligence' and 'educated' as normative characteristics of Whiteness, while 'gangs', 'basketball player', 'entertainer' and 'sprinter' become the 'marginalised and delegitimated categories of Blackness or African Caribbeaness' (Ladson-Billings, 1998: 9). More humorously, Coates' (2002) paper entitled 'I don't sing, I don't dance and I don't play basketball'! emphasises that as a powerful social construct 'race' structures our histories and our sport to the point that beneficiaries do not register the perks or 'privileges of Whiteness', neither do the dominant classifying discourses challenge the concepts that subtly racialise, marginalise and oppress African Caribbeans in the UK.

A critique of Whiteness in sport (Long and Hylton, 2002), my analysis of sport and leisure studies (Hylton, 2005, 2009) and Gillborn's

(2005) examination of education in the UK all emphasise how sport and education policy and practice include dominant ideas and epistemologies whilst allowing others to be marginalised. A consequence of this is the rendering of Blackness as visible and often the *a priori* object for debates around 'race' and sport, whilst Whiteness and the power that is privileged by it remains untheorised, unexamined and invisible. Giroux's (1997) critique of Whiteness starts from the premise that 'race' structures social relations and fosters a differential experience of education, sport and leisure for those living either side of the infamous DuBoisian colour line. In our analysis of Whiteness in sport, Long and Hylton (2002) argue that much of the attention concerning the construction of 'racial' characteristics has examined features ascribed to Black people. The 'other' is Black, peripheral, while 'White' commands the centre, due to a process of the 'normalisation' of Whiteness. Some would go further to argue that the worst incarnation of White supremacy is the normalisation of Whiteness (Gillborn, 2005).

Frankenberg's (1999) view that Whiteness is a 'process' not a 'thing', 'plural' and not 'singular' in nature, begins the task of dismantling Whiteness with White people complicit in its destruction. Essed's (2002) examination of everyday racism allows us to identify Whiteness as a clear target for an antiracist critical pedagogy. Further, our analysis of sports in the UK have depicted how racial hierarchies are constructed and perpetuated in the most mainstream of sports, such as football, rugby league and cricket (Long and Hylton, 2002). The studies evidence how sport is a contested site of White racism, Black resistance and Whiteness processes ranging from the casual behaviour of spectators to the established governing administrative structures. Essed (2002) explains how this everydayness emerges as racist notions inextricably linked to the meanings that make actions manageable and understandable, and examples of this can still be found in the way our sport, leisure and physical education are racialised; these practices become reified due to their repetitive and recursive nature and as a result of such issues Frankenberg's (1999) three reasons why our sport and physical education students should talk critically about Whiteness are particularly useful to start an antiracist agenda. Frankenberg (1999) urges us to:

1. displace the 'unmarked marker' (cultural practice) and identify White status and seeming transparency of White positioning.
2. establish 'a place from which we look' (Frankenberg, 1993, 1999) at 'everyone but White people . . .', necessary for a thorough understanding of racial processes and formations.
3. create opportunity for analyses of White selves.

This is always likely to be a risky strategy and is likely to generate personal stresses and anxieties associated with rethinking normative ideals and one's own identity at the centre of these. McIntyre (1997: 14) would support these points further when she posits that as the next generation of managers and teachers it is critical that White students reflect upon how Whiteness is implicated in the individual, institutional and cultural forms of racism that have afflicted UK society. Jenkins (2004) suggests that although we have more knowledge about ourselves than others, the knowledge of ourselves is at least as imperfect as our understanding of others. The reflexivity required to understand these dynamic racial processes can emerge from critical self-analysis and/or be facilitated through sites, such as higher education, where young people can be encouraged in a supportive atmosphere to become critically introspective.

A critical awareness of Whiteness offers the capacity to further understand how modalities of power are expressed in racialised sites, such as sport, leisure, education or even the media, where Whiteness cannot only be considered but is implicated as a constituent element in forming racialised hierarchies (Westwood, 2002). Further, White people become the focus of these studies because of their privileging in racial processes (Leonardo, 2004). In sport this is more apparent than in other arenas due to the public displays of racialisation and 'Othering' in traditional, crude forms of racism as well as in newer, more subtle forms (Long *et al.*, 2000; Long and Hylton, 2002). In sport and leisure studies the work of Andrews *et al.* (1997), Burdsey (2004), Carrington and McDonald (2001), Long and Hylton (2002) and MacClancy (1996) and others have sharpened the focus of 'race', ethnicity and identity to reinforce the privilege that Whiteness appropriates to more advantaged individuals whether they are conscious of it or not.

African Caribbeans and the media

It is generally accepted that sport is a domain where Black people are often depicted as successful, heroic, winners. It could also be said that in these neutral spaces that African Caribbeaness and ethnic identities are subservient to performances, winning and losing. The global media influence over sport is so powerful that the messages that emerge, from the television to the podcast, help us to understand what is happening in the world a little bit better than before. The reasons for this reside in the significance of sport as a social, cultural and political product of UK society. Our love for sport is such that often the success of the dominant sports in the UK can be an indicator of the state of the nation (Marquesee, 1994). The significance of our mediated sport, however, has not been lost on our social commentators, who have explored the relationship between the media and sport (Campbell, 1995; Hall, 1990; Whannel, 1992). Some of these writers have had a specific focus on issues of 'race', ethnicity and sport to the extent that a reading of this literature presents a caveat to those prepared to accept media discourses uncritically.

For most of us our identity has been constructed in a sense by who we think we are and how we think others view us. It is not purely as simple as this, given my earlier missive in relation to our diversity and the dialectical nature of social processes, but still the media play an influential role in this formation of identities. The media imaginary presents for us images and conceptions that enables us to categorise social groups, phenomena and events on a day-to-day basis. The media are key actors in constructing our ideas about what it means to be African Caribbean in the UK and this heritage is worked, reworked and transformed in the public domain of sport. In 1998 the independent think-tank the *Runneymede Trust* established a Commission on the Future of Multi-Ethnic Britain; here two of the areas for consideration were sport and the arts in addition to the media. In acknowledging the shifting and subtle nature of 'race' and racism, the Parekh Report, as it became known, concluded of the UK media that whatever we read is always likely to be coloured by a dominant discourse that acts as a lens through which to interpret our 'realities'. The Report goes on to argue that:

> If the larger narrative is racist or more benignly representative of a 95/5 society then the story is likely to be interpreted in a racist or majority biased way, regardless of the conscious intentions of reporters, journalists and headline writers. (Parekh, 2000: 169)

However, there are inconsistencies in how the media react to racism, especially as more overt forms would clearly implicate them. It is also a mark of a self-conscious media that, when the former West Bromwich Albion and Manchester United manager and football pundit Ron Atkinson resigned from his job, for the *Guardian* and also ITV Sport it was due to his publicly denounced 'off-the-record' racist slurs on a live link to the Middle East (Howe, 2004). At the end of a dismal performance by Chelsea he vented his spleen at the World Cup winning and French international team captain Marcel Desailly, whom he described as a 'Fxxxing lazy thick nxxxer'. When Atkinson articulated his mitigation – 'I was responsible for putting Black players in the First Division when other managers wouldn't, so how can I be racist?' – it was not accepted. In relation to Atkinson being part of a football culture or institution, there has been much made by cultural studies critics of the place of the media in how 'race' and ethnicity are represented or even re-represented to the public. Some, like Darcus Howe (2004), would say that Atkinson's actions are commonplace and that his words were just the tip of the iceberg. Given Atkinson's *faux pas*, it is useful to consider Campbell (1995: 60), who cites Ahmed Rashad, a former National Football League player and commentator, making an observation about sports announcers when he stated that:

> If you close your eyes and listen, you can tell whether a commentator is discussing a White or a Black athlete when he [sic] says that somebody is a 'natural', so fluid and graceful, you know he's talking about a Black performer. When you hear that this other guy's a hard worker, or that he comes to play everyday on the strength of guts and intelligence, you know that the player in question is White. Just open your eyes. (Campbell, 1995: 60)

On one level, self-preservation is an incentive to challenge overt racism where more subtle forms are left uncriticised. The failure of the West Indies cricket team at Headingley in 2000 led Younge (2000) to illustrate how even in sport the politics of subjugation can be recreated; here he is critical of the UK media excusing the thrashings meted out to the English team by putting defeat down to the natural abilities of the physical West Indians. However, the West Indies team were beaten these reductionist arguments are demoted and no longer become dominant in cricket, but are renewed in football, athletics and other areas where there is conspicuous Black success. Younge posits that 'yesterday's "natural" cricketers are today's "natural" footballers . . . the switch is not in their genes but in our society' (Younge, 2000: 25). Brookes (2002) contends that the sport media has been instrumental in renewing stereotypes based on ideologies of natural differences between socially constructed social groups. Processes of validation and the privileging of dominant ideas legitimate the commonsenseness of physical and psychological abilities and propensities for particular pursuits. Of the media, Hall (1990) argues that these stereotypes, views of Englishness, xenophobia and knowledge of the Black 'other' can emerge from an overt racism that we are less likely to see these days, but still do. Overt racism, encapsulated by Ron Atkinson, embraces openly racist opinions that could be evidenced in many of the early media coverage on Black people in sport (Gordon and Rosenberg, 1989). Hall (1990) goes on to state that the inferential racism of the media is worse than its overt racism. Hall describes inferential racism as:

Those . . . naturalised representations of events and situations relating to race, whether 'factual' or 'fictional' which have racist premises and propositions inscribed in them as a set of *unquestioned assumptions*. These enable racist statements to be formulated without ever bringing into awareness the racist predicates on which statements are grounded. (Hall, 1990: 13)

Gordon and Rosenberg's (1989) examination of a 1988 *Daily Mail* interview with John Barnes gives a clear indication of how inferential racism works in the media. The racism that Barnes suffered in the Merseyside Derby that year was the focus of the initial part of the article, with the rest of the article intent on arguing that racism was not a problem in Britain. The colour of Barnes' skin in the article was trivialised and equated to a fat stomach or being different in some other superficial way. As Gordon and Rosenberg would argue, it is difficult to see journalists from this newspaper presenting an article based on the more political reflections of Black athletes such as Linford Christie, Ian Wright, Thierry Henry or Les Ferdinand, who have been less reticent or apologetic about their experiences of racism in sport and society. Eleven years after the Barnes interview the *Observer* (Mackay and Campbell, 1999: 10) headlined one of its sports pages with, 'Can White beat Black?', as it presented us with an explanation about how the Australian sports media have built up the rivalry between 'ageing Black speed king' Linford Christie and 'young White sprinter' Matt Shirvington. The aim of this article was an attempt to answer 'the most explosive question in sport . . . who runs the fastest: Blacks or Whites'? Christie only came out of retirement to run this race because he was so irritated by the racist premise of the rivalry; however, the *Observer* was keen to present a wealth of 'expertise' from discredited sport scientists who would argue that Black sprinters have superiority over White sprinters. We can see that Hall's (1990) analysis of the media was relevant at the end of the 1990s, and is still relevant today (Hylton, 2009).

Rugby league: an untold story

Melling and Collins (2004) argue that one of the least considered stories in sport is the untold story of Black players in rugby league. My interest in rugby league is one of innocent bystander in a city and county that loves its rugby football (Leeds, Yorkshire). For me, rugby league seemed anomalous in how, as Melling and Collins argue, its White working-classness incorporated so many African Caribbean and other Black players. The rugby league story starts before World War

One in the professional game, and around the 1930s at an international level. In contrast to professional football, where Black players became commonplace from the late 1970s, rugby league has had a conspicuous Black presence since the 1950s. Working in Hull for a few years I would wonder how a player such as Clive Sullivan could get a main street named after him given the relatively parochial and very White nature of the city. Former Great Britain captain, Member of the British Empire (MBE) and even star guest on *This is Your Life!*, Sullivan was a legend in Hull and played for both teams in the city (Hull and Hull Kingston Rovers), but was not the first Black rugby league player to reach these exalted heights (Risman, 2004). In addition, where we had to wait for Viv Anderson to be the first Black England international football player in 1979, the equivalent honour had been bestowed upon George Bennett of Wales in 1935 and England's Jimmy Cumberbatch two years later (Melling and Collins, 2004).

Roy Francis is one of the archetypal rugby legends who played for Hull Football Club in the 1950s before returning to coach the team in his fifties. Gibbons (2004) described his first sighting of Roy Francis' return to the Hull Boulevard:

> Roy Francis was regarded as a god but the real man I saw that day was Black, wiry, unassuming and in his fifties. To me he was an old man, how could he have inspired such anticipation and devotion . . . Ask anyone who remembers Roy Francis what really made him stand out and they will say one of two things, 'best coach we ever had' or 'he was twenty years ahead of his time'. (Gibbons, 2004: 41)

Francis' story is one tinged with sadness and cold reality for African Caribbeans in UK sport, as in his early years of success at Wigan he was forced to leave the club due to the racism he only later admitted to experiencing. Spracklen (2004) and Leeds Metropolitan University (Long *et al.*, 1995) have recognised the 'small but significant problem of racism' in rugby league over the years, which Spracklen argues is 'built into the boundaries of the imaginary community in the form of shared history and meanings of which they do not share, and stereotypes and assumptions' (Spracklen, 2004: 174). Francis was born in Wales in 1919; it is said that he was not picked to play in the Great Britain tour to Australia due to the colour-bar being operated there just after World War Two. However, he did play for Great Britain, and at a time when Leeds United were getting a mass of publicity for signing Albert Johannesen from South Africa, further up the road in Headingley, Leeds Rugby Club (League) were winning top honours with Francis as the manager after his move from Hull. Rugby league can offer us an unfamiliar side to sport that is both heartwarming and yet resonates with many of us in the inability of even the best players and coaches to avoid the realities of racial hierarchies in sport. For some writers sport has been viewed as a tool of resistance in such an unforgiving society; it has provided an opportunity to wrest control for Black sportspeople, to empower them, and to create a level of agency in one area of their lives that is perhaps not as conspicuous in others. In the final section I reflect on these issues, using the work of Britton (1999), Carrington (1999), Ratcliffe (1996) and Williams (1994), who explore 'race', sport and resistance in their sport sociology.

Resistance through sport

Ratcliffe's (1996) analysis of the 1991 Census shows clearly how more concentrated in urban areas the Black population is than the White population. Around 80 per cent of Black Africans and Black Caribbeans live inside Greater London, Greater Manchester and the metropolitan counties of the West Midlands and West Yorkshire (Ratcliffe, 1996: 116). Further, even within these areas, residential patterns reflect a concentration of minority ethnic communities in the inner urban areas. Ratcliffe's (1996) observation of social distributions led him to suggest that the policy-makers have often been colour-blind in their treatment of high concentrations of Black communities. Ratcliffe concludes that a lack of local authority ethnic monitoring of their urban policy can lead to colour-blindness. He posits that 'the use of space as a cultural entity and as an embodiment and focus of material experience is important for an understanding of "race" and ethnicity in urban Britain'. Both Williams (1994) and Westwood (1990) suggest that sport can be used as a site of resistance for Black people. In the case of Black men, sport acts as an arena in which they can restate their masculinity, which is being negated by racism in other areas of their social lives.

Westwood (1990) argues that spaces themselves become racialised and become appropriated by Black and White through a form of 'neighbourhood nationalism'. Westwood (1990) goes further: in her ethnography of young Black men in a provincial city she describes how spaces are defended against outsiders who represent oppressors and those who are privileged in some way. Williams' (1994) case study of Highfield Rangers in the Midlands is one of the few ethnographic studies of sport in Black communities. Rangers, a predominantly African Caribbean team, was established as a response to the exclusion and discrimination its founder members experienced in the 1970s. Williams argues that the Highfield club is a site of empowerment and resistance against the collective experience of racism in sport and the wider society for its members, fans and community. Williams describes this process as a form of community politics, which is a process considered by Carrington (1999) at the Caribbean Cricket Club (the first Black cricket club formed in Britain) in local league cricket; similar analyses include Westwood's (1990) account of pub football and Long *et al.*'s. (2000) three case studies in semi-professional and grassroots football, one of which included the Fforde Grene football team in Leeds. Williams concluded that Highfield Rangers, similar to the Fforde Grene and the Caribbean Cricket Club, are an: 'Inhabited social space where symbolic victories can be achieved as a means of alleviating wider community tensions or of responding to perceived community injustices' (Williams, 1994: 171).

In Carrington's (1999: 14) ethnography of a Caribbean cricket club in the north of England, a long-serving member stated that: 'Cricket is the only thing, to some extent, that binds Black people together as one force. So in a sense it's more than cricket'. Here the symbolic nature of sport, cricket in this case, comes through persuasively as a force for change, or a tool to destabilise dominant hegemonic processes. The significance of cricket as a cultural product is emphasised in its meaning to a society – in this case to African Caribbeans in the UK. The cultural heritage of each group has acted as a binding force of shared symbols of diverse cultures, from food to sport (Carrington, 1999; Hylton, 2003; Westwood, 1990; Williams, 1994). A shared experience of the institution of sport bound the collectivities together and effectively galvanised their resolve to become agents of change where they could challenge symbolic institutions in sport. However, for many of these studies what unified these groups was recognition of the social categories of 'Black' and 'Black and minority ethnic' that facilitated an inclusive Black consciousness. The Blackness of African Caribbeans in these instances in the context of sport became the unifying border from which to include and exclude around the injustices in sport.

Britton (1999) explains how a racialisation of a sporting community acted as a unifying process for a Black voluntary-sector group. This process is mirrored in my ethnographic study of a Black sports pressure group, the Voluntary Black and Ethnic Sport forum (VBES) in the north of England (Hylton, 2003). For Britton (1999) and Hylton's (2003) groups, Blackness itself indicated membership and a foundation for resistance for their shared experiences of racialised exclusions. VBES is committed to equality of opportunity and antiracism in sport and recreation for Black people in Northern England. This commitment was in recognition of the disparity in the representation of Black people as administrators and managers in sport as opposed to purely participants (Hylton/ILAM, 1999; Jarvie, 1991b; Long *et al.*, 2000). VBES is made up of executive members who are all experienced full-time Black sports development professionals based in Yorkshire. They have been drawn from the areas in the county that have the highest Black and culturally diverse populations. Each member has worked for their authority and/or their local community for more than ten years and yet, significantly, none at a senior (principal) officer level. The members of VBES were conscious of the institutional structures that have systematically and summarily excluded Black people from the policy-making and implementation processes in sport, and of why Black people in Yorkshire in the north of England have felt it necessary to resist this.

VBES occupied a space in a regional sport policy network that was paradoxical. The organisation's existence clearly contested the notion of sport as the great leveller, or even as a domain for equal opportunities. The discourse of equality within the public sector, which presents local government sport as equitable in terms of the development and implementation of sports policy and practice, was the target of the business of VBES. Voluntary Black and Ethnic Sport's story is a counter-story, a competing discourse, an alternative paradigm that situates the Black experience of sport in a process that constrains as it liberates, empowers as it disempowers, includes as it excludes (Delgado, 2000; Goldberg, 1993; Ladson-Billings, 1998; Nebeker, 1998). Delgado's (2000) argument that 'in-groups' create their own stories applies here to the public commitments by local authorities to the equality that they often fail to deliver in sport. 'Out groups' such as VBES aim to subvert that reality, hence their forceful objectives that place racism and equality of outcome in local authorities as two of their primary concerns. According to Hain (1976), an organisation with the social and community drive of VBES draws towards it individuals who in the past have been isolated by the organisation and structure of their working or personal experiences. He suggests that these types of organisations enable people to take some control of their own destiny by affecting and effecting change. This was clearly the case for the Black professionals linked to the emergent pressure group, as they saw the sum of VBES being far more influential than its parts. Consequently the forum members have made a point to those established organisations in the sports policy network that *they* are failing and it is time that there was a critical Black voice amongst them. Whatever the motivation for the forum members to be involved, the increased level of agency achieved by volunteers in community or pressure groups is an important factor for them to join such a group. The key members

demonstrated that their ability to influence policy-makers and practitioners in their new position as VBES executive members was a
common reason for them to become involved.

By opening up alternative lines of inquiry that include these often
under-valued sources, VBES produces an oppositional story that rejects
the claims of progress in public-sector sport. Instead it produces contradictions that count as caveats for more complacent local authorities and incentives for more forward-looking ones. The Home Office
report on community self-help outlined how community groups such
as VBES are in fact a paradox (Home Office, 1999). They are necessary
because of the actions or inactions of public authorities. Their emergence occurs as a response to the perceived need of a Black community
that sees a disparity in the quality and quantity of sports facilities and
services available to it. As noted earlier, the emergence of VBES in itself
sends a message to local authorities and other sports governing agencies that others in their network want to go beyond documented affirm-
ations of inequality and racism in sport, and that Black people are
taking action to address these imbalances.

Conclusion

Sport for many African Caribbeans in the UK is very symbolic, redolent of a place that reflects the best of community, unity, history and
agency. Sport offers us the illusion, at least, of an oasis where we can
be ourselves and/or watch others like us be happy and successful.
For many, sport demonstrates that there are robust examples of equal
opportunities, equity, respect and best practice that we can transfer
into other areas of the public domain. It cannot be denied that sport
has many positive connotations for African Caribbeans in the UK and
it is only a weather eye that will spy the anomalies, some of which
have been discussed already; Henderson's use of Blackness to define
English identity; Ron Atkinson's description of Black footballers and
racism across sport; the under-researched and poorly understood
power of Whiteness processes and their formations; the media's pen-
chant for crude description that reinforces difference and stereotypes;
the absence of Black women and other social groups from the academic
and media gaze; and the instrumental use of sport as policy and sport
as resistance all tell an intriguing story of a cultural product (sport?!)
that is at the same time *trivial* as it is *significant*.

The problematic of 'race' thinking for many in sport is its endemic
discourse. The popularity of 'race' thinking is historically located in
multifarious assumptions and deeds that reinforce the legitimacy of

'race' and therefore physical differences in sport. Enduring assumptions argue that humans are divided into a few biologically and phenotypically detached 'races'; the similarities within these groups can then be reduced to ability, behaviour and morality; these differences would be naturally passed from one generation to the next and racial hierarchies exist with White people at the top and darker 'races' at the opposite end (Fenton, 2003). These racialised processes find their expression in how we experience and/or play sport. They impact who we play with, who is included in the WE and who makes up THEM. The subtleties of these processes are such that sport does not extend to us the levels of agency purported by policy-makers and educationalists, and it is only through critical readings of these messages coupled with active resistance that we can effect any transformations in attitudes in sport and wider society.

References

Abbott, D. (2006), *Guardian Weekend* (6 May)

Andrews, D. L., Pitter, R., Zwick, D. and Ambrose, D. (1997), 'Soccer's racial frontier: sport and the suburbanization of contemporary America', in Armstrong, G. and Giuliannoti, R. (eds), *Entering the Field: New Perspectives on World Football* (Oxford: Berg)

Back, L., Crabbe, T. and Solomos, J. (2001), *The Changing Face of Football* (Oxford: Berg)

Bains, J. (2005), *Asians Can Play Football: Another Wasted Decade* (Leicester: Asians in Football Forum)

Bains, J. and Patel, R. (1996), *Asians Can't Play Football* (Solihull: ASDAL)

Billings, A. and Eastman, S. (2002), 'Selective representation of gender, ethnicity and nationality in American television coverage of the 2000 summer olympics', *International Review for the Sociology of Sport*, 37:3–4, 351–70

Birrell, S. (1989), 'Racial relations theories and sport: suggestions for a more critical analysis', *Sociology of Sport*, 6, 212–27

Britton, N. J. (1999), 'Racialised identity and the term "Black"', in Roseneil, S. and Seymour, J. (eds), *Practising Identities Power and Resistance* (London: Palgrave Macmillan)

Brookes, R. (2002), *Representing Sport* (London: Arnold)

Burdsey, D. (2004), 'Obstacle race? "Race", racism and the recruitment of British Asian professional footballers', *Patterns of Prejudice*, 38:3, 279–99

Campbell, C. (1995), *Race, Myth and the News* (London: Sage)

Carrington, B. (1999), 'Cricket, culture and identity: an ethnographic analysis of the significance of sport within Black communities', in Roseneil, S. and Seymour, J. (eds), *Practising Identities Power and Resistance* (London: Palgrave Macmillan)

Carrington, B. and McDonald, I. (2003), 'The politics of race and sports policy', in Houlihan, B. (ed.), *Sport and Society: A Student Introduction* (London: Sage)

Carrington, B. and McDonald, I. (2001), 'Whose game is it anyway? Racism in local league cricket', in Carrington, B. and McDonald, I. (eds), *'Race', Sport and British Society* (London: Routledge)

Carrington, B. and Wood, E. (1983), 'Body talk: images of sport in a multi-racial school', *Multiracial Education*, 11, 29–38

Cashmore, E. (1982), *Black Sportsmen* (London: Routledge and Kegan-Paul)

Coakley, J. (2001), *Sport in Society: Issues and Controversies* (New York: McGraw-Hill)

Coates, R. (2002) 'I don't sing, I don't dance and I don't play basketball! Is sociology declining in significance, or has it just returned to business as usual'? *Critical Sociology*, 28:1–2, 255–79

Delgado, R. (2000), 'Storytelling for oppositionists and others: a plea for narrative', in Delgado, R. and Stefancic, J. (eds), *Critical Race Theory: The Cutting Edge* (Philadelphia, PA: Temple University Press)

Essed, P. (2002), 'Everyday racism', in Essed, P. and Goldberg, D. (eds), *Race Critical Theories* (Oxford: Blackwell Publishing)

Essed, P. and Goldberg D. (eds) (2002), *Race Critical Theories* (Oxford: Blackwell Publishing)

Fenton, S. (2003) *Ethnicity* (Cambridge: Polity Press)

Fleming, S. (1991), 'Sport, schooling and Asian male culture', in Jarvie, G. (ed.), *Sport, Racism and Ethnicity* (London: Falmer Press)

Frankenberg, R. (ed.) (1999), *Displacing Whiteness* (Durham, NC, and London: Duke University Press)

Frankenberg, R. (1993), *White Woman, Race Matters: The Social Construction of Whiteness* (London: Routledge)

Gibbons, T. (2004), 'Roy Francis', in Melling, P. and Collins, T. (eds), *The Glory of Their Times: Crossing the Colour Line in Rugby League* (Skipton: Vertical Editions)

Gillborn, D. (2005), 'Education policy as an act of White supremacy: Whiteness, critical race theory and education reform', *Journal of Education Policy*, 20:4, 485–505

Gilroy, P. (1987), *There Ain't No Black in the Union Jack* (London: Routledge)

Giroux, H. (1997), *Pedagogy and the Politics of Hope: Theory, Culture and Schooling: A Critical Reader* (Boulder, CO: Westview)

Goldberg, D. (2002), *The Racial State* (Oxford: Blackwell Publishing)

Goldberg, D. (1993), *Racist Culture* (Oxford: Blackwell Publishing)

Gordon, P. and Rosenberg, D. (1989), *Daily Racism: The Press and Black People in Britain* (London: Runnymede Trust)

Gunaratnam, Y. (2003), *Researching 'Race' and Ethnicity: Methods, Knowledge and Power* (London: Sage)

Hain, P. (1976), *Community Politics* (London: Calder)

Hall, S. (1990), 'The Whites of their eyes: racist ideologies and the media', in Alvarado, M. and Thompson, J. (eds), *The Media Reader* (Norfolk: BFI)

Hargreaves, J. (1994), *Sporting Females: Critical Issues in the History and Sociology of Women's Sports* (London: Routledge)

Hargreaves, J. (1986), *Sport Power and Culture* (Oxford: Polity Press)

Harrison, L., Azzarito, L. and Burden, J. (2004), 'Perceptions of athletic superiority: a view from the other side', *Race Ethnicity and Education*, 7:2, 159–66

Henderson, R. (1995), 'Is it in the Blood?', *Wisden Cricket Monthly* (July)

Home Office (1999), *Policy Action Team 9: Community Self-Help* (London: Home Office)

Howe, D. (2004), 'It was not a lapse: Atkinson was up to his neck in football's endemic racism', *The New Statesman* (3 May)

Hylton, K. (2009) *'Race' and Sport: Critical Race Theory* (London, Routledge)

Hylton, K. (2005), '"Race", sport and leisure: lessons from critical race theory', *Leisure Studies*, 24:1, 81–98

Hylton, K. (2003), *Local Government 'Race' and Sports Policy Implementation* (PhD Dissertation, Leeds Metropolitan University)

Hylton, K/ILAM (1999), 'Where are the Black leisure managers'? *Leisure Manager* (4 September)

Hylton, K. and Totten, M. (2008), 'Developing sport for all', in Hylton, K. and Bramham, P. *Sports Development: Policy, Process and Practice* (London: Routledge)

Ismond, P. (2003), *Black and Asian Athletes in British Sport and Society: A Sporting Chance?* (Basingsoke: Palgrave Macmillan)

Jarvie, G. (1991a), *Sport, Racism and Ethnicity* (London: Falmer Press)

Jarvie, G. (1991b), 'There ain't no problem here?', *Sport and Leisure* (November/ December), 20–1

Jenkins, R. (2004) *Social Identity* (London: Routledge)

Ladson-Billings, G. (1998) 'Just what is critical race theory and what's it doing in a nice field like education?', *Qualitative Studies in Education*, 11:1, 7–24

Leonardo, Z. (2004), 'Introduction', *Educational Philosophy and Theory*, 36:2, 2

Long, J. and Hylton, K. (2002), 'Shades of White: an examination of Whiteness in sport', *Leisure Studies*, 21:2, 87–103

Long, J., Hylton, K., Dart, J. and Welch, M. (2000), *Part of the Game? An Examination of Racism in Grass Roots Football* (London: Kick It Out)

Long, J., Tongue, N., Spracklen, K. and Carrington, B. (1995), *What's the Difference: A Study of the Nature and Extent of Racism in Rugby League* (Leeds: RFL/CRE/LCC/LMU)

MacClancy, J. (ed.) (1996), *Sport, Identity and Ethnicity* (Oxford: Berg)

McIntyre, A. (1997), *Making Meaning of Whiteness: Exploring Racial Identity with White Teachers* (New York: SUNY)

Mackay, D. and Campbell, D. (1999), 'Can White beat Black'? *Observer* (28 March)

Marquesee, M. (1994), *Anyone But England: Cricket and the National Malaise* (London: Verso)

Melling, P. and Collins, T. (eds) (2004); *The Glory of Their Times: Crossing the Colour Line in Rugby League* (Skipton: Vertical Editions)

Mirza, H. (1997), *Black British Feminism: A Reader* (London: Routledge)

Nebeker, K. (1998), 'Critical race theory: a White graduate student's struggle with this growing area of scholarship', *Qualitative Studies in Education*, 11:1, 25–41

Omi, M. and Winant, H. (2002), 'Racial formation', in Essed, P. and Goldberg, D. (eds), *Race Critical Theories* (Oxford: Blackwell Publishing Publishers)

Parekh, B. (2000), *The Future of Multi-Ethnic Britain* (London: Runnymede Trust)

Polley, M. (1998), *Moving the Goalposts: The History of Sport and Society from 1945* (London: Routledge)

Ratcliffe, P. (ed.) (1996), *Ethnicity in the 1991 Census. Volume Three: Social Geography and Ethnicity in Britain* (London: OPCS)

Risman, B. (2004), 'Clive Sullivan', in Melling, P. and Collins, T. (eds), *The Glory of Their Times: Crossing the Colour Line in Rugby League* (Skipton: Vertical Editions)

Roediger, D. (2002), *Colored White: Transcending the Racial Past* (London: UCL)

St Louis, B. (2004), 'Sport and commonsense racial science', *Leisure Studies*, 23:1, 31–46

Schultz, J. (2005), 'Reading the catsuit: Serena Williams and the production of Blackness at the 2002 US Open', *Journal of Sport and Social Issues*, 29:3 (August), 338–57

Scraton, S. (2001), 'Reconceptualising race, gender and sport: the contribution of Black feminism', in Carrington, B. and McDonald, I. (eds), *Race Sport and British Society* (London: Routledge)

Singer, J. (2005), 'Addressing epistemological racism in sport management research', *Journal of Sport Management*, 19, 404–79

Skellington, R. and Morris, P. (1996), *'Race' in Britain Today* (London: Sage)

Solomos, J. and Back, L. (1995), *Race, Politics and Social Change* (London: Routledge)

Song, M. (2004), 'Introduction: who's at the bottom? Examining claims about racial hierarchy', *Ethnic and Racial Studies*, 27:6 (November), 859–77

Spencer, N. (2004), 'Sister act VI: Venus and Serena Williams at Indian Wells: "Sincere Fictions" and White racism', *Journal of Sport and Social Issues*, 28:2, 115–35

Sport England (2000), *Sports Participation and Ethnicity in England: National Survey 1999/2000* (London: Sport England)

Spracklen, K. (2004) 'Ikram Butt', in Melling, P. and Collins, T. (eds), *The Glory of Their Times: Crossing the Colour Line in Rugby League* (Skipton: Vertical Editions)

Spracklen, K., Hylton, K. and Long, J. (2006), 'Managing and monitoring equality and diversity in UK sport', *Journal of Sport and Social Issues*, 30:3, 289–305

Sugden, J. and Tomlinson, A. (2002), 'Theory and method for a critical sociology of sport', in Sugden, J. and Tomlinson, A. (eds), *Power Games: A Critical Sociology of Sport* (London: Routledge)

Swinney, A. and Horne, J. (2005), 'Race equality and leisure policy: discourses in Scottish local authorities', *Leisure Studies*, 24:3, 271–89

Watson, B. and Scraton, S. (2001), 'Confronting Whiteness? Researching the leisure lives of South Asian mothers', *Journal of Gender Studies*, 10:3, 265–77

Westwood, S. (2002), *Power and the Social* (London: Routledge)

Westwood, S. (1990), 'Racism, Black masculinity and the politics of space', in Hearn, J. and Morgan, D. (eds), *Men, Masculinities and Social Theory* (London: Unwyn Hyman Ltd)

Whannel, G. (1992), *Fields in Vision: Television Sport and Cultural Transformation* (London: Routledge)

Wheeler, J. (2000), *Leicester Racial Equality and Sport Project Preparation Report* (Leicester: Leicester City Council)

Williams, J. (1994), 'Rangers is a Black club', in Giuliannoti, R. and Williams, J. (eds), *Game without Frontiers: Football, Identity and Modernity, Popular Culture Studies 5* (Aldershot: Arena Publications)

Williams, R. (1977), *Marxism and Literature* (Oxford: Oxford University Press)

Younge, G. (2000), 'White on Black', *Recreation* (November), 24–5

12

Creating and sustaining African self-identity in the Western diaspora

Carl Hylton

Introduction

> An ideology for liberation must find its existence in ourselves. It cannot be external to us, and it cannot be imposed by those other than ourselves; it must be derived from our particular historical and cultural experience. Our liberation from the captivity of racist language is the first order of the intellectual. There is no freedom until there is freedom of the mind. (Asante, 1995: 31)

This chapter will focus on some of the psychological, philosophical, cultural and sociological issues that enable people of African descent to survive in a positive manner in the United Kingdom (UK) and the wider western diaspora. The chapter draws out these self-selected themes to show the complexity of the task individuals undertake to keep sane. Some of the themes such as spirituality and cultural style are unconsciously activated, which are probably part of a cultural community resource that is tapped. Other themes such as the use of Africancentricity and creating positives from negative labels are arrived at through personal and collective experiences of racism and class struggles. They are chosen as a way of life after deliberation that sometimes entails personal sacrifices, leading to a different way of life that individuals regard as enlightening and worthwhile. The project is to create a persona that makes sense to the individual, which is coherent – can stand self- and external criticism and can be expressed visually, musically and/or orally to others. It has to hang together – to be logical. You do not need to be converted but should be able to appreciate the logic of the particular stance taken.

My analysis starts from my initial position as a social scientist, community activist and archivist of African descent who is committed to the positive development of people of African ancestry. My academic and community inputs are counter-balanced, with each area of involvement affecting the outcome and analysis of the other. My stance is in tune with Melucci (1989: 205–6), who believes that changing self and changing society are considered as the same process, where the journey is as important as the destination. Where the methods we use to interact with others are of equal importance as the end goals. Individuals cannot arrive at the end of the journey without being changed to some extent by the processes they use to achieve their aims.

The beginning

At the junction of an appreciation of where my world ends and that of another individual begins is the formation of 'me' as a separate living, thinking human being. These philosophical considerations also make us aware of the boundaries between ourselves and the material world around us. It is our recognition of a table or chair – recognising its functions, construction and special dimensions. As small children, we begin to understand where the table or chair starts and ends. These everyday material items take up space and we come to understand that if we locate them in their spatial element, without interference we expect to see them in that space when we next visit it (Piaget, 1990). These arguments may appear trivial and matter-of-fact now that we are fully formed conscious adults, but we need to remind ourselves that this appreciation and worldly knowledge concerning our spatial identity are nurtured and learnt experiences (Bandura, 1977). They have to be acquired and honed during the early phases of our life cycle. For instance, newborn human babies slowly acquire the knowledge that they are separate from their carers and the material world around them. They are at the beginning of the process of self-discovery to gain an understanding of self – or Me – You – Them. They begin to build up the interconnections of their links to others – be they family, friends or inanimate objects (Davey, 2004; Piaget and Inhelder, 1967).

A great deal of the work of a parent or carer is given over to try to present positive examples for their children, in their efforts to help them to be assertive and become good active citizens. This of course is made difficult in western societies where people of African descent are not automatically viewed as positive. Parents and carers have a priority to provide their offspring with positive self-identity traits as building blocks of survival skills. These skills – such as an antenna that tries to pick up reasons for rejection, filtered for potential racist clues – are alternative in the sense that they are opposites to the general normal skills passed on to Caucasian (White) children. They are survival strategies or skills in the sense that they provide children of African/Caribbean descent with the means of overcoming the negative attributes of racist western cultures. The aim is to survive and remain sane (Hylton, 1999b).

The need

To be a fully formed human being requires us to have a sense of who we are, which is a composite picture of ourselves. We have to be able to construct a picture of what makes us tick – to understand that we are human – that we are female or male – that we are located in ties of family, friendship, study and work-colleague networks. We have to understand our place in each of these very different spheres that constitute our total life experiences and make-up. We learn about ourselves, about other humans and about the wider world by imitation, study and our very human trait of self-reflection. Giddens (1991) believes that creative narratives are also important. These are the selective ways we describe our actions to ourselves and others. When an individual begins to operate outside of the self-reflection mode – and particularly where that individual lacks the ability to empathise with other humans and performs hideous criminal actions again the person – we are shocked. Our reaction is to try and find the underlying causes of the 'person's' behaviour. Sometimes a 'knee-jerk' reaction is to place the 'person' who has committed the criminal act outside of the embrace of our humanity. The 'person' is classified as 'sub-human' or 'in-human'. This makes it easier for us to believe that the others, We–Us, are not capable of the outsider's wickedness.

A positive sense of self is therefore linked to being human, being sane and happy, being able to make positive links and friendships with other humans and non-humans, and to operate as a fully formed and rounded person (Maslow, 1943, 1971). We are also able to apportion praise or blame to individual people. This is therefore the recipe for a stable, progressive and safe society, where each individual has a high moral code and an internal mechanism that polices their actions. This type of society is the direct opposite to the aggressive individualism and violence that someone such as political philosopher Thomas Hobbes (1588–1679) would recognise. In his famous work *Leviathan*, he sets out this type of world as being 'solitary, poor, nasty, brutish and short' (Hobbes, 2004). We are all flung into a bottomless pit where we lose all sense of time, space, depth and future. Everywhere there is disunity. We are trying to hold on but everything around us is blurred, disappearing and melting (Berman, 1982: 13–15).

Self-identity helps to create the notion of self-control because we internalise the social, cultural, religious and political rules of our society that help others to predict our individual actions. The issue of self-identity has a direct link with social justice themes concerned with political liberty, freedom of speech and assembly, liberty of conscience and freedom of thought (Rawls, 1999). We require this positive self-identity to counteract racist ideas and to keep us sane (Asante, 1995; Muhammad, 2004).

Wanda Bernard (1995) believes that there are several key strategies that help people of African descent to create a positive sense of self. She uses an Africancentric perspective to analyse the survival strategies of groups of African Canadian and African Caribbean UK men. Spirituality was the key concept that 'kept them sane'. Other strategies included personal values and family support, role models, education and marketing skills, setting attainable goals, political and racial consciousness, employment or self-employment, and a positive African identity.

Richard Wright's (2004) work provides a practical illustration of the human spirit-need to overcome and to create a true persona. His moving account of early childhood into young adulthood is told in novel form in his book *Black Boy*, set against prejudice, racism and the apartheid system in 1920s Mississippi in the southern United States of America (USA). It reminded me of issues in the powerful book and film *The Color Purple*: the book was written by Alice Walker in 1982 and the film directed by Steven Spielberg in 1985 (see Walker, 2004). In *Black Boy*, Wright has to cultivate a deep understanding of how his words and actions are interpreted by members of the southern USA White world, who expect people of colour or former enslaved Africans to act at all times in a servile, docile, happy-go-lucky, non-threatening and stupid manner. He had to deliberately cultivate a particular method of interchange with his White peers. Acting otherwise – as an equal, upright, intelligent man of colour – meant not only that he did not secure employment, but that his very being, his existence, his life was in danger. During this period African Americans were killed for such indiscretions. Wright had to cultivate a safe persona – a safe public identity – while he secretly borrowed radical library books to help him shape a private self-assured self-identity. His secret end goal was to work and save and then to travel north as an escape route to become a writer.

Here we see that if the person cast in the submissive role (the African American) does not play and replay this role it causes the others cast in the dominant role (the southern USA Caucasians) to feel a sense of unease. The cure was to reconstruct the status quo by placing sanctions on the recalcitrant individual to bring the person back to submission. The dominant White identity was and is very much dependent on the submissive Black identity. This scenario is a classical zero-sum interaction, where one person or group's power creates an opposite loss of power for the other person or group. Survival of the 'Black Boy' was dependent on his awareness of these philosophical, cultural and political issues and his methods of using his wits and African spirituality to overcome them.

Black identity

Black identity is usually linked to popularist ideas and actions, centred on style rather than substance – consumption rather than thrift – posing and flashy antics rather than measured pursuits that have spirituality, history and high moral appreciation. The focus is on aggression, sex, physical strength and speed, rather than cerebral pursuits characterised by rational western intellect. Racism makes it difficult to cultivate and sustain positive concepts of African identity – but it is not enough to make this statement, we have to present a clear understanding of the meaning of the term 'racism'. Using the formula 'racism equals prejudice plus power', Chandra Fernando (2000) and the other members of the London-based Coram Family Moyenda Project developed a strong clear analysis of the meaning of the term racism. I was a member of the Moyenda Project team and regard this analysis as a useful tool that can help us counter racist ideas and practices.

> Racism is a set of beliefs that position European ('white') people as superior to visual minority people such as Africans, African Caribbeans and South Asians. Historically Europeans held and continue to hold power and resources to create actions that disadvantage visual minority people. The beliefs that render visual minorities as inferior and Europeans as superior, with rights to dominate other ethnic groups, have roots from the period of colonisation and the trans-Atlantic African slave trade. Ideas from this time that were constructed by Britain and other European countries to justify the social, economic and political exploitation of visual minority people, continue to exist in more direct forms of racist behaviour such as verbal abuse, school exclusion and physical attack – while others are subtle and embedded in the fabric of UK institutions, and are therefore called institutional racism.
>
> Racists categorise visual minority languages (dialects), cultural behaviour, religious and family systems as inferior to their own practices. The combination of these prejudice attitudes against visual minorities and the power to create actions that disadvantage others, is what makes racism different from other types of prejudices. (Fernando, 2000: 1)

To act as a counterbalance against these types of racist practices a growing number of African/Caribbean individuals, families and community organisations are turning to an Africancentric way forward. This is an intellectual and practical survival strategy based on the rejection of Europeancentric ideas and actions to be replaced by African-centred history, concepts and deeds that proclaim a changed consciousness, leading to activities that enhance individual and collective self-worth (Ani, 1994; Asante, 1992, 1995; Browder, 1989). Positive African identity is set against the physical and ideological struggles that are opposed to the antics of the continuing actions of fringe right-wing groups who are bidding for a wider power base through UK electoral political actions (Hylton, 2005). We must never forget this tactic of gaining electoral approval was successfully used by Adolf Hitler and the German Nazi Party to gain political power in 1933, partly using the existing democratic process.

In today's western popular consciousness a Black person or a person of African descent usually carries a host of negatives and stereotypical labels. These different traits can be easily brought forward and listed as: aggressive, athletic, big, consumption led, flashy, live for now, physical, sexual and style-led. Some of the items that might be missing from such a popularist list could include: caring, cerebral, considerate, entrepreneurial, beautiful, gentle, kind, loving and symbolic – images that are not limited to Black youth street culture.

The notion of Black style and symbolic images

Black style can be examined through the brilliant edited work of Carol Tulloch (2004), Senior Research Fellow in Black Visual Culture at Chelsea College of Art. Her book details various aspects of a Black sense of style and self-image. She comments that:

> The term 'Black style' generally conjures up images of black youth and street culture. Although phenomenal in its impact on fashion and style across the world, this is not the only aspect of black life that warrants critical exposure. The book examines everyday dress, occasional and traditional clothing. Thus black style, in this context, is an expression of the ways in which different kinds of people within the African diaspora have negotiated and defined their sense of self in spite of the legacy of inequality meted out through race and class. (Tulloch, 2004: 14)

The manner in which a person carries their body – the various shapes, whether thin, curvaceous or muscular – is always changing over time and has social, political, cultural and ethnic significance. In the west both female and male African bodies have strong historical connotations. Men of African descent are either emasculated as clowns, entertainers or eunuchs who are happy to serve – or objectified as sex beasts, with the focus placed on penis size. While African women are 'regarded as sexually available and equated with the prostitute' – 'Brown sugar' – or desexualised as the 'mammy of the Aunt Jemina type' (Pieterse, 1992: 178). Men and women of African descent have to cope with these contrasting images while still striving to reflect their own concept of self and style viewed in their manner of walking, deportment, speech patterns and dress. This different sense of style can sometimes subvert and reinvent aspects of European/Caucasian style to make it conform to African style. An example of this is the USA baseball cap, where the peak is turned 180 degrees to create a very different effect and sense of style. Kaiser *et al.* note that:

> Over the last few years, the backward baseball cap of the late gangsta rap artist Tupac Shakur, for example, has come to symbolize the creative reapproriation of white style. It is not just what one wears, but how one wears it that is relevant here. (Kaiser *et al.*, 2004: 52)

Hair stories

A very poignant symbolic image of Black identity, style and image is the focus on African hair. For many years Leeds-based poet and cultural performance artist Khadijah Ibrahiim has been collating visual images to illustrate the diversity and creativity of the various hair styles of people of African descent (Ibrahiim, 2006). She has called this project *Hair Stories*. Black hair has always been used as a cultural political vehicle to express individual and collective cultural identity. Sometimes this is achieved by simple or elaborate head ties or wraps – sometimes termed crowns or tams. Even when hair is invisible, powerful statements can be made based on the type of head-covering chosen. But while we can point to positives here, there is deep-seated internal confusion about African hair that is a reflection of the self-hate initiated by colonialism and three hundred years of trans-Atlantic enslavement. African or 'Afro' hairstyles became a symbol of Black militancy in the 1960s and 1970s – on the world stage this was symbolised by the USA political activist Angela Davis and rock–blues legend Jimi Hendrix. The link with the 'Afro' as a sign and symbol of Black beauty and positive African identity is counterposed with notions of 'relaxing' or 'straightening' African hair. Sometimes, it is argued that this is being done as a means of 'taming' and making hair easier to manage – although the underlying message is to get as close as possible to the lanky relaxed look of Caucasian hair styles. This type of stance introduces the notion of 'good hair' and 'bad hair'. According to Bill Gaskins (1997):

> When a Black child was born, I would hear my mother or other Black women refer to the child's hair as good. They'd say, 'That child has a good grade of hair'. I don't ever recall hearing them say that a child's hair was bad. But between them and the television commercials, the concept of good hair was firmly set in my mind. Good hair was hair that was not curly or course in texture. Good hair was not difficult to comb. Good hair had waves if you were male, length and manageability if you were female. I thought something was wrong with us. We weren't rich, we weren't white, and our hair wasn't on television. (Gaskins, 1997: 56)

This ideological battle concerning hair reminds us that self-identity and love of self are constantly shifting and liquid phenomena.

Creating positives from negatives

Self-identity is one aspect of our cultural trait and – like all the other various elements such as language, ethnicity and physical location that make up our cultural heritage – self-identity is not a static entity, but is ever changing over time and space: it is fluid and liquid. Self-identity, 'race' and ethnicities are social relationship links that differentiate us as individual human beings. The idea of self-identity is usually discussed around issues of rejecting negatives to create or recreate positive selves that can compete with other individuals and groups who have high social standings. It could be said that this is about gaining power to act and compete on a more equal social, economic and political framework. David Mason (1995), who is not particularly focussing on self-identity but rather the wider issues of 'race' and 'ethnicity', makes an important point about power and social relationship of difference:

> Thus race was always more than just a way of thinking about and describing human differences. It was a social relationship characterised by an unequal distribution of power and resources. Beliefs about race, and the stereotyped images of others which they entailed, were among the symbolic resources which were mobilised by dominant groups in their efforts to protect their position of power. (Mason, 1995: 8)

Power politics is also about ascribing and labelling OTHERS – giving them negative human qualities in the hope that they become universal burdens to individual and group progression.

Prolonged self-debasement by people of African descent has occurred because western colonialism and trans-Atlantic African enslavement was geared to be self-perpetuating by the abused internalising negative traits of themselves as true and factual. In this scenario people of African descent continue mentally and emotionally to enslave themselves even after the physical restraint of enforcement has been lifted. For example, the granting of physical freedom with the Emancipation Act of 1833 did not automatically change the psychological fetters of dependence and belief in the hierarchy that White is right and White is might.

During the period of African trans-Atlantic enslavement, Caribbean slave owner William (Willie) Lynch became fully aware of the need to find a systematic 'scientific' method of removing the positive self-identity and pride possessed by newly enslaved African men, women and children. In 1712 he was invited to the USA colony of Virginia to speak to other plantation owners. He was aware that the use of 'fear, distrust and envy' would result in self-hate and internal negativity. Lynch advocated pitting young enslaved Africans against old enslaved Africans, males against females, dark skinned against light skinned, short against tall – in effect, any and every African difference was exaggerated. He was clear that the end product was that 'they must love, respect and trust only us' (Hassan-El, 1999: 9). Using these divide and rule tactics would instil a negative mentality that required minimal policing to ensure that the planters felt safe in their beds. Lynch compared the breaking process of dehumanising enslaved Africans to that used to tame wild horses to submit to human will. The method used on humans was to instil fear by publically brutally torturing and killing the strongest male member of the enslaved Africans newly arrived from the African continent.

> Take the meanest and most restless nigger, strip him of his clothes in front of the remaining male niggers, the female, and the nigger infant, tar and feather him, tie each leg to a different horse in opposite directions, set him a fire and beat both horses to pull him apart in front of the remaining niggers. The next step is to take a bullwhip and beat the remaining nigger male to the point of death in front of the female and the infant. Don't kill him, but put the fear of God in him, for he can be useful for future breeding. (Hassan-El, 1999: 15)

This set the process for helping to break kinship, family and gender ties where the African woman moved to a state of 'frozen independence' because she could not depend on the African male for support or protection. According to Lynch:

> By her being left alone, unprotected, with the male image destroyed, the ordeal caused her to move from her psychological dependent state to a frozen independent state. In this frozen psychological state of independence she will raise her male and female offspring in reversed roles. For fear of the young male's life, she will psychologically train him to be mentally weak and dependent but physically strong.
>
> Because she has become psychologically independent she will train her female offspring's to be psychologically independent. What have you got? You've got the nigger woman out front and the man behind and scared. This is a perfect situation for sound sleep and economics. (Hassan-El, 1999: 16–17)

Lynch believed that this pattern of behaviour would 'become self refuelling and self generating for hundreds of years, maybe thousands' (Hassan-El, 1999: 9). It could be argued that he has had some success because African/Caribbean internal negativity today displays itself in the proliferation of misogynist rap/hip-hop music that denigrates African women and glorifies killing other African-descent males (Walker, 2005). There is also a preoccupation with shading, where light/white skin-tones are prized over dark/black skin (Fanon, 1986; Nyaako, 2004: 12–19), and there are continuing tensions between women and men of African/Caribbean descent (Hylton, 1999b: 55--72; James-Fergus, 1997; Nelson, 2005: 8–10).

The power to create and project self- and group identity can recreate a positive from the negative. For instance, during the 1960s the negative notion of 'black' was embraced and used as a positive political tool that was for a time also encompassing for many people of South Asian origins. During the 1970s and 1980s some South Asians began to move away from the phenotypical idea of 'black' as a concept that they could support as describing their ethnic, cultural and religious traditions. They argued that the 'black' identity term was imposed by African Americans and UK activists of African/Caribbean descent. They, Asians, were appendages who now wanted separate religious/cultural identities defined by them, for example Muslim, Indian, Pakistani or Bangladeshi (Modood, 1988). Some urban African Americans and UK African Caribbeans have argued that they are creating a similar transformation with the derogatory term 'nigger'. They claim that when they use it as part of their everyday speech patterns it loses its power to anger, shock and belittle people of African descent. Of course the counter-argument here is that it also makes it virtually impossible to argue that others outside of the African community, including racists, should not use the term as a slur remark. Jerome Williams (2005) in a short article in *The Northern Journal* goes further by linking the use of the term 'black' as offensive as what he terms the 'n' word, 'nigger'. He argues that 'black' when referring to people of African descent has links with the period of trans-Atlantic enslavement.

> Whenever I read about the period of trans-Atlantic enslavement the literature refers to 'us' as 'blacks' among other things. Now, that is no different to saying horse, dog, cattle or any other form of addressing an animal. Have you fed the horses? Have you chained up the blacks? The men were defined and recorded as bulls, the women, cows and the children, pups. (Williams, 2005: 32)

For Williams, the positive move out of this debacle is to force the concept of African humanity on to the agenda by insisting that the term 'black' by itself is unacceptable and the term 'black people' should be used. For this or other types of change identity to occur requires knowledge of choices and the ability to act with whatever power and belief that can be mustered – the key concepts being power and choice.

The power to choose and knowledge of choices

Power can be defined as the ability to do or act with authority, which can be invested in a person or thing such as an organisation or office. Power becomes vested in the person or thing that acts with authority because they have the power to act (*Collins English Dictionary*, 2006). A person who acquires this power is able to influence the behaviour of others, encouraging them to act in a particular manner. There is a widespread common-sense belief that power is a finite item, therefore it has to be taken in both hands as quickly as possible before some other claimant steals the crown. This is the concept of power as 'zero-sum', where the more power I have the less you will have. Using this analogy, power can be expressed as a cake, which is finite. Once it is carved up and shared out, there is no more to be had. An alternative way of conceiving power is to view it in the post-modern sense where the access and authority vested in power is open to everyone; where we all have power to act; where all voices carry equal weight with authority; and where the notion of hierarchy due to acquiring more or less power is not recognised. This is a society of equals.

The power to choose is an important aspect of the distinctive element that separates us from other animals. The notion of self-reflection, where we have the capacity to think about the consequences of our actions, is also important. This self-reflection enables us to make conscious decisions about our future actions based on the outcome of our present and past actions or deeds. This is part of our humanity and our understanding of others and self. Making a choice is the notion of doing one thing as opposed to doing something else – whether we have the power of selection or whether we are constrained or forced into a narrow range of choices. Our choices can be limited by a range of obstacles that include lack of knowledge of the available choices and the inability to weigh or access the choices available and to make a rational selection (Manz, 2003).

The outcome of a perceived lack of choices can be illustrated by one of the key presentations at the November 2005 Mary Seacole Wings Award Ceremony (2005) to celebrate the academic, business and cultural achievements of Leeds' ethnic minority communities. One of the main speakers, Andrew Muhammad, reflected on the theme of lack of choices when he examined the contents of violent DVDs. Young people viewing this material come under the spell that their behaviour strategies and future career options are limited to a range of aggressive, individualist and violent actions linked to drug dealing, gangsterism and prostitution.

The limit or range of a person's social upbringing, education, social class, ethnicity, gender, political outlook and religious or spiritual affiliation can affect choices. Using these criteria it is obvious that people of African/Caribbean descent in the UK and other western democracies have to work very hard to give themselves the opportunities to exercise the power of choice. It is a struggle for them to live the life they want to live: to be educated to the limits of their capabilities, to attain jobs and seniority consistent with their abilities and aspirations, and to be respected. The start of this new life could entail a shift of perception using Africancentric tools.

Social movement for change: Africancentricity

From research in London about Black family survival strategies a London Rastafarian expresses a widely held African/Caribbean viewpoint:

> basically, values from the host society have been adopted, and ways of being with people. Hostility, that's how they [majority UK community] operate, just general hostility. So it is important for us to instil in our children that we don't have to live like hostile beings, and you have to be careful when you are out there. (Hylton, 1999b: 31)

There is a mounting desire from the community of people of African descent for the creation of positive African identities linked to social relationships and family survival issues. A growing number of individuals and community groups are turning to an Africancentric way forward to counteract the negative effects of inner-city western life in the UK. This sub-section provides an introduction to these ideas.

Africancentrics believe that positive survival for people of African descent in the west requires us to regain knowledge of our historic African cultural heritage. This is achieved by a change in our inner consciousness, followed by changed activities in our private and public lifestyles. It is the casting off of an inner yoke of psychological oppression to get to the belief that the African is once more the subject of history with agency, rather than an object doomed to passivity. Individuals take charge of the direction of their life rather than waiting for others to point the way forward. This practical use of theoretical Africancentric concepts can be illustrated by African/Caribbean, cultural and artistic expressions.

According to O'Neal (1998), 'although enslaved Africans were not allowed to retain their own cultural artefacts, the conditions of slavery did not eradicate their aesthetic memory' of West Africa and the Congo (O'Neal, 1998: 167). People of African descent, particularly in the west, have used music, dance and spirituality as three of the main forces to help them to recast or hold on to separate and positive identities that do not rely on European social and cultural norms (Hylton, 1996). In a later article (2006) I remind us about the healing power of the drum:

> Artists of African descent possess a power to heal themselves and others. This creative force is at its apex in the rhythmic pounding of the drum. The beat of the drum is in tune with our hearts – our very soul – there is no escape. That is why we have to move our bodies and in the movement we connect with ourselves and gain release. The power of the drum reunites us to ourselves and reminds us of our own power. It is no coincidence that we humans all love to dance and gain pleasure and release from the act of physical movement. (Hylton, 2006: 7)

Richmond Quarshie's chapter in this publication, 'Black music as a key revolutionary signifier', provides sustained arguments to the effect that 'revolutionary artists are every bit as important as political leaders', where African music forms are used as the voice of struggle, through a spiritual medium that casts musicians who are living the struggle as 'today's equivalent of the prophets' (page 285).

It is widely accepted that Black art functions on a different basis from art with a mainly Europeancentric focus. Black art derives form and strength from organic links with the African/Caribbean community, where the separation of the artistic art forms and the audience is not acknowledged. Art and society are considered as a seamless entity that forms a part of the rank-and-file political struggles against social exclusion and racism. Such struggles are concerned with self-determination issues that redefine and recreate the building blocks for future generations. Art and society are one and the same – where art is life and life is art. Black artistic culture is used as a tool for the creation of individual and collective consciousness. In Leeds this was achieved in the 1960s and 1970s by collectives such as Uhuru (freedom) Arts Group, and from the 1980s with Kuffdem Arts, Gbakhanda Tiata Company, Ashobi Animateurs and the People's Arts Council (PAC) during the 1990s.

Africancentric theory and practice derive their intellectual and practical bases and their strength from the USA, where 'organic intellectuals' (Gramsci, 1891–1937) such as Marimba Ani (1994), Molefi Kete Asante (1995, 1992), Anthony Browder (1989), Rosalind Jefferies, Del Jones (1993) and Nana Sekhmet have a popular appeal, as they also do in the UK and Africa. All these activists are not strangers to the UK because they have visited on many occasions for nationwide lectures, discussions and workshop tours. For instance, Molefi Kete Asante was the key speaker at a Leeds conference in 1998 organised by the Black Men's Forum, *Men of African Descent Overcoming Social Exclusion* (Hylton, 1999a). In addition, others such as James Small, Anthony Browder and Richard Majors also gave lectures and workshops in Leeds in 1993, 1995 and 1997. These activist/theorists believe that knowledge of African history and culture can form the basis of a worldview that transforms individual consciousness to create a collective force. According to Asante (1995: 1):

> The psychology of the African without Afrocentricity has become a matter of great concern. Instead of looking out from one's own centre, the non-Afrocentric person operates in a manner that is negatively predictable. The person's images, symbols, lifestyles, and manners are contradictory and therefore destructive to personal and collective growth and development. Unable to call upon the power of ancestors, because one does not know them; without an ideology of heritage, because one does not respect one's own prophets; the person is like an ant trying to move a large piece of garbage only to find that it will not move.

Correct self-knowledge is the key to create pride and to act as a buffer to counter the self-defacing ideas that emanate from European-centred culture and theories. These revolutionary Africancentric ideas have not emerged out of a vacuum but have a distinguished history of past African nationalism, which include: the ideas and activities of Marcus Garvey;

Franz Fanon's African consciousness movement in Algeria; Steve Biko's Black consciousness movement in South Africa; the Pan Africanism of Dr Nelson Mandela; Malcolm X; the Black Panther programme created in 1967 by Bobby Seale, Huey Newton, Bobby Hutton and Eldridge Cleaver; and the Rastafarian movement in Jamaica, USA and the UK.

Africancentric ideas have been criticised by theorists such as bell hooks (1991) and Paul Gilroy (1993), who believe the Africancentric quest for authenticity and uniformity is a myth. A key element in this struggle for identity reformation is the ability to have control of the power of story-telling and recreation of historical events. I was privileged to participate as a management committee member and, later, Project Director of the community-led Leeds events in 2007 and 2008 to mark the 1807 UK Parliamentary Act that put an end to the kidnapping, capture and transportation of African people across the Atlantic. Below is a self-reflective summary of the Leeds project, which provides an instructive example of continuing cultural and political struggles about identity formation.

The Leeds Bi-Centenary Transformation Project

On 25 March 1807 there was a vote in the UK House of Commons when two hundred and eighty-three Members of Parliament voted for abolition, while sixteen voted against. From this date, UK ship captains could be fined £100 for each enslaved African found on board their ships. While it took a further thirty years before trans-Atlantic enslavement was abolished, the Act of 1807 was significant because Africans could no longer 'legally' be captured and transported into bondage. The importance of these historical events was not lost on today's people of African descent, including the Black community in Leeds. The tight-knit African/Caribbean community in Leeds, similar to other groupings in other major UK cities, wanted to mark this emancipatory event. Local activists wanted to use the 2007 commemorations as an active tool to empower themselves and their communities.

Similar to many other community initiatives, Leeds Bi-Centenary Transformation Project was kick-started by a charismatic local activist; in Leeds' case his name was Arthur France, Member of the British Empire (MBE). The first public meeting occurred in October 2005 at Leeds West Indian Centre, with approximately forty people in attendance. Most of the audience were committed community activists who were determined to try and develop a community-led 2007 project bid to the Heritage Lottery Fund, which was due in the first quarter of 2006. Meeting continuously throughout 2006 a working group of fifteen activists was able to build partnerships with Education Leeds, Leeds City Museum, Leeds Metropolitan University, Leeds Racial Equality Council and local community organisations, including Leeds West Indian Carnival Committee. The result of this collaboration enabled funding to be secured from Education Leeds, Heritage Lottery Fund, Joseph Rowntree Charitable Trust and Leeds City Council.

The Leeds Bi-Centenary Transformation Project was Africancentric, placing the three-hundred-year period of African trans-Atlantic enslavement into historical context in both Africa and Europe. There was an emphasis on telling the story from an African perspective – giving voice to eighteenth-century contemporary African activists such as Olaudah Equiano, Sarah Parker Remond, Frederick Douglass and Ignatius Sancho. Equiano, Remond and Douglass all had close links with the city of Leeds and the Yorkshire region. Also important is the impact this African holocaust had on the descendants of individuals and families of Africans who were forcibly displaced to the Caribbean, some of whom now reside in the UK. The final key theme underlying the Leeds programme was to highlight the extent of the benefits Leeds and other UK cities gained from British involvement in the trans-Atlantic 'trade'. The stress here was on the African trans-Atlantic enslavement that generated the 'triangle trade', which was the motor for British and European capitalist development (Fryer, 1984). Textiles, cutlery, gunpowder, green glass, beads, alcohol and tobacco were transported from the UK to the West African coast, to be traded for African people. They were enslaved and taken to the Caribbean and the Americas to be sold, to work to produce sugar, spices, molasses, rum, tobacco and cotton, which were shipped to the UK, thereby completing the lucrative trading triangle.

The Leeds Project was launched on 25 January 2007 at a half-day ceremony held at Leeds Civic Hall and continued in an evening session at Leeds West Indian Centre. The morning session was attended by local people and dignitaries including African and Caribbean Ambassadors, and the Leeds Lord Mayor Mohammed Iqbal, and with a powerful keynote address from Professor Gus John entitled *Pride in Our Heritage*. He emphasised African history prior to trans-Atlantic enslavement including the spirit of revolt and freedom that made enslavement untenable and created links between enslaved Africans and radical working-class movements in the UK. He stated that:

we have a duty, if we are not to falsify history, to make the connections between the way in which the slavery and plantation system was organised and exploited for the expansion of mercantile capitalism, and the way generations of white working class people here in Britain were exploited and made to acquiesce in the enslavement of Africans on the plantations across Europe. (John, 2007)

The two-year-long programme, which was extended for a further six months, presented activities that involved schools, museums, churches, artists and the wider community participating in exhibitions, scholarships, conventions, day-trips, workshops, lectures, training, performances and Leeds Carnival. Some of these activities were one-off events while others continued throughout the life of the programme. All efforts involved people in a greater understanding of their heritage. Audience participation for some of the programme was passive: for example, as audience members at a play or street theatre. However, even this passive involvement was followed by audience debate and other means of active audience participation. The aim, therefore, was for most of the programme to involve active participation in events such as seminars, debates and discussions, whilst other activities involved groups of young people in research, selection and design of materials that were used in mobile and permanent exhibitions using African artefacts from Leeds Museum stores. Other people, with the help of two writers in residence, developed school curricular and published materials that brought to life the impact of trans-Atlantic enslavement themes.

While members of the African/Caribbean community in Leeds had been successful in devising and remaining in control of a programme of events that allowed them to tell their own stories by having control of their self-identity formation, others were unsuccessful. Black community activists in Leeds proceeded with an Africancentric programme that did not replicate the very notion of physical, spiritual, cultural and economic enslavement that is reminiscent of the trans-Atlantic enslavement period.

There were tensions between African community leadership of 2007 bi-centenary projects and 'liberal' organisations, perhaps with William Wilberforce's evangelical social change as their main focus, who were also keen to stress the issues of contemporary enslavement and people-trafficking. In this regard UK museums and White-led organisations were the main beneficiaries of Heritage Lottery Fund grants for 2007 bi-centenary projects. The £408,000 Heritage Lottery Fund awarded to Leeds Bi-Centenary Transformation Project went against this national trend and also became the largest 2007 award to a 'grassroots' community organisation. I believe that while this should be applauded we must remember the plight of the other African community organisations that did not succeed. One of these organisations was a consortium of Bristol's Black community. Hilary Banks from the Bristol-based Consortium of Black Groups told Black Britain (website) that:

> We are opposed both to government plans as well as to those of Bristol City Council as they do not come from an Afrikan-centred perspective and continue to position Afrikan people as victims. (Black Britain website, 2006)

In 2007 Operation TRUTH 2007 mounted a campaign to oppose events such as *Abolition 200* organised by Bristol City Council and to replace them with African-planned activities organised from a Black perspective (Operation TRUTH, 2007). These were some of the examples of the widespread resistance from African Caribbean organisations that insisted 2007 commemorations should not cast enslaved Africans as victims who were freed by enlightened White radicals such as William Wilberforce and Granville Sharp, but rather should acknowledge that 'free' and enslaved Africans were also agents of their own liberation and that high-profile African activists such as Equiano, Remond and Douglass must be remembered. Likewise, collective struggles of mass resistance and 'slave revolts' such as the Maroon wars in Jamaica, the San Domingo revolution and the Sam Sharpe uprising in 1831 needed to be highlighted (James, 1984; Williams, 1993). These sentiments were endorsed by the long-running Liverpool Slavery Remembrance Initiative, which organises three days of Remembrance in August each year. Their aims are clearly stated:

> Through Slavery Remembrance Day we seek to both commemorate the lives of enslaved Africans and to celebrate the resistance, rebellion and revolution which ended slavery, highlighting the role of enslaved Africans in their own liberation. (Liverpool Slavery Remembrance Initiative, 2006)

From this case study it is possible to summarise that it is obvious that the two-hundred-year anniversary of the ending of the kidnapping, capture and transportation of African people from their homeland gave us all in the UK an opportunity to revisit our shared history. This past history can be classified as unfinished business that has strong resonances for all of us today. It is firstly about what is history: what is remembered, who gets to recall this history, how historical self-identity is constructed, and how the past interacts with the present and future. The struggles of Africancentric community 'grassroots' organisations to be able to dictate the recalling of their history is counter-posed by White-led 'liberal' evangelical organisations who wish to retell this period of history with their ancestors such as William Wilberforce and Granville Sharp as actors located centre stage. The 'bonded Africans' then become passive victims. What was different in Leeds was that 'grassroots' African/Caribbean activists managed to work with others outside of their community while still maintaining their radical agenda for African transformation, self and group identity.

Black and British: a contradiction in terms?

In 1998 Africancentric writer and performance poet Onyeka exploded onto the Black literary and cultural scene with the first of his two hard-hitting novels about the struggles of young African/Caribbeans in South London, who were trying to find positive methods of self and community redefinition for self-survival. The two books were *Waiting to Explode* (1998), subtitled *How to Stay Alive*, and *The Black Prince* (1999). In the introduction to *Waiting to Explode*, Onyeka 'pulls no punches' by stating that: 'To be African and live in the imperial heart that once enslaved us is to face a number of contradictions; one can lose oneself quicker than a fly in ointment'. He goes on to add that:

> The powers that be would like the legacy of this [Black] population to be remembered as the Frank Brunos, Lenny Henrys, and Linford Christies. These are the so called ambassadors of multicultural Britain. But let us remember the ordinary people who clung on to their culture as a matter of survival. Ordinary people made extraordinary not for their sound bite but their ability to resist oppression. (Onyeka, 1998: 5)

In *Waiting to Explode* the features of the main character Tayo, an eighteen-year-old polytechnic student, are made crystal clear early in the first chapter:

> As far back as Tayo could remember he had always looked black in anger. He did not have a blueprint of how to stay alive, but plan or not, he was definitely going to stay alive. Tayo felt that he had been thrown in at the deep end of a very large river. Without coaching or guiding, he logically should have drowned but he was not that easy to kill. He was part of a race that had been subject to every form of abuse and ridicule known in history and yet was still around to tell the tale. He had that same spirit inside of him, uncompromising, undaunted, and angry. As

a baby if anyone ever touched his pram he would scream, he was cross then, but he was as mad as hell now. A fire burnt inside him which he could not fully control. Almost, as if the rage of a hundred slaves butchered in the middle passage had taken out his soul and replaced it with their own. (Onyeka, 1998: 9)

Although Tayo was fostered with a White family during the 1970s, he never wanted to be White; he never dated White girls and he 'had always fought definitions which made him inferior' (Onyeka, 1998: 13). He tried to foster an Africancentric outlook while trying to hold back his physical anger, although he is constantly disrespected by White society including staff and students of his south London polytechnic. Onyeka's powerful novels highlight the very topical discussion point that asks: can people of African descent be accepted in the UK as British or English? The African/Caribbean characters in Onyeka's south London world, although born in the UK, are not accepted, and they face a daily barrage of implicit and explicit racist actions. This is especially the case for individuals such as Tayo who choose to live by a spiritual code that is Africancentric. This tension of Black Britishness and acceptance/unacceptance is explored in Paul Gilroy's work, particularly *There Ain't No Black in the Union Jack* (1992), first published in 1987, and the work of Tariq Modood (1988 and 1992) is particularly tuned to South Asian Muslims' UK experiences.

Public and private identities

This short sub-section explores the positive and negative impact of families in shaping the public and private behaviour patterns of African descent individuals in the west. The outcome of families transmitting a range of survival strategies creates different types of actions and speech patterns in private or with close family and friends when compared to the 'outside world', which is often considered as hostile and unforgiving. Where there is the safety net of familiar and, perhaps more importantly, safe surroundings, individuals can relax and be at ease, being able to 'speak their mind'. There is a lack of fear of criticism of their actions or downright hate, or possibility of feinted acceptance and shallow friendship bonds. Family preparation to meet unforgiving public scrutiny is sometimes regarded as more harsh, stern, physical and authoritarian than in Caucasian families. This statement is a sweeping generalisation that takes no account of regional variations and socioeconomic differences. This image of African/Caribbeans as brutish and short-tempered finds a most perfect match when discussing young males. Some argue that this image is created in early childhood when male children are humiliated by parent/carers after showing emotions of fear (Harris *et al.*, 1995: 33–8). In a hostile world these parent/carers know that any sign of fear will lead to harsh punishment for their children from school authorities and the judicial system.

Young men of African descent soon learn to hide their true emotions from the White world. They adopt a sense of male style that presents an overtly exaggerated sense of masculinity. This is the notion of being 'cool'. Richard Majors and Janet Billson (1992) term this 'a cool pose'. They argue that:

> Some African-American males have channelled their creative energies into the construction of a symbolic universe. Denied access to mainstream avenues of success, they have created their own voice. Unique patterns of speech, walk, and demeanour express the cool pose. This strategic style allows the black male to tip society's imbalanced scales in his favour. Coolness means poise under pressure and the ability to maintain detachment, even during tense encounters. Being cool invigorates a life that would otherwise be degrading and empty. It helps the black male make sense out of his life and get what he wants from others. Cool pose brings a dynamic vitality into the black male's everyday encounters, transforming the mundane into the sublime and making the routine spectacular. (Majors and Billson, 1992: 2)

With this protective over-garment Black men can make sense of their lives and survive with their semblance of pride and dignity intact, in a world that does not give them 'respect', social justice or equal opportunities. This is the face reserved for the public arena using a type of mask that hides the true character of the individual whose style of self-determination is viewed as a threat to White society.

Conclusion

Self-identity is about you, as an individual, creating your own version of who you are and locating your place in historical narratives that place you at centre stage. It is an understanding that it is your story, told by you, because you are best placed to know and understand the present and historical lived experiences. The need for self-identity provides us with a means of labelling and being able to apportion praise and individual blame to human activities. For people of African descent in the western diaspora this self-identity has to be able to withstand an array of negatives historically designed to undermine their individual and communal essence. An ever-changing array of counter-measures has been adopted to help African-descent individuals remain sane in what might be classified as generally racist western cultures.

Due to colonialism and three hundred years of trans-Atlantic enslavement people of African descent in the west have been left psychologically and culturally traumatised. These negative tensions were meant to be self-perpetuating by Africans internalising negatives about self and their community, thereby engendering lack of trust for others who look like them. The idea was to doubt self, family and other Africans, but constantly strive to think, look and act like and to trust Caucasians. All the counter-measures to recreate and sustain African self and group identity in the West has to come to terms with this historical dilemma by facing the issues head-on and finding methods of overcoming these powerful past historical, psychological and cultural forces – while at the same time dealing with existing negatives from the existing White world.

Positive African identity is set against the physical and ideological struggles and antics of the continuing actions of fringe right-wing groups such as the British National Party (BNP), who are bidding for a wider power base through UK electoral political activism.

The essence of positive self-identity is about trying to find a clear understanding of past events, which results in coming to terms with history. The aim is also to look beyond the events of the past few hundred years, to a re-analysis of world history spanning thousands of years into antiquity. This has the effect of placing the true contributions of African ancestors into historical significance of importance. Armed with this re-knowledge it is possible to construct intellectual arguments and practical actions that allow African individuals to regain their lost power. The key to change is to recreate internal consciousness.

One of the key theoretical and practical tools used by people of African descent in the West is the use of Africancentric ideas and actions. This provides the basis of a counter-ideology that has the intellectual weight to help Africancentric adherers to offer theoretical and practical arguments to oppose European-centred beliefs. People of African descent, while grappling to change the negative labels attached to their ethnic group, go about this work with a sense of style. For example, artistic expressions provide a method of resistance that taps into our humanity and helps us to remain sane in a sometimes insane western world.

References

Ani, M. (1994), *Yurugu* (Trenton, NJ: Africa World Press)

Asante, M. K. (1992), *Kemet, Afrocentricity and Knowledge* (Trenton, NJ: Africa World Press)

Asante, M. K. (1995), *Afrocentricity* (Trenton, NJ: Africa World Press, 7th edn)

Bandura, A. (1977), *Social Learning Theory* (Englewood Cliffs, NJ: Prentice Hall)

Berman, M. (1982), *All That Is Solid Melts Into Air* (London: Verso)

Bernard, W. (1995), 'Working with Men for Change' (PhD dissertation, University of Sheffield)

Browder, A. T. (1989), *From the Browder File* (Washington, DC: The Institute of Karmic Guidance)

Collins English Dictionary (2006), *Collins English Dictionary* (London: Harper Collins)

Davey, G. (ed.) (2004), *Complete Psychology* (London: Hodder and Stoughton)

Fanon, F. (1986), *Black Skin White Mask* (London: Pluto)

Fernando, C. (2000), *Racism and its Effects on Parenting* (London: Coram Family Moyenda Project)

Fryer, P. (1984), *Staying Power: The History of Black People in Britain* (London: Pluto)

Gaskins, B. (1997), *Good and Bad Hair* (New Brunswick, NJ: Rutgers University Press)

Giddens, A. (1991), *Modernity and Self-Identity, Self and Society in the Late Modern Age* (Cambridge: Polity Press)

Gilroy, P. (1993), *The Black Atlantic* (London: Verso)

Gilroy, P. (1992), *There Ain't No Black in the Union Jack* (London: Routledge)

Gramsci, A. (1891–1937), *Selections from the Prison Notebooks of Antonio Gramsci*, ed. and trans. Q. Hoare and E. Smith (London: Lawrence and Wishart)

Harris, H., Blue, H. and Griffith, E. (1995), *Racial and Ethnic Identity: Psychological Development and Creative Expression* (London: Routledge)

Hassan-El, K. M. (1999), *The Willie Lynch Letter and the Making of a Slave* (Chicago: Lushena Books)

Hobbes, T. (2004), *The Leviathan* (Whitefish, MT: Kessinger Publishing)

hooks, b. (1991), *Yearning Race, Gender and Cultural Politics* (London: Turnaround)

Hylton, C. (2006), 'The notion of power', *The Northern Journal* (Spring–Summer): 5–7

Hylton, C. (2005), 'Do the right thing', *The Northern Journal* (Spring): 21–3

Hylton, C. (1999a), *Men of African Descent Overcoming Social Exclusion* (Leeds: GBAKHANDA Publishing, Leeds Metropolitan University, Black Men's Forum)

Hylton, C. (1999b), *African Caribbean Community Organisations: The Search for Individual and Group Identity* (Stoke on Trent: Trentham Books)

Hylton, C. (1996), *African and African Caribbean Arts: A Perspective from Leeds* (Leeds: University of Leeds)

Ibrahiim, K. (2006), 'Bigwig n Suga Brown' (poem), in Shirley, M. and Kalu, P. (eds), *Hair* (Manchester: Suitcase Books)

James, C. L. R. (1984), *The Black Jacobins* (London: Allison and Busby)

James-Fergus, S. (1997), 'Rebuilding the African-Caribbean family in Britain', in Dench, J. (ed.), *Rewriting the Social Contract* (London: Institute of Community Studies)

John, G. (2007), 'Pride in Our Heritage', keynote address – *Launch of Leeds Bi-Centenary Transformation Project*, 25 January (Leeds: Leeds Civic Hall)

Jones, D. (1993), *Culture Bandits II: Annihilation of African Images* (Philadelphia, PA: Hikeka Press)

Kaiser, S., Rabine, L., Hall, C. and Ketchum, K. (2004), 'Beyond binaries: respecting the improvisation in African-American style', in Tulloch, C. (ed.), *Black Style* (London: V and A Publications)

Majors, R. and Billson, J. M. (1992), *Cool Pose: The Dilemma of Black Manhood in America* (New York: Simon and Schuster)

Manz, C. C. (2003), *Emotional Discipline: The Power to Choose How You Feel* (San Francisco: Berrett-Koehler Publisher)

Mary Seacole Black Achievers Wings Award Ceremony (2005) at Castle Grove Banqueting (December), Leeds Bi-Centenary Transformation Project

Maslow, A. (1971), *The Further Reaches of Human Nature* (New York: The Viking Press)

Maslow, A. (1943), 'A theory of human motivation', *Psychological Review*, 50: 370–96

Mason, D. (1995), *Race Ethnicity in Modern Britain* (Oxford: Oxford University Press)

Melucci, M. (1989), 'Nomads of the present: social movements and individual needs', in Keane, J. and Mier, P. (eds), *Contemporary Society* (London: Hutchinson Radius)

Modood, T. (1992), *Not Easy Being British* (Stoke on Trent: Trentham Books)

Modood, T. (1988), ' "Black", racial equality and Asian identity', *New Community*, 14 (Spring): 3

Muhammad, A. (2004), *The Hidden Truth: Free Your Mind* (London: Hakiki Publishing)

Nelson, H. (2005), 'What is a successful Black woman?' *The Northern Journal* (Winter): 8–10

Nyaako, K. (2004), 'One for the head and heart to all natti congo Asante, bungabunga, African people', *The Northern Journal* (Autumn): 12–19

O'Neal, G. S. (1998), 'African-American aesthetics of dress: current manifestations', *Clothing and Textiles Research Journal*, 16: 4

Onyeka (1999), *The Black Prince: Leopards In The Temple* (London: Abeng Communications)

Onyeka (1998), *Waiting to Explode: How to Stay Alive* (London: Onyeka)

Piaget, J. (1990), *The Child's Conception of the World* (New York: Littlefield Adams)

Piaget, J. and Inhelder, B. (1967), *The Child's Conception of Space* (New York: Norton)

Pieterse, J. N. (1992), *White on Black: Images of Africa and Blacks in Western Popular Culture* (New Haven, CT: Yale University Press)

Rawls, J. (1999), *A Theory of Justice* (Oxford: Oxford University Press)

Tulloch, C. (ed.) (2004), *Black Style* (London: V and A Publications)

Walker, A. (2004), *The Color Purple* (London: Phoenix)

Walker, M. (2005), 'Is sexism in the media a violation of women's human rights?' *The Northern Journal* (Winter): 14–19

Williams, E. (1993), *From Columbus to Castro: The History of the Caribbean 1492–1969* (London: Andre Deutsch)

Williams, J. (2005), 'Is the use of "Black" as a noun as implicitly offensive as the "N" word?' *The Northern Journal* (Winter): 31–2

Wright, R. (2004), *Black Boy* (London: Vintage)

Internet sources

Black Britain website, www.blackbritain.co.uk (accessed 23 October 2006)

Liverpool Slavery Remembrance Initiative (2006), Liverpool Slavery Remembrance Initiative pamphlet www.liverpoolmuseums.org (accessed 28 October 2006)

Operation TRUTH 2007 (2007), pamphlet www.operationtruth2007.co.uk (accessed 21 June 2007)

13

Black music as a key revolutionary signifier

Richmond Quarshie

Introduction

This chapter constructs a view of music as being a powerful indicator and documentary of the Black experience, rather than only a rhythmic concept. This analysis comes from an artistic perspective whilst drawing on the beliefs, traditions and practices that underpin African spirituality. A number of themes are developed in presenting the thrust of this argument, with the most fundamental being that music is a potent force and spiritual medium that should be revered. This chapter also portends that music and the 'Black struggle' are intricately linked, hence giving rise to the notion of revolutionary artistes. Entering into the realms of spirituality, it contends that music is a conduit allowing for connections to higher forces, elevating the status of some artistes, who have a divine mission, with serious consequences when this is compromised. There is also a focus on the oratory skills that make Black music unique as a voice of struggle. From here it examines the lyrical content, and shows the current state of play along with the complexities and implications for the 'Black struggle', whilst acknowledging the dynamism pushing in several directions. Certain developments are beneficial in terms of the 'Black struggle', whilst others raise serious questions. Whilst acknowledging the contribution of Black musicians across all artistic genres, the chapter concludes on a note that pushes for music to be more in tune with its true essence including the aspirations of 'the struggle'.

Redemption songs: Kuti and Marley

If you play with music, you go die. (Fela Kuti)

It is something of gravitational proportions that these words should continue to reverberate to this day. In Africa, music is revered as a potent force at the heart of everything cosmologically conceivable. The thought of music as a treasure hoard of political awareness is perhaps not so strange after all, and such is this phenomenon that many artistes have emerged in a league of their own, as evidence of their contribution to the 'Black struggle'. In fact, that intricate link between music and politics shines a whole new light on what artistes have to say. As a result, it is not surprising that governments or regimes will move to slap censorship on certain forms of music, lyrics or artistes. Historically and spiritually, music has been an area where Black people have articulated their experiences, and when artistes have been affirmed in their political sensibilities this has been effective in putting forward relevant ideologies and opinions. This includes the dexterous and skilful use of driving rhythms to sometimes mask the 'rawness' of radical thoughts into songs whose impact can be subliminal.

In the book *Catch a Fire*, Timothy White (2000) illustrates Bob Marley's infusion of the teachings and philosophies of the late, great Marcus Garvey into music. *Redemption Song* and *Wake Up and Live* show the end result in a powerful awakening call to the oppressed. Similar to other artistes, Marley also touted an intricate knowledge of 'the struggle' and issues that proved to be relevant. This fact is demonstrated by the inclusion and delivery on *Rastaman Vibration* of *War* (Cole and Barrett, 1976), a speech by Haile Sellasie superbly set to music with emphasis on 'under the philosophy that holds one race superior and another inferior is finally discredited and abandoned'.

In countless interviews, Kuti, the acclaimed Nigerian artiste, elaborated on his tour of the United States of America (USA) in the late 1960s, where he encountered the Black civil-rights movement and the Marxist Black Panther Party, along with Angela Davis and Stokely Carmichael, as being a critical milestone. Once he was armed with this knowledge and his grasp of African affairs, the regime in Nigeria found itself under fire not only from a well-informed militant artiste but also a political force. Interestingly, it was also on returning from the USA, to Jamaica, that Marley immersed himself deeper in the teachings of Rastafarianism. It seemed that the reality of Black tribulation in the 'heart of the beast' was a factor in mobilising the efforts of this pair in their own 'backyards'. From a spiritual dimension, the role that Kuti and Marley went on to play on behalf of the masses was on a par with Garnet Silk's rendition in *The Rod* (Smith *et al.*, 1999), which stated that 'music is the rod and we are Moses'. There is no doubt that both Kuti and Marley were attuned to the struggle before travelling to the USA, and it is striking that travelling also featured in the lives of other great Black leaders. However, neither of them needed to venture far because the fact that they were African contextually meant they were flung into the 'Black struggle' even before birth. Naturally, this is the line that African spirituality will take.

Whilst social class may constitute some advantages for some artistes, what is more important is their alignment with the masses. There is a difference between a songwriter with a good imagination and one that actually lives 'the struggle', even if both were Black, a point that resonates with the line, 'mama you got me born into the wrong class' as heard on *Living on the Frontline* (Grant, 1979). This throws in the issue of 'honesty and integrity' with the wealth amassed by some of these artistes, making it hypocritical of them to voice their utterances against 'high society' whilst indulging the same vices. Even the use of the term 'revolutionary artiste' within this context can be controversial and superficial. One thing that is certain is their notoriety for out-spokenness and radical political opinions, especially as social commentators. Having the awareness and conscious to articulate issues or political opinions that are relevant to the struggle is courageous and admirable.

A spiritual perspective

Exodus, movement of Jah people. (Marley, 1977)

Historically, music has been a means used by Africans to connect to higher forces. It is a widely held belief that musicians are chosen for a purpose to be enacted with humility, honesty and integrity. As such, the phenomenal accomplishments of some artistes cannot be only attributable to them being musically talented or politically astute. One can easily go on to suggest that these are today's equivalent of the prophets. As well as 'revolutionary', 'visionary' and 'king', confidantes of Marley have described him as 'Joseph of the Bible', whilst others have been forthright in the use of 'near prophet' and 'messenger'. Even Kuti proclaimed himself to be the spiritual son of Dr Kwame Nkrumah, one of the foremost exponents of the Pan-Africanist movement. His sense of mysticism was heightened by the accounts of people leaving their families to live at the Kalakuta Republic set-up by Kuti as an independent state in Nigeria.

Whilst the 'Black struggle' is often theorised as a socioeconomic or political process or system, the fight against spiritual wickedness remains resolute. Taking the African view of collectivism, rather than individualism, Moses, for example, would be a multitude, which under-scores the view of the music fraternity, as sung on *The Rod* (Smith *et al.*, 1999). On another plane, a prophet could simply be a messenger sent to reaffirm verbally what has been before, or someone physically doing the deeds of those who have been. Certainly, the term 'near prophet' used by some people to describe Marley is not misplaced when one takes the African view. The proficiency with which he articulated biblical quotations throughout his songs was breathtaking and evocative of the utterances of Dennis Brown (1983) in *Words of Wisdom*:

> I will open my mouth in a parable, and sing the dark sayings of old.
> And much wisdom and knowledge stretch forth their hands,
> Unto you, o children, I cry.
> All the words of my mouth speak righteousness.
> All the days of my life will tell.
> Take heed of the words of Jehovah, or men you will surely fail!

Reggae music is awash with such sayings and this is not a simple case of paraphrasing, especially when they are set to rhythm or rhyme, often they often appear as cryptically coded messages to be sung with thought-provoking potency. Moreover, it is recognised that, as well as political change, the struggle was also about furthering spirituality and consciousness, as witnessed by the fight to hold on to African traditions and beliefs whilst under bondage.

Musicians can also be classified as intermediaries between people and the Creator, in the same way as the linguists operate in the African court. Linguists are appointed to noble families, elders, chieftaincy or royals in various roles from spokesperson, interpreter or advisor. During libation, for example, it is the linguist who would perform this ritual with skill, efficacy and eloquence, including the petitioning of the Supreme Being, Ancestors and Deities. Apart from the ancestral lineage, those enthroned as custodians of the people are regarded as being sacred, meaning that their subjects must speak to them through an intermediary, the linguist. This was also the protocol during the Exodus when the Israelites required divine intervention. By likening revolutionary artistes to the traditional linguists, one is able to appreciate their reverence of old sayings and dexterous lyricism, especially in the distinct language set, including the coded or thought-provoking proverbs.

Those words uttered by Kuti of the deadly consequences of playing with music confirm two important things, the first being the spiritual meaning of music with the other being the power bestowed on musicians as players and wordsmiths. Both can be tied to the fact that in the beginning was the word and the word was with the Creator and the word was the Creator. From this the African perspective conceives the trilogy of word, sound and power and thus the talking drum takes on a powerful dimension, when word is transformed into sound. Unlike any other instrument, the 'big drum' is viewed as sacred, employing a unique tonal system to convey powerful messages. In Africa, the meaning of music is rooted in the word, creation itself, and is most powerful when reflecting all the emotions and realities of life where struggle is one dimension. Rightly so: this is not something to be toyed with – hence the severe consequences as a deterrent.

Often, with revolutionary artistes, there will be noticeable elements of spirituality that go beyond music. In truth, entertainment is secondary, as seen with the accomplished drummer Ghanaba (Guy Warren) declining an offer to perform on the spur of the moment because the spirits had not been petitioned beforehand. This line is no different from Marley (1980) singing in *Redemption Song* of his hands being strengthened by those of the Almighty. Apart from those versed in the African oracle, some artistes will not even realise the purpose for which they have been sent. Therefore, it is not for them to self-proclaim any titles as it is only on their passing that rites are performed to decide whether ancestorship should be conferred. The esteem of this bestowment is confirmed when ancestors are called alongside the Creator whenever the ritual of libation is performed. Implicitly, artistes that are 'brought in the fold' and able to approach music with humility, integrity and conviction are looked upon favourably in the spiritual realm.

The African view is also critical to explain the acts of defiance and determination when the lives of revolutionary artistes are placed in danger. In truth, the Creator and Ancestors would carry these illustrious prophets until their purposes in this existence are fulfilled. For example, the assassination attempt on Bob Marley's life in 1976 did not stop him recording the album *Exodus*, which was a defining moment in his career. The consequences that were to be suffered by Fela for his scathing denunciations – several arrests, imprisonment and beatings at the hands of the Nigerian authorities – are already noted. Even the death of his mother did not dampen Fela's determination, as remonstrated by the song *Coffin for Head of State*. This form of courage, determination and passion at critical points of the 'Black struggle' is indestructible and not surprising because of what it implies by way of the masses being endowed with a voice, direction and leadership.

Small axe: big tree

The view of the soil as the vital life force for the tree is transmitted in a more powerful metaphor about the culture in which one grows.

The saying, 'a people without a knowledge of their history is like a tree without roots' by Marcus Garvey, as adapted by Aswad in the song *Old Time Tradition*, is of that vein, as is the citing of 'we are the branches, the leaves that have life', in *Jah Seed* by Morgan Heritage (2001). In the book *Catch a Fire*, Timothy White (2000) explains that what appears to be a simple allegory on *Small Axe* by the Wailers, in which a woodsman informs a large tree that it is about to be felled, is actually a fascinating three-pronged assertion that is readily understood by all Jamaicans but utterly obscure to almost anyone else. Here, Marley is not only warning oppressors everywhere that they will be cut down to size one day, it also had a particular application to the Jamaican recording industry.

When originally penned the song, *Small Axe* referred to 'the Big T'ree', the island's dictatorial record company triumvirate: Dynamic, Federal and Studio One. The final dimension, perhaps the most powerful, depicts the ordering of enslaved Africans to topple gigantic trees, which are held sacred, hence the pouring of libation accompanied by a woeful song to assure the spirits that it was not the slaves' idea, but rather the will of their masters. When applied to serve a political purpose, this eloquent clandestine code is equally potent. Combined with old sayings, the results were statements with which the masses were instantly able to identify. Along with the irony, derision and wit of a talented and well-informed artiste, the effects are compelling, as seen with how Kuti effortlessly re-painted the political landscape in a format that made those in power uneasy. The enormously popular song *Zombie* even brought the fury of the Nigerian army upon him and his followers in 1977, resulting in the death of his mother.

Transforming standard English codes

Employing the same means, Africans were able to transform standard English into other forms, such as 'Pidgin English' or 'patois', in a tradition that continues with the language of the emerging urban music culture. By applying this in describing everyday situations many artistes were able to bend the rudiments of music to create more space to target their opinions. The thoughts stirred up by 'some will eat and drink with you, then behind dem su-su pon you' (Barrett and Barrett, 1976) as found on *Who the Cap Fit* were not to be underestimated, neither must 'ah, whoa! frighten dem', as Marley (1979a) aptly asked on *One Drop*. These dialects, if they could be described as such, by definition evolve out of cultural determination and resistance to the imposition of foreign languages on Africans. Their infusion into

the music of struggle is also an affirmation of the role of revolutionary artistes as cultural ambassadors. Moreover, this art of language
transformation is still evident in the rapid explosion of urban music
forms today.

The enemy within: 'house slaves' versus 'field hands'

Looking back on the contribution made by key artistes, a host of questions are thrown up concerning leadership. With the link between music
and politics, it is not surprising that politicians go to extremes to
elicit the help of artistes for political ends. However, a distinction is
made between political affiliation and the universal message associated with this discussion. What is clear is that revolutionary artistes
see the need to challenge the wrongs they encounter. For example, during the 1970s, the imperialist and neo-colonial forces working against
the 'Black struggle' were clearly particularised. Whilst not openly
entrenching any political position, Marley (1976) made it clear in
Rat Race that 'Rasta don't work for no CIA'. In the end, it all comes
down to the battle against evil, and anyone venturing onto that side
of the equation would find themselves under fire from the school of
revolutionary artistes.

Historically, it is dismal leadership that has created the platform
for music to become a vehicle for vocalising the plight of the masses.
Without revolutionary leaders, political change is so much harder,
especially where people are unable to affect self-rule even after a revolution. Whilst the masses move when the moment arises, it is essential for the process to be properly steered. Visionary leaders are hard
to come by, let alone when the struggle has been gifted with them but
due praise is not given. In *Redemption Song*, Marley (1980) rightly asks,
'how long shall they kill our prophets, while we stand aside and look'?
When Nkrumah was being overthrown in 1966, no one thought that
one day Ghanaians would lament their dejection of one of its most
illustrious sons. An absence of leadership is bad enough in itself, but
the situation where those elected to positions of power then misrule
the populace is despicably criminal and a seedbed for unimaginable vices. In his book *Omali Yeshitela Speaks*, Omali Yeshitela (2005)
writes:

> In the absence of the independent revolutionary organisations that we
> had in the 1960s, no body speaks out or articulates the interest of the
> masses of African working and poor people. We only get statements
> from the politicians and from liberal and petty bourgeois, middle class

organizations that lead the charge against the black community. Now you've got Africans occupying positions of authority to maintain the system of oppression of the African community. They killed off our revolutionary movement. They killed off our revolutionary leaders. Then they raise black leaders to function for white power.

It is often at critical moments that the works of artistes have been most poignant, when they have stepped in as an alternative voice. With tales of corruption, misrule, dictatorship, embezzlement and self-gratification from community to government circles endemic, many would say not much has changed. Without true revolutionary leaders, power elites serve their own interests, with the masses powerless to do anything, as daily survival subverts the will to resist. Through a sophisticated form of elitism designed to confuse, the people's power is steadily rolled back with their 'own' carrying out the will of the oppressors at the top. This allows them, with minimal power, to control the masses through 'divide and rule' tactics. Once again in *Rat Race*, Marley (1976) finds the phrase with, 'when the cat's away the mice will play, political violence fill your city'. Metaphorically, the 'cat' is the old regime, slave holder or colonial masters swept aside in favour of self-rule with the new leadership; the 'mice' represents the use of subjugation to curtail the masses through political games, including violence if necessary. In this scenario, the new leaders or emergent ruling class remain subservient to those 'pulling the strings'. In time, they graduate from overseers into tyrants whose behaviour becomes indistinguishable from the dominant group, as they now adopt similar values. As a rule, whilst they will not step on each other, the process is still manipulated by the dominant group, making the rest no more than pawns in the game of 'divide and rule'. Implicitly, tensions and conflicts between the ruling classes and the masses are inevitable, as Marley (1979b) highlights with the song *Zimbabwe*:

> To divide and rule could only tear us apart
> In everyman chest there beats a heart
> So soon we'll find out who is the real revolutionaries
> And I don't want my people to be tricked by mercenaries

If the Black ruling class had been instrumental in removing the old order, then this was more opportunism rather than revolution. From the onset their role was part of an elaborate scheme to deny real power to the masses. Fearing an uprising because of their ill-gotten gains under the new settlement, they resorted to brutalising the people with whatever means at their disposal. For example, Fela in *Zombie* highlighted the programming of soldiers into killing machines only to be unleashed on the masses with impunity by a corrupt regime, just as in *Burnin and Lootin* Marley describes waking up in a curfew confronted by strange faces dressed in uniforms of brutality, thus making a rebellion unavoidable. Whilst these scenarios may be difficult to accept, it is also a reminder of what Black people can become if there is nothing in place for the masses to keep those in power in check, hence the notion of the oppressor within. This is the same battle 'house slaves' and 'field hands' fought out on the plantations, with the former scheming to protect the meagre advantages and privileges of loyal servitude, but only now it is the revolutionary leaders versus the liberal and petty bourgeois class. Whilst this battle has been raging for some time, music has been vociferous in bringing it to the fore. This in part explains why Public Enemy and others felt it necessary to voice their endorsement of Louis Farrakhan and the Nation of Islam (NOI).

Even with the influence of hip-hop or rap, the liberal and petty bourgeois class continue to shun artistes for their alignment with radical organisations, thus prohibiting constructive dialogue on issues pertinent to the struggle. Whilst many artistes do not proclaim to be leaders, their revolutionary utterances make it difficult for people not to see them as such. As recently as the flooding of New Orleans, when leaders were 'dragging their feet' about 'race' as a factor in the slow response, Kanye West (Moraes, 2005) stood up and made it plain that, 'Bush does not care about Black people'. Indeed, this is not unusual, as many would recall Margaret Thatcher being pasted by Bob Geldof about the famine in Ethiopia in the 1980s (Garfield, 2004). What is encouraging from the hip-hop experience in particular is the contingent of artistes using their brand revolutionary rhymes to expose the corruptive practices regardless of 'who the cap fits'.

A musical revolution

By the time images of blazing United Kingdom (UK) cities flashed across television screens during the disturbances of 1981, Britain was lurching dangerously into a state of anarchy. Whilst the hardship and struggles of the working class are well documented and discussed, there is not much about the Black experience. Yet it was significant that The Specials topped the singles charts in the same year with *Ghost Town* – a powerful song constructed over a beat that was more heavy reggae than their usual 'ska'. Regardless of the racial backgrounds of the band members, this brilliant song, while making a powerful political statement, was also recognising the influence of reggae in

Britain, especially in the 1970s. Whilst this period was undoubtedly a 'golden age' as far as the music was concerned, it also provides a powerful documentary of the 'Black struggle', the reverberations of which are still being felt. There was no doubt that government thinking altered significantly in the wake of the urban riots in 1981 and, whilst this may be seen as a major coup in political terms, the part musicians played in highlighting the issues was critical.

The notion of musicians deputising as mouthpieces for 'the people' is already highlighted, and the music of the 1970s was no different. However, in terms of the problems facing the targeted populous, the music scene was where a far more radical approach could be articulated without censorship. It is true that people would look for inspiration from all directions if they felt they had no voice, notwithstanding the endurance of hardship. In terms of leadership – with most of the 1960s revolutionary leaders murdered, incarcerated or covertly sidelined – the context was ripe for radicalism. Of course people will always buy music for music's sake, especially if they have the means to do so. For example, whilst partying to the gyratory reggae beats at the elite clubs of Jamaica, how many of the 'high society' of 1970s were sympathetic to the abysmal life of their poor neighbours as expressed by the lyrics? It is only when their way of life is threatened that they take notice, a scenario aptly captured in the classic movie *Rockers* (Hulsey and Bafaloukos, 1978).

Whilst Public Enemy may be renowned universally for opening the eyes of mainstream rap music to political opinions, their contribution to 'the struggle' was even more critical. This can be seen by reflecting on the reality of daily life in the Black neighbourhoods long after the sacrifices of the USA civil-rights movement. By the time Public Enemy came to the fore, there was already a notion of struggle across the spectrum of Black music, not only in rap. However, their infusion of creativity and new elements to the radical form of hip-hop of the early 1990s, unreservedly promoting Black consciousness whilst bending the rudiments of music with mind-blowing hard-core beats and rhymes, took North America by storm. To some extent the riots that erupted in Los Angeles in 1992 after the notorious beating of Rodney King (Von Hoffman, 2003: 227) also reflected the mood of that era after years of deprivation and frustration. The significance of these events was similar to the British experiences leading up to the inner-city disturbances of 1981.

With mainstream politics devoid of radical views, young people saw the need for an approach that at times, conflicted with their predecessors'. In some way, Marley's prognosis of 'the generation gap' in *One Drop* (1979a), or 'we're the generation try break through tribulation' in *Exodus* (1977), seemed right. This was nothing more than an acknowledgement that young people were prepared to carry the mantle handed to them, based on their analysis. In his article, Olende (2005) writes;

> To young West Indians in Britain who suffered discrimination at school and work and were targeted by the police with the notorious sus-stop and search-laws, Rastafari offered an oppositional culture, giving a sense of self respect and identity . . . Young blacks in British inner city areas were not simply absorbing the music of the Caribbean. As an established community they made their own music, reflecting life in Britain.

With its infusion of elements for mass appeal by artistes such as Bob Marley, the air of acceptability about reggae music also signalled the UK contingent to interject their own versions and experiences. Before long, Aswad, Steel Pulse, Matumbi, Misty in Roots and others, with the assistance of the sound systems, rose to that challenge with impact. In terms of the sociopolitical context, reflecting this revolutionary cultural mood, songs such as *Back to Africa, Concrete Slaveship* and *Corruption* by Aswad were just as significant as Johnny Clarke's (1976) reworking of *Declaration of Rights*:

> Look, oh Lord, they brought us down here
> Have us in bondage, right through these years
> Fussing and fighting, among ourselves
> Nothing to achieve this way, it's worser than hell, I say
>
> Get up and fight for your rights my brothers
> Get up and fight for your rights my sisters
> Took us away from civilization
> Brought us to slave in this big plantation . . .

Having artistic control enabled UK artistes to create music that could be employed to carry a philosophical, sociological or political message, with a life of its own. Whilst all the ingredients for commercial viability are maintained, the result is not only a piece of music but a powerful cause-championing vehicle. It will be interesting to know if the record companies handling artistes such as Marley were aware of the revolutionary thinking and political thoughts that emerged as a result of their music.

This discussion would be incomplete without noting Rastafari as a way of life combining the different notions of self-identity and consciousness, whilst making a politico-cultural statement. Even the challenges illustrated by the song *Since I Throw the Comb Away* by the Twinkle Brothers (1980) could not stop this tide. Not only did 'Rastafari' double up as a supplementary system of education in its own right, it represented a cultural rebirth, with converts changing their western names to others such as Asher, Levi or Judah in a clear rejection of those of slave masters. Soon groups were organising across the country with 'reasoning' as an art form, reminiscing the days of the ancient kingdoms of Ghana, Mali and Songhay. The quest for self-knowledge brought a host of radical literature to prominence, including the publication of leaflets and newsletters, perhaps the closest to a revolutionary free press in Britain.

Although developments were at an advanced stage, the television screening of *Roots* in 1977 became a defining moment. The theme song was turned into a powerful 'dub plate', a must for every sound system, which drove revellers into a warrior-like trance. Apart from music, sound systems ventured into other areas, including the retail of clothing items, books, 'ital food' and artworks. Towards the late 1970s, sections of society were already sensing the racial tensions, and the creation of the *Rock Against Racism* movement in 1978 showed musicians to be further ahead than the politicians. Olende (2005) acknowledges that the anti-fascist struggle and the coming together of punk and reggae as anti-establishment allies was a major breakthrough. As well as the economic climate, years of racism and brutality, containment and the infamous 'sus' laws had become a flashpoint of confrontation with the police. The images of the police shielding the far-right fascist groups during marches in contrast to the heavy handedness towards 'left-wing' protestors or at Black gatherings simply made matters worse.

During this intense 1970s and 1980s period, the Notting Hill Carnival should have been an occasion to 'wind down' whilst taking in a cultural explosion of music, sound systems, food and togetherness, but it was to become a scene of confrontation with the institutionally racist police. The images of burnt-out police cars in the aftermath, resembling something of an enervated 'beast', alleviated any fears about the impregnability of the police as a force. As captivated by songs such as *Three Babylon* and *Babylon* by Aswad, the situation with the police was at the point of crisis. The mood was reflected up and down the country, as performance poet Linton Kwesi Johnson remonstrated with *Dread Inna Inglan* (1978):

> Dem frame up George Lindo up in Bradford town
> but de Bradford blaks dem a rally round
> me seh dem frame up George Lindo up in Bradford town
> but de Bradford blaks dem a rally round

Maggi Tatcha on di go
wid a racist show
but a she haffi go . . .

Dissipating a revolution

The disturbances of 1981 brought many issues to the fore not only for the Black community but also for the wider UK masses. One can only imagine the panic in the corridors of power when the then Thatcher Government woke up to find cities ablaze with 'posses' of disenchanted and disillusioned youths running amok. It is unimaginable that the Government would not have studied the causes, especially the political ideologies that motivated the reaction seen across cities. Any government that believed its policies of containment were working then to have it all fly back in their face would want to know what had gone wrong. However, their motives would not necessarily have been about making things better for the Black community; rather the opposite. In the ideological onslaught on the working class by the Thatcher Government, it was hard to see how the Black community could escape the consequences. Since the 1980s, the 'Black struggle' has taken on a whole new dimension, which has not been fully understood in its proper context. Essentially, whilst the issues remain untouched, it has changed dramatically from a tactical viewpoint with venomous sophistication. One can no longer take for granted that the arts provide a space for artistes to freely express or articulate views without constraints; even that notion is now questionable. Whilst there would have been moves to clamp down on the spirit of defiance that exploded onto the streets in 1981, not a lot of thought has been given to how that process was to be carried out. The term 'cultural terrorism' (Quarshie, 2005) captivates how this has worked in relation to reggae, and unless the Black community wises up to the plan to deprive them of their heritage, culture and motherland, the sacrifices made during centuries of struggle will come to nothing.

The shift towards monetarism in the 1980s set out to snuff out every last stronghold of socialist thought around the globe. In his book, White (2000) confirms the concerns over the impact Marley was having throughout the world. There is no way that interest would have been centred on one person, because by the 1980s there was a whole movement in place, with the likes of Peter Tosh and others being considered equally as militant. The fatal assumption made in all this was that Rastafarianism was essentially a socialist or left-wing ideological concept. This is an under-estimation of the 'Black struggle' and a tactic of 'demonisation' to undermine its cultural and spiritual significance. The impact of reggae in the UK guaranteed that the music had an outlet to the lucrative global market. If this musical revolution was to be locked off, the process had to begin in the UK.

In his book, White (2000) makes it clear that Marley did not approach politics from an ideological standpoint. However, the assumption about this typifies an approach to the study of different cultures that is founded on ethnocentrism and continued to this day. Preiswerk and Perrot (1978) in their book *Ethnocentrism and History* define ethno-centrism as follows:

> As the attitude of a group which consists of attributing to itself a central position compared to other groups, valuing positively its achievements and particular characteristics, adopting a projective type of behaviour toward out-groups and interpreting the out-groups through the in-group's mode of thinking.

On these assumptions the thought of pro-Black reggae artistes with the clout to develop initiatives in Jamaica, Nigeria or anywhere else would have been unpalatable. One cannot under-estimate the strength of anti-establishment feelings in the UK during the 1980s, as seen with *Rock Against Racism*: alliances emerged that demonstrated the highest level of political thinking and organisation, as well as the notion of music as part of a progressive struggle. The fact that the punk move-ment viewed it as critical to create this form of alliance with reggae is an indication of reggae's popularity and significance. The emergence of a quasi-reggae movement in the form of ska was another thorn in the side of a government determined to crush the working class. As seen with *Ghost Town*, The Specials had adopted reggae's tradition of protest to express opinions about the devastative effect of Thatcher's policies. Given the racial mixture of these groups, ignoring this devel-opment whilst the country had just witnessed disturbances that were a product of horrendous living conditions, oppressive policing and gov-ernment policies would have been perilous. The message resonated with the record-buying public and was rapidly incorporated into the repertoires of other bands. It was clear that, with musicianship and political courage, these groups could cause problems for any government.

In his article, Olende (2005) confirms that, generally, the politics was dropped from reggae in the 1980s. What seems clear is that in the aftermath of the inner-city disturbances a significant shift in cul-tural policy took place, with Black music in particular being driven underground, utilising a policy that continues to this day. It seems that any development within the music scene is being watched with close interest at the highest level. Claire Hughes (2005), in her article, describes similar responses to 'acid house':

> The dawning of 'acid house' prompted a wave of public panic, exacerbated by the British press, which had us believing that anyone listening to this new music was a crazed drug addict . . . Government response to the ensuing hysteria, fuelled by press coverage of the raves put on by promoters such as Sunrise, Biology, Fantasia and Spiral Tribe, paved the way for the 1994 Criminal Justice Bill. Never before had legislation been brought in so quickly by any government.

However, this did nothing to stop the wave of urban music such as street soul, dance, jungle, drum and bass, garage, ragga and bashment, which are all reggae influenced and an indication of the African fighting spirit. Because of their origins, these are not simply styles of music; they also represent a political, social and artistic movement signifying their own elements of the struggle.

Beats of mass destruction

Considering its underground origins, the increasing success of 'urban music' should be watched very carefully with an 'open mind'. In contrast to where Black music was, whilst the oratory skills remain resolute, the current scene is less edgy, considering the fiery revolutionary lyrics of yesteryear. Without simplifying the countless genres that make up today's Black music, this discussion would be meaningless without references to reggae/ragga, rap/hip-hop and soul/R and B. Going by some of the recent material, serious questions are being asked about the direction in which things are going especially as, after centuries of struggle and the popularity of Black music, not much progress has been made in terms of Black ownership in the music industry.

Reflecting on the kind of hip-hop or rap that peaked in the 1990s – giving rise to a new form of consciousness in a defiant rejection of oppression even if it meant condemning the community's own shortcomings – something is seriously amiss. Instead of revolutionary rhymes about racism and capitalism, it appears that artistes only seem capable of reconstructing vocabulary in contempt of woman as 'bitches' and idolisation of 'pimps', 'rides' and guns. For example, if we consider what is now known as 'gangsta rap', despite its popularity, the sensationalising of the 'n' word or 'ghettoisation' of the Black experience is stooped in controversy and backwardness. This trend is not unique of hip-hop or rap as everywhere across the genres, it seems, artistes have developed a fascination with how far to take things in the direction of immorality.

It is clear that self-regulation will not resolve anything, as the industry is content to sit tight with the huge sums of money flowing in. With everybody 'dragging their feet' about debating this matter as a point of struggle, the artistes continue churning out this material and wiping out ground gained during centuries of struggle. With the popularity of rap or even reggae, the sensationalism of the lyrics with their powerful imagery and symbolism is all the more worrying. Since the first record with women referred to as 'bitches', generations have emerged that know no other term of reference. Sadly, even White teenagers can be heard emulating this language with the belief that it is cool to talk 'Black'.

Racism in the music industry is scarcely acknowledged, therefore there are no strategies for tackling the problem. At the same time, this may come across as a brave assertion in view of the popularity of some of today's Black artistes. Indeed, with certain genres of Black music actually dominating the market, how could one dare bring an accusation of racism? However, a closer examination shows nothing much to have changed within the fraternity, with its 'Black music, White business' philosophy still firmly rooted. One reason why the industry remains buoyant and unscathed by any criticism is of course the perception of Black artistes doing well. Some of these artistes will even defend the industry dismissing any condemnation as nonsense. In the meanwhile, the 'blaxploitation' by these 'snow-capped' record companies goes on, with wider ramifications. If, similar to art, music is supposed to be a safe area for self-expression that stimulates the imagination about issues pertaining to society even in all its complexity, then there is deep trouble. Stories of Black artistes being forced to 'tone down the lyrics' as a condition of being signed are not uncommon. It is frightening to think what the world would have been denied if Island Records or Chris Blackwell had placed similar conditions on Marley. The same can be said of numerous other Black artistes across the music spectrum.

In the same way that cultural policies are instrumental in engineering the societal fabric, so can music. For example, in the USA, the backlash to 'disco' (Weinraub, 2002) saw bonfires of records being burned to appease frenzied mobs. Perhaps such scenes were too wickedly wise to warrant that much condemnation at the time. Yet there was a time when similar acts were being perpetuated against 'niggers' instead of records. The attempt on Bob Marley's life in Jamaica and brutal acts against Fela Kuti and his entourage in Nigeria were equally significant. Even when Black people are responsible for these dreadful acts, what justification can there be for such senseless attacks on cultural expression? Until the 'Black music, White business' paraphrase is critically analysed, evaluated and discoursed, the 'Black struggle' will continue to be set back by confusion. The image of a Black woman, not forgetting that it also references the archetype of the African matriarch, on pornographic-like visuals impacts far beyond the selling of music. One is careful not to do a disservice to Black artists of consciousness 'keeping it real' in creative and commercial terms. It is so easy to forget that being heard or seen on mainstream media is not a recipe to jettison certain principles and values.

The notion of the Black community spending hard-earned cash on the negativity churned out by the music industry invokes a sombre mood. The question must be asked as to how much of this is self-perpetuated. As long as things remain the same, the music industry can always cite 'commercial viability' as justification. The rarity of artistes in the mainstream promoting the type of revolutionary lyrics and imagery of previous decades is disappointing. When asked in an interview with Siobhan Murphy (2006) of the *Metro* to comment on his part in the film *Get Rich Or Die Trying*, Asher 'D' (Ashley Walters), said he was the opposite to 50 Cent because he would not promote that stuff in his music. Moreover, in relation to the promotion of gun crime, the mentality of rap artistes in the USA, especially those who are willing to do whatever it takes to sell their product, is duly questioned. At the same time, it is acknowledged that one art form cannot be blamed. When artistes such as Asher 'D' go the 'extra mile' in refusing such roles, there could be a more meaningful impact.

Where politicians have become a turn-off, artistes are getting through to people. Given the issue of ownership within the music industry, this can be counter-productive and very difficult to control. Without Black people in influential roles, record companies continue to exert tremendous pressure on gullible artistes, who despite their phenomenal success lack the consciousness or awareness to reject this modern form of slavery, continuing the cycle of garbage music. The issues have to be seen in a strategic context, including the related elements such as the imagery and media in terms of the disservice being done to the 'Black struggle'. With the industry earning huge amounts, governments will be reluctant to act against such a significant source of revenue, and a useful propaganda tool. Unless there is a radical shake-up amongst the artistes, the notion of 'blaxploitation' will continue, with its racist elements, at the expense of the 'Black struggle'.

Conclusion: getting back on track

It is a fact of struggle to find music that suffices as a parallel, succinct recording or documentation of that experience. In no shape or form is it suggested here that music is necessary a triggering factor, as it will be the conditions within people's lives that determine the desire for any form of change. Music, undoubtedly, can be a reliable measure of the level of consciousness within a society. This phenomenon, given the African perspective, is bound to be even more poignant when it comes to the 'Black struggle' hence the scope of analysis undertaken in this chapter.

Even with the questionable elements, Black music is still unrivalled and continues to be invaluable as a site of struggle. At critical moments in the past artistes have stood up to voice their own opinions on issues, and some of these movements have been significant enough to be labelled as a 'golden age'. In the 1920s, for example, Harlem in the USA witnessed an unprecedented outburst of creative activity among Black Americans in all fields of art. What begun as a series of literary discussions soon became a Black cultural movement known as the 'Harlem Renaissance'. Whilst this is a well-documented fact, certain points are worth noting, including the focus on the unique cultural heritage of Black people as a source of celebration and esteem. One only has to hear the artistes of that era to appreciate the transcendence of expression and its significance. Similarly, Jamaica and Britain of the 1970s could be seen in the same light with reggae being the creative force, as can the USA of the 1990s with hip-hop.

Throughout the struggle, the stimulating power of music has been an inspiration, and one can appreciate why oppressors have constantly tried to strip Africans of this heritage. The fact that music still remains central within the cultural profile is also testimony to the spirit of resistance and determination. The oratory tradition, evolved from the African continent, remains intact and thriving. In truth, these things are so deeply inscribed into the make-up and psyche that their removal can only be by the will of the Creator and not oppressors. In applying this in-built faculty to music as a voice of struggle, revolutionary artistes have elevated themselves in seeking the highest accolade, that of the Creator. Marley (1980) in *Redemption Song* brilliantly emphasises this notion of a spiritual connection:

> Old pirates, yes, they rob I, sold I to the merchant ships,
> Minutes after they took I from the bottomless pit.
> But my hand was made strong by the hand of the Almighty.
> We forward in this generation triumphantly.

Won't you help to sing these songs of freedom
Cause all I ever had redemption songs, redemption songs

Music is also able to provide an indication of the well-being of the community, and is also important for cultural identity purposes. Especially in the face of adversity, it has urged Africans to be defiant through repertoires of powerful songs designed to infuse morality, community, character, self-respect and pride, including those reserved for special social or cultural events and often combined with ritual and dance. Once the Creator, Ancestors and Deities have been petitioned, exposure to this awesome fusion of hypnotic drumming, chanting and singing can impact in ways unimaginable from a trance to the spurred-on might of warriors. This is an indication of the power wielded by musicians or artistes, hence the warning that this is not a plaything. Adapting *Killing Me Softly* by Roberta Flack (1973), the question is asked as to what could be more powerful than the words of a conscious song articulating the plight of the masses along with a subtle reminder of the consequences of venturing 'against that grain'.

With music, artistes have the means to communicate with people around the world who are equally anxious to hear views on all topics including the 'Black struggle'. After setbacks, it is encouraging to see genres of music undergoing something of a renaissance with the emergence of radical opinions. It is even more positive and productive that people from all walks of life are debating the lyrical content of songs. For example, *Welcome to Jamrock* by Damian Marley (2005) has sparked off an interesting debate. Whilst some see the song as a brilliant piece of social commentary, others are perturbed by the references to guns. Damian points out that the lavish life tourists live whilst at the all-inclusive resorts in Jamaica does not accurately reflect the harsh realities of life in the island's poorest communities, nor the country's high homicide rate. What is important is that once again music is triggering constructive debate about the lives of the masses, arguing for something to be done. Even if commercial pressures dictate what is heard, artistes cannot afford to lose sight of their roots and the divine obligation that comes with talent. Perhaps this is where some of the new generation of Black artistes need to be more conscious in their approach. More thought needs to be given to ownership, in order to stimulate the composition of music relevant to today's context for the masses. This cannot be achieved without Black people 'in the driving seat' or influential positions, so that music can regain its centrality as an art for the advancement of humanity. Furthermore, this can only occur if it is allowed to flourish in a spirit of freedom, communicating across boundaries and breaking down barriers.

Revolutionary artistes are every bit as important as political leaders, and it is vital that their potential contribution to the 'Black struggle' should exist without interferences or any infringement of the freedom and right of creative expression. Artistes must also make this an issue and challenge companies that insist on such constraints, including the dilution of certain forms of music as terms for acceptance. If necessary, artistes must be prepared to walk away from those companies and rededicate themselves more purposefully by setting up their own organisations by themselves or with like-minded others. As long as the 'Black struggle' is there to be fought, experiences of it will always be articulated through Black music. This is a tradition that must be valued and interwoven with emerging genres to take in the energies and emotions of the artistes of the day. As a vibrancy and vitality of creativity, this should be celebrated as a source of pride, testimony of triumph over adversity and a blow to oppressors. Revolutionary artistes must be affirmed in the knowledge of doing the Creator's work, which should reinforce their determination, diligence, humility, tolerance and business acumen. The wisdom of Fela Kuti is there for those with nothing better to do than peddle loose lyrics whilst their communities remain in crisis. In the end, providing critical elements remain focused, nothing can thwart music's centrality as a voice of struggle.

References

Garfield, S. (2004), 'Live aid: the man', *The Observer* (17 October)

Hughes, C. (2005), 'Can dance music and politics really mix?' *Independent* (30 September)

Hulsey, P. and Bafaloukos, T. (1978), *Rockers* (Jamaica: Rockers Film Co-operation)

Moraes, L. (2005) 'Kanye West's torrent of criticism, live on NBC', *Washington Post* (3 September)

Murphy, S. (2006), '60 Second interview with Ashley Walters', *Metro* (15 March)

Olende, K. (2005), 'Roots reggae and resistance from Jamaica to Brixton', *Socialist Worker Online*, 1965 (27 August)

Preiswerk, R. and Perrot, D. (1978), *Ethnocentrism and History: Africa, Asia and Indian America, in Western Textbooks* (New York: Nok Publishers International)

Quarshie, R. (2005), 'Commercial valiability or cultural terrorism', *The Northern Journal* (Spring): 30–3

Von Hoffman, A. (2003), *House to House, Block by Block: The Rebirth of America's Urban Neighbourhood* (Oxford: Oxford University Press)

Weinraub, B. (2002), 'Arts in America: here's to disco it never could say good bye', *The New York Times* (10 December)

White, T. (2000), *Catch a Fire: The Life of Bob Marley* (New York: Henry, Holt and Company)

Yeshitela, O. (2005), *Omali Yeshitela Speaks* (St Petersburg, FL: Burning Spear Uhuru Publications)

Music sources

Barrett, A. and Barrett, C. (1976), *Who the Cap Fit* (performed by Bob Marley and the Wailers) (Paris: Island Records)

Brown, D. (1983), *Words of Wisdom* (Hertfordshire: Intersong Music Ltd, Music Collection International)

Cole, A. and Barrett, C. (1976), *War* (performed by Bob Marley and the Wailers) (Paris: Island Records)

Flack, R. (1973), *Killing me Softly with His Song* (Atlanta: Atlantic 2940)

Grant, E. (1979), *Living on the Frontline* (Barbados: Ice Records)

Grant, N. (1980), *Since I Threw the Comb Away* (performed by Twinkle Brothers) (London: EMI Virgin Music Ltd)

Kuti, F. (1999), *Suffering and Smiling – Part 2* (Chicago: Universal Music International)

Kwesi Johnson, L. (1978), *Dread Inna Inglan* (United Kingdom: Music Collection International)

Manning, D., Manning, L. and Collins, B. (1976), *Declaration of Rights* (performed by Johnny Clarke) (London: EMI Virgin Music Ltd)

Marley, D. (2005), *Welcome to Jamrock* (Colorado, New York: Universal Music Group)

Marley, R. (1980), *Redemption Song* (London: Island Records)

Marley, R. (1979a), *One Drop* (Paris: Island Records)

Marley, R. (1979b), *Zimbabwe* (Paris: Island Records)

Marley, R. (1977), *Exodus* (London: Island Records)

Marley, R. (1976), *Rat Race* (Paris: Island Records)

Morgan Heritage (2001), *Jah Seed* (Jamaica: VP Records)

Smith, G., Dixon, B. and Dodd, C. (1999), *The Rod* (performed by Garnet Silk) (Jamaica: Brickwall Record Distribution)

Musical inspiration

Aswad
  Babylon
  Back to Africa
  Concrete Slaveship
  Old Time Tradition
  Three Babylon

Bob Marley and The Wailers
  Burnin and Lootin
  One Drop
  Small Axe
  Wake Up and Live

Fela Kuti
  Coffin for Head of State
  Zombie

Sound of Blackness
  Journey of the Drum

Specials
  Ghost Town

Twinkle Brothers
  Since I Throw the Comb Away

14

Spirituality and Black family life

Garnet Parris

Introduction

Black spirituality should be seen as a term that encompasses the totality of beliefs, power, values and behaviours that moulds the understanding, capacity and consciousness of Black people in relation to divine realities. Within this framework, spirituality enables people to interpret, adapt and formulate their understanding of God within a specific context. This chapter presents an introduction to the Black church movement in the UK and the Nation of Islam, as well as mainline Islamic influences within the African Caribbean population in the United Kingdom (UK).

Black church movement in the UK

The African Indigenous Churches and the African Caribbean Churches have made significant steps in developing themselves and their communities as a people who can face adversities and move on and upwards in their goal to equality.

The terminology for African Churches was discussed at a consultation of the World Council of Churches on this subject convened at the Mindolo Ecumenical Centre, Kitwe, Northern Rhodesia (modern-day Zambia) on 6–13 September 1962. Here it was agreed that Churches in Africa should be divided into the following main classes:

- African Independent Churches (AICs)
- The Older Churches
- Ethiopian
- Zionist

(Ayegboyin and Ishola, 1997: 18–19)

One of the main AIC groups present in the UK is the Musama Disco Christo Church (MDCC). The MDCC is one of the oldest indigenous churches in West Africa. It has been described as a church that readily draws on traditional Akan religion and culture in the search for more satisfactory answers to the problems of contemporary life (Ayegboyin and Ishola, 1997). The founder of MDCC was concerned to re-assert the values of African institutions and customs in the face of what he considered to be an all-out rejection of them in favour of European ways. The organisation of the Church in some respects seemed to tally with the traditional Akan state structure based on Nana Akaboa (King or the Highest or Supreme Head). The Church practises 'controlled polygamy', but is against any form of divorce. The Church worship is particularly popular with the West African community. Ayegboyin and Ishola (1997) provides a detail account of the various African Indigenous Churches in the UK.

The typical beginning of what we now call 'Black MAJORITY CHURCHES' owed a lot to Christians arriving from the Caribbean and sharing information with each other about Christian meetings taking place in their homes. The majority of the Black churches from the Caribbean are mainly Pentecostal in origin and have links with the United States of America (USA). This often meant that for some time they maintained links with USA headquarters, though many of the denominations in the UK are now autonomous. The irony of these USA links was that most of these Pentecostal churches had their headquarters in southern states, with White leadership at the helm who often believed that it was important to reserve leadership positions for 'White' brethren. Thus, while racism was overt in the wider society, the covert racism in their church structures was not always openly challenged. The denominations that fit these particular categories are:

- the New Testament Church of God,
- the Church of God of Prophecy
- the New Testament Assembly (all Trinitarian)
- the Bethel Church of Jesus Christ (Apostolic/Oneness)

Another tradition within this movement is the Holiness Churches, who also have their earliest roots in the USA. This movement emerged from within North American Methodism in the mid-nineteenth century and had strong theological and social emphases. Socially, it championed women's rights, the abolition of trans-Atlantic enslavement and a commitment to ministry with the poor and oppressed, wedded to a desire to work for peace (Becker, 1995: 14).

A final group worthy of mentioning is the Seventh Day Adventist Church, which again had its beginnings in the USA. There are two other strands represented in Britain, namely the Seventh Day Baptist Church and the Church of God (Seventh Day), which is a Pentecostal

Church. Gerloff (1992: 24) sums up the important social-justice role of UK Black churches by stating that 'Socially, the Black Church in Britain is therefore of extreme importance for human rights, challenging racial discrimination, empowerment of people, intercultural empathy, and peace in multicultural societies of Europe generally'.

Islamic faith traditions

A further factor in the life of the Black community is the presence of Islamic influences, in the common understanding of Islam, the world-wide sister/brotherhood and the Nation of Islam (NOI), which is under the leadership of Louis Farrakhan, whose emphasis is on the need for strong families and Black empowerment. In terms of activity, these groups are having some impact in the inner cities of the UK where they try to steer young Black men away from crime and point them towards other types of economic activities. In the UK, in densely Black-populated areas such as Brixton, Shepherd Bush, Hackney and Tottenham, residents and sometimes civic authorities have welcomed NOI members and praised their efforts to create clean, safe, drug- and alcohol-free environments. The NOI has now gained widespread popularity and acceptance in the Black community and manages to mobilise Black politics and leadership. The movement appears to be a voice that displays a strong organisation and solidarity, and is taking root in the Black diaspora. Among African Caribbeans, the NOI is welcomed as a necessity, because there is the feeling that a strong Black organisation – whether it is political, nationalist or religious – is important to raise awareness of Black issues and problems (Tinaz, 2001).

A question of struggle – the case of the Black church movement

The various Black spiritual movements have provided a haven for their members in the face of overt racism. Families have found strength to move on in their daily lives because of the strength and support they found within church life. In the case of the African churches, the reality for many was that, in the midst of the racism they experienced, churches were places where they felt affirmed, both in terms of faith and culture. On Sundays, they would be transported back to a world where the language and traditions were familiar and, for some, the surroundings were protective and helpful.

The reality for many, however, is that the experiences of fathers and mothers in building and maintaining these traditions is no longer valued as it was in the past, because young people of African/Caribbean descent are not necessarily to be found in the Black Majority Churches. Our youths, particularly those of the African Caribbean community, are very much in the forefront of current difficulties, as our prisons have large Black populations and gun crime is a factor that dominates 'our' youth gangs (Conversation with Bishop Dr Joe Aldred, Chair of Council of Black Led Churches in Birmingham, 12 June 2006). In the face of these issues, what has been the Black church's response? Birmingham provides a good case study.

The Black-led churches have responded to the triple problem of guns, drugs and crime through specific initiatives: for example, initiating a national project called 'Bringing Hope', which tackles the aforementioned problems. 'Bringing Hope' was started in Birmingham by the Council of Black Led Churches and Birmingham Churches Together, after the fatal shooting of two Black girls at a New Year's Eve party on 31 December 2002. In Birmingham, a worker for this project is now supported financially by the City Council of Birmingham. An initiative of the Church of God of Prophecy is now a national project called 'Black Boys Can', which is an intervention by the Black churches into the education of Black boys. This is principally concerned with supplementary schooling for Black youths. In Birmingham, a Black initiative, the 'Young Disciples' programme, seeks to reach Black youngsters on the fringes of society with aims to change negative behaviours into positive directions. Black leaders are involved in Primary Health Care Trusts, in Police Authorities and in many other spheres that affect the lives of their people as citizens of the UK.

In my interview (12 June 2006) with Bishop Dr Joe Aldred, Secretary for Minority Ethnic Christian Affairs, Christians Together in England, he discussed the reality of a National Black Leaders Forum being formed. This would be serviced by a small secretariat of Black leaders who could speak to government departments and quangos about issues that impact on Black British people and address religious, political, social and economic issues of the day. Will they be heard? They are already involved in important discussions with government, and the 2005 church-going population survey indicated that 10 per cent of those attending church in the UK belong to a Black church, hence their significance in representing the Black community and the strength of their case (2005 English Church Census). This is a significant figure when we remember that Black minority ethnic people make up 2.2 per cent of the UK's population in England and Wales (Census 2001 – Ethnicity and Religion in England and Wales). There are also other community initiatives from Black minority church organisations that should be acknowledged: for example, Church of God of Prophecy has initiated a housing project for its elderly members in Birmingham, the running of which may be soon transferred to a housing association, and the New Testament Church of God has a national prison ministry.

More important than the actual church organisations is the role of para-church organisations that use a multidisciplinary approach to the issues affecting the Black community. A key organisation in this area is the African Caribbean Evangelical Alliance (ACEA), which is a para-church organisation representing the interests of Black churches. ACEA has five areas of major concern, namely parenting, youth, education, Black mental health and governance. They hold a national brief for most churches within the Black community and, unlike sectarian Black church organisations, they are not bogged down by bureaucracy and can respond quickly to issues; in addition, they employ staff who are particularly adept at dealing with a plethora of issues. In ACEA, the churches can plan strategically how they can respond to various issues, a factor that is missing in the various sectarian Black churches that are primarily concerned with property, doctrine and teaching rather than community issues. ACEA therefore should be seen as an extension of the Black church leadership's vision for the wider Black communities working in a multidisciplinary manner. The presence of Black church leaders in key areas is not necessarily strategic but an indicator of individual commitment. It is through ACEA that Black leaders will have their national forum.

Due to different histories the African Caribbean faith community in the UK and its leadership cannot really be compared to African American churches in the USA, which are heavily involved in the political and economic spheres (Lincoln and Mamiya, 1990). The African churches likewise have links with ACEA, but in the main they have not yet taken on the social and political challenges that are facing Black/African communities in the UK. Many of them are still concerned with the business of finding or maintaining property and consolidating membership.

Conclusion

The richness of a spirituality that has enabled Black churches and their communities to survive, build and educate themselves needs to be cherished. Leadership of the Black church now means that government ministers expect them to be involved in resolving problems of the community, consequently theirs is a significant presence at various government forums. The Black church has undertaken its own research on knife and gun crimes.

Although the African Caribbean concerns over the education of Black boys are to be commended, there should be some learning from the African churches and their communities that seem to do well educationally with their young people. Leaders need to be involved more creatively in providing scholarships to young Black people so that we can have an impact on the country economically and politically. The church must ask where our politicians and business and industrial leaders going to emerge from in the future. The answer must lie in the efforts of leadership of the community, as unlike the USA we do not have Black colleges or a history of such investment in our community's education. Our leaders need to be proactive in the areas of social, economic, foreign, environmental and poverty policy issues, and to achieve these demands working across many spheres with others who may not share all our ideals, but certainly wish to build and develop the Black community.

In my opinion, spiritual struggles within Black families result from the array of religious offerings in the UK marketplace and the corrosive impact of racism in family and community life. It is no longer the norm that parents go to church or other religious institutions and their children follow without question in the traditions of their parents. Now, there are different beliefs within the same household and some of the intergenerational stresses may well come from these differences, since different interpretations often create barriers rather than unity. Interestingly, these differences are not as divisive within some West African households, for I am occasionally reminded by some of my West African Christian students that their households in Africa often reflect different religious commitments. Similarly, we need to reassess how racism still impacts on our lives away from the headlines. Finally, it is also my considered opinion that it is in the different approaches to societal problems and the different interpretations of issues in Black life that we encounter in various religious communities in the UK, that we will continue our spiritual struggles in Black family life.

References

Ayegboyin, D. and Ishola, S. A. (1997), *African Indigenous Churches, An Historical Perspective* (Lagos: Greater Heights Publication)

Becker, V. (1995), *Black Christians: Black Church Traditions in Britain* (Birmingham: Centre for Black and White Christian Partnership and Westhill RE Centre)

Gerloff, R. I. H. (1992), *A Plea for British Black Theologies: The Black Church Movement in Britain in its Transatlantic Cultural and Theological Interaction* (Frankfurt: Peter Lang)

Lincoln, E. C. and Mamiya, L. H. (1990), *The Black Church in the African Experience* (Durham, NC: Duke University Press)

Internet sources

2005 English Church Census: www.eauk.org/index.cfm

Tinaz, N. (2001), *Globalization and the Influence of Black Religio-nationalist Movement in Black Diaspora: The Case of Nation of Islam in Britain* www.cesnur.org/2001/london2001/tinaz (accessed 20 October 2007)

15

Conclusion: can you didgeridoo?

Carl Hylton and Bertha Ochieng

This edited work presents research, social policy and theoretical issues directly relating to individuals and families of African and African Caribbean descent in the UK. The work provides analyses of the issues from a Black perspective utilising academics, practitioners and artists who share a common African heritage. They all have expertise in the particular areas they cover for their chapters by providing foundation insights about the key issues and make-up of Black families in the UK. The final section of an edited book of this type is normally reserved to draw out the common and uncommon threads of the different preceding chapters. We will do this to some extent but will use the device of presenting past and present practical and theoretical work we have been involved with during the past three years as a vehicle for linking some of the various chapters and describing the reasons for the book and the outcome of the work. The significance of three years covers the period we spent in the writing and editing of this book project. It is no coincidence that during the time we dedicated to developing, writing and editing this work we have been involved in these types of projects. We believe that these practical community development and social policy issues are closely linked to the issues of Black families in struggle – we argue that these issues are another aspect of 'the site of struggle'. This we hope will confirm, firstly, that there is a 'continuing struggle', in which progressive African/Caribbean academics, researchers, practitioners and artists are involved. The written academic format such as the chapters in this work are only one aspect of that 'struggle', which for people of African/Caribbean descent is more than an academic project, but is about continuing lived experiences that have profound effects on their life-chances.

The main thrust for this edited book project is to fill a void in the academic literature using an unusual method of delivery. The story concerning aspects of Black family life in the UK collated into one volume provides an excellent teaching aid – although we also wanted the volume to be a true reflection of lived experiences rather than a cold academic subject matter. The story is told from various points of view including areas such as rites of passage (Trevor Gordon, Chapter 10), sports (Kevin Hylton, Chapter 11), music (Richmond Quarshie, Chapter 13), and spirituality (Garnet Parris, Chapter 14), which are not usually covered in a sociological family-oriented manner. Another of our key concern was to commission writers who were not only academic or professionally qualified to expound on a particular aspect of Black family life, but who, because of their African/Caribbean ancestry, 'walk the walk' of the lives they were analysing. These writers had very direct connections with their academic subject matter. For example, Richmond Quarshie is a member of reggae band *Harlem Gem*; Laura Serrant-Green and Bertha Ochieng are former clinical nurses; and Jerome Williams is a Business and Economic Development Advisor. In effect, the act of producing a chapter for this edited book project was more than an academic exercise and a flexing of their intellectual muscles. They were telling the story 'as it is'. Similarly Carl Hylton is editor of a community journal based in Leeds called *The Northern Journal* (TNJ), which is based on people of African descent telling their own stories from their perspective – telling the story 'as it is'. TNJ creates a local focus for debate on civic issues such as regeneration, representation, health and education. In this volume William (Lez) Henry (Chapter 8), is keen to remind us that his analysis is from an 'insider' perspective that is rarely valued by mainstream White scholarship.

One may argue that the significance of this book has been weakened with the input of our experiences and that of our authors; while this may be the case, the data from research and previous published work in most instances corroborated our individual experiences. In general, our writing was thus informed, *inter alia*, by our own identities as people of African descent. Keeping them separate was not possible; equally, acknowledging and exploring this overlap was also not an easy task. We believe that our own experiences have given credibility and assisted in the compilation of a comprehensive critical volume of Black families.

In essence, the volume has explored the 'everyday' experiences of Black families in the UK; this was done by examining and situating Black families' everyday life into a wider structural perspective. It was acknowledged from the outset of the project that there is currently a dearth of information on Black families' experiences in the UK. However, the material available indicates that UK Black families are subjected to significant discrimination and social exclusion; this

fact has also been reinforced by the various authors who have analysed different aspects of Black family lives. This discrimination and
marginalisation continues to contribute to Black families' disadvantaged
position in Britain. The approach we adopted in writing this book
was crucial as it made Black families the focus and allowed the different authors to put Black families' everyday experiences into their
broader context.

For Black people, the family remains the key tenet of their individual
well-being. Family members continue to rely overwhelmingly on
each other for all forms of social support. This is analysed most
clearly in this volume in the works of Franklin Smith (Chapter 2) and
Alice Sawyerr, Carl Hylton and Valerie Moore (Chapter 7). Therefore,
the exploration of Black families' experiences is a rational and efficient
approach that should be used with any organisation working with
Black families. It is imperative that policies and strategies aimed at
Black families are planned and delivered using a much clearer understanding of their 'everyday' experiences, respecting their individuality and participation. There is a need not only to acknowledge the
experiences of Black families, but also to appreciate their existing
strengths. Currently, most policies aimed at Black families are detached
from their lived experiences. For strategies to succeed, they will
have to be an integral part of the identities of the Black communities,
and not separated from them; there has to be a direct relationship.
Recognising this will be an important development in moving towards
policies and strategies that are of value not only for the Black communities, but for the wider British population. There is therefore a need
for further work in this area in order to establish the influence the
concept of self-identity has on the everyday experiences of Black and
other minority ethnic groups in the UK.

A number of our authors have demonstrated that racism and discrimination continue to exist in UK public institutions such as the labour
market, sports and welfare system. These systems mirrored values
of the majority; in essence, they met the needs of and benefited the
majority ethnic UK population. For instance, our research found that,
in employment, families suffered all the cultural deprivations and dis-
abilities that traditionally affect working-class groups irrespective of
ethnicity. Poor educational opportunities partly contributed to the
disproportionately high levels of low-status jobs, underemployment
and unemployment among African Caribbean men and women. Black
families should not be settling for second-class citizenship in exchange
for some of the improvements that have been made with 'race' amendment acts. The expression 'equality of opportunity' should be taken

up on its literal meaning: equal treatment and parity to progress irrespective of ethnicity. It must be recognised that racism is dynamic, and that we should therefore continue to analyse the experiences of families of African descent in the context of a changing public discourse. In addition, there is now a need for more systematic research into the social construction of racism and critical evaluation of its impact on the everyday experience of Black families. Equally, there is a need to assess the nature and structure of racism, especially in terms of its multiple dimensions and components. This will include an understanding of the living conditions created by racism and the systematic assessment of its overall consequences.

Structures to combat racism and discrimination should be visible to all. As a less politically powerful group Black families are particularly affected by inequitable social policies, and because they share common experiences of racism and social exclusion they ought to pursue a strategy founded on the unity of the oppressed. This approach was recently adopted by a group of Black academics in the North of England and saw the building of the Northern Black Workers Network (NBWN), with Bertha Ochieng as the network's first nominated chairperson. The Network, which currently has more than two hundred members, endeavours to provide an authoritative voice for Black workers in further and higher education across the north of the UK. In addition, it seeks to uphold the ethics and principles of race equality legislations and to work towards improving career prospects and opportunities for Black workers. Whilst recognising the differences between Black communities, the Network also strives to advance the commonality of experiences and advocate the need for a common strategy to overcome the many inequalities faced by Black workers in further and higher education.

Can you didgeridoo?

During the final editing of this work one of us (Carl Hylton) was approached by an Africancentric Leeds activist who was developing a music project that involved workshops to learn to play the didgeridoo. Hylton was asked to be on the project management committee – and he agreed. Hylton was deeply moved that he had been singled out as someone worthy of being involved with this very creative music/cultural project. The reason for the choice of this wind instrument mirrors some of the arguments in Richmond Quarshie's work (Chapter 13) in this volume, where he argues about the cultural, spiritual and political effect of music and musicians as key signifiers of

African survival strategies. Quarshie provides passionate arguments about the powerful effects of conscious music on the Black psyche. He believed that conscious artists of African/Caribbean descent can and do perform the role of spiritual, moral and political leaders, able to speak directly to 'the people' in a language and style that connects with their inherent spirituality. Here, music is not only for dancing – although movement is important – here, music becomes a key signifier to reaffirm contemporary struggles by using historical knowledge about past events that have sometimes been distorted or forgotten. The musician acts as griot, prophet and spiritual leader – releasing latent talents we have bottled up inside ourselves. The Leeds activist had deliberately chosen the didgeridoo because of its links with Black people of African descent – of course played by Australian aborigines. The didgeridoo, perhaps the world's oldest wind instrument, has a deep mellow sound that produces a calming effect. He wanted to use these features to help other Black people of African descent in Leeds to find peace and cultural depth. This was more than a focus concerned with playing an instrument for 'playing's sake' – he was aware that this ancient instrument is linked to religious rituals. He appreciated the significance of making music with the instrument. He talked about the spiritual aspect of involvement, where didgeridoo players have the opportunity to remake their connections with their ancestors. Also, the technical mastery of the continuous breathing required to successfully play the didgeridoo will give the player a sense of power. Involvement in this project is meant to transform the individual through a 'rites of passage' programme. There are also direct links here with the work in this volume by Tony Sewell (Chapter 4), Trevor Gordon (Chapter 10) and Garnet Parris (Chapter 14).

Transformation project: curriculum development

Earlier in this volume Carl Hylton (Chapter 12) described the successful development of the Leeds Bi-Centenary Transformation Project. A section of this Project developed Key Stage 1–2 and 3–4 curriculum packs dealing with issue from before, during and after trans-Atlantic African enslavement. This included historical analysis of African history and culture and individual and communal anti-enslavement resistance strategies. The wider Transformation Project and the curriculum section provided valuable information to the local African-descent communities of Leeds and locality – by increasing their self-esteem and confidence. The spiritual issues analysed by Garnet

Parris in this volume (Chapter 14) provide a similar process as the effects of this two-year funded Transformation Project.

End note

The various works in this volume provide sustained arguments that present alternative models of Black family life-styles in the UK. The importance of the various images is in the nature of their reflection of reality and actual lived experiences. The outcome is academic, with the perception that the lives of Black families are real and occur outside the confines of university debates. Contributors to this volume understand this important concept because of their African heritage. They are academic, although also particularly aware of the 'real' issues affecting UK Black families, and they recognise that as 'insiders' their aims interacts with the communities they are analysing – that is, a concern for physical and mental survival in a hostile, insane environment that does not reward people of African ancestry.

Black families' experiences have been placed within the broader contexts of economical, cultural, spiritual, psychological and moral discourses. For example, in this volume Perry Stanislas (Chapter 9) explores a comparative analysis of the cultural and political strategies of African Caribbean and West African families in the UK. Tracey Reynolds (Chapter 5) uses her in-depth research on UK Caribbean mothers to examine issues of 'race' and gender family politics where mothering is both racialised and gendered. Locating these families' experiences in wider perspectives suggests comprehensive structural approaches that are more encompassing than currently widely available. At present too much attention is being focussed on trying to address the challenges that Black families encounter by altering individual behaviour and not enough on tackling the circumstances that control Black lives. In this respect, the issues tackled in this volume may be a microcosm of wider challenges to Black families. Since no group or profession has a monopoly on understanding the complexities of these issues, there is need for policy-makers to build new alliances with local communities. It is through this 'bottom-up' approach that strategies will best serve the interests of families of African descent. It is possible to respond and work in cooperation with people and communities to improve and change their living circumstances.

In the past, specific beliefs, cultural values and behaviours have been cited as the basis for the supposed failures of many Black families in UK. However, throughout the various chapters in this volume there was not enough evidence to support the notion that the beliefs and value systems of Black families might be such as to dissuade them from having better experiences in UK schools and mainstream employment. It was the policy-makers' lack of appreciation, along with the marginalisation of and the discrimination against the Black community that have resulted in such poor experiences. It is important to acknowledge that their beliefs and values stemmed from many different factors, including a response to environmental and material constraints, a consequence of historical–political factors such as the experiences of discrimination and racism; an active social process linked to broader socioeconomic patterns, the process of acculturation; and the psychosocial processes associated with the dynamics of culture itself.

The arguments in this volume suggest that there is a requirement to understand the relationship between the Black community and the 'host' society, with their interrelated past, not forgetting the wider geographical aspects of that history. This may function as a prerequisite to remedial actions for the achievement of better living conditions and assist effective approaches to promote harmony and citizenship. It will take extensive political action and economic planning to reverse the widespread racism and discrimination that characterise the treatment of most UK families of African descent. This demonstrates that once again experiences of unemployment, discrimination, marginalisation and racism should be placed as central and pivotal rather than on the periphery when considering improving Black families' experiences. The space left by the macro-structural constraints of social exclusion, closure and subordination inhibits their choices. These are important issues as a significant, and growing, proportion of the British population is Black. The relevance of socio-economic structures, racism and discrimination in the lifestyle choices of Black families is currently conceived of in a limited fashion and there is a need to conceptualise such factors.

Future studies on the relationship between ethnicity and the state need to take into account aspects of individuals' experiences. Therefore, the multidimensional and contextual nature of socioeconomic factors and experiences of racism and discrimination, and the intricate connection of African Caribbean life situations must be recognised. These were important areas for our better understanding in explaining how African Caribbean families' lives are constructed in contemporary society and how this affects their participation in the building of the UK state. While there is scope for further research and study, there is hope that the present work will become the key text for an introduction to the study of Black families on academic and social policy courses in the UK and beyond.

Index

acculturation 34, 36–7, 64, 156, 222, 318
adolescents 55–63, 69, 71–2
  Black adolescents 56–7
  see also African Caribbean boys;
    youth culture
African Caribbean boys 42, 83–4
  see also adolescents; youth
    culture
African Indigenous Churches 18,
  305–6
  see also Black churches
antiracism 250
  antiracist 243

Black community 10, 17, 47, 55, 57,
  70, 126, 143, 154, 157, 205–6,
  224, 226, 242, 252, 272, 295,
  299, 307–10, 318
  African community 218, 223, 267,
    290
  African Caribbean community
    13–14, 124–5, 135, 143, 188–90,
    192, 199–200, 202, 308
  see also Somali community;
    Ugandan community; West
    African community
Black boys 50, 76, 78, 83, 151, 205,
  217, 308, 310
  'Black Boys Can' 308
Black British 32, 36, 39, 145, 147,
  149, 308
Black Britishness 16, 235, 277
Black churches 18, 165, 306–9
  Black church movement 14, 307

Black Majority Churches 49, 306,
  308
  see also African Indigenous
    Churches
Black elders 143–4, 146–50, 153–4,
  156–61
Black fathers 12, 23, 48, 56, 60–1
  absent fathers 150, 200
  African Caribbean fathers 60–1
  West African fathers 191
  see also Black men
Black feminist perspective 192
  Black feminist 104–5
Black men 24, 36–7, 44–5, 48, 50,
  61–2, 106, 126, 206–7, 240, 249,
  278, 307
  100 Black Men of London 207
  Leeds Black Men's Forum 48
  see also Black fathers
Black mothers 56, 101–2, 104, 107
  African Caribbean mothers 13,
    56, 121
  see also Black women
Black Panther Party 284
'Black struggle' 283–5, 287, 289,
  292, 295, 299–302
  the struggle 17, 68, 112, 117, 178,
    206, 276, 270, 283–6, 289,
    291–2, 297, 300
Black women 103, 190, 201, 208,
  240–1, 252, 265
  Black women's experiences 105
  Black women's roles 105
  see also Black mothers

childcare 48, 58–60, 62, 101, 193
  'good childcare' 150
childhood 69, 111, 115, 225, 229,
  261, 278
child-shifting 33, 37, 105, 106, 109,
  110, 157
colonialism 15, 26, 36, 102, 170, 173,
  176, 178, 214, 217–18, 223, 226,
  264, 266, 279
Commission for Racial Equality
  (CRE) 127, 154, 225
  see also institutional racism;
  racism
Commonwealth 24, 26, 146, 223, 225
  Black Commonwealth citizens
  222
  Commonwealth Students
  Children Society 30
  'New Commonwealth' 25
community 9, 13–14, 18, 57, 67, 70,
  78–9, 80–1, 83, 89, 93, 95–8,
  100, 104, 113, 127, 131, 133,
  135–7, 156, 183, 196, 198,
  204–7, 215, 218, 241, 217–18,
  221–2, 224, 227, 236, 248, 250,
  252, 258, 269, 270, 272, 274–5,
  279, 301, 309–10, 313
  community cohesion 16, 124, 205
  community organisations 205,
  263, 273, 275
  see also community activist
community activist 258, 272
  see also community
conjugal relations 201
coping strategies 78, 79, 82, 98, 169
Council of Black Led Churches 308
crime 67, 83, 195, 202–3, 205, 217,
  307, 308
  gun crime 299, 308, 310
culture 3, 12, 17, 21, 23, 47, 49, 61,
  65, 70–1, 77, 81, 84–5, 87, 95,
  103, 156–8, 184, 188, 193, 195,
  214, 220, 222, 226, 237, 246,
  263, 271, 276, 287–8, 293,
  295–7, 316, 318

British culture 12, 23, 36, 145–6,
  180
  youth culture 6, 61, 86

Diop, Cheikh Anta 217, 230
discrimination 22, 41, 45, 55, 57, 63,
  65, 71, 82, 123–4, 127, 131,
  136–9, 169, 189, 225, 249, 293,
  313–14, 318
  gender discrimination 152
  racial discrimination 12–14, 22,
  41, 44, 48, 50, 138, 145, 194,
  199, 223, 235, 307
  racism and discrimination 14,
  72–3, 100–1, 117, 124, 315,
  318
  social discrimination 70, 127
discipline 40, 56, 62, 66–9, 88, 91,
  113–14, 173, 175
Dual Heritage 7, 36, 39, 43, 50,
  190–1, 215
DuBois, William Edward
  Burghardt 81, 83, 102
  DuBoisian 243

enslavement 103, 136, 182, 195, 218,
  273–4
  African enslavement 25, 36, 81,
  102–3, 214
  trans-Atlantic African
  enslavement 11, 15, 23, 30,
  103, 113, 195, 214, 222, 266,
  316
  trans-Atlantic enslavement 15,
  30, 104, 106, 214, 217–9, 221,
  226–7, 264, 268, 272–4, 279,
  306
equal opportunities 124, 139,
  204–5, 251–2, 278
  Equal Opportunities Commission
  227
equality 55, 71, 124, 175, 238,
  250–1, 305, 314
  gender equality 201
  racial equality 127, 236, 315

ethnicity 2–7, 9, 13, 18, 56, 71, 100, 117, 124, 128, 132, 151, 160, 188, 235–6, 240, 244–6, 249, 265, 269, 314–15, 318
  see also Policy Research Institute on Ageing and Ethnicity
ethnic market 135
  ethnic markets 134
  minority ethnic markets 135
  non-ethnic markets 135
ethnic minorities 38, 41–2, 44, 79, 124, 126, 138–9, 172
Ethnic Minorities Business Task Force 137
ethnic niche 133, 135, 138

Fanon, Frantz 26, 178, 189, 190–1, 195, 272
Foucault, Michel 82–3

health 3, 9, 10–11, 66, 115–16, 143, 146–50, 155–6, 158, 160, 202, 313
  health-care 3, 14, 153, 159, 164, 193, 224
  mental health 69, 144, 149, 159, 160–1, 202, 309
  see also National Health Service;
healthy lifestyle 66
  healthy sexual behaviour 64
  sexual health 10, 68
  see also health; National Health Service
human rights 307

inequality 3, 65, 72, 179, 238, 252, 263
  economic inequality 72
  racial inequality 111–12, 116, 236
  social inequality 9
'informal wife' 197
institutional racism 27, 47, 55, 76, 123
  institutionalised racism 171, 173, 225, 227–8, 262
  see also Commission for Racial Equality (CRE); racism

kin 30, 58, 103, 105, 109, 157
  Discretionary kins 29
  Fictive kins 29
  Kinship 13, 21–3, 26–7, 29, 31–3, 62, 100, 102, 105–6, 110, 195–7, 208, 266
  see also kindred bonds
kindred bonds 29
  see also kin

Leeds Racial Equality Council 273
lone parents 32, 59, 126, 150

Marley, Bob 283, 284–93, 287, 295–6, 298, 300
matriarch 106–7
  African matriarch 299
  Black matriarch 106
  matriarchal 15, 30, 214
McPherson Report 11
migration 2, 15, 21, 26, 29, 37, 49, 58, 102, 109, 113, 117, 144, 146, 155, 157, 160–2, 188–91, 194, 196, 198, 219, 223
  Immigration Acts 25
  Immigration to the United Kingdom 24
monogamy 197
Mother country 146, 214, 218, 222, 225–6

National Health Service 26, 143, 146, 164
  Department of Health 38, 40, 148, 158
  Primary Health Care Trusts 308
  see also health; healthy lifestyle
Nation of Islam 18, 297, 306–7

Obeah 49

patriarchal 15, 214
peer group pressure 12, 76

Policy Research Institute on Ageing
and Ethnicity 147, 160, 164
see also ethnicity
polygamy 197, 306

Racial Equality Unit (REU) 148
racism 2–3, 5, 11–16, 21–2, 25, 33,
42, 45, 47–8, 50, 56, 62, 65–6,
68, 71–3, 76, 79–80, 101–2,
111–12, 138, 143–5, 148,
159–61, 164, 169–75, 177,
183–5, 188–9, 199, 204–5, 207,
214, 223–6, 235–6, 238, 242–52,
258, 261–2, 271, 294, 297–8,
306–7, 310, 314–15, 318
cultural racism 181, 238
neo-scientific racism 177
scientific racism 176
see also Commission for Racial
Equality (CRE); institutional
racism
Rastafari 293–4
Rastafarians 49, 269
Rastafarianism 284, 295
see also Rastafarian movement
Rastafarian movement 49, 272
see also Rastafari
Rock Against Racism 294, 296
see also racism

self-employment 131, 138, 261
self-identity 16, 49, 259–61, 265,
274, 276, 278–9, 293, 314
social cohesion 236
social exclusion 14, 22, 124,
169–70, 175, 178, 271, 313,
315, 318
socialisation process 9, 58, 62,
67, 69
adolescents' socialisation
processes 59
Black children's socialisation
process 12
Child socialisation process 56
social networks 62, 89

Somali community 155–6
see also Black community;
Ugandan community; West
African community
spirituality 17, 48, 56, 62, 69–70,
258, 261–2, 270, 283, 285–7,
305, 309, 313, 316
State, the 37, 44, 47, 68, 132, 147,
151, 157, 163–4, 201, 235, 318
the State sector 80
see also State's social care system
State's social care system, the 40
the State's education system 44
the State's responsibility 143
see also the State

Ugandan community 155
see also Black community; Somali
community; West African
community
unemployment 13, 45, 123–6, 130,
132, 144–5, 194, 199–200, 205,
228, 314, 318
under achievement 12, 33, 42–3, 50,
76, 79, 80, 217

'visiting unions' 195

West Africans 15, 39, 191–4,
197–200, 202–4, 208
see also West African community
West African community, 198, 306
see also Black community; Somali
community; Ugandan
community; West Africans
working-class 55, 84, 108, 180, 273, 314
working-classness 247
World War Two 26, 105–6, 145–6,
150, 159, 171, 180, 222, 248

youth culture 6, 86
Black youth 144, 150–1, 263, 308
West African youth 202
see also adolescents; African
Caribbean boys